POLITICAL CHANGE AND MATERIAL CULTURE
IN MIDDLE TO LATE BRONZE AGE CANAAN

HISTORY, ARCHAEOLOGY, AND
CULTURE OF THE LEVANT

Edited by
JEFFREY A. BLAKELY, *University of Wisconsin, Madison*
K. LAWSON YOUNGER, *Trinity Evangelical Divinity School*

1. *The Horsemen of Israel: Horses and Chariotry in Monarchic Israel (Ninth–Eighth Centuries B.C.E.)*, by Deborah O'Daniel Cantrell
2. *Donkeys in the Biblical World: Ceremony and Symbol*, by Kenneth C. Way
3. *The Wilderness Itineraries: Genre, Geography, and the Growth of Torah*, by Angela R. Roskop
4. *Temples and Sanctuaries from the Early Iron Age Levant: Recovery after Collapse*, by William E. Mierse
5. *Poetic Astronomy in the Ancient Near East: The Reflexes of Celestial Science in the Literature of Ancient Mesopotamia, Ugarit, and Israel*, by Jeffrey L. Cooley
6. *A Monetary and Political History of the Phoenician City of Byblos in the Fifth and Fourth Centuries B.C.E.*, by J. Elayi and A. G. Elayi
7. *The Land before the Kingdom of Israel: A History of the Southern Levant and the People Who Populated It*, by Brendon C. Benz
8. *Baal, St. George, and Khidr*, by Robert D. Miller II
9. *Scribal Tools in Ancient Israel: A Study of Biblical Hebrew Terms for Writing Materials and Implements*, by Philip Zhakevich
10. *Camels in the Biblical World*, by Martin Heide and Joris Peters
11. *Political Change and Material Culture in Middle to Late Bronze Age Canaan*, by Shlomit Bechar

Political Change and Material Culture in Middle to Late Bronze Age Canaan

SHLOMIT BECHAR

EISENBRAUNS | University Park, Pennsylvania

Library of Congress Cataloging-in-Publication Data

Names: Bechar, Shlomit, 1982– author.
Title: Political change and material culture in Middle to Late Bronze Age Canaan / Shlomit Bechar.
Other titles: History, archaeology, and culture of the Levant ; 11.
Description: University Park, Pennsylvania : Eisenbrauns, [2022] | Series: History, archaeology, and culture of the Levant ; 11 | Includes bibliographical references and index.
Summary: "Examines the relationship between politics and material culture during the transition from the Middle Bronze Age to the Late Bronze Age in the southern Levant by studying architectural and ceramic changes"—Provided by publisher.
Identifiers: LCCN 2022019034 | ISBN 9781646021932 (hardback) | ISBN 9781646022984 (paper)
Subjects: LCSH: Canaanites—Material culture. | Canaanites—Politics and government. | Architecture, Ancient—Palestine. | Pottery, Ancient—Palestine. | Palestine—Antiquities. | Palestine—History—To 70 A.D.
Classification: LCC DS121.4 .B43 2022 | DDC 933/.01—dc23/eng/20220511
LC record available at https://lccn.loc.gov/2022019034

Copyright © 2022 The Pennsylvania State University
All rights reserved
Printed in the United States of America
Published by The Pennsylvania State University Press,
University Park, PA 16802–1003

Eisenbrauns is an imprint of The Pennsylvania State University Press.

The Pennsylvania State University Press is a member of the Association of University Presses.

It is the policy of The Pennsylvania State University Press to use acid-free paper. Publications on uncoated stock satisfy the minimum requirements of American National Standard for Information Sciences—Permanence of Paper for Printed Library Material, ANSI Z39.48–1992.

Dedicated to my parents,
Ariela Shimon-Bechar and Eliyahu Bechar

CONTENTS

List of Illustrations ix
List of Tables xiii
Acknowledgments xv

CHAPTER 1. Introduction 1
   1.1. General Introduction 1
   1.2. Research Questions and Aims of Study 2
   1.3. Geographical Framework 3
   1.4. Chronological Framework 4
   1.5. Historical Background: The Sixteenth–Fourteenth Centuries BCE in the Ancient Near East 8
   1.6. State of Research 27
   1.7. Economic Models and Pottery Production: Theoretical Framework 29
   1.8. Economic Model for the Southern Levant 31
   1.9. Methodology 32
   1.10. Research Outline 34

CHAPTER 2. The Transition from the Middle to the Late Bronze Age: Architectural Aspects at Hazor. 36
   2.1. Background 36
   2.2. The Architectural Evidence 37
   2.3. The Built Environment of the Lower City 65
   2.4. Crisis Architecture 70
   2.5. Historical Implications 72
   2.6. Conclusions 73

CHAPTER 3. The Middle Bronze Age–Late Bronze Age Transition in the Levant: Architectural Aspects 74
    3.1. Introduction   74
    3.2. The Southern Levant   76
    3.3. Northern Levant: Lebanon   90
    3.4. Northern Levant: Syria   110
    3.5. Summary and Conclusions   121

CHAPTER 4. Pottery Assemblages from the Middle and Late Bronze Ages 125
    4.1. Methodology   125
    4.2. Typological Scheme   132
    4.3. Discussion by Site   166
    4.4. Discussion and Summary   218

CHAPTER 5. Discussion and Conclusions 223
    5.1. Introduction and Summary of Previous Chapters   223
    5.2. Historical Implications   224
    5.3. Changes in Ceramic Traditions and Consumption   231
    5.4. Final Conclusions—From a Super Power in the MBA to a Great Vassal in the LBA   234

Bibliography 241
Index 257

ILLUSTRATIONS

Figures

1.1. Map of the Levant, with sites mentioned in this study   9
2.1. Map of Tel Hazor and the different excavation areas   38
2.2. MBA and LBA strata in Area F   41
2.3. MBA and LBA strata in Area C   44
2.4. MBA and LBA strata in Area H   48
2.5. MBA and LBA strata in Area K   52
2.6. MBA and LBA strata in Area P   55
2.7. MBA and LBA strata in Area M   57
2.8. MBA and LBI strata in Area A   60
2.9. LBII Stratum XIV in Area A   62
3.1. Map of the Levant, with sites mentioned in this study   76
3.2. MBA and LBA strata in Tel Qashish, Area A   78
3.3. MBA and LBA strata in Yoqne'am, Area A1   80
3.4. MBA and LBA strata in Yoqne'am, Area A4   82
3.5. Strata R-5 and R-4 in Beth-Shean   84
3.6. Strata R-3 and R-2 in Beth-Shean   86
3.7. Beth-Shean, Stratum R-1b   87
3.8. Beth-Shean, Stratum R-1a   88
3.9. MBA strata in Kamid el-Loz, Area II   92
3.10. LBA strata in Kamid el-Loz, Area II, continued   93
3.11. LBA strata in Kamid el-Loz, Area II, continued   95
3.12. MBA and LBA strata in Kamid el-Loz, Area VI   96
3.13. LBA strata in Kamid el-Loz, Area VI, continued   98
3.14. MBA strata in Kamid el-Loz, Area IV   100
3.15. MBA and LBA strata in Kamid el-Loz, Area IV, continued   101
3.16. MBA and LBA strata in Kamid el-Loz, Area III   102
3.17. MBA and LBA strata at Tell el-Ghassil   104

3.18. MBA and LBIa strata in Tell Arqa 106
3.19. LBIb and LBII strata in Tell Arqa 109
3.20. MBA and LBI strata in Qatna, Area J 112
3.21. MBA strata in Qatna, Area T 115
3.22. Qatna, Area T, Phase II 116
3.23. LBA Palaces in Qatna 118
3.24. Map of the Levant with sites mentioned in the study, indicating when major architectural changes occurred 123
4.1. Bowls and kraters 133
4.2. Kraters and cooking pots 144
4.3. Large storage vessels 150
4.4. Small storage vessels 154

Photos

2.1. Aerial photo of Area F, looking south 42
2.2. A wall from Stratum 1b, cutting the Strata 2 and 3 courtyard, looking southeast 49
2.3. On the right, structures and installations of Strata 1b–1a, looking east 53
2.4. Aerial view of the MBA staircase, sealed by walls of the LBA administrative palace; north to the right 58
2.5. Aerial view of the LBA administrative palace, north to the right 58
2.6. The MBA palace and the Southern Temple, sealed by the LBA courtyard of the Ceremonial Precinct, north to the right 61
2.7. Aerial view of Building 7050 and its eastern courtyard, north at top 63
3.1. Yoqne'am, the MBA–LBI retaining wall on the left (W.387) with the MBA glacis (L.2559), sealed by the LBA remains 83
3.2. Tel Arqa, strata 13 and 12. On the left, terraces of Stratum 12, in the center, terraces of Stratum 13, looking east 107
3.3. Qatna, the Royal Palace 119

Graphs

2.1. Changes in the architectural fabric of the lower city between the different strata 69
4.1. Shallow bowls (SB), organized by period 134
4.2. Deep bowls (DB), organized by period 135
4.3. Hemispherical bowls (HB), organized by period 135
4.4. Open bowls (OB), organized by period 136
4.5. Closed carinated bowls with low neck (CB1), organized by period 136
4.6. Closed carinated bowls with high neck (CB2), organized by period 137
4.7. Open shallow carinated bowls (CB3), organized by period 138

4.8. Open deep carinated bowls (CB4), organized by period   138
4.9. Miniature bowls from Hazor, by strata   140
4.10. Closed kraters (CK), organized by period   140
4.11. Closed kraters with ridged rim (CKR), organized by period   141
4.12. Necked kraters (NK), organized by period   142
4.13. Necked kraters with ridged rim (NKR), organized by period   142
4.14. Necked kraters with a gutter rim (NKY), organized by period   143
4.15. Bowl-like kraters (K1), organized by period   143
4.16. Pithos-like kraters (K2), organized by period   145
4.17. Upright cooking pots (UCP), organized by period   146
4.18. Rounded cooking pots with a simple rim (CP1), organized by period   146
4.19. Rounded cooking pots with a thickened rim (CP2), organized by period   147
4.20. Rounded cooking pots with a triangular rim (CP3), organized by period   147
4.21. Rounded cooking pots with a y-shaped rim (CP4), organized by period   148
4.22. Holemouth cooking pots (HCP), organized by period   148
4.23. Miniature cooking pots (MCP), organized by period   149
4.24. Pithoi (P), organized by period   151
4.25. Storage jars with a simple rim (SJ1), organized by period   152
4.26. Storage jars with a worked rim (SJ2), organized by period   153
4.27. Jugs with a simple rim (J1), organized by period   155
4.28. Jugs with a worked rim (J2), organized by period   155
4.29. Dipper jugs (J3), organized by period   156
4.30. Biconical jugs (J4), organized by period   157
4.31. Juglets with a simple rim (JT1), organized by period   157
4.32. Dipper juglets (JT2), organized by period   158
4.33. Juglets with a worked rim (JT3), organized by period   158
4.34. Flasks (FL), organized by period   159
4.35. Chocolate on White Ware, organized by period   161
4.36. Red, White, and Blue Ware, organized by period   161
4.37. Eggshell Ware, organized by period   162
4.38. *Charom* Ware from Hazor, by strata   163
4.39. Cypriot Bichrome Ware, organized by period   164
4.40. Mycenaean imports, organized by period   164
4.41. Cypriot imports, organized by period   165
4.42. Hazor: Bowls   167
4.43. Hazor: Kraters   169
4.44. Hazor: Cooking Pots   170

4.45. Hazor: Large Storage Vessels   172
4.46. Hazor: Small Storage Vessels   174
4.47. Hazor: Varia (miscellaneous families)   175
4.48. Tel Qashish: Bowls   177
4.49. Tel Qashish: Kraters   178
4.50. Tel Qashish: Cooking Pots   180
4.51. Tel Qashish: Large Storage Vessels   182
4.52. Tel Qashish: Small Storage Vessels   183
4.53. Tel Qashish: Varia (miscellaneous families)   185
4.54. Yoqneʿam: Bowls   187
4.55. Yoqneʿam: Kraters   188
4.56. Yoqneʿam: Cooking Pots   190
4.57. Yoqneʿam: Large Storage Vessels   191
4.58. Yoqneʿam: Small Storage Vessels   193
4.59. Yoqneʿam: Varia (miscellaneous families)   194
4.60. Beth-Shean: Bowls   198
4.61. Beth-Shean: Kraters   200
4.62. Beth-Shean: Cooking Pots   201
4.63. Beth-Shean: Large Storage Vessels   203
4.64. Beth-Shean: Small Storage Vessels   205
4.65. Beth-Shean: Varia (miscellaneous families)   206
4.66. Tell Arqa: Bowls   209
4.67. Tell Arqa: Kraters   210
4.68. Tell Arqa: Cooking Pots   211
4.69. Tell Arqa: Large Storage Vessels   213
4.70. Tell Arqa: Small Storage Vessels   214
4.71. Tell Arqa: Varia (miscellaneous families)   215

TABLES

1.1. List of Kings Mentioned in the Text   13
2.1. Hazor's Strata   39
2.2. Different Usage of Space in Area F (in M²)   67
2.3. Different Usage of Space in Area C (in M²)   67
2.4. Different Usage of Space in Area H (in M²)   67
2.5. Different Usage of Space in Area K (in M²)   68
2.6. Different Usage of Space in Area S (in M²)   68
3.1. Stratigraphy of the Different Sites Mentioned in the Study   75
4.1. Average of the Consumption of Vessels in All Examined Sites   166
4.2. Consumption of Bowls at Hazor   167
4.3. Consumption of Kraters at Hazor   169
4.4. Consumption of Cooking Pots at Hazor   171
4.5. Consumption of Large Storage Vessels at Hazor   172
4.6. Consumption of Small Storage Vessels at Hazor   174
4.7. Consumption of Bowls at Tel Qashish   177
4.8. Consumption of Kraters at Tel Qashish   179
4.9. Consumption of Cooking Pots at Tel Qashish   181
4.10. Consumption of Large Storage Vessels at Tel Qashish   182
4.11. Consumption of Small Storage Vessels at Tel Qashish   184
4.12. Consumption of Bowls at Yoqne'am   187
4.13. Consumption of Kraters at Yoqne'am   189
4.14. Consumption of Cooking Pots at Yoqne'am   190
4.15. Consumption of Large Storage Vessels at Yoqne'am   192
4.16. Consumption of Small Storage Vessels at Yoqne'am   193
4.17. Consumption of Bowls at Beth-Shean   198
4.18. Consumption of Kraters at Beth-Shean   200
4.19. Consumption of Cooking Pots at Beth-Shean   202
4.20. Consumption of Large Storage Vessels at Beth-Shean   204

4.21. Consumption of Bowls at Beth-Shean   205
4.22. Consumption of Bowls at Tell Arqa   209
4.23. Consumption of Kraters at Tell Arqa   210
4.24. Consumption of Cooking Pots at Tell Arqa   212
4.25. Consumption of Large Storage Vessels at Tell Arqa   213

ACKNOWLEDGMENTS

> Archaeology is the search for facts, not truth. If it's truth you're looking for, Dr. Tyree's philosophy class is right down the hall.
>
> —from *Indiana Jones and the Last Crusade*

This research is the result of a long journey that began in 2014, and it would not have been feasible without the aid and support of many people. Some, not mentioned here, helped me by a supportive word, a hug, or a cup of coffee in times of need or want.

First, I would like to thank Yossi Garfinkel, who was my advisor, for all his support during my writing, for pushing me forward and for lending a hand when needed. I am grateful for all his stimulating comments and suggestions during our many talks.

I also wish to thank Arlette David and Shlomo Bunimovitz (z"l), for their support, encouragement and insightful comments, which encouraged me to approach my research from various perspectives.

I started writing this research under the supervision of Sharon Zuckerman, who passed away in November 2014. Sharon was my first mentor and teacher, and much more than that. I looked up to her and enjoyed working with her. She has been very much missed.

I would like to thank Amnon Ben-Tor for his encouragement, motivation, and his belief in me.

I am deeply grateful for all the help, advice, and excellent comments I received from one of my truest and most supportive friends, Nimrod Marom, who is an inspiration to me.

I would also like to thank Leore Grosman, Nathan Wasserman, Sarit Paz, Mark Leone, and Philipp Stockhammer for their ongoing help, support, and encouragement.

Several people have helped me get access to bibliographic items that were out of my reach. Some cannot be named here for reasons of international politics. I owe immense gratitude to Cory Crawford, Daniel Bechar, and my wolfpack, Andrew Knapp and James Nati.

Viviana Moscovich proofed this research and I am very grateful for her care, patience, and advice, making sure every dash is the right kind and every comma is in place.

The publication of this manuscript would not be possible without the help of Jim Eisenbraun and Jen Singletary. I would also like to thank the two readers of this manuscript for their useful comments which made this manuscript so much better. Jackie Haynes also helped me with making the manuscript better, and much more than that.

I would like to thank my "library friends" Ortal Harush, Ido Wachtel, Shulamit Miller, Yael Rotem, Anat Mendel, and Deby Sandhaus and my anthropologist friend, Lior Chen, for their support and the long days and evenings sitting and writing, discussing issues in my research, helping me solve dilemmas, and reaching conclusions. Thank you for everything!

I am also very grateful for the support and encouragement I received from my "Hazor family," who are all just amazing.

This journey would not have been feasible without the help and support of my friends and family. My friends from the kibbutz not only encouraged my work and allowed it to be "my reason for a plate" every Friday night but also contributed to my research through stimulating discussions that helped me reach some of the most significant conclusions.

Last, I would have achieved nothing without my family, present at every step of the way and giving me their full encouragement, confidence, and help. My discussions with my parents—from technical Excel issues to historical conclusions—not only improved my work but also inspired me and pushed me forward. My siblings, Michal, Daniel, and Naʻama also inspire me, each in their own way. I am so grateful for all you did for me.

I am truly fortunate to have been surrounded by all this love and support, and I am absolutely in awe of it.

CHAPTER I

Introduction

1.1. General Introduction

The Middle Bronze Age (henceforth, MBA) was a period of true urban culture in the southern Levant. New cities, featuring massive fortifications, large temples, cult places, and impressive palaces, were built. The material culture of the period, including, among other objects, fine pottery vessels, gold and silver jewelry, bronze objects, and bone and ivory inlays and scarabs, is rich and well executed, produced using sophisticated technology, and at times imported from other regions. This period can be (and has been) regarded to as the heyday of Canaan.

The beginning of the MBA in the southern Levant is dated to circa 2000/1950 BCE, contemporary with the beginning of the Twelfth Dynasty in Egypt. This period is marked by the reestablishment of urban institutions, following the five centuries of the Intermediate Bronze Age characterized by small rural villages and more modest material culture (Greenberg 2002, 105–9; Cohen 2015). The origin of this renewed urbanization, as well as the significant transformation, has been ascribed by some scholars to the arrival of newcomers from the north (Na'aman 1982, 132–34) or a cultural diffusion from the northern to the southern Levant (Dever 1987). Other scholars see the new urban culture of the southern Levant as part of the long process that took place during the MBIIa,[1] beginning in the coastal area and slowly infiltrating to the interior of the country until it became fully urbanized during the MBIIa–MBIIb transition (Cohen 2002).

The end of the MBA and the beginning of the Late Bronze Age (henceforth, LBA) are traditionally dated to the Hyksos expulsion from Egypt and the rise of the New Kingdom in Egypt (e.g., Weinstein 1981, 1; A. Mazar 1992, 226–27; Dever 1992). The Hyksos, a group of west-Asiatic origin, of which most scholars assume a Canaanite origin, took over Lower Egypt around 1650 BCE and

---

1. I discuss the terminology of the period below.

I

ruled from the city of Avaris (identified at Tell ed-Dabʻa in the Nile Delta) during the Fifteenth Dynasty. Their reign ended around 1530 BCE, an event documented in the Egyptian sources of the Eighteenth Dynasty.

However, several scholars argued in favor of a later date for the MBA–LBA transition, based on architectural and ceramic finds, as well as scarabs. According to these scholars, the transition between these two periods should be dated after Thutmose III's 1457/6 BCE military campaign to the Southern Levant and his conquest of this region (discussed below).

This chronological debate introduces the question of the degree of influence of the Egyptian historical events on the inner development of the southern Levant, more specifically in northern Canaan, and how these are reflected in the material culture. The transition between the material culture of the MBA and the LBA is characterized by its continuity, which makes it difficult to suggest a precise date for it. Consequently, it is also the first transitional period whose definition is based on historical events rather than on changes in the material culture.

1.2. Research Questions and Aims of Study

The research questions of this study are twofold. First, it aims to identify when the changes in the material horizons of the MBA and the LBA take place. Second, this study seeks to examine how the political changes that occurred in this region affect the material culture and this transition. Each of these questions will be elaborated below.

1.2.1. The Transition Between the MBA and the LBA

The first question refers to the material culture—when did significant changes in the material culture take place during the transition from the MBA to the LBA? Traditionally, this transition is defined based on the historical events that occurred in this region—the expulsion of the Hyksos and the destruction of many cities in southern Canaan.

Several scholars have already stated that the examination of historical and archaeological evidence is crucial for the explanation of cultural processes and change. Bunimovitz (1995, 320) noted that, by using the archaeological and textual evidence in the examination of cultural changes in Canaan during the LBA, he was able to identify sociocultural changes at the end of the MBA. These changes, according to him, would reshape the social and cultural landscape of the country and have a long-term and profound impact on local society. The question that remains to be answered is whether the changes identified by

Bunimovitz should indeed be attributed to the end of the MBA or perhaps occur only in the LBI. In the present study, it will be shown that, in contrast to previous scholarly work and based on architectural and ceramic changes, the most significant changes occurred between the LBI and the LBII.

1.2.2. Do Political Changes Affect Material Culture?

The second research question deals with the historical aspect of the changes identified in the analysis of the material culture. This question aims at examining the historical processes that occurred at the time of the defined geographical and chronological frameworks to determine whether any of the political changes could be the culprits in the changes in the material culture. If so, what are the implications thereof?

The changes in the material culture identified in the transition from the LBI to the LBII will be attributed to the conquest of Canaan by the Egyptian Empire. I will discuss and deal with the economic and social implications of this conquest. The Egyptian conquest opens another question—was this conquest the result of a single event (the Battle of Megiddo), or was it the result of a long process that enabled the conquest? Based on the material culture and textual evidence, I will argue that Canaan witnessed an economic decline during the LBIa, in the period after the expulsion of the Hyksos from Egypt and before the conquest of southern Levant by Thutmose III. Consequently, I will maintain that the conquest was ultimately enabled by this long economic decline, which began with the expulsion of the Hyksos and the fall of some important Syrian cities to the north of Canaan.

1.3. Geographical Framework

The focal point of this research is the city of Hazor. This is due to the extensive excavations and publications that this site has witnessed since the first excavations in the 1950s as well as to my personal connection to the site, as a team member and codirector of the Hazor excavations. Thus, this research was conducted with full access to the material of the largest MBA and LBA cities of southern Levant, including the unpublished material from Areas M and S.

Consequently, the geographic framework of the present study is defined in light of Hazor and includes its realm and the sites in its vicinity, comprising also the northern part of the Cisjordan (from Beth-Shean in the south to Hazor in the north), Lebanon, and southern Syria (see the map in fig. 1.1).

According to several sources, Hazor is considered the southernmost Syrian city of the Mesopotamian world. One of these sources is the Mari archive, where Hazor is the only southern Levantine site mentioned. One of the tablets found in the archive is referred to as a dream-book. In this Middle Babylonian document, the dreamer lists the cities he traveled to in his dream. His departure is probably from the city of Babylon, and his final point is Hazor. The city mentioned before Hazor (that is, the next large kingdom to the north of Hazor) is Qatna (Oppenheim 1956, 260, 268). Therefore, based on the literary evidence, it seems logical to place Qatna as the northernmost limit of the geographical framework of this study, the assumption being that any site to the north of Qatna must have been part of its realm and not of Hazor's. Since Hazor probably controlled the Jordan Valley road, it is safe to locate its southern border in Beth-Shean, where a large settlement dated to the second millennium was found (which I discuss in chapter 3). Similarly to the area north of Qatna, any sites to the south of Beth-Shean would probably be in the latter's realm. The western border of this study is the Mediterranean Sea, and the eastern border is the Jordan River and the Lebanese Biqʻa.[2]

1.4. Chronological Framework

"One of the longest and most obscure eras in the history and culture of Palestine is the Middle Bronze Age. Not without reason, the opinions of scholars have been divided on its nature and character, on its beginning and end, and on its breakdown into periods and phases; even up to this very day it is one of the most controversial topics in historical and archaeological research." These words were written by B. Mazar in his 1968 publication, but they could have been easily written today, as they are still very relevant, especially in light of the ongoing heated debate on the MBA chronology. Therefore, it is crucial to define the subphases of the MBA and present the debate on MBA chronology.

1.4.1. MBA Terminology

The MBA was initially divided into two phases by Albright, the MBI and MBII, the latter further subdivided into three subphases—MBIIa, MBIIb, and MBIIc. Albright's MBI is today referred to by Israeli archaeologists as the Intermediate Bronze Age (some refer to it as the Early Bronze IV), leading scholars to term the three MBA subphases MBI, MBII, and MBIII (Dever 1980, 1987). However, Albright's terminology is still in use (see, for example, A. Ben-Tor et al. 2017a),

---

2. One site, Tell Sakka is located to the east of the Lebanese Biqʻa but was added to the study because it is the only site in southern Syria that yielded both MBA and LBA remains.

and there are virtually no differences between the different terminologies. Albright's terminology will be used here for reasons of personal convenience.

1.4.2. Traditional Dates for the Second Millennium

Dever has rightfully argued that "all chronological arguments for the ancient Near East begin with relative sequences, based on exceedingly complex chains of evidence that are largely circumstantial; with even one piece of new data, one link may break, and the chain will fall apart. Moreover, the attempt to move from relative to absolute chronology often results in a classic circular argument, in which appeal is made to one unspecified variable to explain another" (Dever 1992, 1).

Traditionally, the MBIIa is dated to 2000/1950–1750 BCE, the MBIIb to 1750–1650 BCE, and the MBIIc to 1650–1550/1500 BCE, the latter marked by the expulsion of the Hyksos from Egypt (Ilan 2003, 332). However, these dates are still in debate (see D. Ben-Tor 2018 for a summary of the different suggested dates for the MBA).

In the northern Levant, the MBA is divided into two phases, based on the chronology of Ebla. The MBI, dated to 2000–1800/1770 BCE, is equivalent to Mardikh IIIA, and the MBII, dated to 1800/1770–1600 BCE, is equivalent to Mardikh IIIB. The end of the MBA in the northern Levant is marked by the destruction of Ebla around 1600 BCE. However, some suggest a later date (ca. 1560/1500 BCE) based on the ultra-low chronology (discussed below; Akkermans and Schwartz 2003, 291; Morandi-Bonacossi 2014, 414–15; Charaf 2014, 434–37).

As for the LBA, all dates rely on Egyptian historical events. Thus, the LBI is traditionally divided into the LBIa and the LBIb, separated by the date of the Battle of Megiddo (1457/6 BCE). The LBIIa begins after Thutmose IV reign, circa 1390 BCE, and the LBIIb begins with the Nineteenth Dynasty, around 1300 BCE (Weinstein 1982, 12–15; Panitz-Cohen 2014, 542–43; Morris 2015, 140).

In the northern Levant, the LBA is divided into two phases, the LBI and the LBII, separated by the conquests of Suppiluliuma I's under the Hittite New Kingdom and the end of the Mitanni kingdom, circa 1340 BCE (Luciani 2014, 509–10).

1.4.3. C14 and Absolute Dating

The absolute date of the expulsion of the Hyksos is still debated, as is the entire chronological framework of the MBA. The traditional date of the Hyksos expulsion and the beginning of the New Kingdom is 1550 BCE (Shaw 2000).

Radiocarbon analyses have supplied earlier (older) dates pointing to the first half of the century, circa 1570 BCE (Bronk Ramsey et al. 2010, table 1). However, the stratigraphy of Tell ed-Dabʻa does not fit well with this picture, and the results from the excavations at the site indicate a date of 1530 BCE for the beginning of the New Kingdom (Bietak 2013). An even later date, 1524 BCE, was suggested for the beginning of the New Kingdom, based on the synchronism between lunar data, archaeological evidence, and king lists (Krauss and Warburton 2009, table 1). Still, C14 dates from this site indicate a date that is 120 years earlier (Kuschera et al. 2012), resulting in a severe discrepancy between the radiocarbon dates and the archaeological remains and their interpretation, a conundrum that has not yet been solved. The 120-year difference between the archaeological evidence and the radiocarbon dates has led to a much-heated debate. Recently, C14 dates have placed the beginning of the MBA at 2000/1900 BCE; the transition from the MBIIa to the MBIIb at 1850/1800 BCE; the transition from the MBIIb to the MBIIc at 1700 BCE and the beginning of the LBA at 1600 BCE (Höflmayer 2017). In my opinion, these dates are problematic, as they leave about 250 years for the MBIIc–LBIa, a period considered as transitional. As will be shown, the LBIa is considered here a period of decline. If this period lasted indeed circa 150 years, as indicated by the radiocarbon-based chronology, a comprehensive explanation is needed by the advocates of these higher dates—could a 150-year decline period persevere after the flourishing MBIIb–c, which lasted approximately 200 years?

Scholars who adhere to radiocarbon dates and find them more reliable point to flaws in the archaeological-historical dating of the material from Tell ed-Dabʻa (e.g., Höflmayer et al. 2016; Höflmayer and Cohen 2017, 3–4). Scholars who rely on the archaeological evidence have pointed out the numerous problems relating to the historical implications of the early dates and call for a more cautious use of radiocarbon dates. These are supported by further evidence from several sites in Egypt and the Levant (e.g., Beitak 2013; D. Ben-Tor 2018).

The present study does not rely on absolute dating but rather on relative dating, and thus cannot contribute to this argument, aiming to remain outside of it. However, I believe that there is, undoubtedly, a problem to be solved and that neither side can ignore the results and conclusions of the opposing scholars. With that, a recent study by Manning et al. (2018) has identified fluctuations within radiocarbon dates based on the growing season of the organic material examined as well as differences between central and northern European C14 offsets. This find leads to an undisputed conclusion: radiocarbon dates should be used with caution (see also Finkelstein 2016) and, in my opinion, should never disregard the archaeological evidence. The results from radiocarbon analysis are a dating tool with its caveats, as are also imported and local pottery, historical events, glyptic objects, and stratigraphy. Radiocarbon dates should never be considered on their own and should be viewed as a part of the whole picture.

In the present study, I will argue that the LBIa cultural horizon still forms part of the MBA cultural horizon. Thus, returning to Dever's argument quoted above, since this study is based not on absolute dates but on relative dates, it can remain outside the heated debate on MBA chronology. Its contribution to this debate is in showing that the end of the MBA should actually be dated later, as the MBA material culture shows no break at the traditional beginning point of the LBA.

1.4.4. The Periodization of the Transition

"A 'period' of history is an arbitrary fabrication, a mere part torn from its context, given a fictitious unity, and set in fictitious isolation, yet by being so treated, it acquires a beginning, and a middle and an end" (Collingwood 1927, 324).

Beginning in the nineteenth century CE, and up to 1922, the periodization of Palestine was based on "ethnic periods" (for example, the Amorite period, the Jewish period, the Israelite period, the Semitic period, and so forth). These terms were very different from each other and therefore did not allow for a consensus among scholars (Finkelstein 1996, 104). It was only in 1922 that a widely accepted terminology was created. In an article named "A New Chronological Classification of Palestinian Archaeology," scholars were, for the first time, presented with a table that was set up by four representatives of the three schools of archaeology in Jerusalem (the American, British, and French schools). However, this was simply a chronological table with no explanation as to how it came to be. This system includes both technological-evolutionary terms (Stone, Bronze, Iron, and Modern Ages) and ethnic-racial terms (Canaanite, Palestinian, Jewish, Philistine, and so forth; Garstang et al. 1922).

In a letter to Fischer, written the evening of the aforementioned meeting, Albright states that the division and nomenclature of the Bronze Age were his responsibility, while the corresponding treatment of the Iron Age should be ascribed to Garstang and Phythian-Adams (W. F. Albright, letter to Fischer, July12, 1922, TS).[3] Since the periodization of Palestinian archaeology in general and the Bronze Age in particular was led by W. F. Albright, let us focus on his notions.

Based on an earlier article by Albright, we know that the division between the MBA and the LBA is based on the expulsion of the Hyksos from Egypt and the beginning of the Eighteenth Dynasty. Albright dated these events to circa 1580 BCE (Albright 1920, 79), a date rounded to 1600 BCE in the chronological table of Garstang et al. (1922).

---

3. I examined Albright's personal letters during a visit to the American Philosophical Society's Library, within the framework of an International Graduate Research Fellowship at the University of Maryland during the months of January–April 2015. This was made possible by a joint grant of the University of Maryland and the Hebrew University of Jerusalem.

Albright identified the Hyksos's invasion of Egypt[4] with the Israelites' entrance into Goshen (Albright 1920, 65) and concluded that the Israelite era in Egypt was identical with the Hyksos's ruling era of Egypt (Albright 1920, 65–66). However, Albright dates the Exodus to approximately 1260 BCE (Albright 1920, 66), which means that he did not identify the Hyksos's expulsion from Egypt with the Exodus, contrary to Josephus, who identified the two events as one (*Against Apion* 1.26–31). This creates a conundrum concerning Albright's view of the relationship between the Hyksos and the Exodus—on the one hand, he explicitly tells us that the Hyksos and the Israelites are one and the same, and on the other hand he dates the Exodus to approximately 350 years after the expulsion of the Hyksos from Egypt. This disparity cannot be solved. However, as stated above, we must consider 1600 BCE as the date he attributed to the Hyksos expulsion from Egypt.

Because there is no clear cultural break between the MBA and the LBA, it is not clear why the Hyksos expulsion was chosen as the significant historical event to mark the transition between the two periods. The conquest of Canaan by the Egyptian Empire at around 1457/6 BCE could just as easily have been chosen as the date of transition. Alternatively, the two periods could have been conglomerated into one period (Finkelstein 1996, 116). The latter suggestion would probably not have been well accepted in Albright's time, since archaeological research and scholarly work was influenced by work done in Greece, where the tripartite periodization was adopted. Albright aimed at keeping the terminology of Palestinian archaeology in harmony with the Greek terminology (Wright 1961, 87; Finkelstein 1996, 104–5).

1.5. Historical Background: The Sixteenth–Fourteenth Centuries BCE in the Ancient Near East

As noted above, the geographical area under discussion is sandwiched between competing territorial states—Egypt and Mitanni in the sixteenth and fifteenth centuries and Egypt and Hatti in the fourteenth and thirteenth centuries (see fig. 1). The area under discussion in general, and Hazor in particular, is part of the Syrian world and is involved in the palace economies of the region. Therefore, it is crucial to understand the historical and political context of these regions—Egypt and the northern Levant—during this time, as well as their economic influence and their chronological significance (see table 1.1).

---

4. Today it is accepted that the Canaanite settlement of northern Egypt was part of a gradual process and not an invasion (Dever 1992).

1.5.1. The Southern Levant

1.5.1.1. Canaan in the MBA

The MBA is characterized by a prominent change from the Intermediate Bronze Age. This change is attributed by most scholars to the arrival of newcomers from the north, based on new architectural features and techniques found in newly founded cities, on studies conducted on human skeletons, and on the appearance of Hurrian names in tablets found in the southern Levant (Ilan 2003, 332; Na'aman 1994, 183).

In the MBIIa, and more so in the MBIIb, urban centers were built throughout the country. The city of Hazor is one of these new urban centers, and its establishment, according to many scholars, changed the social and political fabric of Canaan. In addition to urban, fortified centers, small and rural settlements

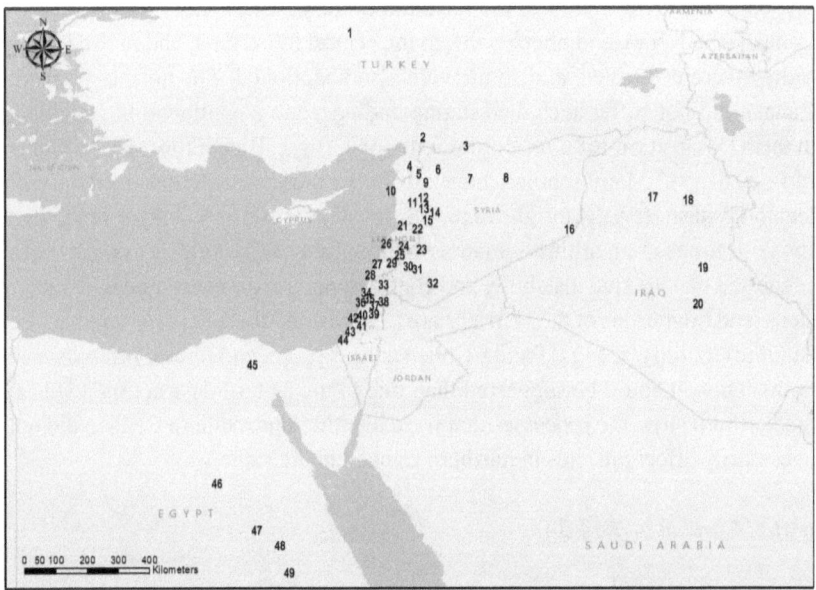

FIGURE 1.1 Map of the Levant, with sites mentioned in this study: (1) Hattusa (2) Zincirli (3) Carchemish (4) Alalakh (5) Tell Afis (6) Aleppo (7) Emar (8) Tuttul (9) Ebla (10) Ugarit (11) Tell 'As (12) Khan Shaykhun (13) Hama (14) Dnebi (15) Qatna (16) Mari (17) Assur (18) Nuzi (19) Eshnuna (20) Babylon (21) Tell Arqa (22) Kadesh (Tell Nebi Mend) (23) Yabrud (24) Tell Hizin (25) Tell el-Ghassil (26) Byblos (27) Sidon (28) Tyre (29) Kamid el-Loz (30) Damascus (31) Tell Sakka (32) Khirbet Umbashi (33) Hazor (34) Tel Qashish (35) Yoqne'am (36) Tel Mevorach (37) Megiddo (38) Beth Shean (39) Shechem (40) Aphek (41) Gezer (42) Jaffa (43) Ashkelon (44) Tell el-Ajjul (45) Tell ed-Dab'a (46) Cusae (47) Abydos (48) Thebes (49) Edfu.

were also recorded in several surveys conducted across the country, later abandoned in the LBA. During the MBA, trade relations with Cyprus began, focusing mainly on copper ingots, but imported Cypriot pottery also appears in the southern Levant, as well as Minoan pottery from Crete (I discuss this in chapter 5). A relationship between the local population and the Hyksos rulers is evidenced by the appearance of Egyptian goods and their imitations in many sites (A. Mazar 1992, 197–218; Burke 2014, 408–11).

Apart from Hazor and Ashkelon, two of the largest sites in the country, which probably functioned as royal capitals, the remaining sites are much smaller. All were defined on a seven-tiered settlement hierarchy (defined for both the northern and the southern Levant). These include the large fortified political centers (the two mentioned above), secondary fortified provincial centers (such as Megiddo and Beth-Shean), smaller fortified towns (such as Timnah and Tel Qashish), unfortified villages, fortresses (such as Tel Mevorakh), watchtowers, and farmsteads (Burke 2008).

Sometime in the middle of the sixteenth century BCE, many sites in southern Canaan (the Negev and Shephelah), in the central hill region, and in the Jordan Valley were destroyed, and some were also abandoned. The northern part of Canaan did not suffer such devastating endings, and a continuation is evident in them (Weinsterin 1981, 10; Bunimovitz 1989, 11–34; Bietak 1991, 58; A. Mazar 1992, 226–27).[5] Many scholars have attributed these destructions to the Eighteenth Dynasty (e.g., Albright 1949, 96, 101; Dever 1987; A. Mazar 1992; Ilan 1995), at times in an arbitrary manner (Bunimovitz 1989, 10).[6] It has also been suggested that internal instability and conflicts, natural disasters, nomadic incursions, and migrations of the Hurrians are to be blamed for these destructions (see Bunimovitz 1995, 322–23; Panitz-Cohen 2014, 541–42; and further references in both). Thus, it could be suggested that, due to the lack of destruction levels at the northern sites, the processes that were identified in southern Canaan did not necessarily affect the sites in northern Canaan in the same way.

1.5.1.2. Canaan in the LBA

In the past, scholars did not agree on whether the southern Levantine LBA was a period of decline (e.g., Albright 1949, 101; Knapp 1987) or a period of rich material culture (e.g., Liebowitz 1987). However, it seems that the current scholarly

---

5. Noteworthy and exceptional in this regard is the large city at Kabri, which was abandoned at the end of the MBIIb (Yassur-Landau et al. 2015).

6. It is interesting to note that in his discussion of the end of the MBA A. Mazar refers to the Hittite destructions in Syria but suggests that the only influence of these destructions on the southern Levant is the thin stream of Hurrian people fleeing Syria that appear in the southern Levant (A. Mazar 1992, 226).

work has agreed that the southern Levant was both prosperous and in decline, as there are technological advances juxtaposing the domination and exploitation of the country by the Egyptian Empire (e.g., Bienkowski 1989; A. Mazar 1992, 232; Bunimovitz 1995, 320; Panitz-Cohen 2014, 541).

Following the expulsion of the Hyksos from Egypt, it was believed that the kings of the New Kingdom, the first kings of the Eighteenth Dynasty, battled against some Canaanite rulers, mainly those in the south. These battles continued until Thutmose III's campaign to Canaan in 1457/6 BCE (discussed further below). This campaign brought the southern Levant under Egyptian rule. This also led to administrative changes that would remain until the end of the Bronze Age (Weinstein 1981, 10–12).

As for the settlement pattern, many of the southern sites were abandoned at the end of the MBA and were not resettled in the LBA. Actually, the entire arid area of the country—the Jordan Valley, the Negev and the central hill—are very sparsely populated in the LBA. The settlements are concentrated in the coastal area, the Shephelah, and the northern valleys. Compared to the MBA, the overall settlement is much more sparse, with fewer settlements in the whole country (a decrease in the number of settlements) and a population reduction. Some scholars have argued that, during the LBIIb, a gradual increase in settlements is evident (e.g., Bunimovitz 1995, 320–24), though others suggest that this is only due to the establishment of the Egyptian posts, whereas the Canaanite settlement sites still remained abandoned (Gonen 1984, 69). Another change is reflected in the increase in the nomadic population, which includes the Shasu and ʿApiru (or Habiru). In other words, the LBA political-territorial organization is much more diverse and much less integrated than that of the MBA. Based on the documents found in the country, it seems that the population of the southern Levant was mostly West Semitic, mixed with a non-Semitic population, mostly of Hurrian origin (Mitannian, discussed below), though migration of people from Anatolia, Syria, and the Aegean must have also influenced the local population at the end of the LBIIb (A. Mazar 1992, 236–41; Naʾaman 1994; Bunimovitz 1996; Panitz-Cohen 2014, 543–47).

Based on the el-Amarna letters, scholars have tried to reconstruct the number of city-states, especially their areas of control and borders, leading to between thirteen and twenty-four different cities (e.g., Finkelstein 1996; Naʾaman 1997; Savage and Falconer 2003). The letters dealing with local Canaanite rulers document their petty bickering and requests to the Egyptian king.

1.5.2. *Egypt*

It should be mentioned that the absolute dates provided here are based on the Egyptian low chronology, accepted today by most scholars (Beitak 1991, 27;

Dever 1992, 13; Kitchen 2000, 43–44; Zeeb 2004, 83; D. Ben-Tor 2011, 203). In other words, as far as the Egyptian chronology is concerned, there is almost a consensus among the scholars (contra Mesopotamian chronology).

1.5.2.1. Historical and Political Context

1.5.2.1.1. EGYPT IN THE SECOND INTERMEDIATE PERIOD

During the Second Intermediate Period, Egypt was divided into two kingdoms: one in Lower Egypt, ruled by the Hyksos or "rulers of foreign lands," with their capital in Avaris, identified in Tell ed-Dabʿa; the other in Upper Egypt, ruled by the Egyptians, with their capital in Thebes.

The Egyptian rule of Upper Egypt is attributed to the 16th and 17th dynasties, whose kings ruled from Thebes. The Sixteenth Dynasty had both kings and local rulers who ruled from cities other than Thebes, such as Abydos and Edfu. Fortresses were built in Lower Nubia, which was under Egyptian rule during the late Middle Kingdom. The Egyptian fortresses in Nubia were abandoned most likely toward the end of the Thirteenth Dynasty. Some Egyptian commanders of these fortresses transferred their alliance to Nubia, and others merely abandoned their garrisons. These commanders came under the control of the ruler of Kush, which was the Nubian king of Upper Nubia, their capital located at Kerma. The Nubians were cattle breeders and warriors who also benefited from their proximity to gold-mining regions. The Kushite kingdom and the Hyksos had close trade relations, which eventually resulted in allied military ties (O'Connor 1997, 48; Quirke 2001, 263; Bourriau 2003, 195–97).

At the end of the Seventeenth Dynasty, probably for a period of about thirty years, the Egyptians and the Hyksos were in constant battle until the Hyksos were finally expelled from Egypt. These battles were probably fueled by the economic inferiority the Egyptians experienced due to their position between the Hyksos and the Nubians (O'Connor 1997, 62–63). The Egyptian king Kamose recaptured the gold mining region of Buhen in Nubia, thus driving the Nubians further to the south. Kamose also carried out a military expedition against Avaris. These two battles are known from two "Kamose Stelae," on which a great deal of our knowledge is based (Redford 1997, 13–15). Kamose's campaign to Avaris, probably a raid against the city, did not succeed. Following the deaths of Kamose and Apophis, his Hyksos counterpart and foe, new kings reigned in both kingdoms—Ahmose, the first king in the Eighteenth Dynasty in Upper Egypt, and possibly Khamudi, the last king of the Hyksos kingdom in Lower Egypt according to the Turin king list. Textual evidence of Ahmose's campaign against the Hyksos is recorded in the biography of "Ahmose, son of Ibana," who was an officer in the Egyptian army, serving in the military campaigns of the pharaoh Ahmose. This biography was found on a relief in his tomb in El-Kab.

TABLE 1.1 List of Kings Mentioned in the Text

Date[a]	Egypt	Mitanni	Hatti	Northern Levant and Upper Mesopotamia
Eighteenth century	Second Intermediate Period			Shamshi Adad Naram Sin Ishme-Dagan Yasmah Addu Zimri Lim Hamurabbi Samsuiluna
Seventeenth century			Hattusili Mursili I	
Sixteenth century	Kamose Apophis Ahmose Khamudi		decline	
Fifteenth century	Thutmose I Thutmose II Hatshepsut Thutmose III Amenhotep II	Parrattarna	decline	Idrimi
Fourteenth century	Thutmose IV Amenhotep III Akhenaten	Artashumara Tushratta / Artatama Kili Teshub	Suppiluliuma I Mursili II	
Thirteenth century	Seti I Ramses II			

[a] Kings are placed in chronological order in the different regions, but no absolute dates were used. In addition, it was not attempted to synchronize the different kings. In order to avoid confusion, kings that are not mentioned in the text were not incorporated in this table. The dates used are based on the middle chronology

Records of the battle at Avaris are also known from the reliefs in Ahmose's mortuary temple in Abydos and in Josephus's account of these events. These sources describe the fall of Avaris and the expulsion of the Hyksos by Ahmose (Bourriau 2003, 197–203; Morris 2005, 27–28).

The Hyksos's rule of Lower Egypt is attributed to the Fifteenth Dynasty. The textual evidence from the Second Intermediate Period Lower Egypt is scarce, and most of our knowledge is based on the material culture (D. Ben-Tor 2009, 1). There is evidence for trade between the Hyksos and Canaan, Cyprus, and the Minoan palaces, as well as the Kushite kingdom, as evidenced by the material culture found in Tell ed-Dabʻa, and the literary evidence referring to the materials they imported (based on the Kamose stele). However, it is not clear what they provided in exchange (Bourriau 2003, 182). The Kamose stele also mention the taxes that the Hyksos imposed on all Nile traffic and their control over Cusae (about forty kilometers south of Hermopolis and the administrative center of this region during the Middle Kingdom), indicating this is one of the ways they earned their income. This Hyksos control over Cusae and the taxes imposed by them are also evident from a papyrus dated to the days of Merneptah (end of the thirteenth century BCE) referring to a quarrel between Seqenerna and Apophis, one of the latest Hyksos kings (Bourriau 2003, 183, 188, 198).

Though it is commonly agreed that the Hyksos had some type of relationship with the inhabitants of the Canaanite city-states during the MBA, it is not clear whether these were blood ties, trade relationships, or marital connections (Redford 1992, 119–22; Bietak 2010; D. Ben-Tor 2009, 2011). The "Hyksos" scarabs found all over the southern Levant were mostly locally made. Not only was scarab production not found in the northern Levant, but Second Intermediate Period scarabs, in general, are absent from this area. According to D. Ben-Tor, this suggests a hiatus in trade relations between the northern Levant and Egypt during this period (D. Ben-Tor 2009, 3; 2011, 28–30).

We do know that during its ruling days of Lower Egypt, the city of Avaris imported large amounts of pottery vessels, some probably containing liquids from the central and southern Levant (Beitak 1991; Maeir 2010, 113; D. Ben-Tor 2018, 46). The material culture identified in Tel a-Dabʻa comprises both Egyptian and Canaanite shapes and some Cypriot imports. The number of Canaanite shapes increased in time—from 18% in the late Twelfth Dynasty to 40% during the Hyksos period (Beitak 1991, 31–47; 2010, 151–52, 163). It is interesting to note that even after Ahmose's conquest of the site, an apparent continuation is seen in the ceramic traditions (Egyptian shapes as well as Canaanite types), at least until the reign of Thutmose III (Beitak 2010, 170).

The conquest of Avaris by Ahmose, the first king of the Eighteenth Dynasty and the founder of the New Kingdom, marks the end of this period. According to Egyptian texts and chronology, this conquest and the reunification of Egypt are dated to 1532–1528 BCE (Bourriau 2003, 172; Bard 2008, 195–97). It is noteworthy that even more than sixty years after the expulsion, during the days of Queen Hatshepsut, the rulers of Egypt were still boasting this expulsion (Bourriau 2003, 188).

1.5.2.1.2. THE EARLY EIGHTEENTH DYNASTY

As stated above, Ahmose, the first Pharaoh of the Eighteenth Dynasty, is also the founder of the New Kingdom. Following the removal of the Hyksos, he sets sail down to Nubia to regain Egyptian control over the region. After his triumphs, Ahmose began rebuilding Egypt and its monuments (Bourriau 2003, 203–4). Ahmose not only defeated the Hyksos in Avaris but continued to attack Sharuhen, the Hyksos stronghold in southern Canaan, as well as the city of Kerma, the capital of the Kushite kingdom (Bryan 2003, 207–8). The first kings of the Eighteenth Dynasty mainly focused on extending Egyptian control southward for this region's material rewards (that is, gold; Bryan 2003, 214). This is also evident from the Kamose stela, where Nubia is considered part of Egypt, but not so with the southern Levant.

The constant trade relationship between Canaan and Egypt is manifested beginning with the first dynasties of Egypt. After a long hiatus, these trade relationships began again in the Middle Kingdom and continued up to the MBII Hyksos. It is only in the LBII that we find an actual Egyptian presence north of the Negev[7]—Beth-Shean being the northernmost stronghold (A. Mazar and Mullins 2007), although Jaffa (Burke et al. 2017) and Aphek (Gadot 2010) should also be mentioned. It is also apparent from the Egyptian and Egyptianized ceramic assemblages. These vessels become more common in the southern Levant only during the reign of Thutmose III, and even more so during the Nineteenth Dynasty. According to Martin, this indicates that the early pharaohs of the Eighteenth Dynasty did not aim at establishing a permanent military or political presence in Canaan, evident only after Thutmose III's campaign (Martin 2011, 273–74). However, it should also be noted that some scholars question whether these so-called Egyptian fortresses actually housed Egyptians and suggest they should be considered an "elite emulation" of the local population. Higginbotham suggested that these were used by Egyptianized Canaanite rulers or officials in the Ramesside period (Higginbotham 2000), though this has been widely criticized (e.g., Hoffmeier 2004; Koch 2014, 167, and see further references there).

It seems that until the LBIb, during the Old and Middle Kingdoms, the Egyptian policy was not to conquer Canaan, but to secure their economic interests in

---

7. Evidence for Egyptian presence was noted in the EBI in the Negev region, though its nature is still debated (Rowan and Golden 2009, 71)

the region. Consequently, Egyptian presence in Canaan was only accomplished in the New Kingdom, during the days of Thutmose III (Redford 1979, 274; Hoffmeier 2004, 133; Martin 2011, 273–74). Nevertheless, the Egyptian annals indicate an Egyptian military presence before the Battle of Megiddo, possibly in the city of Megiddo itself (Hoffmeier 2004, 134).

As for the Egyptian relations with Syria, Thutmose I was the first pharaoh to battle with Mitanni, a north-Syrian kingdom located to the east of the Euphrates. He emerges triumphant from this battle and subsequently conducts an elephant hunt. His son, Thutmose II, also battles with the northern kingdom, but contrary to his father, he takes Shasu prisoners.[8] After his victory, Thutmose II focuses his efforts on restraining and managing the Shasu threats, aiming at securing safety along the roads. Following Thutmose II's death, his wife, Hatshepsut, acted as ward and regent of her nephew, Thutmose III. Under her rule, mining activities in Sinai as well as trade with Lebanon, Punt, and Libya were resumed (Morris 2005, 31–34). It is not clear whether Hatshepsut campaigned in Canaan (Morris 2005, 34) or refrained from it (Redford 1992, 151).

During the days of Thutmose III's sole reign, he led several campaigns to the Levant (Redford 2003). The most relevant to our discussion here is his Battle of Megiddo, launched during his 23rd year of reign. This battle is well known for Thutmose III's deceitful actions against the Canaanite kings, choosing the least expected road. After his surprise attack and seven months of siege against the Canaanite kings assembled at Megiddo, Thutmose won the battle, and the Canaanite kings took an oath of loyalty to Egypt and returned to their homes in Canaan. Consequently, the Canaanite cities became vassal cities, and sons or brothers of the vassal kings were held at the Egyptian court until the death of the vassal, in order to educate or rather indoctrinate them into Egyptian culture. These were also highly valuable hostages. In some cases the Pharaoh would also replace the local kings, creating new dynasties. Following the Battle of Megiddo, Thutmose engaged in expeditions to the north almost annually to retain his control.

Thutmose's eighth battle, in his 33rd year of reign, was a great victory against the kingdom of Mitanni. This battle extended further north than Carchemish and into the Mitannian heartland, finding the king of Mitanni unprepared. This battle is well known due to Thutmose's crossing of the (Euphrates) river, after which he set up a stela. On his return home, via the land route and not the sea route, Thutmose engages in an elephant hunt and passes through Qatna, where he examines the bow-manufacture industry and participates in a marksmanship show. In his 35th year of reign, Thutmose III campaigned against the kingdom of

---

8. Shasu are seminomadic people known in Sinai, Transjordan, the central hills, and Syria (Morris 2005, 33, and see references there).

Mitanni again, but this time the battle ends at a draw and probably not in a great victory as he prided himself. The last recorded battle is dated to his 42nd year of reign. This battle was due to an uprising in the Akkar plains (the region of Tell Arqa), probably led by the king of Kadesh. Thutmose reaches the region by the *via maris*, passing through the southern Levant, until he finally captures and destroys the city of Tunip (but not Kadesh), though the city quickly returned to Mitannian hands (Redford 1992, 156–60; Redford 2003, 222–25, 229–30, 238–40; Bryan 2003, 237–39; Morris 2005, 115–26).

Amenhotep II (or Amenophis II), Thutmose III's son, was the next ruler. He carried out two campaigns in the Levant aimed at expanding Egypt's boundaries. The first was against Syria and the second against rebelling kings in the southern Levant. This is also the first time that we hear of peace with Mitanni, Hattusa, and Babylon, as the kings of these kingdoms brought gifts to Amenhotep II following his battles in the Levant. As part of this peace, Amenhotep II's son, Thutmose IV, married the daughter of the Mitannian king Artatama I.[9] We know that, in some cases, Amenhotep II ordered the mass deportation of the local population and that following his seventh-year campaign he left Canaan and brought with him 2,214 people as well as several hundred children and wives of Canaanite rulers. It is not clear how many prisoners he took following his ninth-year campaign set against rebelling rulers in the southern Levant. The numbers range from about 1,000 prisoners to 85,000 or 101,000 prisoners, as documented in the different texts recording this campaign. Even though these numbers are still debated, it is clear that either mass deportations were carried out during this campaign (in which case the numbers might be exaggerated) or that these people came under Egyptian rule, in which case the numbers reflect a census of the area. Thutmose IV continued these mass deportations. In his mortuary temple in Thebes, it is noted that he deported the population of Gezer (though this is also in debate). However, the marriage between Thutmose IV and the Mitannian princess and the continuation of the peace between the sides was beneficial to both and brought peace to the region. There may have also been a dynastic marriage between Egypt and Babylon, and there is also evidence for possible relations between Egypt and Assur as well as a peace treaty with Hatti. This period of peace affected Egypt's foreign policy during the remainder of the Eighteenth Dynasty (Redford 1992, 163–69; Bryan 2003, 244–45; Morris 2005, 127–35).

1.5.2.1.3. THE AMARNA PERIOD: THE LATE EIGHTEENTH DYNASTY

Egypt enjoyed a period of peace, stability, and great wealth during the days of Amenhotep III. Surrounding states were seen as partners in foreign trade, and

---

9. The marriage was arranged between Amenhotep II and the father of Artatama I, Saussatar, who was the reigning king. Artatama was his successor (Redford 1992, 165).

Amenhotep III's court was an international diplomatic center where several diplomatic marriages took place (Redford 1992, 269; van Dijk 2003, 265). However, during his days, Amenhotep III also faced conflicts in the Lebanese mountains as well as the Central Hills of the southern Levant. These conflicts merited direct Egyptian intervention in the local internecine wars leading to the removal of the Ammuru king Abdi-Ashirta and the king of Shechem, Laba'yu, the former probably killed by his own countrymen and the latter by people from the neighboring town of Gina (Redford 1992, 170–71; Morris 2005, 223–27).

His son, Amenhotep IV or Akhenaten, was the next ruler of Egypt. Akhenaten transformed the Egyptian religion, changing the focus from the god Amun, as the primary god, to Aten, and moving the capital from Thebes to Amarna (van Dijk 2003, 267–70).

Akhenaten led his main military campaign, during his 12th year of reign, against Nubia, at the same time when the Hittite kingdom defeated the Mitannian kingdom, Egypt's ally (van Dirjk 2003, 270). During the time of Akhenaten's reign, and probably also his father's, the tradition of annual campaigns to Canaan, which began in the days of Thutmose III, were no longer upheld, and Egyptian troops arrived in the region only when necessary (Morris 2005, 233). During this period, the Egyptian administrative system in the Levant consisted of three provinces: Canaan, governed from Gaza; Phoenicia and Ammuru, governed from Sumur; and Upe, governed from Kamid el-Loz and perhaps later from Damascus (Morris 2005, 239–40).

In the days of the last rulers of the Eighteenth Dynasty, evidence for Egyptian campaigns in Canaan are rare, and it seems that Egypt mainly focused on keeping its influence in the area while still battling the Hittites. A peace treaty between the two sides may have existed after these conflicts, during the days of Horemheb, as recorded in the later peace treaty signed between Ramses II and Hattusili III. In general, it seems that the administration system that was laid after Thutmose III's campaign continued to exist in the Amarna days, the only main difference being that the pharaoh did not send annual campaigns to collect tribute and taxes and to display his strength (van Dijk 2003, 284; Morris 2005, 265–70). It also seems that the area of southern Syria, between Hazor and Qatna (including the latter), changed hands several times between the Egyptian, Mitannian, and Hittite kingdoms (Redford 1992, 166–67).

1.5.2.2. Economic Influence of Egypt

According to Egyptian records, following the Hyksos expulsion, the Egyptians focused on recolonizing Nubia and apparently had little economic interest in Canaan (Aḥituv 1978; Redford 1979, 273–74; 1992, 149; Bourriau 2003, 203–4;

Hoffmeier 2004). It has also been suggested that during the fifteenth century BCE the primary efforts of the Egyptians in the Jordan Valley and the Jezreel Valley were to control or limit the access of Canaanite cities to an interregional trade system and economically exploit the southern Levant (Knapp 1992, 89–90).

It seems that in the days of Hatshepsut, the queen was interested in rebuilding Egypt and keeping peace and not in military campaigns against Canaan. In fact, between Thutmose I's campaign in northern Syria and Thutmose III's Megiddo battle, Egypt seems to have "withdrawn" from Canaan. The impression is that, during this time, most of the territory in northern Canaan was under Mitanni influence, as evidenced in the king of Kadesh's statement that the cities of the Galilee were loyal to him. This influence ultimately led to the Battle of Megiddo in 1457/6 BCE (Redford 1992, 151–56). Sometime after the battle and the conquest of the southern Levant, Amenophis II (son of Thutmose III), and his son, Thutmose IV, each carried out mass deportations from Canaanite cities (especially in the hill country and the Shephela) and Syrian cities (Redford 1992, 208–9). As noted above, following his campaign, Thutmose III appointed new vassal kings in the rebellious cities in order to ensure their loyalty to the Egyptian Empire. Moreover, the sons, princes of these vassal kings, were brought to Egypt for indoctrination (Hoffmeier 2004, 134–35). These mass deportations not only resulted in changes in the physical and spatial organization of cities, their environs, and their hinterland but probably also affected the subsistence strategies of Canaanite society (Buminovitz 1996).

It was only after Thutmose III's campaign that Egypt sought to secure the agricultural resources and its permanent control over interregional trade routes, thus creating a system of domination and exploitation that, according to Knapp, resulted in the vassal city-states of the LBA (Knapp 1992, 92). These city-states were partially independent and partially incorporated under Egyptian rule. Na'aman states that, based on the textual evidence, these cities did not send agricultural goods to Egypt but mainly silver, cattle, and personnel. However, he suggests that the agricultural goods, such as grain, wine, and honey, were indeed sent to Egypt, but that the texts do not mention them since they were sent either as trade goods or tribute (Na'aman 1981, 184; Morris 2005, 124).

As for the economic relationship between Canaan and Egypt following this campaign, it seems that, according to Egyptian records, the Egyptians utilized agents in order to oversee the harvest and the storage of grains in Canaan. It has been suggested that these grains were not primarily transferred to Egypt but were rather used by the Egyptian troops when campaigning in the region or destined for the local population (Hoffmeier 2004, 135), a suggestion that has recently acquired some support (Finkelstein et al. 2017).

1.5.3. Northern Levant

1.5.3.1. Historical and Political Context

Between the sixteenth and fourteenth centuries BCE, a number of forces acted in the northern Levant: the Amorites, the Hurrians, the Hittites, and the Egyptians, with political power changing hands frequently. The struggle for control is reflected in an earlier letter dated to the eighteenth century BCE, stating the five kingdoms in Mesopotamia and northern Levant that were constantly in a battle for power: Babylon, Larsa, Eshnunna, Qatna, and Yamhad (Roaf 1990, 108–10; Van De Mieroop 2007, 85–86). In the sixteenth century, following the defeat of Yamhad (Aleppo), as well as the defeat of Hammurabi's Babylonian Empire by the Hittite king Mursili, the Near East was divided into new kingdoms: Egypt, Mitanni and the Hittites in the Levant, and the Kassites and Elamites in Mesopotamia (Roaf 1990, 132). The Syro-Levantine city-states were located between these great powers, always depending on either the Egyptians, the Mitannians, or the Hittites. At the end of the sixteenth century and the beginning of the fifteenth century, Mitanni grew stronger and was able to conquer the whole northern Levant—from Nuzi in the east to Alalakh in the west—and was even able to take over some cities in the southern Levant (though the extent of this is yet unknown). This expansion threatened Egyptian power and control over the southern Levant, bringing about military struggles between these two empires (Novak 2013, 340, Na'aman 1982, 183). These struggles enable us to synchronize between the Egyptian chronology and that of the northern Levant and Mesopotamia.

1.5.3.2. Chronology

The period under discussion, the sixteenth–fifteenth centuries BCE, is known as the Ancient Near East's "Dark Age" (Van de Mieroop 2007, 117, 121). In contrast to Egypt, the chronological schemes for the northern Levant and Mesopotamia are much more speculative and are mainly based on astronomical observations of Venus recorded in the Venus tablet of Ammisaduqa (Enuma Anu Enlil Tablet 63). These astronomical observations were preserved in a few tablets dating to the first millennium BCE. However, the astronomical observations probably derived from the Babylonian Hammurabi dynasty, dating to around the seventeenth century BCE (Cryer 1995, 658). These observations, based on celestial cycles repeated every sixty-four years, have created a debate among scholars regarding Mesopotamian chronology, divided between ultra-high chronology, high chronology, middle chronology (with a division between a high and low middle chronology, separated by eight years), low chronology (with low and lower chronologies again separated by eight years), new chronology, and ultra-low chronology (Schwartz 2008, 450; Manning et al. 2016, 1).

The absolute dates for this period in the northern Levant are based on Egyptian and Hittite dates (Van de Mieroop 2007, 122). However, the Hittite chronology is in many cases very hard to anchor since Hittite kings bearing the same name have no sequential numbers (Cryer 1995, 658; Schwartz 2008, 450). There is also no kings' list providing their reign lengths. In addition, there are several suggestions for the length of Suppiluliuma I's reign, the establisher of the Hittite New Kingdom, ranging between twenty and forty years (Van De Mieroop 2007, 156).

Two large archives were discovered in Alalakh, one in Stratum VII and the other in Stratum IV, both dated to the second millennium BCE. These archives, together with the biography of King Idrimi (inscribed on his statute), who ruled Alalakh probably around the middle of the fifteenth century (Zeeb 2004, 87–88), add information regarding the period but also create many puzzles. Some attempts have been undertaken to give absolute and relative dates to these archives. Zeeb (2004) has shown that they support the ultra-low chronology, whereas Na'aman (1976 and 1979) has shown that they fit well with the middle chronology. With that, recent dendrochronological studies, combined with C14 analysis, have supported the middle chronology or the low-middle chronology, based on material from the Anatolian sites of Acemhöyük and Kültepe, placing the death of Shamshi-Adad I at approximately 1776 BCE or 1768 BCE (Manning et al. 2016, 20–21; 2018).

Bietak (1991, 27), Cryer (1995, 659) and Zeeb (2004, 83) already pointed out that the second millennium should be dated based on Egyptian chronology, which is more secure than the Mesopotamian chronology that has two-hundred-year differences between the high, middle, low, or ultra-low chronologies. In fact, Hittite history cannot be dated without Egyptian, Assyrian, or Babylonian chronology (Van De Mieroop 2007, 156). Therefore, when discussing the history of the northern Levant, no absolute dates will be given.

1.5.3.3. The Kingdom of Mitanni

The kingdom of Mitanni is located in northern Syria, between the Euphrates bend and the Tigris. In its heyday, Mitanni controlled territories to the east of the Tigris, on the southern coast of Anatolia, and it probably controlled or exerted an influence on city centers in the southern Levant. Though known from written records as Washukanni, the capital of Mitanni has not been identified archaeologically.[10] The ethnicity of the Mitannians is still debated—whether it was of

---

10. One common suggestion for its identification is Tall Fakhariyah on the Habur River in modern Syria (Wilhelm 2013, 7062).

Hurrian or Indo-European origin—based on the languages and names appearing in Mitannian texts. It has also been suggested that, based on the West Semitic names and language (Akkadian) in use in cities in Mitanni's control (such as Qatna and Tell Hadidi), there was a process of acculturation undergone by the Mitannians and of emulation by the Semitic population. The Mitannians refer to themselves (as do the Assyrians) as Hanigalbat.

It is not clear how the Mitannian kingdom was exactly established. It has been suggested that, following the Hittite destruction of Aleppo, a power vacuum may have enabled this new state to develop.

By the first half of the fifteenth century, the Mitannian king Parrattarna controlled an area that included Kizzuwatna on the west, Nuzi on the east and Kadesh on the south. This was the most powerful kingdom in western Asia and the main impediment to Egypt's expansion during its Eighteenth Dynasty. This kingdom consisted of regions ruled by local rulers, both loyal and vassal to the Mitannian king, evident, for example, in the biography of Idrimi, the ruler of Alalakh, who was Parrattarna's vassal. Idrimi fled from Aleppo to Emar, becoming thereafter a leader of the Habiru. With their support and strength, he captured the city of Alalakh and its surroundings and became loyal to Parrattarna. As mentioned above, the Mitannian rulers backed up rebellions of Egyptian vassals both in the southern Levant (Thutmose III's campaign was discussed above) and in the northern Levantine coast, leading to animosity between these two great powers.

In the days of Amenhotep II, the Egyptian king of the Eighteenth Dynasty, peace was established between Mitanni and Egypt. During this time, and after a quiet period in the region, the Hittites and Mitannian kingdoms were at war again, seemingly since Mitanni aimed to protect, among other things, Egyptian interests in the area. This war ended in Mitanni becoming a vassal of the Hittite kingdom.

Things worsened for the Mitannian kingdom in the Amarna period when it suffered both internal and external difficulties leading to the end of its prosperous period. The internal problems originated in a feud between two branches of the royal family who competed for the throne, trying to overthrow the other by seeking support from outside powers.

Tushratta was placed on the throne by the murderer of his older brother Artashumara. This battle of powers was frowned upon by Egypt, and it was only after Tushratta executed his brother's murderer that Egypt resumed its diplomatic ties with Mitanni, as evidenced in the Amarna letters, since Tushratta corresponded with Amenhotep III, planning a diplomatic marriage between his daughter and Amenhotep. However, at the same time, Artatama, Tushratta's brother established a rival kingship, which was initially supported by Hatti. As mentioned above, it is Artatama's daughter who married Amenhotep II's son,

Thutmose IV, in a diplomatic marriage. After this, Artatama's son, Shuttarna III, probably murdered his uncle Tushratta and shifted Mitanni's alliance from Hatti to Assyria.

The Hittite king Suppiluliuma, in response, took the side of the exiled son of Tushratta, Kili-Teshub, and helped defeat Shuttarna III. Kili-Teshub was placed on the throne by Suppiluliuma I as his vassal.

Consequently, the west of the Mitanni kingdom was now under Hittite domination while the east was under Assyrian control. With claims to the Mitannian throne by those backed up by both Hatti and Assyria, the area of the Mitanni kingdom became a buffer zone between these two empires until the end of the LBA.

Following Suppiluliuma's death (at the end of the fourteenth century BCE), Hatti weakened, and the Assyrians gradually took over the Mitannian territory, though the Mitannians usually resisted, helped either by the Hittites or the Arameans, a new entity in northern Syria at this time. Eventually, however, the Assyrians established several administrative centers in the region as far as the Euphrates River on the border of the Hittite kingdom (Akkermans and Schwartz 2003, 327–29; Morris 2005, 234–37; Van De Mieroop 2007, 143, 150–54, 165).

1.5.3.4. The Hittite Kingdom

The Hittite Kingdom was most probably established by a ruler called Hattusili sometime in the seventeenth or sixteenth century BCE, a period also known as the Hittite Old Kingdom. It was situated in central Anatolia, and its capital was the city of Hattusa.

Hattusili expanded his kingdom to the south (that is, northern Syria), where he conquered the kingdom of Yamhad, including the city of Alalakh, but not the city of Aleppo itself. At the end of his days, his sons and nephew rebelled against him, and he appointed his grandson, Mursili I, as his heir. Though Mursili I's reign is not well known, there are records of his sacking of Babylon and Aleppo, thus disrupting the power balance in northwest Syria, leaving the entire region in political fragmentation, without a set of strong rulers to dominate the area. Mursili I was murdered by his brother-in-law, in turn later murdered as well. These internal instabilities prevented the Hittites from further expanding their kingdom, remaining in the heartland of Anatolia, becoming a major player again only in the fourteenth century BCE (Van De Mieroop 2007, 121).

Somewhere at the end of the seventeenth century or the beginning of the sixteenth century, Hatti entered a period of decline, also known as the Hittite Middle Kingdom. During this time, its two major rivals were Mitanni and Egypt, which were now allies, pulling forces together against Hatti. Its other rivals were the Gasga, a people from the southern coast of the Black Sea, perhaps responsible for the later destruction of Hattusa. Another rival was the vassal state of Arzawa, ruled by Madduwatta who conquered southwestern Anatolia and Cyprus in the mid-fourteenth century BCE.

However, in the fourteenth century BCE, Suppiluliuma I established the New Kingdom of Hatti, dominating the Anatolian regions to the south and east of Hattusa. He was also able to conquer all of western Mitanni, making it his vassal. The Hittite kingdom extended south as far as Damascus. Aleppo, Ugarit, Kadesh, and Amurru also became his vassals. In its heyday, Hatti's borders might have extended as far as the Black and Aegean seas. Suppiluliuma and his son both died of a plague brought by his soldiers, probably from campaigns in Syria. Mursili II, another son of Suppiluliuma, became the new king and was able to defeat Hatti's rivals: the Gasga in the north and Arzawa in the west.

In Akhenaten's days, in the fourteenth century BCE, there is evidence a peace treaty was in place between the Hittites and the Amurru led by Abdi-Ashirta, the ruler who led the conflict in the Lebanese mountains, sabotaging Egyptian interests there. However, the wars between Mitanni and Hatti were at full scale, ending in the demise of the Mitannian kingdom, sometime around 1340 BCE.

In the days of the Nineteenth Dynasty, during the thirteenth century BCE, Egypt emerged again as Hatti's rival. This rivalry culminated in the Battle of Kadesh, fought between Ramses II and Muwatalli, leading to the first ever known peace treaty (Van De Mieroop 2007, 156–59; Morris 2005, 236–37).

1.5.3.5. The Northern Levant

1.5.3.5.1. THE PERIOD BEFORE MARI'S DESTRUCTION

Shamshi-Adad, the first king of the discussed period, began his rule in the city of Ekallatum. Approximately ten years after he began his reign, Naram-Sin of Eshnunna captured Ekallatum, and Shamshi-Adad had to flee to Babylon. When Naram-Sin died, Shamshi-Adad returned to Ekallatum and later conquered Assur, extending his kingdom. This "Kingdom of Upper Mesopotamia" comprised the area extending from Assur in the east to Tuttul in the west and from the Habur Valley in the north to Babylon in the south, where the local conquered rulers became Shamshi-Adad's vassals. Among these, Qatna is worth mentioning as one of Shamshi-Adad's allied cities. Since the area of Shamshi-Adad's kingdom was very large, he placed his sons in strategic cities: His eldest, Ishme-Dagan, in Ekallatum, and his younger son, Yasmah-Addu, in Mari. Yasmah-Addu was reprimanded both by his father and by his brother for being weak and lazy. He was originally married to the daughter of the previous ruler of Mari (Yahdum-Lim), and later took another wife—the daughter of the king of Qatna, a marriage arranged by his father. Following Shamshi-Adad's death (the circumstances of which are unclear), local powers tried to take over the kingdom. Recently, it has been suggested that the death of Shamshi-Adad I should be placed at approximately 1776 BCE or 1768 BCE (Manning et al. 2016, 20–21; 2018).

Zimri-Lim, a previously unknown Amorite, took over Mari. Ishme-Dagan lost most of the kingdom except for Ekallatum and Assur, and northern Syria became an accumulation of small independent states. Their palaces were centralized establishments and became the dominant forces.

Hammurabi was an Amorite king who ruled Babylon, a kingdom to the south of the Upper Mesopotamia Kingdom. His reign began after his father's death, in the last decades of Shamshi-Adad's life. Following the death of Shamshi-Adad, Hammurabi was able to conquer the entire area of southern Mesopotamia, including Elam, Larsa, Eshnunna, and Mari, which were all incorporated in his kingdom. A vast archive was found in Zimri-Lim's palace, comprising approximately twenty thousand tablets and documenting internal and international affairs of the palace and kingdom. Hammurabi's destruction of Mari ended its role as a great power and political force in the region.

Hammurabi was succeeded by his son Samsuiluna, who had to face a great rebellion in the south. By the end of his reign, many of the southern cities were abandoned but the northern Babylonian kingdom continued to flourish for decades later. However, this kingdom was surrounded by sparsely inhabited regions. The cities of Babylon, Aleppo, and Alalakh were finally conquered by the Hittite king Mursili I, sometime in the sixteenth century BCE (1595 BCE according to the middle chronology or 1531 BCE according to the low chronology), who probably also destroyed other allied Syrian cities in the west.

The cities of western Syria flourished during the seventeenth century BCE, based on their trade ties (and possibly also blood ties) with the Hyksos in Egypt. Several Egyptian objects were found in the cities of Byblos, Ugarit, and Qatna, pointing to the existence of such relationships (Akkermans and Schwartz 2003, 308–26; Van De Mieroop 2007, 106–19).

As noted above, Mursili I most probably also conquered the cities allied with Aleppo; among these, Ebla is noteworthy due to its key role in Syrian chronology (mentioned above). This city was destroyed sometime around 1600 BCE, according to the middle chronology, a destruction dated on the base of historical events. Following this destruction, the city never fully resumed its role as a major power as it was in the MBA and was considered a small town in the LBA (Matthiae 2009, 169; Pinnock 2014, 234–35).

Though the Mesopotamian chronological conundrum described above is beyond the scope of the present research, it does have implications on southern Levantine chronology, due to the role of Hazor in this discussion. Hazor is the only southern Levantine site mentioned in the Mari archive of Zimri-Lim, and thus must have existed before Mari's destruction. It has therefore been argued that the material from Hazor supports the new chronology (A. Ben-Tor 2005).

As will be described in chapter 2, Hazor was established in the transition from the MBIIa to the MBIIb (Maeir 2000; A. Ben-Tor and Bechar 2017). Therefore, if we accept the traditional date of this transition at 1750 BCE (Sharon 2014)[11] and allow for a more flexible date for Shamshi Adad I's death (dated to 1776/1768 based on C14), after which Zimri-Lim becomes the ruler of Mari and corresponds with Hazor, then it seems that the debate could be reduced to a few years and not centuries.

1.5.3.5.2. THE POST-MARI PERIOD

Following the sacking of Mari, Babylon, and Aleppo, the Near East is considered to have been in a "dark age," when urbanism was at an all-time low. Several cities were destroyed or abandoned, and thus very few texts survived from this period. This is also when the Hurrian kingdom of Mitanni in northern Syria and the Kassite kingdom in the region of southern Babylonia were established. During these "Dark Ages," Mesopotamia, Anatolia and Syria saw a sharp reduction in the inhabited area and an increase in seminomadic groups (Van De Mieroop 2007, 123–24; 133).

At the end of the sixteenth century and during the fifteenth century BCE, this picture changed, as several equivalently powered territorial states arose again—Egypt, Babylonia and Assyria, all regional powers or empires. Mitanni now ruled the region of northern Syria, whereas Hatti controlled the region of central Anatolia and northwestern Syria. Egypt controlled parts of the region as well, especially the northern Levantine coast and the region south of Qatna, establishing two provinces in the northern Levant—Upe and Amurru—with an administrative center ruled by an Egyptian official. Both Mitanni and Egypt had a system of local rulers who were their vassals—they kept their power but were expected to send tribute to the ruler of the kingdom (Akkermans and Schwartz 2003, 329; Van De Mieroop 2007, 133).

1.5.3.5.3. THE NORTHERN LEVANT IN THE FOURTEENTH CENTURY

During this period, which is parallel to the Amarna period discussed above, the kings of the Near East correspond with each other, showing respect to their equals. The exchange of gifts between kings and courts was a significant aspect in maintaining these good relations, and some complaints were professed by the kings regarding the quality and quantity of these gifts.

---

11. However, consider an earlier suggestion for this transition, based on C14 dates (Höflmayer et al. 2016, Tell el-Burak, Tell el-Dab'a, and Tell Ifshar). In my opinion, the date the authors suggest (the beginning of the eighteenth century) is too early, as is the date suggested for the transition from the MBIIb to the MBIIc (Höflmayer et al. 2016, Tel Kabri), circa 1700 BCE. These dates would create a very long timespan for the MBIIc and the LBIa, a period of about 250 years, which was previously considered to be only about 100 years.

However, there were also rivalries and conflicts between these regional states, especially border wars when one side was trying to expand its territory, or wars aimed at readjusting the power relations between the powers (Van De Mieroop 2007, 136, 143–44). Following Hatti's sacking of Mitanni, sometime around 1340 BCE, the latter's vassal cities, such as Ugarit, Kadesh, Amurru, and all the northern Syrian cities (e.g., Aleppo, Emar), became Hittite vassals. The Akkar Plain was the base for Egyptian military campaigns in Syria but later was the heartland of the Amurru kingdom, which acted as a buffer zone between the Hittite and Egyptian Empires. The cities of the middle Euphrates (for example, Ekallatum and Emar) remained in Mitannian control until Suppuliliuma I's campaign against the Mitanni kingdom. Following this campaign, the region of the middle Euphrates became the eastern border of the Hittite kingdom.[12]

The division of control over the Levant between Egypt and Hatti was clear, until the beginning of the Nineteenth Dynasty, when the Egyptian kings Seti I and Ramses II tried to expand their domination further north, ending in the Battle of Kadesh between the Hittite king Muwatalli and Ramses II (Akkermans and Schwartz 2003, 329, 335–51; Van De Mieroop 2007, 165).

It is interesting to note that Aegean pottery was only found in coastal sites of the northern Levant and not in sites of the Middle Euphrates or the Habur region (Akkermans and Schwartz 2003, 352–53). This stands in sharp contrast to their prevalence in southern Levantine inland sites and emphasizes the Southern Levant's commercial links with the Aegean.

1.6. State of Research

The transition between the MBA and the LBA is marked by a clear continuation in the material culture (Sharon 2014, 50). This is also apparent in different excavation reports that incorporate a grouped discussion of the ceramic assemblages of these periods (e.g., Yoqneʻam, Lachish, and the recently published Hazor volume). However, some sites do include separate typological schemes for each period (e.g., Tel Dan, Beth-Shean, and Tel Mevorakh). A comprehensive definition of the transitional aspects of the LBI at several sites has not been attempted yet, except in Kassis's 1964 Ph.D. dissertation. His thorough work is focused around Megiddo, since many other sites, one of them also Hazor, were not published at the time. Another exceptional work is Bonfil's typological scheme of Tel Qashish (2003). The continuation between these two periods was pointed out by a number of scholars.

---

12. The LBA city of Carchemish was most probably the main center of the middle Euphrates, of which very little is known (Akkermans and Schwartz 203, 344).

Based on her research on the stratigraphy and pottery of Tel Qashish and her reexamination of Megiddo's stratigraphy, Bonfil has argued that there is a correlation between changes in the material culture (architecture and pottery) at the end of the MBII and the beginning of the LBI and the military campaign of Thutmose III (Bonfil 2012). According to her, this change is apparent in the transitions between Strata X and IX at Megiddo, Strata XXI and XXb at Yoqneʻam, Strata VIII and VIIb at Qashish, and Strata XII and XI at Tel Mevorakh (Bonfil 2012, 138, 140). Bonfil argues, in fact, that contrary to the previous notion it was not Megiddo's Stratum IX that was destroyed by Thutmose III but rather Stratum X. She attributes Stratum X to the last phase of the MBII and Stratum IX to the first LBA level (Bonfil 2012, 139).

She notes that a marked continuity is present in Hazor between the MBII and the LBI and suggests that this might be due to Hazor's political status, which perhaps gave the city independence from Egypt's direct rule during these periods (Bonfil 2012, 139–40). It should be mentioned that the lack of a destruction level between Strata 3 and 2 and Strata XVI and XV at Hazor does not necessarily indicate that Hazor did not take part in the Canaanite campaign against Egypt. According to Egyptian textual evidence, Megiddo was the gathering point of the Canaanite princes. Consequently, Thutmose III and his forces had no need to conquer all the cities in the southern Levant in order to ensure his victory (Weinstein 1981, 11).

Bonfil's suggestion regarding Yoqneʻam stands in contrast to A. Ben-Tor and Ben-Ami's (who have presented the relevant data from Yoqneʻam) interpretation of the finds that testify to the material continuity between Strata XXI and XXb, albeit an occupational gap (A. Ben-Tor and Ben-Ami 2005, 241), and between Stratum XXb and Stratum XXa, which was then destroyed by Thutmose III (A. Ben-Tor and Ben-Ami 2005, 242). Thus, it seems then that Bonfil's argument needs to be reexamined.[13]

This continuation was also evident from a thorough examination of the scarabs found in the southern Levant. D. Ben-Tor has shown that most of the Eighteenth Dynasty scarabs found in LBI contexts in Canaan are dated to the days of Thutmose III and that the locally produced scarabs of the MBII continue to be produced through the LBIa, pointing to cultural continuity until the Egyptian conquest of the southern Levant (2011, 32).

Naʾaman has also argued for a continuation from the end of the MBII to the LBI but suggested to lower this transition. By identifying northern names in

---

13. The present study concludes that the most significant changes in the architecture of the city occurred between Strata XXa and XIX, whereas the most significant ceramic changes occurred between Strata XXb and XXa. In other words, Bonfil's conclusions do not correspond with these changes.

cuneiform tablets found in the southern Levant, he was able to show that the Hurrian infiltration to Canaan began in the seventeenth century BCE. Na'aman argued that "the infiltration of northern groups ... was a major factor in the collapse of the Canaanite urban system" (Na'aman 1994, 183). Regarding terminology, he claims that the end of the MBII, the MBIIc, defined by urban deterioration, should be attributed to the LBI (1994, 184).

Other scholars have suggested that the transition from the MBA to the LBA should be dated to after Thutmose III's conquest, based on the continuity in the material culture (e.g., Dever 1987; Finkelstein 1996, 116–17).

In summary, there is a growing tendency to link the last phase of the MBA (the MBIIc) with the beginning of the LBI (the LBIa). The questions still standing are what is the ceramic evidence for linking them and, based on that, whether it is actually justified to link them together.

1.7. Economic Models and Pottery Production: Theoretical Framework

The current study will have repercussions on economic aspects and conclusions, and thus the discussion's theoretical framework should be outlined. Most of this outline is based on the comprehensive study by Timothy Earle on Bronze Age economic systems in Denmark, Hawaii, and the Mayan Empire (Earle 2002).

1.7.1. Economic Types of Specialization

Specialization, standardization, and pottery production are widely discussed in the literature (e.g., Rice 1984; Brumfiel and Earle 1987; Costin 1991; Arnold 2000). In the present study, the economic aspects of two types of specialization are discussed:

Independent specialists: Goods and services are made for unspecified people—anyone who wants to purchase these goods and services has access to them through an exchange. Production by these type of specialists is motivated by two factors. The first is efficiency, which lowers the production costs and thus the cost of the product itself. By doing so, the demand for the product may increase, which is essentially the goal of the producers. The second is standardization, which typically characterizes large-scale independent-specialists' production. Standardization creates efficient production since tasks become routine, reducing the cost of production.

Attached specialists: goods and services are provided to a patron, usually an individual member of the elite or institution. This relationship is based on the patron's need for secure and reliable access to the goods or services provided by the specialists. The secure access is translated into control over the distribution of the goods and services, usually including luxury goods as well as weapons. Efficiency and standardization are not an issue in this type of specialized production. On the contrary, objects tend to be highly elaborated and individualized. Consequently, only a few specialized craftspersons can make the objects, and imitations can easily be detected. The status of attached specialists can vary widely, and usually the individuals' profession does not set their social status (see also Schloen 2001, 304). In other words, the attached specialist can bear a status anywhere between elite and slave (Earle 2002, 128–29).

1.7.2. Models of Economic Development and Political Evolution

There are three models of economic development that also affect the political evolution of a society:

The Commercial Development Model. According to this model, based on the works of Smith (2007 [1776]) and early Marxists (e.g., Engels 1972 [1884]), the division of labor creates an efficient economic system and low-cost products. Therefore, the development of complex societies is dependent on independent specialized production and self-regulated markets. According to Earle, the problem with this model is that it explains rapid technological or economic development of societies but not noncapitalist economies. As evidence, in the economies Earle studied in the Hawaiian islands and the Andes, complex political systems developed without a wide-scale system of independent specialization (Earle 2002, 130–31).

The Adaptionist Model. This model, based on the works of new or processual archaeologists (e.g., Binford 1962), posits that society adapts itself to the environment by creating solutions to the local challenges of survival. These solutions include new technologies or new social organizations that result in the evolution into more complex societies. Earle argues that this model is also problematic since it assumes an evolutionary development where an increase in specialization results in an increase of exchange and correlates with developing complexity. He claims that these assumptions, again, do not fit the evidence from the Hawaiian islands and the Andes (Earle 2002, 137–39). According to him, these economies were not dependent on specialization. The specialization and exchange that did exist in these societies were not dependent on a central management (Earle 2002, 144).

The Political Model. According to this model, specialization is not the result of environmental or demographic conditions, and it is also not the primary factor that contributes to political and social complexity. This model posits that specialization is a key element for rulers, and their institutions might use specialization in order to strengthen their political and economic control. Based on this model, specialists were attached to a patron or to governing institutions to produce special products or provide special services. Thus, the specialists supply more control and power for their patrons—the patrons are the ones who decide how to distribute the specialized products and to whom. These goods are inalienable—their value and distribution are set by the social and political relationships within which they are produced. On the other hand, when production is carried out by independent specialists, they can decide to whom their products will be distributed. In this case, the goods are alienable—a social or political relationship between the producer, the distributer and the consumer does not necessarily exist (Earle 2002, 144).

1.8. Economic Model for the Southern Levant

Schloen, following Regner and Polanyi, all agree that the economic system of the Bronze Age was not a market exchange system, where products are uniformly traded based on their agreed value, disembedded from the social relations between the parties. Schloen argues that the economic system was rather one of redistribution or reciprocity. These modes of exchange consider the identity and status of both parties and their social relations. These modes are common, according to Schloen, in all patrimonial societies, where the social relations dictate and mediate most economic activities. Only the long-distance trade was somehow based on market exchange.[14] He maintains that the long-distance trade is conducted between strangers, the merchant and the consumer, but that this was marginal in the broader and local agrarian economic systems of the Bronze Age. In any case, Schloen claims that long-distance trade was not a significant element in the local economy and in social changes (this is also based on Stein's study; see Stein 1998). The long-distance trade was a symbolic means to legitimizing political dominance and relations (Schloen 2001, 80–88).

With Earle's political model in mind, it seems that Schloen's model could be easily accepted for inalienable goods; in other words, luxury goods and goods produced by attached specialists. It seems that Schloen would argue that alienable goods, such as flint tools or pottery vessels, also have an inalienable element to them as they are exchanged based on the identity and status of both consumer and distributor. However, Earle would argue that these types of goods would have been made by independent specialists, and, therefore, their distribution

---

14. Schloen claims that these long-distance exchanges were also based on personal social relations between contemporary kings (2001, 83–84).

would not be based on social or political relationships. Pottery distribution in the MBA and the LBA will be discussed in chapter 5, showing that MBA pottery was probably produced by attached specialists and therefore fits nicely in Schloen's model. The LBA pottery was most likely produced by independent specialists, making them alienable goods, therefore fitting Earle's political model.

1.9. Methodology

Architecture and ceramic assemblages are the bread and butter of "biblical archaeologists." Their changes may reflect political shifts, changes in the local population, changes in the modes of production and trade, and so forth.

When trying to identify changes in the material culture, an absolute chronology cannot be used, and we must deal with the relative chronology to try to point to the relative time when we can identify a change in the material culture. This can be achieved by examining the architectural and ceramic evidence of different sites that share a common feature.

1.9.1. Architecture

Architecture is a material means for nonverbal communication (Rapoport 1990). Due to its visibility and durability, it often serves as a medium of political, social, ideological, and symbolic expression (Abrams 1989, 48). By examining the ways by which the architecture of a built space communicates meaning and social practices, scholars can describe, to a certain degree, the sociopolitical processes that produced and were reproduced by that architecture (Pantou 2014, 369). Therefore, alterations in built structures have been used to identify social, political or economic changes within a given society (e.g., Abrams 1989; Liebmann et al. 2005; Maran 2006; Pantou 2014; and the numerous examples within these). Some modifications to the architecture can indicate a crisis in the society (Driessen 1995, 63–66).

This study will first investigate the architectural changes from the MBIIb to the LBIIa at Tel Hazor in order to pinpoint the stratigraphic changes that occurred at the site. The premise of the present study is that major architectural changes will also enable defining the transition from the MBA material horizon to that of the LBA at Hazor. Following the study of Hazor's architectural changes, these will be also examined at other sites located within this study's geographical framework. Similar to the study of Hazor, the examination will span the sixteenth–fourteenth centuries—that is, the MBIIb–LBIIa. Only sites where both MBA and LBA architecture was uncovered have been included in this study (and I will present additional caveats in chapter 3).

1.9.2. Ceramic Assemblages

In a general description of the changes in settlement patterns in the southern Levant, Na'aman argues that the deep change seen in this period (a wave of destruction and abandonment in every region in Canaan) is contemporaneous with the historical events (the Egyptian conquest of the region at the beginning of the Eighteenth Dynasty). According to him, this justifies a new name for the period—the LBA. He indicated that, in contrast to this deep change, there is an eminent continuation in the ceramic remains throughout the sixteenth century BCE. Na'aman states that this may indicate that the ceramic evidence is not always a criterion for historical changes. According to him, settlement patterns are more sensitive to historical changes than the ceramic scheme (Na'aman 1982, 175). This statement will be examined here—since mostly southern sites were destroyed and abandoned, and not the northern states, does this assertion hold also for the northern sites? In his dissertation, Bunimovitz stated that, in order to understand the transition between the MBA and the LBA, a thorough comparison between the different ceramic assemblages should be undertaken. However, he quotes and agrees with Kempinski in that regional differences are present in the ceramic remains during this period and, therefore, such a comparison should be made cautiously (Bunimovitz 1989, 36–37).

This study will include a comprehensive analysis of all assemblages from the sites located within the geographic framework. Published ceramic assemblages dated to MBA and LBA and their subperiods were found only at five sites—Beth-Shean, Tel Qashish, Yoqne'am, Tel Hazor, and Tell Arqa. These assemblages were examined using a macrotypology, which comprises a minimal number of general types (36), and not a by microtypology commonly used today (Karasik and Smilansky 2008). Using a macrotypology enabled me to track the pace of the change in the assemblages and examine whether social, economic, or political processes took place. In other words, analyzing the pace of change in low resolution (macrotypology) will enable identification of the apparatus of change before discussing the change's cause. This analysis will therefore examine what changed, at what pace, and which characteristics in the material assemblage changed before others. This sort of examination allows for discussing possible processes that might have enabled the occurrence of a historical event to take place, bringing the start of a new period. It will also allow examining whether processes highlighted in the material culture could have enabled the conquest of Canaan by Egypt or if this conquest is what led, in fact, to changes in the material culture.

Adams conducted a comprehensive study on changes in Nubian ceramic traditions from 200 to 1550 CE when Nubia changed its religious ideology from Egyptian religion through Christianity and finally to Islam. In this thorough research, he has shown that the most abrupt changes in the ceramic assemblages identified by him did not always go hand in hand with social changes. However, he also noticed that the introduction of Christianity to the Nubian region in the sixth century CE led to architectural, artistic, and literary changes, while the ceramic *traditions* only altered about 250 years later. On the other hand, he did notice changes in the forms of the vessels when the religious beliefs transformed from paganism to Christianity but also that changes in *forms* occur, nevertheless, every two to three centuries (throughout the historical times), not accompanying political changes (Adams 1979, 732).

Thus, changes in ceramic traditions do not always reflect socioeconomic or historical events. However, Adams claims that in nonindustrial societies, arguments based on "from pottery to history" are safer (Adams 1979, 733). Since the present study clearly deals with nonindustrial societies, interpreting changes in the ceramic assemblages in light of historical events will be attempted, though cautiously.

1.9.3. Imported Ware: Why Should It Be Considered?

In his comprehensive study of pottery assemblages from Nubia, one of the families that Adams examined was manufactured in Aswan, which is considered imported pottery. He noted that the different families that he examined evolved with very little influence on each other. Each family evolved at its own pace. He also posits that, if each family were considered by itself in the historical and political reconstruction, a different conclusion would be reached, and none of these conclusions would be accurate (Adams 1979, 733). It is therefore important to examine the development of the local pottery in light of the imported Aegean pottery. In chapter 5, I will show how this pottery had a great influence not only on the local assemblages but especially on the production systems of the local plain ware.

1.10. Research Outline

The following chapters of this research will deal with architectural and ceramic changes, throughout the MBA and LBA, in the geographical area described above.

Chapter 2 will describe the architectural changes that took place at Hazor, the focal site of this study. The architecture and the city plan of almost all excavated areas will be studied, of both the acropolis and the lower city. It will be shown that the most significant changes occurred between the strata dated to the LBI and the LBIIa. The architectural fabric of Hazor and the changes within the city plan and use of the areas will be examined, showing that profound changes took place in the function of specific areas in the lower city of Hazor. Finally, it will also be suggested that a crisis occurred at Hazor during the LBI, most probably in the LBIa.

Chapter 3 will deal with sites within the described geographical framework and will examine the architectural changes that took place in these sites. In most of them, the major changes are reflected between the LBI and the LBII or between the LBIa and the LBIb, supporting and strengthening the evidence noted at Hazor in chapter 2.

Chapter 4 will examine the ceramic changes in assemblages from five sites within the geographical framework of this study dating to the MBA and the LBA. The ceramic assemblages will be analyzed based on macrotypology. This method is unique and seldom used by others. It also stands in sharp contrast to the very popular microtypology used today. It will be shown that, again, the most significant ceramic changes occurred between the LBI and the LBII, or between the LBIa and the LBIb, when pottery became less varied, more regular, and more mass-produced.

Chapter 5 will discuss the results of the previous chapters. It will be argued that the historical event that led to the changes in the material culture is the conquest of the southern Levant by the Egyptian Empire, following Thutmose III's campaign. It will also be suggested that the local economic decline following the expulsion of the Hyksos and the fall of the Syrian cities in the north enabled this conquest. It will be argued that the influx of Aegean imports (which included mainly closed but also open shapes) contributed to the lack of variety in shapes and decorations noted in the LBA local assemblages. It will also be suggested that the MBA ceramic production was based on attached specialists, which are less efficient, investing vast energy and resources in the production of vessels, while the LBA ceramic production was based on independent specialists, who promote efficiency and standardization. The general conclusion of this study is that the new administrative system, created following Thutmose III's campaign, led to significant changes in the ceramic production system as well as to architectural changes probably needed due to the decrease in the size of the local population.

CHAPTER 2

The Transition from the Middle to the Late Bronze Age: Architectural Aspects at Hazor

2.1. Background

Tel Hazor is the largest tel in modern-day Israel (fig. 2.1). It encompasses an area of approximately eighty-four hectares, comprising an acropolis as well as a lower city.

Excavations at the site have, so far, been conducted by two major teams of the Hebrew University of Jerusalem.[1] Yigael Yadin headed the first in the 1950s, as well as a supplementary season in 1968. Yadin excavated in both the acropolis and the lower city. Excavations at the site were renewed in 1990 by Amnon Ben-Tor, continuing to the present day, and codirected with me since 2015.[2] The renewed excavations are limited to the acropolis, focusing on two areas previously excavated by Yadin. Three seasons of excavations were conducted in Area S in the lower city by Sharon Zuckerman during the years 2008–2010.

Yadin dated the first second-millennium settlement at Hazor to the MBIIa/b transition period, terming this settlement pre-Stratum XVII (Yadin 1972, 121–22). According to him, the establishment of "Greater Hazor," the city mentioned in the Mari archive, should be dated to the MBIIb (1972, 107–8). This claim was ascertained by the renewed excavations (Ben-Tor and Bechar 2017, 1–2), though it was decided to change Yadin's chronological strata scheme based on the ceramic and architectural finds uncovered in the renewed excavations (see table 2.1). This chapter expands on the claims of the renewed excavations and aims to complete the given picture with evidence exposed in the lower

---

A portion of this chapter was originally published in Shlomit Bechar, "Changes in the Architectural Fabric of Hazor's Lower City from the Middle Bronze to the Late Bronze," in *Transitions, Urbanism, and Collapse in the Bronze Age: Essays in Honor of Suzanne Richard*, ed. J. C. Long Jr. and W. G. Dever (Sheffield: Equinox, 2021), 81–94. © Equinox Publishing Ltd. 2021.

1. John Garstang was the first to excavate the site in 1928. However, the finds from his excavation have never been fully published and therefore will not be dealt with here.

2. Excavations were codirected by Amnon Ben-Tor and Sharon Zuckerman between 2006 and 2014, and after Zuckerman's untimely death, I codirected them beginning in 2015.

city and in the northern slopes of the tel. The following discussion is arranged by area, beginning with the lower city and continuing to the acropolis.[3] Since the aim of this chapter is to try to pinpoint the time of architectural changes between the MBA and the LBA, this discussion only includes the MBIIb–LBIIa Strata, excluding Stratum 1a of the lower city and Stratum XIII of the acropolis, which are dated to the LBIIb. The architectural evidence will be first presented and discussed, followed by an analysis of the built environment of the lower city. Characteristics of crisis architecture will also be discussed as related to the transition from the MBA to the LBA. Last, the historical implications following the conclusions of this chapter will also be presented.

2.2. The Architectural Evidence

Architectural remains at Hazor dating to the MBA and the LBA have been unearthed in nine areas of excavations, two of which are on the acropolis and the rest in the lower city. As noted above, the city is first established in the MBIIa/b transition (Stratum XVII/4). This city was encompassed by a large fortification system. It is not well known in the lower city (Stratum 4), whereas on the acropolis (Stratum XVII) the MBA palace and the Southern Temple were established during this stratum. It is also possible that the road leading from the lower city through the northern slopes of the acropolis (Area M) to the center of the acropolis (Area A) was built during this time. The next phase, dated to the MBIIb–c (Stratum XVI/3), is much better known architecturally in the entire site. The fortifications still continue to be in use. In the acropolis, the temple and palace continue to be in use and a complex of standing stones was built in an open area near the supposed entrance to the palace. In the lower city, a domestic quarter was found in the southwestern corner (Area C) and in the east (Area D). Monumental temples were built in the northernmost part of the lower city (Area H) and in its eastern part (Area F). The paved road leading up to the acropolis (Area M) continued to be in use during this stratum. In Stratum XV/2 of the LBI, the gates continue to be in use. The domestic nature in the southwest (Area C) and the east (Area D) continued during this time. The temple in the east (Area F) was decreased to half its original size. In the temple in the northernmost part of the lower city (Area H), a large courtyard with several installations was built. On the acropolis, it seems that the southern part of the

---

3. This description will be accompanied by schematic plans of each discussed area, apart from Areas D and E where mainly tunnels and cisterns were found. In the accompanying plans, the walls are shaded black, walls that continued to be in use from a previous stratum are shaded dark gray (unless otherwise specified), floors and pavements are only mentioned by locus number, and benches are marked but not filled in. Blocked entrances are shaded in diagonal lines.

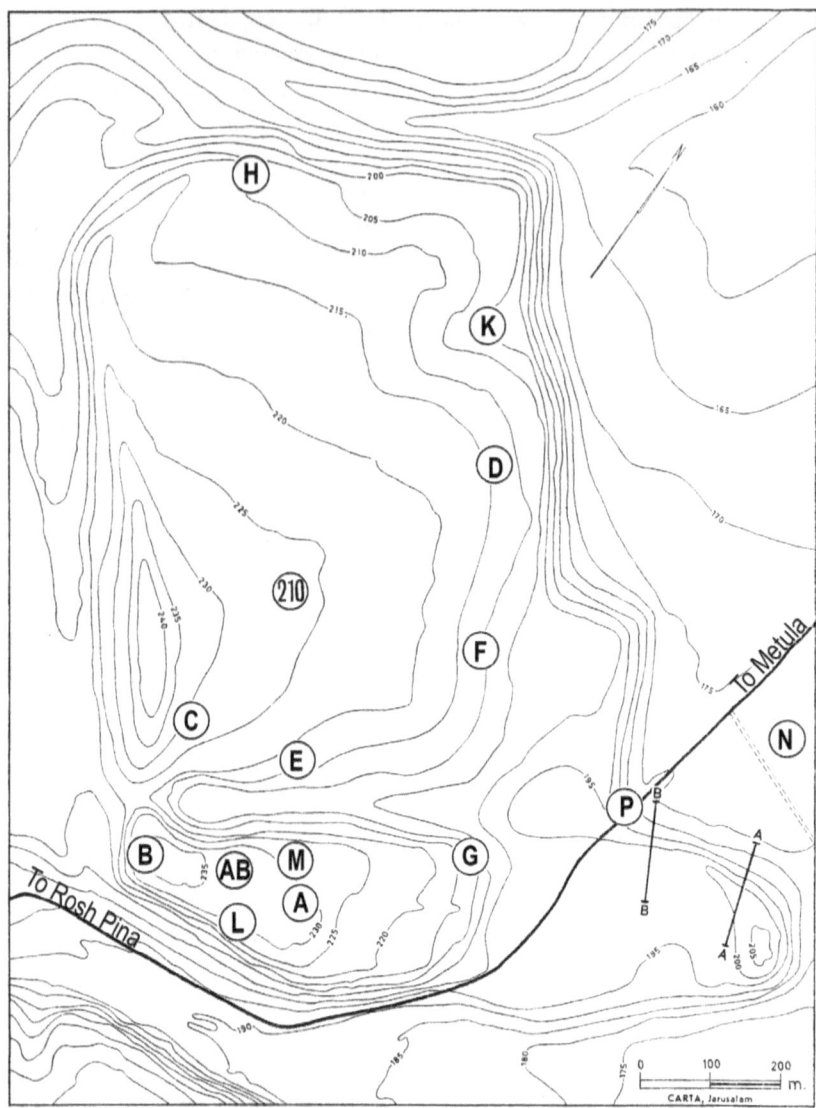

FIGURE 2.1 Map of Tel Hazor and the different excavation areas.

acropolis was abandoned. The Southern Temple was covered and ultimately taken out of use. Minor changes were also noted in the paved road leading from the northern slopes of the tel (Area M) to the center of the acropolis (Area A). In the LBIIa, Stratum XIV/1b, major building projects commenced in the entire city. In the southwestern corner of the lower city (Area C), a small temple was built, surrounded by several workshops or domestic units. The domestic nature

TABLE 2.1 Hazor's Strata

Stratum of the Acropolis	Stratum of the Lower City	Period by Yadin	Period Following Ben-Tor and Bechar 2017
XVII	4	MBIIa/b–MBIIb	MBIIa/b–MBIIb
XVI	3	MBIIb–MBIIc	MBIIb–MBIIc
XV	2	LBI	LBIa[a]
XIV	1b	LBIIa	LBIb–LBIIa
XIII	1a	LBIIb	LBIIa–LBIIb

[a]The following discussion will refer to Stratum XV/2 as LBI and Stratum XIV/1b as LBIIa, in order to avoid confusions.

in the east (Area D) continued during this stratum. The monumental temple found in the east (Area F) went out of use and the area was now a domestic quarter. The monumental temple in the north (Area H) continued to function as a royal temple with some changes to its layout and its courtyard. On the acropolis, a ceremonial precinct with temples and courtyards was built above the earlier palace (Area A). On the northern slopes of the acropolis (Area M), the paved road went out of use and a large administrative palace was built.

The following is a detailed description of these changes, by the different areas. It will be shown that the major architectural changes took place between the LBI and the LBIIa (Strata XV and XIV on the acropolis and Strata 2 and 1b in the lower city). It will also be shown that the fabric of the city was also changed between these two strata. Finally, it will be suggested that this was due to a decline in the city of Hazor.

2.2.1. Area D (Yadin et al. 1958, Plate CLXXXIII)

Several plastered bottle-shaped cisterns were uncovered in this area. These were probably originally used to store water. Evidence for residential buildings and a number of tombs were found near the cisterns. In the MBIIb–c, one of these cisterns (L.9024) was turned into a tomb. Two kilns should probably also be dated to the MBII—one used as a pottery kiln and the other for the metallurgy industry.

In Stratum 2 of the LBI, Cistern L.9024 was used as a silo. A sterile accumulation was identified between Strata 2 and 1b (of the LBIIa), leading Yadin to suggest a hiatus during the LBIb. A similar situation was identified in Cistern L.9027.

The finds attributed to Strata 1b (LBIIa) and 1a (LBIIb) are nearly impossible to distinguish. In these strata, some of the cisterns were used to store ceramic vessels (e.g., L.9017) and some as tombs (e.g., L.9027; see Yadin 1972, 38–42; Yadin et al. 1958, 100–141).

2.2.2. Area F (Figure 2.2, Photo 2.1)

The earliest building activity in this area, attributed to Stratum 4 of the MBIIb (Ben-Tor 1989, 135, 147) is a system of extensive underground tunnels cut in the rock, about one hundred meters long, sloping toward to the outer perimeter of the city on the west. These tunnels originated in different directions and locations but converged to one tunnel (Yadin 1972, 42–44).

Directly on top of these tunnels, in Stratum 3 (of the MBIIb–c), a large rectangular building was erected. Yadin interpreted this building as a temple based on parallels from Assur (Yadin 1972, 96–97) and the fact that cultic places tend to keep their nature throughout the ages (I discuss this below in the section on Strata 2–1). However, the finds did not aid in the clear identification of the building's function (Ben-Tor 1989, 138). Yadin reconstructed this building as a "double temple" with two identical and parallel wings and three rooms in-between (Yadin 1972, fig. 23). In the final publication, the editors noted that, in many cases, the preservation of the walls of this building was so poor that it was actually impossible to confirm or deny Yadin's reconstruction (Ben-Tor 1989, 138).

The poor preservation of the walls was also evident in Stratum 2 (of the LBI) where part of the building is likewise based on reconstructions (Ben-Tor 1989, 150). In fact, in both Stratum 3 (MBIIb–c) and Stratum 2 (LBI) buildings, the excavators did not identify the southern wall of the building, and, therefore, the entire southern part of the building is also a reconstruction. In Stratum 3, the reconstruction is based on the assumption of this being a "Double Temple," whereas in Stratum 2 it is based on it being a "Square Temple" (Ben-Tor 1989, 139, 151). Yadin also based his reconstruction of this building as a temple on its similarity to the temple found in Amman (Yadin 1972, 98–99 and fig. 24), though recently, it has been suggested that the latter actually functioned as a watchtower (Burke 2007, 46–47). All the outer walls of the temple, built already in Stratum 3, continued to be in use in Stratum 2 (Ben-Tor 1989, 152).

The heart of the Stratum 2 building is a plastered courtyard (L.8074) surrounded by walls of different widths. A narrow entrance, made by the southern and western walls surrounding this courtyard, leads to it. Short walls were built perpendicular to the outer faces of the courtyard's walls. These walls did not abut the inner faces of the outer walls, leaving narrow openings between them (Ben-Tor 1989, 151–52).

A row of stones (W.8571), built on the line of the inner face of the courtyard's northern wall (W.8563), connects the northeastern corner of the courtyard with its eastern outer wall. The editors do not accept this reconstruction due to the poor preservation in this area and the fact that it was not built *directly* on the same line as wall W.8563. However, Dunayevsky, the expedition's surveyor,

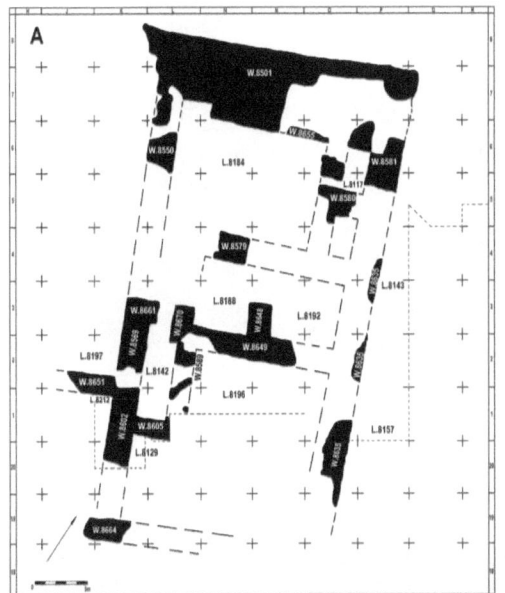
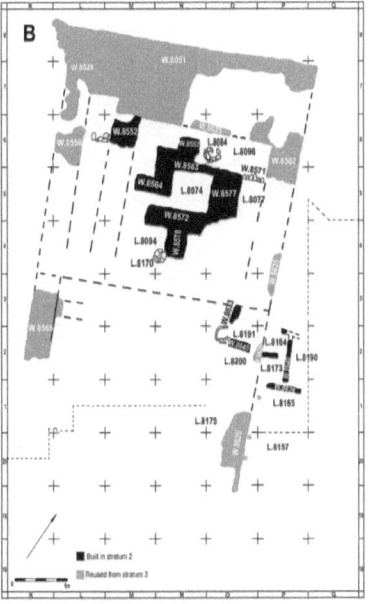
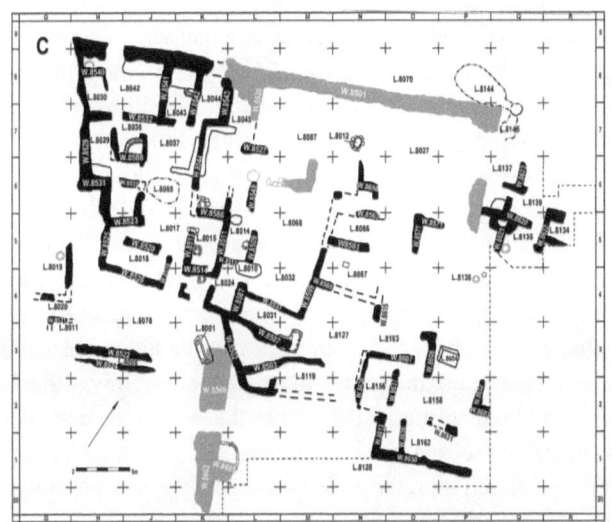

FIGURE 2.2 MBA and LBA strata in Area F—(A) Stratum 3 (after Ben-Tor 1989, plan xxviii); (B) Stratum 2 (after Ben-Tor 1989, plan xxix); (C) Stratum 1b (after Yadin et al. 1959, plate ccx).

PHOTO 2.1 Aerial photo of Area F, looking south (from Yadin et al. 1961, pl. lx).

suggests that this row of stones is, in fact, the protruding eastern wall (Ben-Tor 1989, 152). Thus, if this reconstruction is accepted, it appears that this wall divides the building in two, closing the free passages between the different rooms surrounding the courtyard. Another possible suggestion is that this is a later addition to the building, which may explain why this row of stones is not built exactly on the same line as wall W.8563. Only one floor (L.8094) was identified in these rooms, made of small pebbles abutting wall W.8578, which is also the southern protruding wall (contra the editors, Ben-Tor 1989, 152).

Several narrow walls and floors of two rooms were identified to the south of the "Square Temple." W.8635 of the earlier "Double Temple" (the eastern wall of that building) was probably the western limit of these rooms. Another narrow wall, an installation and a stone pavement were built to the west of these rooms, directly on top of W.8635. These rooms are of the same nature as those to the east (Ben-Tor 1989, 153–56). Therefore, it can be suggested that the Stratum 3 wall was no longer in use in Stratum 2. Another possibility is that here, as well, two phases can be identified—the first in the eastern rooms, which used the earlier wall, and the second in the western rooms, which sealed the earlier wall. This latter explanation is preferred. Four tombs were also attributed to Stratum 2 (Ben-Tor 1989, 156–58).

Here is the place to mention a few elements that were not discussed by either Yadin or the editors of Hazor III–IV. These include two rounded installations built of stone, found inside the "Square Temple." One, L.8170, is built in the southwestern room next to the protruding southern wall (W.8578), blocking the passage between the two southern rooms. The second, L.8084, is built in the northeastern room, on the line of wall W.8563, and thus cancels the northern half of the wall. These two installations together with other elements mentioned above allow suggesting that there are two phases for Stratum 2 in Area F. During the first phase, the "Square Temple" was built reusing walls of the Stratum 3 "Double Temple" in the building itself and in the south, by the narrow walls. During the second phase, some of the entrances to the rooms were blocked, and W.8653 of Stratum 3 went out of use.

According to Yadin, the inhabitants of Strata 1b–1a (LBII) knew the tunnels' system in this area and dug several pits to reach them. He postpones the discussion of the LBII activities in this area (such as the preparation and straightening of the area, digging into the tunnels and earlier strata, etc.) to volumes III–IV. He also suggests a hiatus in the settlement in this area between Strata 2 (LBI) and 1b (LBIIa) (Yadin et al. 1958, 129). However, no such discussion appears in Hazor III–IV.

In Stratum 1b (dated to the LBIIa) the area undergoes a complete change. Although still cultic in nature, evident by the large altar in the southwestern part of the area, it now comprises mainly meager walls, courtyards, and installations bounded by a thick wall in the north (W.8501). The walls and courtyards form a number of buildings supported by terraces (e.g., buildings 8039 and 8068). At times it was nearly impossible for the excavators to differentiate between Strata 1b and 1a (of the LBIIb). During Stratum 1b, the main cultic area lies to the south and west of the small buildings. The prime feature of this cultic area is a large limestone altar (L.8001). The area also includes what Yadin refers to as a "Square" (L.8078), a drain channel (L.8005), as well as a "cult place" (L.8019) and a niche (L.8011) near it. A Stratum 3 wall (W.8569, dated to the MBIIb–c) was used as a platform for the altar, which was surrounded by large amounts of bones. The inhabitants of Strata 1b–1a (LBII) reused the tunnels dug in Stratum 4 (of the MBIIb, discussed above) and, in many of them, large amounts of pottery vessels were found. Two tombs were uncovered in the area. One, L.8144–8145, yielded large amounts of local and imported pottery and was in use only during Stratum 1b (LBIIa). It was sealed in Stratum 1a (LBIIb) by wall, W.8624, built over its entrance (not depicted in the plan). The other tomb, L.8065, dug in Courtyard L.8037, also yielded large amounts of pottery, though not as much as tomb L.8144–8145 (Yadin 1972, 100–101; Yadin et al. 1958, 130–45).

2.2.3. Area C (Figure 2.3)

The earliest finds in this area were built directly on virgin soil. The excavators could not differentiate between the finds of Stratum 4 (of the MBIIb) and those of Stratum 3 (dated to the MBIIb–c), and thus they are described together. These include two residential units built on terraces, with shared walls

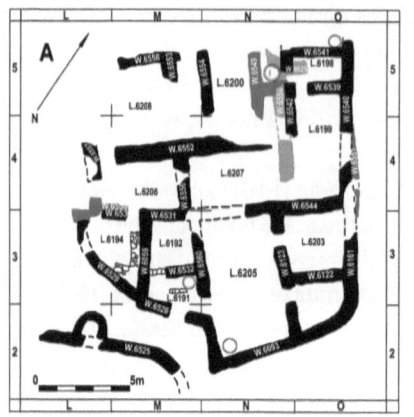
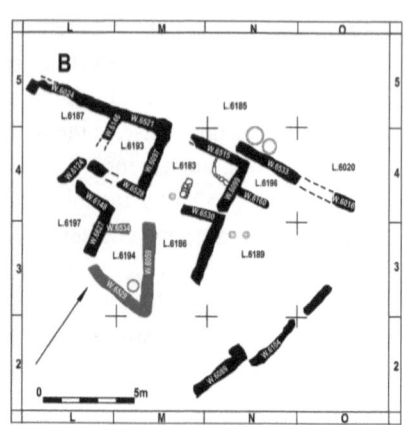
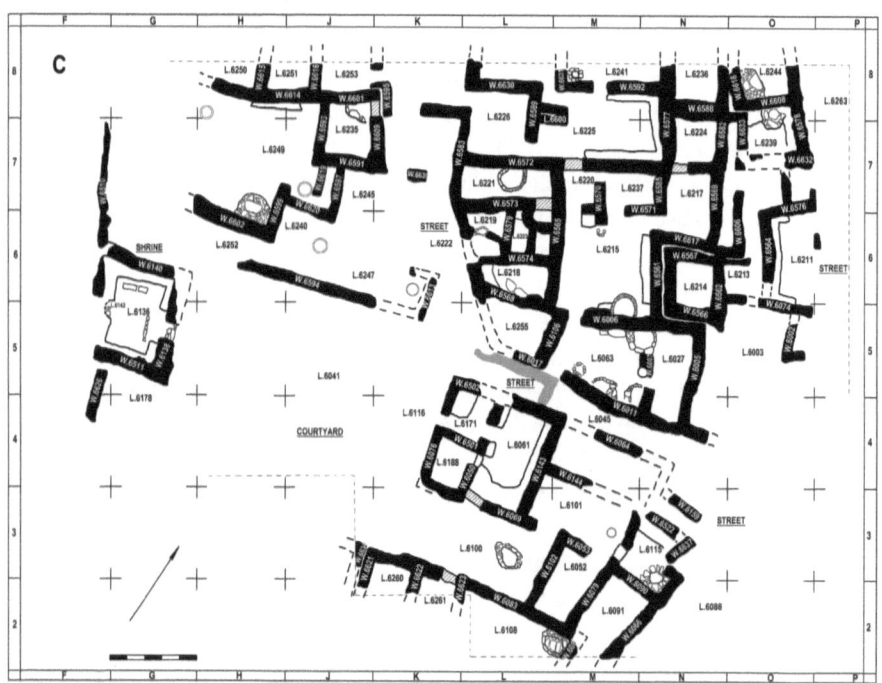

FIGURE 2.3 MBA and LBA strata in Area C—(A) Strata 4–3 (after Yadin et al. 1959, plate CCVII); (B) Stratum 2 (after Yadin et al. 1959, plate ccvii); (C) Stratum 1b (after Yadin et al. 1959, pl. ccviii).

(W.6544 and W.6531). The two units are surrounded by three alleys—in the west, south, and east.

The southern house (building 6205) is better preserved and is composed of a courtyard flanked by rooms on the west and east. At least two phases could be identified in this house. The second phase is characterized by blocked entrances (such as the small wall blocking the entrance between L.6192 and L.6191) and raised floors such as that of Courtyard 6205. This led, in the second phase, to a change in the function of the oven found here, which was turned into a burial place (Yadin et al. 1960, 78) and consequently a new oven was built in room L.6191. Seventeen burials were found in this house, eleven of these were infant burials in storage jars, one adult interment and five disturbed tombs (Yadin et al. 1960, 81–85).

Two phases were identified in the southwestern part of the northern building (6200), based on an addition of a bench to wall W.6059. In the northeastern part of this building, three phases were identified (shaded differently in fig. 2.3: Strata 4–3) based on walls erected one on top the other (Yadin et al. 1960, 79–80). Fourteen burials were found in this house: six infant burials in storage jars, two adult burials, and five disturbed tombs (Yadin et al. 1960, 81–85). At the end of Stratum 3, Building 6200 was covered by a layer of ashes (Yadin et al. 1960, 77), leading Yadin to suggest that this stratum came to an end in a violent conflagration (Yadin 1972, 31). However, since this is of limited extent in Area C in general, this might seem an exaggeration. It would be more cautious to say that Building 6200 came to an end in a fire, but not necessarily the entire Stratum 3 of Area C, and of course not the entire stratum of the lower city.

The inhabitants of Stratum 2 (of the LBI) filled the remains of Stratum 3 (MBIIb–c) with a constructive fill and leveled the area to avoid building on terraces as was done in the previous stratum (Yadin et al. 1960, 92).

A few fragmentary walls were attributed to Stratum 2 but do not add up to a clear plan. Three walls from Stratum 3 continue to be in use (W.6534, W.6059 and W.6529), all walls of the southern room of building 6200. This suggests that despite the fact that the Stratum 3 building was destroyed by fire, the inhabitants of the subsequent city were still able to use its walls. An oven was situated on the corner formed by walls W.6059 and W.6529. In Stratum 2, the area kept its domestic nature. Near the fragmentary walls, cooking facilities (such as the ovens near wall W.6533 and in room L.6194), and storage installations (such as silo in room L.6183) were found (Yadin et al. 1960, 92–93).

In Stratum 1b (LBIIa), the area completely changed its nature—from small domestic units to an area of cultic and industrial nature. The tops of two Stratum 2 walls (W.6521 and W.6416) were used as floors (Yadin et al. 1960, 99). Similarly to the other areas (discussed above and below), the architectural differences between Strata 1b and 1a were very minor, most of the walls continuing to be in use (Yadin et al. 1958, 76). Three streets divided the area.

On the west, abutting the earthen rampart built in the MBII, a small "shrine" was built in the form of a rectangular room with benches built around all its walls. Two limestone slabs were placed next to the northern wall and probably served as offering tables. A niche (L.6142) was cut out of the western wall, and the steles and statues discovered in the subsequent Stratum 1a (LBIIb) niche were most likely originally placed here (Yadin et al. 1958, 84–85). Building 6061 was erected to the east of the shrine and across the entrance to the shrine. The "shrine" and Building 6061 were separated by an open courtyard (L.6041). Building 6061 had two phases—in the first phase, the building had two rooms, each entered from a different street. In the later phase, the western room was divided into two rooms, and the entrance to the eastern room was blocked. Consequently, in the second phase, only one entrance was accessible to the building, from the west, thus creating an axis with the entrance to the shrine (Yadin et al. 1960, 98).

To the north and east of the shrine, a large quarter was exposed, which extends over the limits of the Stratum 3 quarter (Yadin et al. 1960, 95). It is delimited by three streets (L.6045 on the south, L.6222 on the west and L.6088 and L.6263 on the east). Another quarter lies to the south, but most of it has not been exposed. The northern quarter included at least two structures (building 6063 in squares M/P-4/8 and building 6225 in squares K/N-5/8), each with two phases based on the blocked entrances. Another building, which also had two phases, was exposed to the west of this quarter, near the earth rampart (building 6249 in squares H/K-5/8). In the later phase of all three buildings, several openings in the walls were blocked, including the opening in wall W.6572 (square M-7) between the two eastern buildings (Yadin et al. 1960, 98). Several installations (noteworthy are the numerous silos) and benches were built throughout the buildings (Yadin et al. 1960, 98–104). The function of the two eastern buildings probably had something to do with the production of pottery, based on some potter's wheels found in them (Yadin et al. 1960, 100–102). It is also possible that the identical clay vessels found stacked on a bench in Room L.6211 (square O-6; Yadin et al. 1960, 105–6) were probably associated with the potter's workshop identified here. Yadin suggested these pottery workshops were associated with the temple activities (Yadin 1972, 35), though, in fact, there is no evidence connecting the pottery manufacture with the small temple, other than their close proximity.

A cistern was found in the southwestern corner of Room L.6241 in Building 6225. Interestingly, this cistern was filled with a constructive fill between Strata 2 and 1b, similarly to the cisterns in Areas D and E (Yadin et al. 1960, 103).

Signs of destruction between Strata 1b and 1a were identified in the "shrine" (Yadin et al. 1958, 85), as well as in building 6063 (Yadin et al. 1960, 99–100).

2.2.4. Area H (Figure 2.4, Photo 2.2)

The earliest temple was built in Stratum 3 (of the MBIIb–c), cutting the earthen rampart built in Stratum 4, dated to the MBIIb (Ben-Tor 1989, 220). It is the first in a series of four temples built one on top of the other. The main differences between these temples can be seen between Strata 2 (LBI) and 1b (LBIIa), and the discussion will focus on these two temples (the earlier and later temples of Strata 3–2 and 1b–1a, respectively), with the minor changes within them attributed to the different strata.

The earlier temple is a rectangular building divided into two parts. Its southern part is divided into three rooms by two partition walls (W.2535 and W.2526). The northern part is a large room with a niche (L.2187) in its northern end, within wall W.2574. It is highly likely that pillars supported the roof of this room (Ben-Tor 1989, 215–19).

In Stratum 3 (MBIIb–c), the entrance to this building was from the south, through two steps built of basalt slabs. The steps, the entrance to the northern hall and the niche are all built on a single axis, giving the temple its symmetricity (Ben-Tor 1989, 219–20).

The area to the south of the temple is a large open courtyard that is paved with closely packed very small pebbles. It is at least thirty meters long and is limited by a narrow wall to the south, though the nature of this wall is unclear. Two rooms were built (squares F-11/12) abutting the temple from the east (Ben-Tor 1989, 219–20).

Small differences between Strata 3 (MBIIb–c) and 2 (LBI), inside the temple, include the raising of floors, the building of wall W.2565 (squares C/D-14), and the erection of a raised rectangular installation next to this wall. The latter two led to the closing of the niche that was part of the northern room during Stratum 3, thus canceling the straight axis of the building and creating a small entrance to the niche. The northern room was paved, and a layer of plaster covered the pavement. Two shelves or benches were built abutting the southern walls of this room (Ben-Tor 1989, 223–27). Two benches were also built abutting the southern façade of the temple (Ben-Tor 1989, 229).

The main difference between Strata 3 (MBIIb–c) and 2 (LBI) is the organization of the area surrounding the temple. This area is divided into two large paved courtyards (northern and southern), separated by a propylaeum constructed of two broad rooms with a threshold built of three basalt slabs in the southern room. The widths of these slabs differ, and their length does not fit that of the opening, thus indicating they probably originated in Stratum 3, most likely from the stairs leading into the temple. Benches were built abutting all walls of the southern room of the propylaeum, and one bench was built in the northern room, abutting the western wall. Two raised square installations (probably used as a *bamah* or

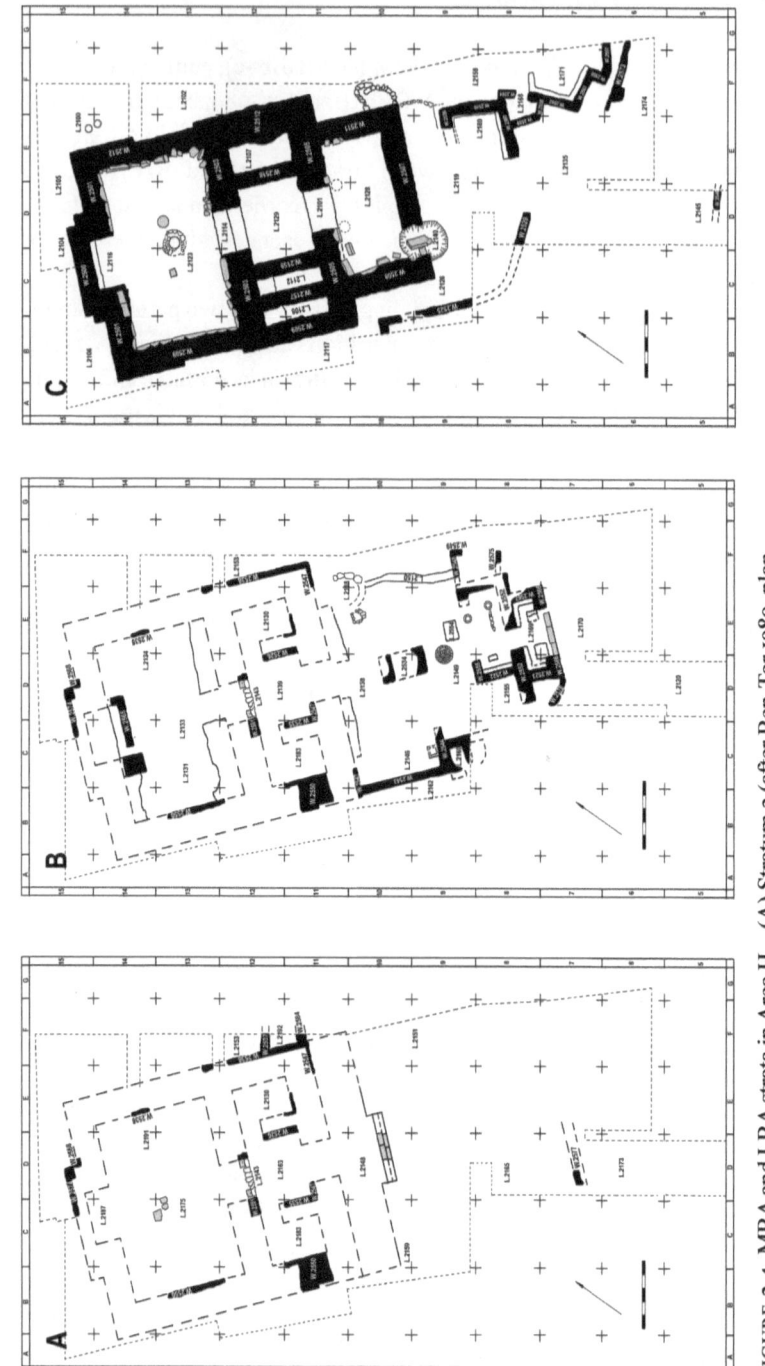

FIGURE 2.4 MBA and LBA strata in Area H—(A) Stratum 3 (after Ben-Tor 1989, plan xxxvii); (B) Stratum 2 (after Ben-Tor 1989, plan xxxviii); (C) Stratum 1b (after Ben-Tor 1989, plan xxxix).

PHOTO 2.2 In the center of the photo, a wall from Stratum 1b, cutting the Strata 2 and 3 courtyard (basalt stairs belong to Stratum 3); looking south-east (from Yadin et al. 1961, pl. cvii: 4).

pillar bases), similar to the one built next to the niche in the temple itself, were found on both sides of the entrance to the southern room. The northern room has a wide opening leading into the northern courtyard. Several installations of an unknown nature were built in this room (one is rectangular and might be a *bamah* or a pillar base). Two rooms were built abutting the propylaeum: one in the west (squares D-7/8) and the other in the east (squares F-8/9).

In the center of the northern courtyard, a raised platform (L.2534) was built, and another, though smaller, was constructed to the south (L.2554). A circular installation was built between these two rectangular platforms. The vast amounts of broken pottery vessels, bones and ash indicate that these installations probably served as altars, and the circular installation probably accompanied them.

In the western part of the northern courtyard, a pottery kiln (L.2160) was found, and in the eastern part, a drain channel was exposed (L.2150). This drain channel was made of three incense burners and a stone-built channel. The channel is connected to a round installation (L.2188). No buildings were found to the east of the temple (Ben-Tor 1989, 228–30).

The propylaeum and the large rectangular altar (L.2534) are all placed on a single axis that shifts from the axis of the temple but is almost aligned with that of the entrance to the niche.

Though the excavators claim that Stratum 2 came to an end in a destruction, evident from the thick mudbrick debris (Ben-Tor 1989, 227, 240), this phenomenon is seemingly similar to that evident on the acropolis where, before the building activities of stratum XIV, the area is filled with a thick mudbrick fill (discussed below, Area A). Hence, apparently, the Stratum 2 temple was not destroyed but rather abolished and filled with mudbricks, most likely those that made up the superstructure of the temple walls.

The later temple, attributed to Strata 1b (LBIIa) and 1a (LBIIb), is different from the earlier temple. Its walls are narrower, built directly on top of the walls of the Stratum 2 temple (LBI). This strengthens the above conjecture regarding the end of the Stratum 2 temple since, in order to use the walls of the Stratum 2 temple as a foundation for the temple of Stratum 1b, the mudbrick superstructure had to be taken down.

The main difference between Strata 2 (LBI) and 1b (LBIIa) is an addition of another room to the southern part of the temple, thus canceling the courtyard of Strata 3–2. This also changes the structure itself, turning it into a tripartite building.

Another significant change is in the entrance to the temple. In Stratum 2 (LBI), and most likely also in Stratum 3 (MBIIb–c), this entrance to the complex was from the south. In Strata 1b (LBIIa) and 1a (LBIIb) the entrance is from the east where a new propylaeum is built (squares F/G-6/9).

In the northern room, similar to the earlier temple, a niche was built in the northern end (L.2116), though this later one is narrower, and a bench or shelf was built against its northern wall. The walls of the niche of the later temple are wider than those of the earlier temple, and the outer part of the northern wall of the niche is stepped, similar to the outer walls of Building 7050 on the acropolis; see below. This niche was probably closed off to the northern room, since depressions, which were interpreted as door sockets, were found on either side of the niche. In the center of the northern room itself, two basalt bases of pillars were found; the pillars must have supported the roof of this room. The walls of this room are lined with basalt orthostats, here in their original use, since these orthostats were cut to fit the walls of the northern room in an exact manner.

A square basalt bowl attributed to Stratum 1b was found in this room, and several stone objects found in Stratum 1a probably originated in Stratum 1b as well. A pit was dug between the two pillar bases, with few objects found within it. The upper part of the pit was lined with stone.

A stepped threshold connected the northern and middle rooms of the temple. Two rooms were built on either side of the central room—the western room probably functioned as a stairwell that likely led to the roof or the second story of the building.

A flat threshold connected the middle and southern rooms (the latter is the room added to the temple in Stratum 1b and served as a porch), and two round basalt pillar bases flanked this entrance. The walls of this room, apart from the southern wall, were lined with basalt orthostats. This wall was partly destroyed, probably at the end of Stratum 1b (LBIIa), by a pit that cut it and all remains through to Stratum 3 (MBIIb–c). A basalt lion orthostat was found in this pit, probably buried at the end of Stratum 1b (LBIIa). The entrance to this room from the courtyard was not identified due to the destruction of the southern wall. However, the excavators reconstruct the entrance in the middle of the wall, based on the assumption that the lion orthostat was in use in this temple. Stratum 1b came to an end in a violent destruction (Ben-Tor 1989, 240–47; see further discussion on this destruction in Bechar et al. 2021).

2.2.5. Area K (Figure 2.5, Photo 2.3)

A large gate and parts of the fortification system of the lower city were uncovered in this area. Only the southern half of the gate was exposed, and the northern half is presumed symmetrical, as shown in the plan (Ben-Tor 1989, 275–76; see also fig. 2.5). Five strata were discerned here.

The earliest remains of the gate are attributed to Stratum 4 (MBIIb) and include the gate's tower, which was probably square. The city wall abutted the tower from the south. To the south of the tower, a large piazza sloped down to the east, where remains of what seems to be a rampart were identified (Ben-Tor 1989, 277–80).

Significant changes were distinguished between Strata 4 (MBIIb) and 3 (MBIIb–c). The tower and the city wall were sealed, and a new city wall and gate structure were built. The southern half of the gate now includes two chambers and three piers. A narrow corridor was used as a passage between the two chambers. The western end of the Stratum 4 tower was now used as a bench in the western chamber. The entrance and exit of the gate were paved with basalt slabs. The new city wall was built to the east of the former Stratum 4 wall. It was built as a casemate wall that abutted the southern gate tower and continued to the north where three rooms of the casemate wall were excavated. The casemate wall ended at the northernmost room of the three and continued to the north as a single-wall fortification. A similar picture was identified in the south, where about thirty meters south of the gate a single fortification wall was identified (W.5539). It is suggested that the casemate walls were part of a citadel, together with the gate towers, whereas the single walls were used as the supporting walls of the earth rampart that encompassed the lower city. This entire complex was supported by a revetment wall that was preserved to a height of more than five meters and built of cyclopean boulders (Ben-Tor 1989, 280–84).

No changes were discerned between Strata 3 (MBIIb–c) and 2 (LBI) apart from the raising of the floors. The bench of the gate's western room, created by the tower of Stratum 4 (MBIIb), was raised to fit the new level of the floors.

Some changes were identified between Strata 2 (LBI) and 1b (LBIIa), mainly in the city wall rather than in the gate itself. The southern casemate wall was destroyed and a new wall, as well as some architectural features, were built above it, sealing the Strata 3–2 wall. The new wall was built of mudbricks, and its faces were covered with stones on the east and plaster on the west (in contrast

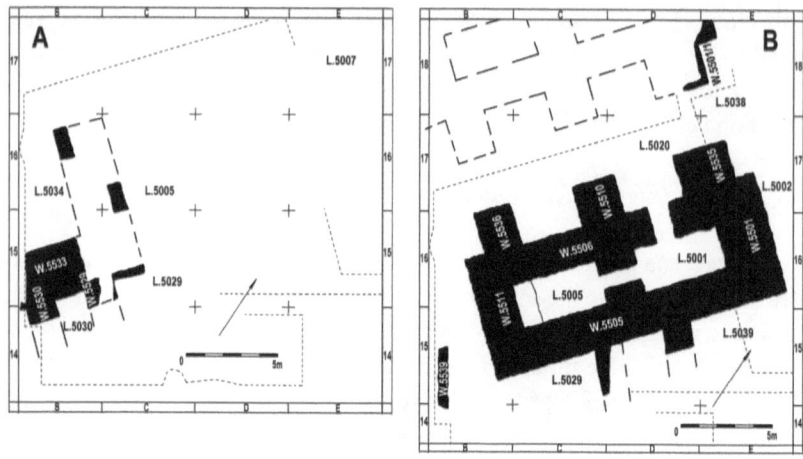
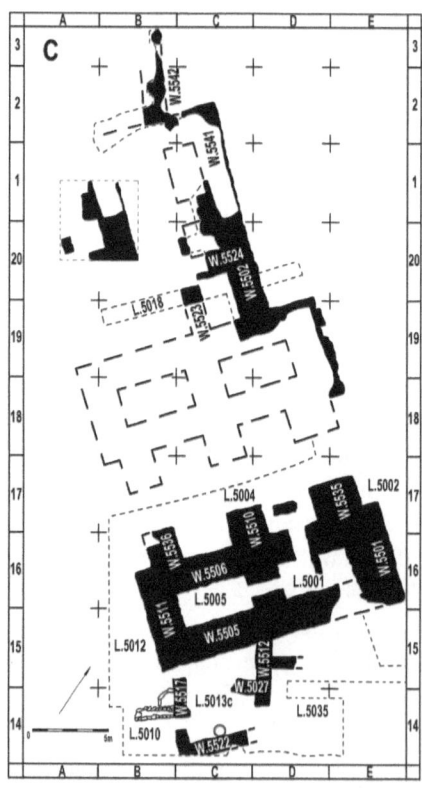

FIGURE 2.5 MBA and LBA strata in Area K—(A) Stratum 4 (after Ben-Tor 1989, plan xlii); (B) Strata 3 and 2 (after Ben-Tor 1989, plan xlii); (C) Stratum 1b (after Ben-Tor 1989, plan xliii).

PHOTO 2.3 On the right, structures and installations of Strata 1b–1a; looking east (from Yadin et al. 1961, pl. cxli: 1).

to the earlier walls built of stone with a possible mudbrick superstructure). The architectural features near this wall and the gate include a structure, a courtyard, and open spaces. The structure (L.5035) comprises two rooms, one opening to the courtyard. Opposite the entrance to the room, a bench was built. The only difference between Strata 1b (LBIIa) and 1a (LBIIb) is the bench that went out of use in the latter stratum. Several installations were exposed within the courtyard. Its floors were raised three times during Strata 1b–1a, and new installations were built each time.

The northern casemate wall continued to be in use with no changes at all—the same floors were used in Strata 2 and 1b. The area came to an end in a violent destruction at the end of Stratum 1a, followed by a post-destruction habitation stage[4] (M. Dothan and Dunayevsky attribute the destruction to Stratum 1b and the post-destruction phase to Stratum 1a, and this explanation is acceptable here).[5]

---

4. This is a problematic point. If we accept Yadin's theory, Area K is the only place on the tel where post-destruction occupation was identified. Although it is known that Yadin did not accept Dunayevsky's theory (which both M. and T. Dothan agreed with) that the Stratum 1a city was not fortified, it seems that, in the final publications, he accepted this theory (Ben-Tor 1989, 170, 264, 297).

5. Dothan and Dunayevsky's attribution fits well with a recent publication that argues that the lower city was destroyed in Stratum 1b, together with the acropolis, followed by a short-term settlement in Stratum 1a (Bechar et al. 2021).

2.2.6. Area P (Figure 2.6)

A large gate with a large structure attached to it were uncovered in this area. Four phases were revealed here, though their attribution to the strata of the lower city is not certain. Mazar's main deliberation was whether to attribute Phase C to Stratum 4 (MBIIb) and Phase B to Strata 2 (LBI) and 1b (LBIIa) or to attribute Phase C to Strata 3 (MBIIb–c) and 2 (LBI) and Phase B to Stratum 1b (LBIIa). He prefers the first (Mazar 1997, 382; I discuss this further below).

The gate was most likely built in the local Phase D, ascribed to Stratum 4, probably together with the earthen rampart. It is very likely that the original plan of the gate was followed by that of Phase C, which probably consisted of a gate with two towers made up of four rooms and six piers (Mazar 1997, 354–55). The walls of the Phase C gate were a bit narrower than those of the previous Phase D (Mazar 1997, 357). Phases C and B came to an end in destruction, evident by an ash layer (Mazar 1997, 357, 360).

Only the northern tower was excavated. This tower consisted of two chambers connected by a narrow corridor during Phases C and B (Mazar 1997, 359). During phase B, the western room (and possibly also the eastern room) was divided into two smaller rooms (Mazar 1997, 359). The entrance to the gate was through a basalt threshold, though it is not clear whether it was built in Phase C or B. The inner faces of the pillars were probably all lined with basalt orthostats (Mazar 1997, 360–61). The major difference in the gate structure was noted in Phase B, when a massive building was built, facing the inner city.[6] This building is supported by a rounded projection, built on the corner of the building and the gate. A large piazza was laid to its west (Mazar 1997, 362–63).

To the south of the gate, six well-built stone terraces were identified, constructed in Phase D or C, and having later additions in Phase B. They probably supported the city wall that filled the gap between the gate and the earthen rampart (Mazar 1997, 367).

Few architectural features were attributed to Phase A (Stratum 1a, LBIIb), such as fragments of orthostats, a wall sealing the basalt threshold, and a pavement. However, it is not clear whether the gate functioned in this phase (Mazar 1997, 363).

This is the place to add something regarding the dating of the phases. The assemblage of Phase C includes mainly MBA sherds, though there are a few

---

6. The plans of the publications indicate that this building is attributed to Phase B (Plans 4–5). In the text, Mazar claims that the building has two phases. He suggests that it might have been constructed already in Phase C (Mazar 1997, 363, 365), though later he states that one of the floors found in this building, attributed to phase C, was laid prior to the construction of the building (Mazar 1997, 363). Yadin also dates this building to the LBII (Yadin 1972, 64–65). Thus, it was decided to attribute this building to Phase B.

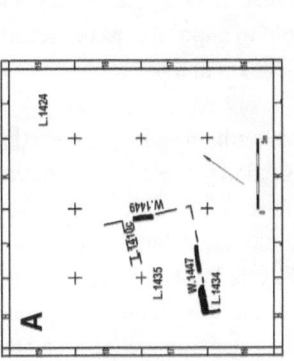
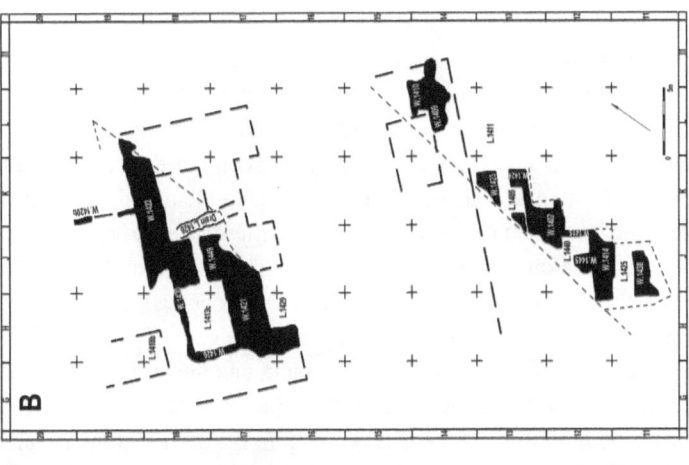

FIGURE 2.6 MBA and LBA strata in Area P—(A) Stratum 4, Phase D (after Mazar 1997, plan v.1); (B) Strata 3 and 2, Phase C (after Mazar 1997, plan v.2); (C) Stratum 1b, Phase B (after Mazar 1997, plan v.4).

LBA remains such as those in Mazar 1997, fig. V.2: 12, which is a LBA krater (see also Mazar 1997, 362) and fig. V.5:33, which is a LBI krater. It also includes several sherds that belong to the Eggshell Ware (Mazar 1997, fig. V.5: 8–9, 11–12). These were dated to the MBIIb–c (Dever 1974, 45; Maeir 2007, 250), though a later MBIIc–LBI date was suggested by others (Bonfil 2003, 280; Bechar 2017, 236–37). The later date is also indicated from their MBIIc–LBI contexts at Dan (Ilan 1996, 218, fig. 4.95:12 and fig. 4.99:10, 16). These indicate an MBII–LBI date for Phase C.

In my opinion, Phase B should be dated to the LBII, based on the ceramic assemblages found on the floors of this phase (see especially Mazar 1997, fig. V.3: 7–22). Thus, Mazar's first option (paralleling Phase C with Strata 3 and 2 and Phase B with Stratum 1b) should be preferred. In his discussion, Mazar, almost incidentally, states that Phase B is attributed to Stratum 1b (Mazar 1997, 362).

2.2.7. Area M (Figure 2.7, Photos 2.4 and 2.5)

The earliest finds, dating from the second millennium, in this area, are a monumental road leading from the lower city to the acropolis. This road, dated to the MBA, is oriented north–south and probably continued to the ceremonial road exposed in the center of the acropolis (discussed below, Area A). The road includes three sections of staircases with large paved courtyards between them. In the south, a monumental wall and a ramp were also identified, both lining the stairs from the west. The monumental wall is built of alternating white and brown mudbricks, creating a checkerboard design. The bottom of the wall was lined with extremely large limestone monoliths. Only one was exposed in its entirety, measuring circa 2 meters long and 1.5 meters high.

In the second phase of use of this road, the ramp and the monumental wall went out of use, and two walls, forming an L-shape, were built. Upon uncovering the limestone monoliths and exposing them to the dry air, they began to crumble, indicating that these ashlars must have needed some maintenance in antiquity to avoid their deterioration. It is possible to suggest that the reason for building the L-shape walls was to seal these ashlars due to the inability to maintain them.

In the north, a wall was built at the top step of the northern staircase, diverting the path to the east. We, the excavators, dated this second phase of use to the end of the MBA or the beginning of the LBA.

In the LBII, the area completely changed its nature. A large administrative building (termed "the administrative palace") was built, sealing the road. The entire southern part of the area went out of use at this stage. This palace has only partially been exposed, and at present only its entrance (termed "the

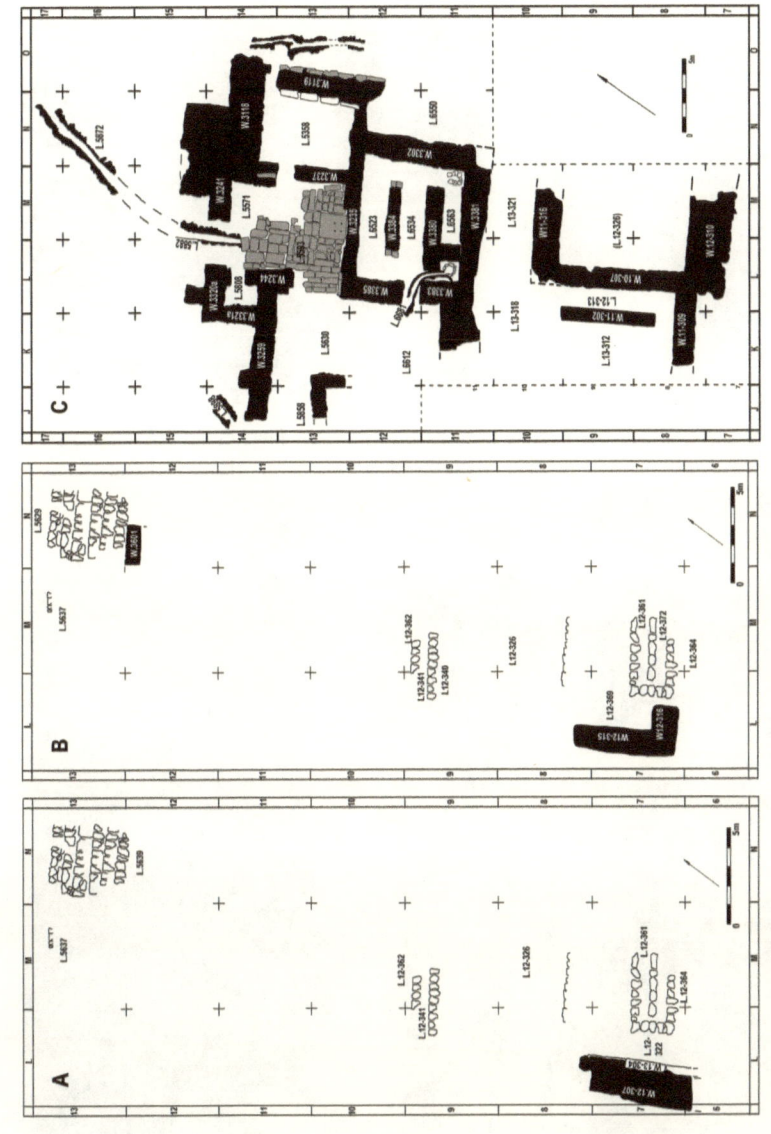

FIGURE 2.7 MBA and LBA strata in Area M—(A) Stratum xvi; (B) Stratum xv; (C) Stratum xiv.

PHOTO 2.4 Aerial view of the MBA staircase, sealed by walls of the LBA administrative palace; north to the right. Courtesy of the Selz Foundation Hazor Excavations in Memory of Yigael Yadin.

PHOTO 2.5 Aerial view of the LBA administrative palace, north to the right. Courtesy of the Selz Foundation Hazor Excavations in Memory of Yigael Yadin.

podium complex") is known. This complex includes a courtyard paved with basalt orthostats, surrounded by a number of rooms. The eastern rooms seal the earlier MBA road. In the southern part of the complex, a podium made of basalt was exposed. Four depressions were drilled into its upper face, indicating that it probably supported a chair on which a king's representative sat. A horseshoe shaped installation was built in front of the podium. Several distorted bowls, known as scoops, were found near this installation and the podium, probably used in some kind of libation ritual that took place in regard to the podium and the installation. Several drain channels were exposed in this complex, all of them found partially roofed.[7]

Five basalt steps were found west of the podium. These led to a paved courtyard, which, in turn, led to a monumental staircase in the west. This staircase has not been fully excavated, and it probably led to the main entrance of the "administrative palace" located farther to the west. Thus far, only four partial halls can be attributed to the "administrative palace." The eastern halls seal the MBA road and stairs. The southeastern hall used the large paved courtyard of the MBA road as its floor. Thirteen pithoi filled with burnt grain were found in the southwestern hall, leaning against its walls. A circular installation filled with ash and dozens of vessels was found in the northwestern hall. Numerous pithoi and other pottery vessels as well as raw materials that were probably used in the palace's workshop were also found in this hall. This hall is now understood to be a storage hall of the palace. The western extension of this building and the continuation of the monumental staircase are currently being excavated.

2.2.8. Area A (Figures 2.8 and 2.9, Photos 2.6 and 2.7)

This is the largest excavation area at Hazor. It is situated in the center of the acropolis. Since it has been excavated by Yadin's two expeditions (in the 1950s and 1968), and the renewed excavations, this is the place to synchronize their results. The northeastern part of the area is the most problematic since it is the only place that has been excavated by all expeditions mentioned above. Therefore, the discussion, which aims to be as brief as possible, will include the different opinions of Aharoni, Yadin, Dunayevski, and Bonfil in the most concise manner and conclude with my own opinion. The discussion will tackle each architectural unit separately, showing its development throughout the strata. Finally, a short summarizing description of each stratum will be provided. The full plan of each stratum is represented in the schematic plans.

In the MBIIb, Stratum XVII, a large palace was built, together with a Syrian-type *migdal* temple (termed the Southern Temple to differentiate it from the

---

7. They are presented here as open drain channels for reasons of convenience.

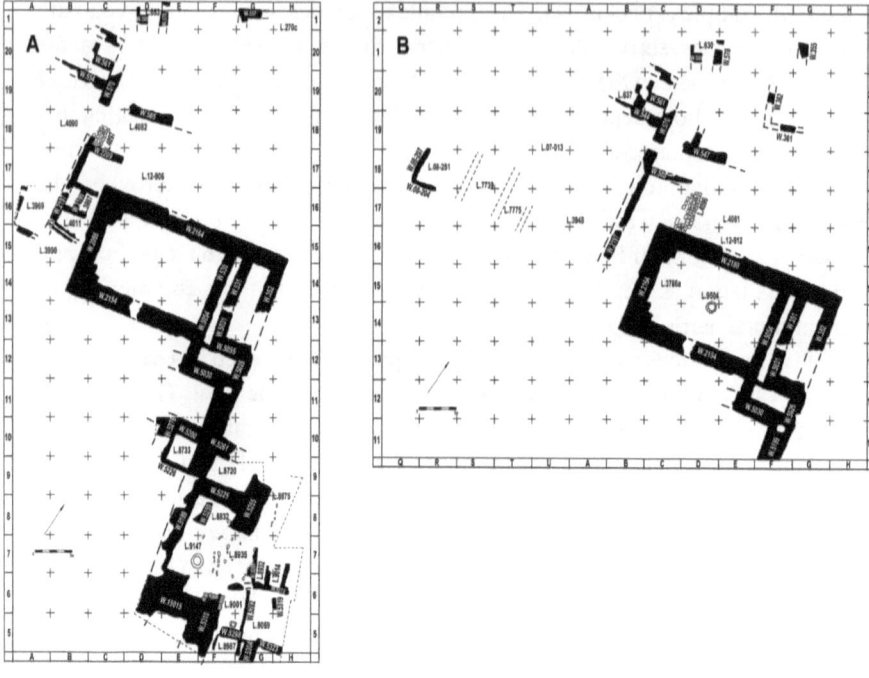

FIGURE 2.8 MBA and LBI strata in Area A—(A) Strata xvii and xvi; (B) Stratum xv.

LBA temple exposed to the north, which is termed the Northern Temple). Six phases were identified near the supposed entrance to the palace, and five phases within the Southern Temple.

The five phases of the Southern Temple consist mainly of the raising of floors and were attributed to Strata XVII–XV. At the end of Stratum XV (LBI), the temple changed its nature. All the ceramic vessels that were in use in the Southern Temple were buried in a pit (a *favissa*).[8] In stratum XIV (LBIIa), the entire temple was filled with a thick earthen fill, and it seems it was turned into an open cultic area. Only the western part of the temple was roofed as indicated by two pillar bases found there. The walls of the western part of the temple were lined with dressed limestone blocks, already used in the previous strata (Ben-Tor et al. 2017b, 35–45).

A road leading from the east to the west was found north of the Southern Temple, probably continuing the road found at the northern slopes of the tel (discussed above, Area M). It probably began at the yet-unknown MBA acropolis gate and led to the center of the acropolis and the major structures located

---

8. It is unknown whether these were buried in one event or during multiple events.

PHOTO 2.6 The MBA palace and the Southern Temple, sealed by the LBA courtyard of the Ceremonial Precinct; north to the right. Courtesy of the Selz Foundation Hazor Excavations in Memory of Yigael Yadin.

there. This road is known from Stratum XVI (MBIIb–c) and was not excavated below it. It continues to the area between the MBA Southern Temple and the LBA Northern Temple, where a large paved courtyard was found (L.4082). The pavement of this courtyard includes also Aharoni's Southern Paving (L.381a, L.382a, and L.346b; Ben-Tor 1989, 12) and Bonfil's 9D pavings (L.610, L.549c, L.566, and L.600; Bonfil 1997, 48–49), creating together a very large, paved piazza. A staircase was uncovered at the western end of the pavement. In the earlier phase of Stratum XVI (MBIIb–c), the staircase was attached to the northwestern corner of the Southern Temple, indicating their contemporaneity. In the later phase of Stratum XVI, the staircase was located further to the north, bound by the mudbrick wall W.2206 in the south and W.565 in the north. The large, paved piazza abuts this staircase. This road continued to be in use in the LBI Stratum XV, its floors raised (Ben-Tor et al. 2017b, 59–62). In Stratum XIV of the LBIIa, a new staircase was built in this same location, leading to both the Northern and the Eastern courtyards.

As noted above, a MBA palace was found in the south, built in Stratum XVII (MBIIb) and continuing until the end of Stratum XVI (MBIIb–c). Most of the palace is unknown since it still underlies the Eastern Courtyard of the LBA Ceremonial Precinct. In the area to the east of the palace, several small rooms were built in relation to the monumental walls of the palace. The small rooms were connected to the palace by pavements and floors that abutted both. The use of standing stones was identified already in the second architectural phase of this area (of the MBIIb) and continued to the last MBA phase.

A large complex of small standing stones was built in the fourth phase, attributed to Stratum XVI (MBIIb–c). This complex includes thirty-seven standing stones (made of both limestone and basalt), built in several rows, as well as

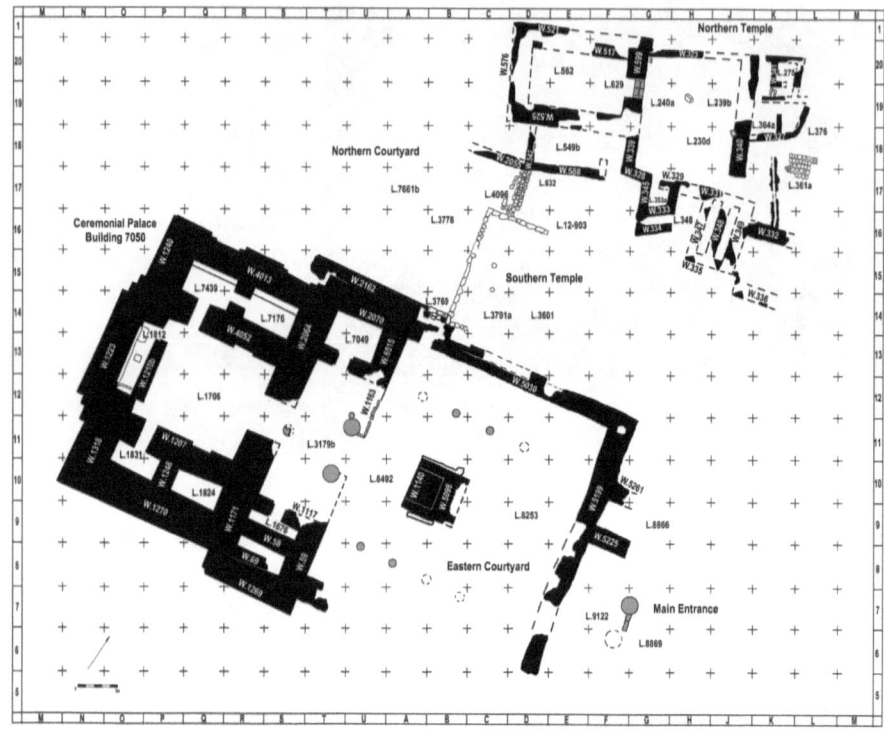

FIGURE 2.9 LBII Stratum xiv in Area A.

offering tables placed in front of them (Ben-Tor et al. 2017a, 45–54). It is noteworthy that no architectural or ceramic remains dating to the LBI were found above Stratum XVI (MBIIb–c) or below Stratum XIV (LBIIa) in this part of the city.

In Stratum XIV (LBIIa), the area completely changed its nature. The complex of standing stones, as well as the palace itself, were both carefully filled with layers of a constructive fill, and a large courtyard was built above these structures. This large construction fill probably destroyed any evidence for floors in most of the uncovered palace rooms (Ben-Tor et al. 2017b, 70). It may be suggested that this constructive fill was partly made up of the mudbricks that were part of the superstructure of the MBA palace (see examples in Ben-Tor et al. 2017b, photos 4.7, 4.17, and 4.22).

The LBA courtyard (termed the Eastern Courtyard to differentiate it from the Northern Courtyard, which is discussed below) was divided into a lower courtyard, its entrance, which is the main entrance to the courtyard, flanked by two large pillars, and an upper courtyard. The passage between these courtyards was most probably through a staircase that has not been identified. In the upper

PHOTO 2.7 Aerial view of Building 7050 and its eastern courtyard, north at top. Courtesy of the Selz Foundation Hazor Excavations in Memory of Yigael Yadin.

courtyard, a large raised platform was found, interpreted as an altar. This courtyard led to the main entrance to the Ceremonial Palace, located on the highest point of the acropolis. This building (also known as Building 7050) had a main hall that was surrounded by rooms to the north, south, and west. The entrance to the upper courtyard was also through the north. Here, the road, built already in the MBA, was raised in the LBII and led to the Northern Courtyard. It also led to another, northern, entrance to the Eastern Courtyard (Ben-Tor et al. 2017b, 70–109). The function of Building 7050 is still in debate. While some scholars believe this building to be a palace (e.g., Ben-Tor 2020), others believe this to be a temple (e.g., Zuckerman 2010). Though this is not the place to determine between these two opinions, I believe that the arguments for a temple are more compelling and outweigh other arguments.

The area to the west of the Southern Temple consists of a series of pavements, meager walls, and an installation, all attributed to Stratum XVII (MBIIb). These were severely disturbed by later Middle and Late Bronze Age walls and installations. In stratum XVI (MBIIb–c), a large building is reconstructed to the west of the Southern Temple. The eastern end of this building comprises walls W.2197 and W.570, with an assumed entrance to the building between them. At least two rooms were exposed to the west of wall W.570 (Bonfil 1997, 30, 35), belonging to the building in the west. This building in the west most likely continued to be in use in Stratum XV (of the LBI): three trenches were found in the west (the area of the Northern Courtyard), interpreted as "phantom walls" of this western building. The builders of the subsequent LBII phase were probably to blame for the robbery of this building. At this time (LBII), these walls are taken down, and the entire area is turned into a paved courtyard, termed the Northern Courtyard, as it lies north of Building 7050 (Ben-Tor et al. 2017b, 66–70).

In the north, the nature of the area is similar to that of the western building and the small rooms outside the entrance to the MBA palace. It includes small rooms built of meager walls. Bonfil attributed this building to Phases 9B and 9A, dated to the LBI (1997, 36–42). The building is cut by the Northern Temple, which has only one phase of use. However, both Aharoni and Bonfil date its construction to the LBI and claim that it continued until the LBII (that is, that it was built during Stratum XV and continued until Stratum XIV or XIII). The date of construction of the temple is based on the ceramics found below its floor, dated to the EBA and the MBA (Ben-Tor 1989, 13; Bonfil 1997, 54–55). In my opinion, the construction of this temple should be attributed to Stratum XIV (of the LBIIa), based on the fact that the temple has only one building phase. The fact that bowls with "band decoration" were found in this temple does not necessarily date it to the LBI (Bonfil 1997, 84). As has been shown elsewhere (Bechar 2017, 242), these bowls appear in the Ceremonial Precinct until the end of the LBII, and though they are an early marker of the LBA, they are not restricted to the LBI. In addition, it should be noted that such bowls are most common in Tel Atchana (Alalakh) in Level IV (Woolley 1955, 322 and 332, type 3b, plate LXXXVIII: e). This level has been dated from the mid-fifteenth to the mid-fourteenth centuries BCE (Fink 2010, 2).

In summary, at the end of Stratum XV, a significant change occurred in the plan of the area. All the buildings built in Stratum XVII ceased to exist—the palace, the complex of standing stones, the Southern Temple, the western building, and the building in the north. The first three were filled with earth layers. Courtyards were built above the complex of standing stones and the palace, and the walls of the western building were taken down, the area being turned into a courtyard. The Southern Temple was filled and was turned into an open cultic area. The building in the north was cut. Two new buildings were built in the area—the Northern Temple and the Ceremonial Precinct, creating a new city plan.

2.2.9. Architectural Conclusions

It seems that the major changes in all areas of Hazor took place in the transition from the LBI to the LBII (from Stratum XV to Stratum XIV on the acropolis, and Stratum 2 to Stratum 1b in the lower city). These changes caused a complete alteration in the urban plan of the city. The only places where minor changes occurred are the gates of the city in Areas K and P, which continue with almost no changes between Strata 3 (MBIIb–c) and 2 (LBI) and few changes in Stratum 1b (LBIIa).

In Area C, the residential quarter completely changed its nature, turning into a ritual and industrial quarter. In Area M, the road leading from the lower city to the acropolis was sealed off by the building of the palace, leading to a change in the course of the road. In Areas A, F, and H, though their nature remained the same (mostly cultic), their entire plan changed. In all three areas, the temples were covered and symbolically buried in preparation for the rebuilding of the temple (as in Area H), either creating an open cultic space (as in Area F and the Southern Temple of Area A) or altogether changing the nature of the area (as in the standing stones complex in Area A). In Area F, the closed temple became an open cultic area. In Area H, another unit was added to the temple, canceling the earlier courtyard. In addition, the entrance to the complex was moved from the south to the east. In Area A, the closed Southern Temple was filled and turned into an open cultic area; the open cultic area of the MBA (complex of standing stones) was covered by a courtyard leading to a new building, and two new monumental cultic buildings were built (the Northern Temple and Building 7050).

2.3. The Built Environment of the Lower City

2.3.1. Methodology

As was seen above, in general, most of the excavation areas of Hazor are composed of public and monumental buildings (fig. 2.1). These include the orthostats temple (Area H, Strata 3–1a, MBIIb–c to LBIIb), the double temple (Area F, Stratum 3, MBIIb–c) the square temple (Area F, Stratum 2, LBI), the palace and standing stones complex (Area A, Strata XVII–XVI MBA), the ceremonial precinct (Area A, Strata XIV–XIII, LBIIa–b), the grand staircase (Area M, Strata XVII–XVI, MBA), and the administrative palace (Area M, Strata XIV–XIII LBIIa–b).

For the purposes of the study of the changes in the built environments of Hazor, only the lower city was considered. The reason for choosing the lower city is that the acropolis of Hazor includes *only* monumental buildings and open spaces, whereas the lower city also includes nonmonumental buildings. Areas A and M, in the acropolis of Hazor, have been the main excavation areas of the renewed expedition. Consequently, the size of the total excavated area in the acropolis (about 0.66 hectares) is well over that of the lower city (about 0.46 hectares). Thus, including the acropolis in the present study would create biased results, as domestic architecture is missing from the most extensive and principal excavation areas of the past thirty years.

In order to examine the differences in the architectural fabric of the lower city, it is crucial, first, to define the different architectural elements. The *private architecture* includes all nonmonumental buildings that cannot be attributed to public buildings. In other words, this would include buildings identified by Yadin as workshops, shops, and houses. The reason for allocating workshops and shops as domestic architecture is that in some cases, in my opinion, there is no conclusive evidence to support their interpretation as workshops or shops. In addition, workshops and shops are not necessarily owned by the ruler of the city or the head of the temples. They may be owned by private people, for the wellbeing and subsistence of these private individuals. Also, if we would accept Yadin's interpretation, it seems that the city was empty of residential buildings during the LBII. Courtyards of houses are also calculated as part of the private architecture.

Public built structures include any structure that is monumental, as well as structures that have a public function such as nonmonumental temples.

Open areas are any areas that functioned as open spaces; large courtyards outside temples are considered open areas, but streets are not since it is difficult to calculate their total area. Besides, the small area that they *do* comprise would not contribute to the present study.

2.3.2. Architectural Remains

For the purposes of the current study, Areas D, E, and P have not been examined. Though nonmonumental architecture has been exposed in Areas D and E, this architecture includes mainly installations, some walls, and rock-cut cists that were all severely disturbed. The stratigraphy of these two areas is very ambiguous (and recall above the discussion of Area D). In addition, both of these areas include a total of about twenty-five excavation squares, some of which are composed mainly of bedrock without any archaeological remains. Thus, any discussion of these areas would not contribute to the present study. The gates of the city were found in both areas K and P. However, Area K was considered, for the present study, since private architecture was exposed near the gate during the LBA, whereas no such architecture was excavated in Area P, and only the fortifications of the city were exposed.

The following is an overview of the different type of architectural elements identified in each of the excavated areas (F, C, H, K, and S).

Area F. The public area identified in Stratum 3 measured 1325 m², 1150 m² in Stratum 2, and did not exist in Stratum 1b. Private architecture covering 100 m² was identified in Stratum 2, and 2000 m² in Stratum 1b. Open spaces were only identified in Stratum 1b, in a 150 m² area (see table 2.2).

Area C. A total of 400 m² of private architecture was calculated for Stratum 3, 125 m² for Stratum 2 and 725 m² for Stratum 1b. Public architecture was only identified in Stratum 1b, covering a total area of 175 m². Open spaces extended over 225 m² in Stratum 2 and 175 m² in Stratum 1b (see table 2.3).

Area H. No private architecture was found in Area H. As for public architecture, a total area of 425 m² was identified in Stratum 3, 650 m² in Stratum 2,

TABLE 2.2 Different Usage of Space in Area F (in m²)

Stratum	Private Architecture	Public Architecture	Open Space	Total
3 (MBIIb–c)	—	1325 (100%)	—	1325
2 (LBI)	100 (8%)	1150 (92%)	—	1250
1b (LBIIa)	2000 (93%)	—	150 (7%)	2150

TABLE 2.3 Different Usage of Space in Area C (in m²)

Stratum	Private Architecture	Public Architecture	Open Space	Total
3 (MBIIb–c)	400	—	—	400
2 (LBI)	125 (36%)	—	225 (64%)	350
1b (LBIIa)	725 (64%)	225 (20%)	175 (16%)	1125

TABLE 2.4 Different usage of space in Area H (in m²)

Stratum	Private Architecture	Public Architecture	Open Space	Total
3 (MBIIb–c)	—	425 (55%)	350 (45%)	775
2 (LBI)	—	650 (79%)	175 (21%)	825
1b (LBIIa)	—	725 (78%)	200 (22%)	925

and 725 m² in Stratum 1b. The open space of Stratum 3 extended for 350 m², 175 m² in Stratum 2, and 200 m² in Stratum 1b (see table 2.4).

Area K. The public architecture of Strata 3–2 has an area of 325 m², and a total of 475 m² was calculated for Stratum 1b. In the latter, about 137.5 m² of private architecture and 25 m² of open space were calculated (see table 2.5).

Area S. This area is located in the center of the lower city. It was initially excavated by Yadin's expedition (square 210/A1). Excavations in this area were renewed in 2008–10 by Sharon Zuckerman. The architectural remains found during the renewed excavations have not yet been published and, therefore, were not discussed in the previous section of this chapter. However, based on the unpublished material,[9] it can be stated that this area includes mainly domestic architecture.

---

9. I would like to thank Ido Wachtel for his assistance and for allowing me to analyze the architectural evidence from Area S. Ido Wachtel and I are responsible for the publication of the material remains from Area S due to the untimely death of Dr. Sharon Zuckerman, the excavator of this area.

TABLE 2.5 Different Usage of Space in Area K (in m²)

Stratum	Private Architecture	Public Architecture	Open Space	Total
3 (MBIIb–c)	—	325 (100%)	—	325
2 (LBI)				
1b (LBIIa)	137.5 (21.6%)	475 (74.5%)	25 (3.9%)	637.5

TABLE 2.6 Different Usage of Space in Area S (in m²)

Stratum	Private Architecture	Public Architecture	Open Space	Total
3 (MBIIb–c)	100 (80%)	—	25 (20%)	125
2 (LBI)	—	—	125 (100%)	125
1b (LBIIa)	162.5 (87%)	—	25 (13%)	187.5

In Stratum 3, the area includes a few fragmentary walls without a clear connection between them, as well as a few burials. Open spaces were also identified.

In Stratum 2, the entire excavated area functioned as an open courtyard.

In Stratum 1b, a series of rooms and courtyards were identified. These might have functioned as shops or workshops, based on their similarities to the Area C domestic units.

A total of 100 m² of private architecture was identified in Stratum 3, and 162.5 m² in Stratum 1b. Only 25 m² of open space were identified in both Stratum 3 and Stratum 1b, and 125 m² were identified in Stratum 2 (see table 2.6).

2.3.3. Discussion

The evidence presented above clearly shows a difference in the usage of space among the excavated areas of Hazor's lower city. As can be seen in graph 2.1, most of the excavated area in the lower city, in both Stratum 3 (MBIIb–c) and Stratum 2 (LBI), is occupied by public structures (70% and 74%, respectively), whereas private architecture composes most of the excavated area in the lower city during the LBIIa Stratum 1b (60%).

It is also interesting to note that, in most cases, at Hazor and other tel sites in the southern Levant, areas of cultic ceremonies tend to keep their nature through time. This is evident in the Area H temple, as well as in the different temples in Area A. A different picture emerges from the evidence in Area F. Monumental structures were exposed here in Strata 3 (MBIIb–c) and 2 (LBI), interpreted by

GRAPH 2.1 Changes in the architectural fabric of the lower city between the different strata.

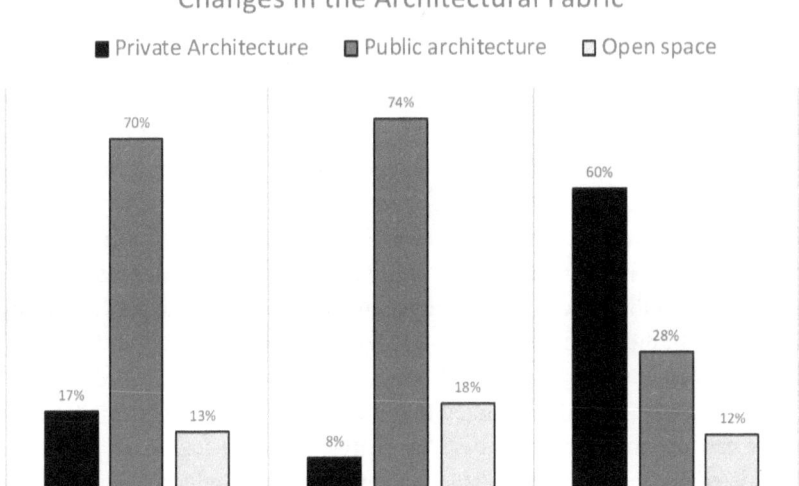

Yadin as temples, mainly based on the fact that a large altar was found in Strata 1b (LBIIa) and 1a (LBIIb). Yadin himself claimed that the reason for this interpretation is the fact that cultic places tend to keep their nature (Yadin 1975, 69, 71). However, the architecture in this area is no longer monumental but domestic. Yadin suggested the priests of the cultic area resided in these buildings. In other words, this is, in fact, domestic architecture that serves cultic purposes. Even so, it seems that the cultic area sacrificed its monumental character for residential purposes. It would be interesting to investigate this observation further within other tel sites in the Levant, but this goes beyond the scope of the present study.

Though open spaces are most prevalent in Stratum 2 (of the LBI, occupying 18% of the excavated area in the lower city), the difference is not significant when comparing Stratum 2 to both Strata 3 and 1b (where the open space comprises 13% and 11% of the excavated area, respectively). However, such a difference may also hint to a distinct trend, especially since parts of the acropolis were also deserted at this time (Ben-Tor et al. 2017b, 66–70, and note the previous discussion, as no architectural remains were uncovered where the MBA complex of standing stones was previously found). Thus, it seems that the major changes in the fabric of the city occurred in the transition from Stratum 2 to Stratum 1b—that is, from the LBI to the LBII. This fits well also with the overall changes in the city's architectural plan.

2.4. Crisis Architecture

The term *crisis architecture* was coined by Driessen (1995) to identify architectural modifications made in response to social, political, and economic distress in society. This kind of architecture can be identified by the appearance of a combination of three elements: (1) a decrease in energy input in the construction and maintenance of a building, (2) a change in the original function of a building, and (3) a change in the original plan of a building (Driessen 1995, 67).

It should be noted that a crisis does not necessarily need to lead to destruction. In other words, the fact that a destruction level was not uncovered at Hazor within the discussed strata does not imply that Hazor did not witness a crisis. It seems that, although continuity is apparent in the architectural plan of the city until the LBI, there is a decline and a reduction in the buildings at this phase. These phenomena will be dealt with using the terminology *crisis architecture*, as defined above. It will be argued that the reduction of the occupied area at Hazor can also indicate in this case the distress of the society in question. It is considered here to be a partial abandonment, which may reflect changing socio-cultural conditions in the society or a reduction in the number of inhabitants in the city (Driessen 1995, 68–70).

Zuckerman has shown how features of crisis architecture were evident at the end of Stratum 1a before the violent destruction of the site (Zuckerman 2007). It will be shown here that features of crisis architecture are also apparent at the end of Stratum 2 (LBI).

2.4.1. Administrative and Domestic Features

Area C. Changes in the domestic buildings of Area C include the reduction of the two residential units to a single building.

Area M. The monumental wall defining the staircase leading to the acropolis is sealed off, as is the ramp of the staircase. The sealing of the wall might have been due to the inability to keep up the maintenance of the large walls and the mudbrick superstructure (discussed above). This also led, of course, to a change in the original route leading to the center of the acropolis.

2.4.2. Cultic Features

Zuckerman has suggested that alterations in monumental cultic buildings hint to a more profound change in the ritual context of the building, indicating a process of decline, especially if it is followed by an intentional obliteration of the temple (Zuckerman 2007, 7). It will be shown that this is the case in all the ritual contexts in Stratum XV/2.

Area F. The double temple of the MBA is reduced to a square temple in Stratum 2 (LBI), which can be seen as a partial abandonment of the structure. This can be regarded as a sign of decline. It can also indicate a decreased need in space, caused by either a reduction in settlement size or sociocultural changes (Dreissen 1995, 68).

Two phases of use were identified in the reduced square temple. During the second phase of use in the square temple, several alterations took place inside the temple and its vicinity. These include the construction of two installations and a wall that closed off the passages between the rooms in the temple, and constructing meager walls that canceled the southern part of the eastern wall. Using the installations to close off the rooms probably also led to altering the original function of these rooms, though the installations' function is unknown (both were found empty). The blocked passages of the inner temple also led to a change in the original plan of the building.

The reduction of the temple to half its size, which is evident especially in the second phase of Stratum 2, when the meager walls seal the monumental wall, also indicates a decrease in energy input in the building's maintenance. This is another feature of crisis architecture, pointing to the social processes that occurred in the city (discussed further below).

Area H. The large courtyard outside the Stratum 3 (MBIIb–c) temple is reduced in size, in Stratum 2 (LBI), by adding the propylaeum, which is in itself built of basalt stones in secondary use. The secondary use of basalt stones may indicate a decrease in energy input in the building's construction. In addition, the niche of the temple is closed off by a narrow wall that also obliterates the symmetrical axis of the temple, thus slightly changing the original plan of the temple. A similar situation was also evident in the Stratum 1a temple as shown by Zuckerman (2007, 17–19). Adding the potter's workshop and the different rooms and installations built around the temple may have led to a change in the original function of the area.

Area A. Very few remains were attributed to Stratum XV (LBI), all of them interpreted as a continuation of the MBII buildings, such as the Western Building and the Southern Temple. However, since no activity dated to the LBI was identified in the area of the Complex of Standing Stones and the Early Palace, it can be suggested that the southern part of the acropolis was not in use during Stratum XV and only the center and the road leading to it were used. This cancelation of the southern part of the acropolis can be seen as a partial abandonment, indicating a reduction of the site's occupied area. This may imply a severe population decrease (Dreissen 1995, 68–70; 2003, 257).

In summary, crisis architecture was identified in all the areas described above. Based on this, as well as on the architectural conclusions brought above, it seems that in Stratum XV/2 (LBI) most of the activities taking place at Hazor occurred in the lower city. However, even here, the settlement and its buildings were reduced in size and space. Thus, the reduction in settlement size during Stratum XV/2 can also be seen as reflecting the distress of the inhabitants of the city. This can be viewed as a partial abandonment of certain areas of the city, indicating, again, socioeconomic changes (I discuss this further in chapter 5). In addition, the analysis of the architectural fabric of the city has shown that open areas were most prevalent in Stratum 2 in the lower city, suggesting a decline in the need for built structures. This, in addition to the (at least) partial abandonment of the acropolis, strengthens the conclusion reached above that the city went through a decline during the LBI. This of course does not necessarily indicate a complete decline of the entire city. It does, however, indicate a decline in the excavated areas and especially those with monumental architecture.

2.5. Historical Implications

As has been noted above, and also previously noted, the MBA-to-LBA transition at Hazor is considered peaceful (Ben-Tor 2015, 74; Zuckerman 2007, 12). However, this is based on the assumption that this transition occurred following the Hyksos expulsion from Egypt, dated to approximately the middle of the sixteenth century BCE. In other words, it is based on the notion that this transition should be seen as occurring between the MBII and the LBI (Strata XVI and XV on the acropolis, and Strata 3 and 2 in the lower city). However, based on the architectural remains presented here, it seems that the major changes in the material culture at Hazor occurred between the LBI and the LBII (Strata XV and XIV on the acropolis, and Strata 2 and 1b in the lower city). This is also evident in the changes in the built environment of the city. It is suggested here that this major architectural change was due to the decline and deterioration of the city during Stratum XV/2, and maybe even a partial abandonment of the city during that time. Thus, this transition is *not* peaceful but rather a transition that brought a change in the entire city plan and the nature of the different quarters and areas of the city. This is not to suggest that the transition was caused by war or violence but rather that it did in fact cause turmoil and instability.

Zuckerman has suggested that the deterioration of the monumental buildings in Stratum XIII/1a (of the LBIIb) indicate a crisis in the power of the city's political and religious elite (2007, 23). This is not necessarily the case at the end of Stratum XV/2 (of the LBI). It is proposed here that the deterioration in the monumental buildings and the abandonment of the southern part of the acropolis was due to an economic decline that most probably occurred in the southern Levant following the Hyksos expulsion from Egypt. This, in turn, led to the partial abandonment of the site and the changes in the function of some of the buildings. In addition, seventeen out of the nineteen Egyptian statues found at Hazor can be dated to the Middle Kingdom. Another is dated to the Old Kingdom. It has been suggested that these were brought to Hazor by the Hyksos (Marée 2017, 583). Therefore, these statues indicate that the rulers of Hazor and the Hyksos were in close commercial and diplomatic contact, close enough to justify such gifts. Thus, the cessation of these relations due to the expulsion of the Hyksos would probably lead to an economic decline at Hazor. These conclusions will be further discussed in chapter 5.

2.6. Conclusions

This chapter aimed to identify the major architectural changes at Hazor during the MBA–LBA. It has been shown that the major differences occurred between Strata XV and XIV on the acropolis, and Strata 2 and 1b in the lower city. It has also been shown that crisis architecture is evident at the end of Stratum XV/2, which might indicate the economic decline of the city, caused by the expulsion of the Hyksos from Egypt and probably also affected by the Egyptian military campaigns in the northern and southern Levant. This may have brought some inhabitants to leave the city, thus leading to a reduction in the size of the settlement.

Despite the previous dating of Strata XV and XIV in the acropolis, and Strata 2 and 1b in the lower city, I have suggested elsewhere (Ben-Tor and Bechar 2017), strengthening the claim here, that the transition between these strata should be dated to the end of the LBIa, which, in my opinion, still forms part of the MBA material horizon (which I will discuss in chapter 4).

CHAPTER 3

The Middle Bronze Age–Late Bronze Age Transition in the Levant: Architectural Aspects

3.1. Introduction

This chapter aims at investigating the architectural changes that took place between the MBIIb and the LBIIa in northern Canaan, encompassing both the northern part of the southern Levant (modern-day northern Israel) and the southern part of northern Levant (modern-day Lebanon and southern Syria), to pinpoint the stratigraphic changes at different sites (table 3.1). This study, based on architectural remains, will focus *only* on settlement sites where significant MBA and LBA remains were found (that is, more than a few squares of excavation) and published. It should be emphasized that only sites that have *both* MBA and LBA strata were considered for this study. There are some sites that have been fully published (for instance, Sarepta); however, these sites have only MBA or only LBA strata and therefore cannot contribute to the present study.

Consequently, burial sites or surveyed sites will not be included. Unfortunately, since not all publications include sufficient architectural plans (for example, Sidon and Tel Sakka), the present research includes these only when available and add to the discussion (for example, the plans from Tel Nebi Mend, which do not contribute to the debate, will not be included).

The geographical framework of this study focuses on the site of Tel Hazor (discussed in detail in chapter 2), its realm, and the sites in its vicinity. This includes the northern part of Cisjordan (from Beth-Shean in the south to Hazor in the north), Lebanon, and southern Syria (fig. 3.1). The site of Qatna being, as yet, the next *known* large kingdom situated to the north of Hazor, has been chosen as the northernmost site since any site to its north must have been part of its realm and not of Hazor's.

The sites in the southern Levant (Qashish, Yoqne'am, and Beth-Shean) are presented first, followed by those in Lebanon (Sidon, Kamid el-Loz, Tell el-Ghassil, and Tell Arqa) and southern Syria (Tell Sakka, Tell Nebi Mend, and

TABLE 3.1 Stratigraphy of the Different Sites Mentioned in the Study

Relative Chronology	Hazor: Lower City	Hazor: Upper City	Tel Qashish	Yoqn'eman	Beth Shean	Tel Arqa	Kamid el-Loz	Tell el-Ghassil	Tell Sakka	Qatna Area J	Qatna Areas T and K
MBIIb	4	XVII	IX	XXIII	R-5 = XI	13	City 1	X	4	J14	Area T Phases V–II
MBIIc	3	XVI	VIII	XXII	R-4 = XB		Anomie 1	IX	—	J13	
				XXI			City 2 MBP2 T5–T4	IX		J12	
				XXb	R-3 = XA		Anomie 2 MBP1	VIII		J11–J10	
LBIa	2	XV	VIIb	XXb–XXa	R-2 = pre IX	12c 12b	City 3 P5–P1	VII	3	J9–J7	?
LBIb			VIIa	XXa	R-1b = IXB	12a	T3–T1				
LBIIa	1b	XIV	VI	XIXb	R-1a = IXA	11		VI			Area K Palace
LBIIb	1a	XIII	V	XIXa	VIII VII			V (LBIIa–LBIIb)			

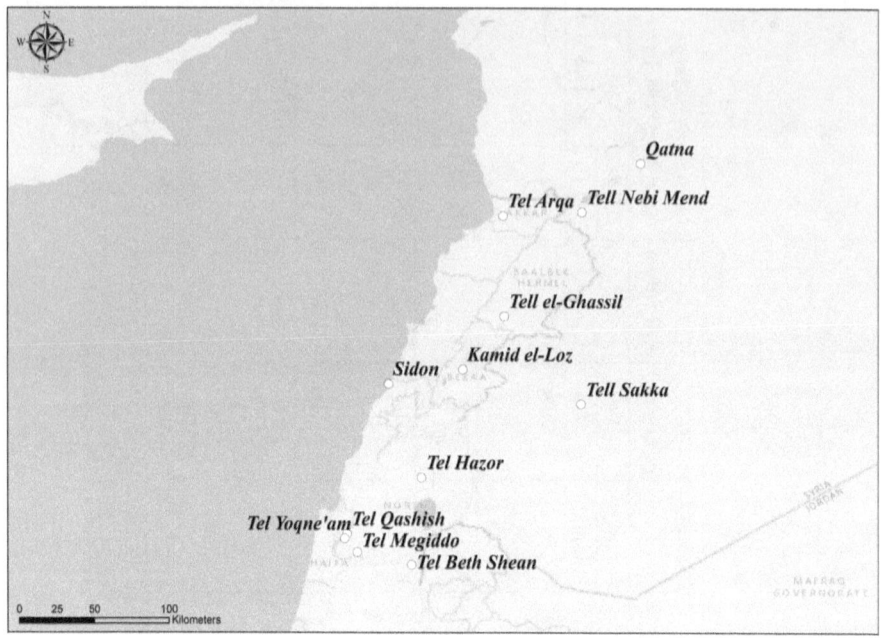

FIGURE 3.1 Map of the Levant, with sites mentioned in this study.

Qatna). For each site, a summary of the relative strata is first given, based on the published material, followed by a discussion aimed at identifying the transition point, extrapolating the results to the different regions.

3.2. The Southern Levant

3.2.1. Tel Qashish (Figure 3.2)

Tel Qashish was first excavated in the 1920s by Garstang, who found only EBA remains. Excavations at the site were renewed in 1978 by the Hebrew University of Jerusalem, as part of the Yoqne'am Regional Project, and continued at the site until 1987 (Ben-Tor et al. 2003, 1–2).

The earliest MBA architectural remains (Stratum IX) date to the MBIIb (fig. 3.2: A). These include a fortification system that comprises a thick wall (about 1.7 meters wide), a glacis, and a tower, as well as several narrow walls abutting it and interpreted as domestic structures. Though Stratum IX is subdivided into three phases, these are mainly characterized by the raising of floors and minor architectural changes (Ben-Tor and Bonfil 2003, 190).

Remains attributed to Stratum VIII, dated by the excavators to the MBIIc based on the ceramic evidence (Ben-Tor and Bonfil 2003, 230, 244), were uncovered only in the southern part of the area (fig. 3.2: B). Almost all the floors attributed to this stratum are stone paved, and some fragmentary walls were also found. The few LBI sherds from this stratum (e.g., Ben-Tor and Bonfil 2003, figs. 93:20, 96:10) and the excavators' claim that parallels to this stratum's assemblage are to be found in assemblages of the MBII–LBI transition period (Ben-Tor and Bonfil 2003, 244) suggest dating this stratum to the MBIIc–LBI transition. This is also clearly stated, in fact, in the discussion of Stratum VII, where the excavators suggest dating Stratum VIII to this transitional period (Ben-Tor and Bonfil 2003, 245). The fortification system of Stratum IX was seemingly still in use in Stratum VIII, since the excavators affirm that it went out of use in the subsequent Stratum VIIb (Ben-Tor and Bonfil 2003, 247).[1] Interestingly, although the excavators posit that significant changes were observed between Strata IX and VIII, it seems that the main difference occurred, in fact, between Strata VIII and VII, similar to the changes found by them in the ceramic assemblages (Ben-Tor and Bonfil 2003, 244).

As noted above, the fortification system of Strata IX–VIII goes out of use in Stratum VII (fig. 3.2: C), when residential units are built on top of it. In Stratum VII, dated to the LBI, the area of the Stratum VIII fortification system comprises at least two residential units connected by a central, partly paved, large courtyard (Ben-Tor and Bonfil 2003, 247–48). The excavators dated this stratum to the LBI based on the imported ware found in the assemblage and on parallels mostly to be found in the Megiddo and Tel Mevorakh LBI assemblages.

Only minor changes occurred between Strata VIIb and VIIa (dated to the LBIa and LBIb, respectively), mainly the raising of floors. The main difference between the two strata is the addition of two walls that define the previous courtyard, making it part of the residential units and perhaps also joining them together (Ben-Tor and Bonfil 2003, 257).

Another significant change occurred between Strata VII and VI (dated to the LBIIa, based on the ceramic evidence (Ben-Tor and Bonfil 2003, 264–65, 276) when all the residential buildings went out of use and a tower was built on them (fig. 3.2: D). A pavement and earth floors made up a large courtyard to the south of the tower.

In summary, the major changes at the site took place between Stratum VIII of the transitional MBA/LBA period, when the site is fortified, and the LBI Stratum VII, when the site has no fortifications.

---

1. Thus, in this study, the fortification system was included in the plan of Stratum VIII.

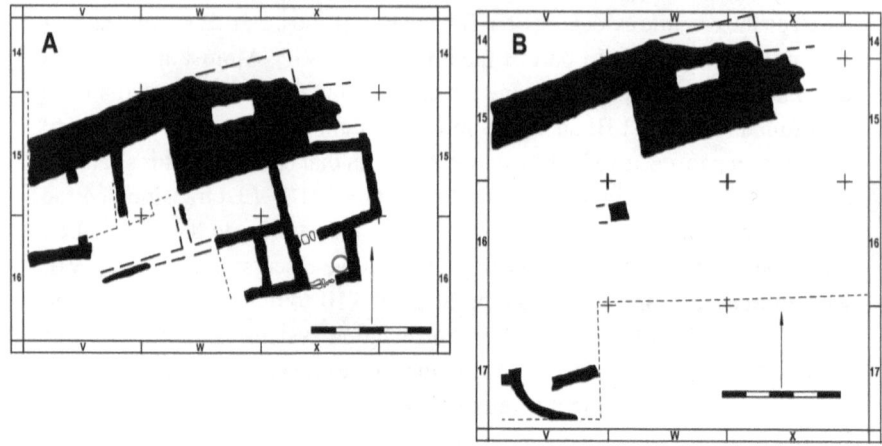
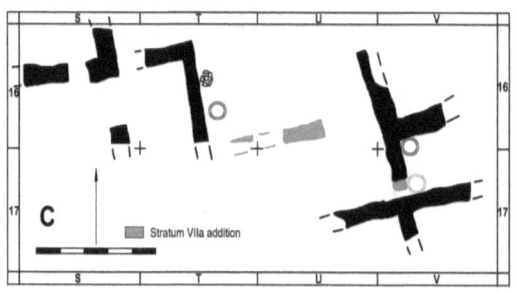
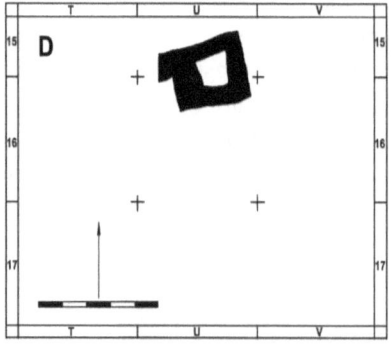

FIGURE 3.2 MBA and LBA strata in Tel Qashish, Area A—(A) Stratum IX (after Ben-Tor and Bonfil 2003, plan 24); (B) Stratum VIII (after Ben-Tor and Bonfil 2003, plan 32); (C) Stratum VII (after Ben-Tor and Bonfil 2003, plans 34 and 36); (D) Stratum VI (after Ben-Tor and Bonfil 2003, plan 38).

3.2.2. Yoqne'am (Figures 3.3–3.4 and Photo 3.1)

Excavations in Yoqne'am were conducted between 1977 and 1988 by the Hebrew University of Jerusalem as part of the Yoqne'am Regional Project (Ben-Tor 1996, 1).

The first MBA settlement at Yoqne'am is dated to the MBIIa. Five strata (XXIII–XIXb) were attributed to the MBIIb–LBIIb in two excavation areas (Areas A-1 and A-4). Stratum XX is subdivided into Stratum XXb and Stratum XXa, Stratum XXb representing the transitional MBIIc/LBI phase. Burials were found beneath all MBA and LBI floors of the domestic units, but none underneath LBII floors.

3.2.2.1. Area A-1

Stratum XXIIIA (MBIIb). A defense system was built in this stratum in the northern part of the city (fig. 3.3: A), comprising a 3-meter-wide wall made of a stone foundation with a mudbrick superstructure and an integrated tower. A new glacis was built against the northern (outer) face of the city wall. Some additional walls formed three rooms of a domestic nature (Livneh and Ben-Tor 2005, 24–26).

Stratum XXII (MBIIb–c). A new city wall is built (fig. 3.3: B), half the width of the previous wall (1.5 meters). Due to erosion, the presumed tower and glacis were not preserved in this stratum. Inside the city wall, a large floor was found in the west, with no associated architectural elements. This floor might have been part of a street or piazza. In the east, a few walls were uncovered, abutted by a floor. The nature of these walls is unclear (Livneh and Ben-Tor 2005, 27–30).

Stratum XXI (MBIIc). In this stratum, dated to the MBIIc, the settlement was no longer fortified (fig. 3.3: C). It was surrounded by a one-meter-wide wall, which probably marked the border of the city, functioning more as a fence than a fortification wall. An earth floor was found in the east, abutting the inner face of the wall. A domestic building, comprising two rooms and a courtyard, was found in the west (Livneh and Ben-Tor 2005, 30).

Stratum XXb (MBIIc/LBIa). This stratum represents the transitional MBIIc/LBI phase (fig. 3.3: D) and shows significant changes in the area. On the previous boundary wall, a structure was built, of which only its southern part survived. In the west, a new structure was uncovered, built in an orientation somewhat similar to the building of the previous stratum (Ben-Ami 2005, 157). This stratum ended in a conflagration, visible only in this area (Ben-Ami 2005, 160).

Stratum XXa (LBI). In this next phase, dated to the LBI (fig. 3.3: E), a new building was constructed, reusing one of the walls of the Stratum XXb building (marked in gray) and following its orientation. West of the room, a pavement

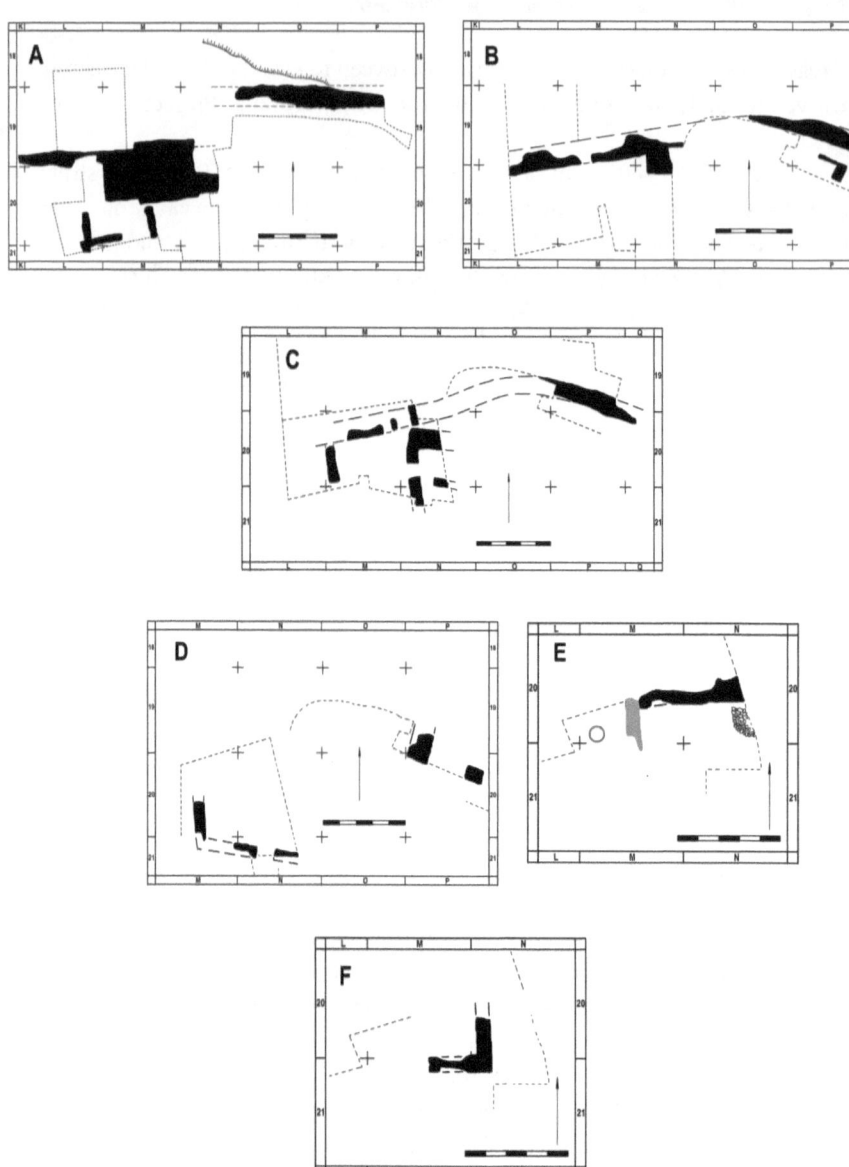

FIGURE 3.3 MBA and LBA strata in Yoqne'am, Area AI—(A) Stratum XXIII (after Livneh and Ben-Tor 2005, plan II.6); (B) Stratum XXII (after Livneh and Ben-Tor 2005, plan ii.7); (C) Stratum XXI (after Livneh and Ben-Tor 2005, plan ii.8); (D) Stratum XXb (after Ben-Ami 2005, plan iii.2); (D) Stratum XXb (after Ben-Ami 2005, plans iii.6a and 6b); (E) Stratum XXa (after Ben-Ami 2005, plan iii.7); (F) Stratum XIXb (after Ben-Ami 2005, plan iii.8).

and a *tabun* were identified, while on the east, a round stone-built surface was uncovered (Ben-Ami 2005, 161).

Stratum XIXb (LBIIa). In the LBII phase of this stratum (fig. 3.3: F), the corner of a house, built in an orientation different from the previous structures, was exposed. A large pavement and an earth floor were found to the south of this corner (outside the room). This stratum ended in a conflagration (Ben-Ami 2005, 162–64).

3.2.2.2. Area A-4

Stratum XXIII (MBIIb). In the eastern slopes of the tel, a massive fortification system was found, attributed to this stratum (fig. 3.4: A) and comprising a fortification wall and a glacis. The fortification wall is similar, both in its construction techniques and in its width (3 m), to the Area A-1 wall (see above, and fig. 3.3: A). Inside the city, an earth floor and a mudbrick wall were found.

Stratum XXII (MBIIb–c). In this stratum, the previous city wall (marked in very light gray on the plan, fig. 3.4: B) went out of use, being replaced by a small wall and a pavement built on top.

Stratum XXI (MBIIc). This stratum yielded only one burial. This burial cut the pavement of Stratum XXII and the fortification wall of Stratum XXIII (both date to the MBIIb). The ceramic evidence found within this burial may indicate either a MBIIc or LBI date (Livneh and Ben-Tor 2005, 34–39).

Stratum XXb (MBIIc/LBI). Prior to the building activities witnessed in this stratum, a large constructive fill was laid on top of the earlier remains. A large domestic building was built on this fill (fig. 3.4: C), composed of several rooms surrounding a courtyard. West of this building, a thick wall (ca. two meters wide), probably a retaining wall, was found, similar to the one attributed to Stratum XXI (MBIIc) of Area A-1 (Ben-Ami 2005, 141–47).

Stratum XXa (LBI). The plan of the building did not change (fig. 3.4: D). The floors were raised, and the walls were built directly on top of those of Stratum XXb (marked in gray). A narrower addition to the retaining wall was constructed. This phase ended in a conflagration (Ben-Ami 2005, 147–51).

Stratum XIXb (LBIIa). After the destruction in Stratum XX, a large, one-meter thick fill was laid before the LBII strata constructions were erected. The retaining wall went out of use, and the new structure characterizing the LBII strata (XIXb and XIXa) was built in a completely different orientation (fig. 3.4: E). In Stratum XIXb, benches were built along two walls of the structure. To the north, an alley was uncovered with two installations on its floor (Ben-Ami 2005, 151–53).

Summing up, the major architectural changes at Yoqne'am are seen between Stratum XXa, dated to the LBI, and Stratum XIXb, dated to the LBII. These changes are reflected in the complete change in the orientation of the buildings.

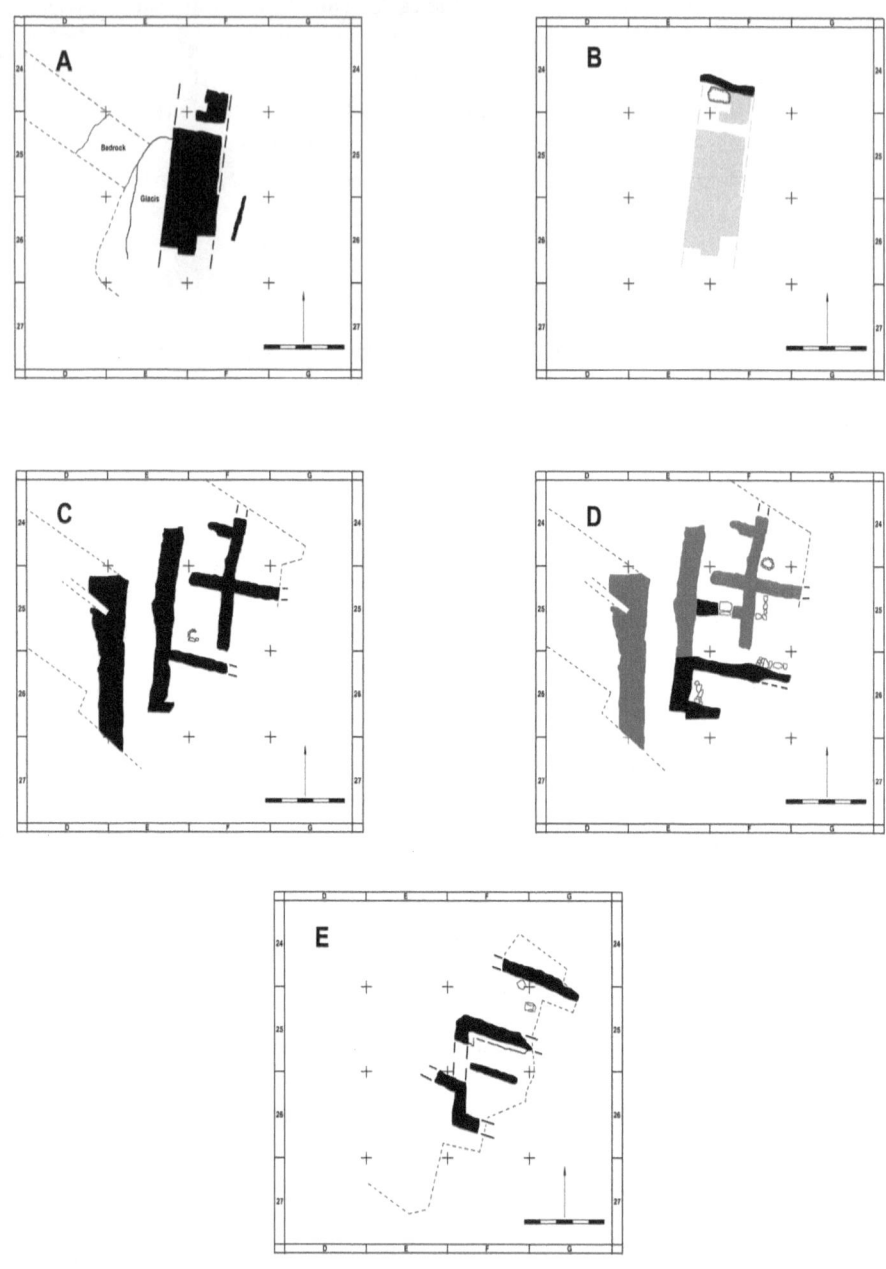

FIGURE 3.4 MBA and LBA strata in Yoqne'am, Area A4—(A) Stratum XXIII (after Livneh and Ben-Tor 2005, plan ii.9); (B) Strata XXII–XXI (after Livneh and Ben-Tor 2005, plan ii.9); (C) Stratum XXb (after Ben-Ami 2005, plan iii.2); (D) Stratum XXa (after Ben-Ami 2005, plan iii.3); (E) Stratum XIXb (after Ben-Ami 2005, plan iii.4).

PHOTO 3.1 The MBA–LBI retaining wall on the left (W.387) with the MBA glacis (L.2559), sealed by the LBA remains (from Ben-Ami 2005, photo III.10). Courtesy of Amnon Ben-Tor.

3.2.3. Beth-Shean (Figures 3.5–3.8)

Tel Beth-Shean was first excavated in the 1920s and the 1930s by the University Museum of the University of Pennsylvania. Excavations were renewed in 1989 by a team from the Hebrew University. The second volume of the final reports of the renewed excavations includes the analysis of the MBA remains uncovered by the University Museum Expedition (UME) together with those of the Hebrew University.

The ensuing discussion addresses only the finds from Area R, this area being the only one where stratification of the MBA and LBA layers was uncovered. Following each expedition publication method, the strata excavated under the UME will be marked in Roman numerals, while strata excavated by the Hebrew University team will be marked in Arabic numbers, headed by the excavated area (Mazar and Mullins 2007, 6).

3.2.3.1. The Middle Bronze Age

In Stratum R-5, the earliest MBA layer dated to the MBIIb–c (see table 3.1 and fig. 3.5: A), a large crater was found that probably functioned as a dump (Mullins

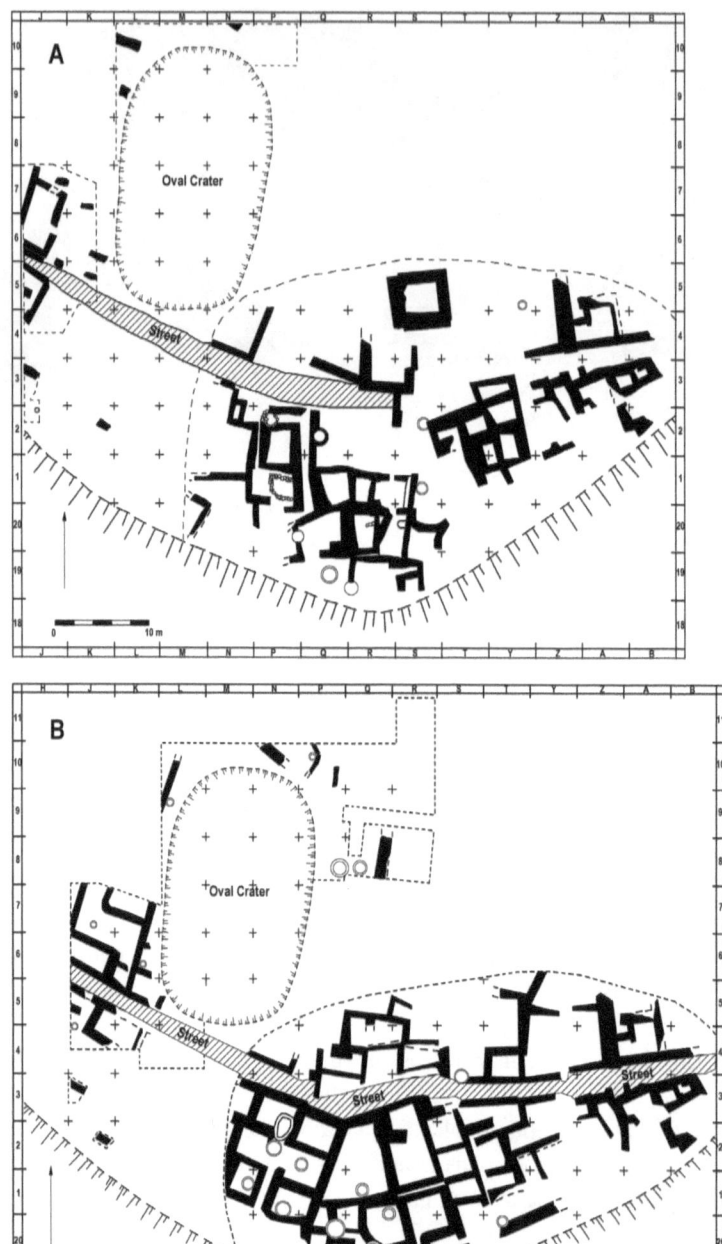

FIGURE 3.5 Strata R-5 and R-4 in Beth Shean—(A) Stratum R-5 (after Mazar and Mullins 2007, figure 1.2); (B) Stratum R-4 (after Mazar and Mullins 2007, figure 1.3).

and Mazar 2007, 47). This crater was in use until the end of Stratum R-4, dated to the MBIIc (fig. 3.5: B).

To the east of the crater, a large open courtyard with several hearths was in use from Stratum R-5 to Stratum R-3 (also dated to the MBIIc). The crater was surrounded by several domestic units to the north, west, and south, built on both sides of a street parallel to the edge of the tel. In Stratum R-3 the crater was filled and sealed, thus going out of use (fig. 3.6: A). Nonetheless, the area kept its domestic nature and the residential quarter expanded over the crater as several installations, floors, and walls were built over it (Mazar and Mullins 2007, 13–15). In general, a natural growth progression and continuity are evident in the MBA town of Beth-Shean (Mullins 2002, 33).

No evidence of a fortification system was exposed in the MBA settlement of Beth-Shean. It seems this city was a small town probably occupying only the southern part of the tel (Mazar and Mullins 2007, 15–16). This town ended in a destruction, partially evident in the southern and western parts of the area (Mullins 2002, 32–33).

3.2.3.2. The Late Bronze Age

No LBIa remains were exposed by the UME. The Hebrew University expedition uncovered a small temple, built over the aforementioned crater, with a few rooms and installations to its north, west, and south, and paved open spaces to its north and west attributed to Stratum R-2, dated to the LBIa (fig. 3.6: B). This is the first temple in a series of LBA–Iron Age temples uncovered in this area. This building was interpreted as a temple based on the benches found within it and an upright standing stone found on a platform. In addition, a posthole with remains of charred wood was recovered in the northern end of this platform and interpreted as the Asherah.

The meager evidence for this stratum at Beth-Shean was interpreted as indicating a time of regression and partial abandonment during the LBIa. This temple was abandoned at the end of its use, most probably due to damage indicated by its sinking floors, caused either by earthquakes or the settling of the crater's MBA fills. The floors of the building were cleaned before being abandoned. This temple was covered by a Stratum R-1b courtyard, dated to the LBIb (Mullins 2002, 33–38; Mazar and Mullins 2007, 17–18; Mullins and Mazar 2007, 112–39).

Based on the continuity of some architectural elements from Stratum R-3 to Stratum R-1b (such as the streets and the place of the R-2 temple), the excavators believe there was a short span between the end of the R-2 temple (LBIa) and the new settlement of R-1b (fig. 3.7). Within this time, in the fifteenth century BCE, Beth-Shean became an Egyptian garrison stronghold, probably following

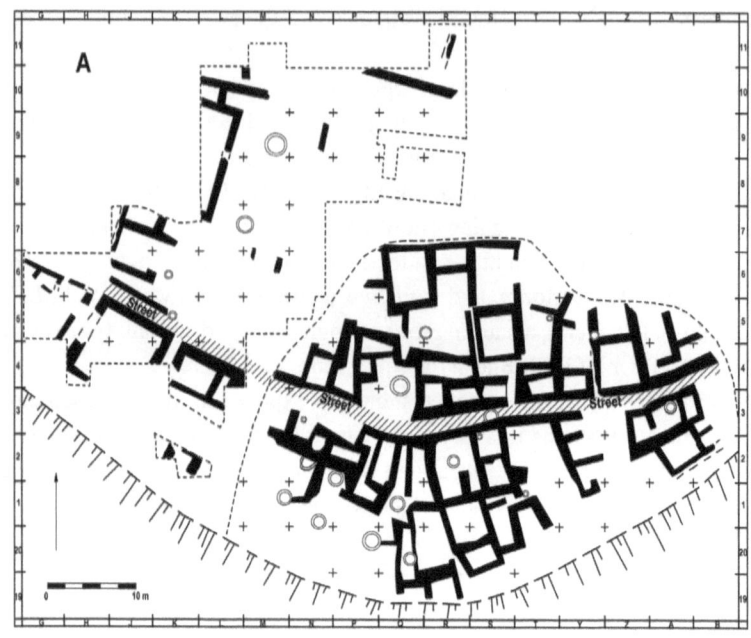

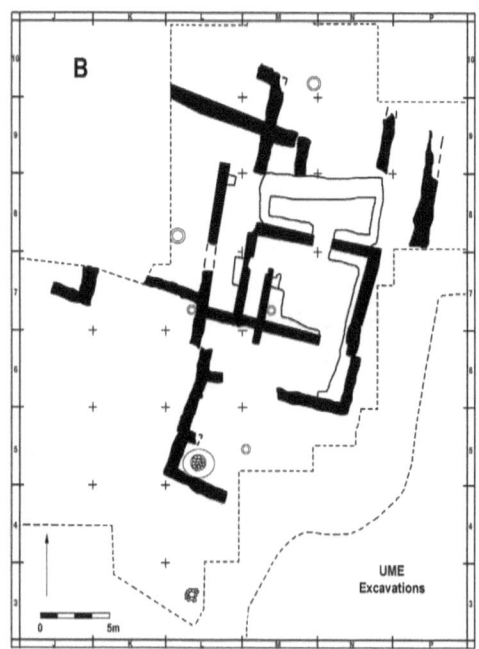

FIGURE 3.6 Strata R-3 and R-2 in Beth Shean—(A) Stratum R-3 (after Mazar and Mullins 2007, figure 1.4); (B) Stratum R-2 (after Mullins and Mazar 2007, figure 3.18).

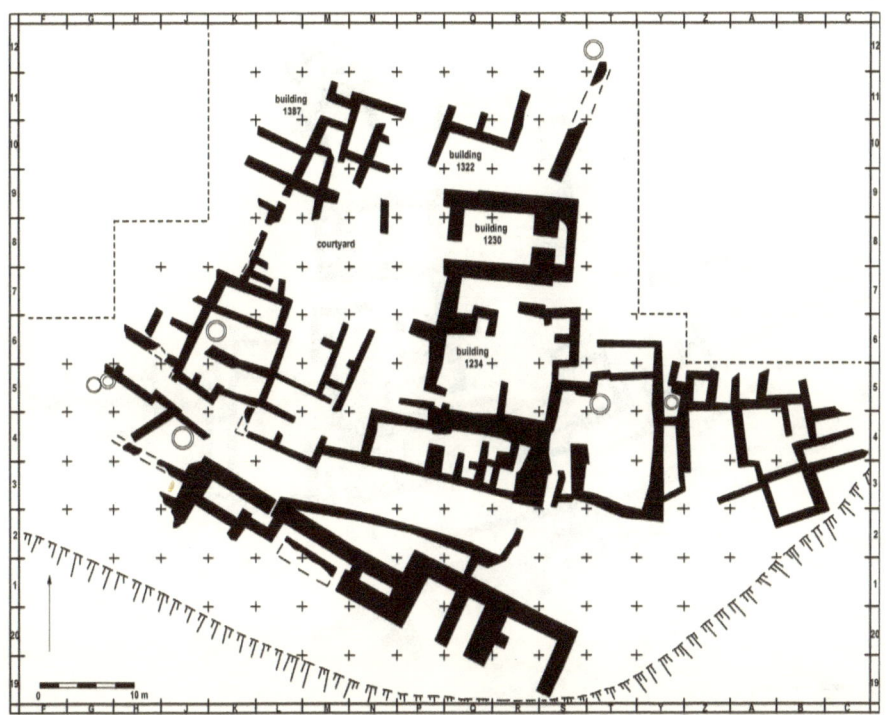

FIGURE 3.7 Beth Shean, Stratum R-1b (after Mazar and Mullins 2007, figure 1.7).

Thutmose III's campaign (Mazar and Mullins 2007, 18–21; Mullins and Mazar 2007, 139).

The UME exposed one stratum dated to the LBI: Stratum IX. However, the Hebrew University excavators discerned that this stratum should be divided into two stages, termed R-1b and R-1a, dated to the LBIb and LBIIa, respectively. Stratum R-1 presents an entirely new city plan with no architectural connections with the previous Stratum R-2.

A large cultic complex was built in Stratum R-1b (LBIb). A large courtyard (which sealed the previous R-2 temple, discussed above) was found to the west of the complex, with four possible identified entrances (Mullins 2002, 80). The complex includes at least two ritual buildings, 1230 in the north and 1234 in the south. The southern building, termed the "Mekal Temple," had several auxiliary rooms to its south and east. Building 1322 was also identified as a temple although this identification is still debated (Mullins 2002, 83–82). In the final publication, Mullins and Mazar (2007, 195) suggest that Building 1230 was actually the main temple, while Building 1234 served as the subsidiary area for the cultic practices.

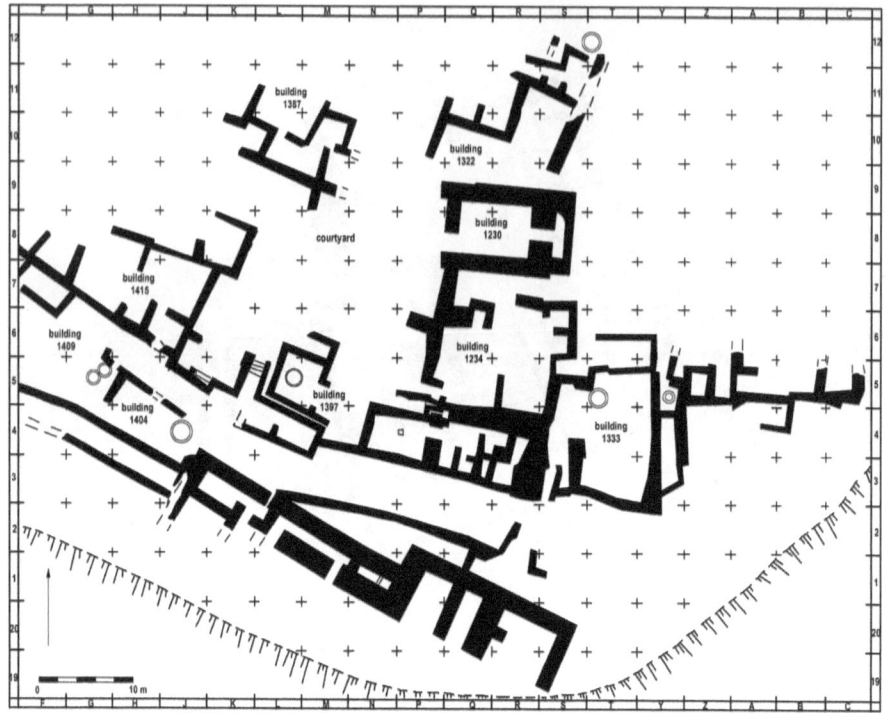

FIGURE 3.8 Beth-Shean, Stratum R-1a (after Mazar and Mullins 2007, figure 1.8).

Very few changes took place between Strata R-1b and R-1a (LBIIa) in the eastern part of the area (where the cultic complex is located), mainly the raising of floors (fig. 3.8). The courtyard was surrounded by several quarters comprising rooms and installations to its west. The two stages of Stratum IX were best exhibited in these quarters, including, mainly, the canceling of walls during stage R-1a (Mullins and Mazar 2007, 195). Northwest of the courtyard, Building 1387 was found, interpreted as a domestic building (Mullins 2002, 99–100) or as an auxiliary building to the cultic complex (Mullins and Mazar 2007, 140).

At the southern edge of the tel, the UME exposed a line of rooms built in casemate style and interpreted it as either the city's fortification or a *temenos* wall of the R-1 temple. However, the Hebrew University excavations revealed that this was in fact a large building, probably a large residential unit that served the Egyptian official of Beth-Shean during the Eighteenth Dynasty (Mullins and Mazar 2007, 177–78).

Levels VIII and VII, uncovered by the UME, were reconstructed as an "Egyptian Garrison" including a temple, a fortress, the Commandant's house, and other residential buildings. These levels were dated to the LBIIb (James and

McGovern 1993, 4–5) and are thus beyond the scope of the present discussion (I discussed the chronological framework of this study in chapter 2).[2]

Summing up, the city of Beth-Shean was seemingly reduced in size in the LBIa. Although the area changed its nature from a residential quarter to a cultic area between Strata R-3 (MBIIc) and R-2 (LBIa), the major architectural differences were identified between Strata R-2 (LBIa) and R-1b (LBIb), when an entirely new city plan was laid out. The transition between these strata is attributed to Beth-Shean being established as an Egyptian garrison sometime during the fifteenth century BCE.

3.2.4. Tel Megiddo

Tel Megiddo was excavated by four expeditions: the German Society for the Study of Palestine in 1903 and 1905; the University of the Chicago's Oriental Institute expedition, from the mid-1920s and the 1930s; the four excavation seasons conducted by the Hebrew University in the 1960s; and last, the renewed Tel Aviv University excavations, carried out from 1994 to the present day. Unfortunately, although the publications of the Oriental Institute include extraordinary amounts of data, it was not possible for me to use them in this study.

The Oriental Institute's publications of Strata XI–VIIa have been heavily studied (e.g., Epstein 1965, Kenyon 1969, Dunayevsky and Kampinsky 1973), each suggesting an alteration in the chronological allocation of the strata. Since the Oriental Institute's area plans offer only a schematic description with no elevations, it is nearly impossible to use this report in a critical manner. In addition, the finds of the renewed excavations by the Tel Aviv University have also led to an alteration in the stratigraphic scheme (Finkelstein et al. 2000, table 1.1; Finkelstein et al. 2006, table 1.1).

While the publications of the renewed excavations offer considerable and significant information, only three published areas include finds related to the present study's discussion topic: Areas M, N, and F.

Area M, located in the German expedition's excavation trench between two buildings—the Nordburg and Chamber f—is divided into a western and eastern Area M. It is probably the most difficult area to understand, since not only was the stratigraphy of Shumacher's excavations debated but the attribution of its levels is still debated among the excavators themselves (Franklin 2013; Finkelstein 2013). In addition, the definition of the Western Area M levels was altered after the Eastern Area M was published.

---

2. Similarly to Hazor, the ceramic assemblages from these strata will not be considered in chapter 4.

The other two areas (N and F) are very small and comprise only a few excavation squares. Thus, their contribution to the subject is scant.

The recent publications of Area K, not available before this book was in press, will greatly contribute to the issue since significant MBA and LBA remains were uncovered there (M. Martin, personal communication).

3.3. Northern Levant: Lebanon

3.3.1. Sidon

Excavations at the "College site" in Sidon were carried out by the British Museum from 1998 to 2012, where several dozen burials dating from the MBIIa were unearthed. Only a few MBIIb burials were exposed. Several associated walls built in the MBIIb probably served to define courtyards. Pits lined with chalk, *tabuns*, and hearths were found in these courtyards together with tools such as pestles, mortars, and grinding slabs. Large amounts of animal bones, grains, fruits, and nuts were also found. According to the excavator, these finds may all represent the remains of feasting activities that occurred as part of the funerary rituals (Doument-Serhal 2009a, 240).

The burial area and its courtyards were expanded throughout the MBIIb phases. Sometime during the MBIIb (Phase 5), a ten-meter-long mudbrick drainage channel with a stone cover was built to the north of the cemetery, which included both the graves and the walls associated with it. The excavators posit that this was not a subterranean channel, based on the care taken in its construction. It is not clear whether this channel was used in the funerary rituals preformed here.

In the last phase (Phase 6), the openings in the cemetery's walls were blocked, indicating the cemetery's end of use (Doument-Serhal 2006, 140–51; 2009b, 24–43 and fig. 19a).

A large building was found in the southern part of the site (Doument-Serhal 2009a, fig. 52). It has only been partially exposed and so far consists of five rooms. According to the excavators, this building was first constructed in the MBIIb, around 1700 BCE, and continued to be in use until the end of the LBA—with its floors being raised several times but with no architectural changes. The building was extended further to the north at the end of the LBA (Doument-Serhal 2006, 151; 2009b, 44–45). An interesting ceramic assemblage was found in one of its rooms (Doument-Serhal 2010, 123 and fig. 18). This assemblage consisted of hundreds of oil lamps and shallow bowls, with very few storage vessels and cooking pots. Together with other evidence, this assemblage led the excavator to interpret the building as a temple where communal ritual activities related to the funerary feasting ceremonies took place (Doument-Serhal 2009a, 239–42).

In the northern part of the site, a large, sunken building paved with large slabs was found. However, this building does not fall within the scope of this discussion since it was dated to the thirteenth century BCE based on the ceramic assemblage, a scarab, and C14 evidence (Doument-Serhal 2002, 193–205; 2004, 75–78). No excavations were conducted below this building, its earlier levels remaining as yet unknown.

In summary, Sidon exhibits rich evidence of funerary rituals, mainly in the MBA, when a large cemetery is associated with what seems to be a temple. The activities in the temple continue until the end of the LBA, although their relation to the earlier MBA cemetery is not clear. It seems that the association of LBA rituals with funerary ceremonies in the temple are based on the earlier remains, and the fact that cultic activities seemingly continue to be performed at the same place during the LBA (Mettinger 1995, 142). Therefore, architectural continuity is apparently exhibited in a single building in Sidon from the MBIIb to the end of the LBA.

3.3.2. Kamid el-Loz (Figures 3.9–3.16)

This site was first excavated between 1963 and 1981 by a German team from the Universität des Saarland. Excavations were renewed in 1997 by the Albert-Ludwigs-Universität, Freiburg.[3] Both teams uncovered finds dated to the Bronze Age, most of them attributed to the LBA (Heinz et al. 2010, 9). The stratigraphy of the site is divided into several phases termed "Cities" and "Anomies"[4] (see table 3.1). The first urban settlement at Kamid el-Loz (City 1) is dated to the beginning of the MBIIb, the last Bronze Age settlement (City 3) is dated to the LBII. The discussion will be presented by excavation area.

3.3.2.1. Area II

A palace was found in Area II.[5] In the earliest phase (City 1) the building comprised two rooms paved by stone slabs (fig. 3.9: A). Following this building's

---

3. The square numbers and orientation of the Saarland University's expedition do not align with those of the renewed excavations, by the Freiburg University. Trying to create this sort of alignment based on the publications was extremely difficult and basically impossible, also due to the inconsistencies in the latest publication. Therefore, the plans accompanying this part are based on those published by the Saarland University's expedition.

4. Anomie is the phrase used by Heinz to define the intermediate periods between the urban phases of the city.

5. It should be mentioned that in several cases no scale was found in the plan of the area. This was very problematic when complete squares were not excavated, preventing the creation of a scale.

FIGURE 3.9 MBA strata in Kamid el-Loz, Area II—(A) Building MBP3 City 1 (after Heinz 2016, figure 58); (B) Buidling MBP2, City 2 (Heinz 2016, figure 94); (C) Building MBP1, Anomie 2 (after Heinz 2016, figure 135).

destruction and a period of "Anomie," a new palace, MBP2, was built over the remains of the earlier building's destruction, attributed to the second urban period (City 2) and dated to the MBIIc (fig. 3.9: B). Thus far, nine rooms of the later palace were identified, built around a large courtyard (R10). This palace was destroyed in a large conflagration evidenced by the burnt wooden beams and mudbricks as well as broken pottery vessels found on its floors (Heinz 2016, 83–86).

Following the destruction and abandonment of the city, another intermediate period existed at Kamid el-Loz (Anomie 2). During this period, the inhabitants leveled the ruins of Palace MBP2 and built on it a small building (MBP1, fig. 3.9: C) comprising three rooms constructed around a courtyard (Heinz 2016, 116). This building also ended in a fierce fire (Heinz 2016, 118). The site began resettling in the LBI (City 3), according to the excavators, and the city continued to exist until the end of the LBII, undergoing three construction phases.

Phase C. The ruins of the previous palaces, MBP2 and MBP1, were leveled and a new palace, P5, was built on top of their ruins (fig. 3.10: A). The entrance to this palace was through a long hallway that led to a large hall. So far, this

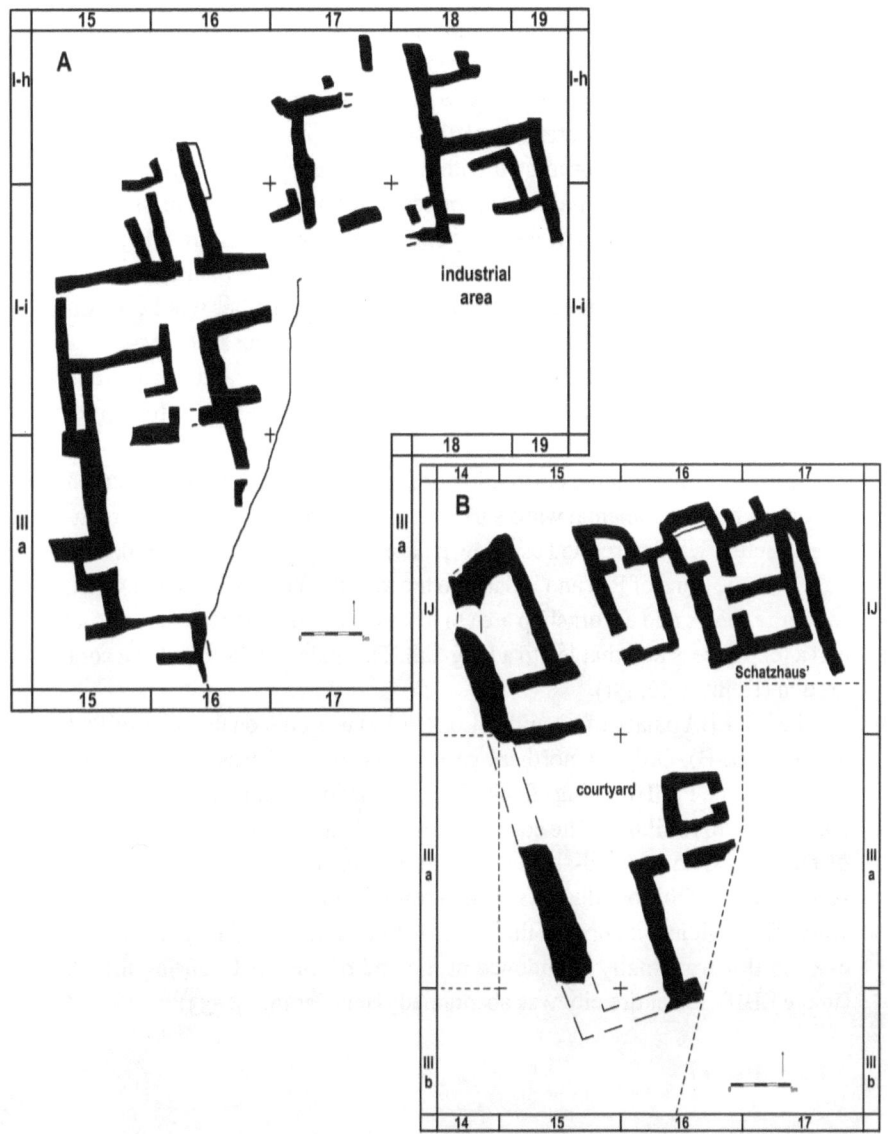

FIGURE 3.10 LBA strata in Kamid el-Loz, Area II, continued—(A) Palace P5, City 3, Phase C (after Heinz 2016, figure 153); (B) Palace P4, City 3, phase B (after Heinz 2016, figure 161).

building comprises four rooms and a large courtyard. An industrial area was constructed within this building against its outer walls and includes several metallurgical workshops (Heinz 2016, 130–32). Although Palace P5 ended in a fire, the metal workshops did not (Heinz 2016, 133).

Phase B. Following the palace's destruction, a new palace (P4) was built (fig. 3.10: B). The latter presented several building phases, beginning in the LBIb. It is distinctly different from the previous buildings due to the elite burial place that was incorporated within its premises as a subterranean tomb (the "Schatzhaus"). The palace comprises at least four rooms in its western wing, and at least two rooms and the "Schatzhaus" in its eastern wing. A passage connects the two wings and leads to a courtyard. The palace's modifications (P4d–P4a) include the rearranging of its rooms. In other words, the outer structure did not change, only its inner organization (Heinz 2016, 135–39). The "Schatzhaus" was in use only during Phase P4d. Phases P4c and P4a also ended in a fire (Heinz 2016, 147–48). Metal working was shifted east of its former location (Heinz 2016, 139).

Phase A. Following the destruction of P4a, a new building was constructed, but only a few monumental walls survived in the northern part of this structure. The structure was interpreted as a new palace (P3, fig. 3.11: A). This palace was built over the ruins of P4a and is dated to the transitional LBI/LBII. It comprises two large rooms and a workshop area to its east and, similarly to Palace P5, also had a long access hall that led to a long hall. This palace also ended in a conflagration (Heinz 2016, 151).

The last LBA palace of Kamid el-Loz (P1/P2) was built on the ruins of Palace P3 (fig. 3.11: B). Only the northern part of this structure was preserved, similarly to palace P3. Two wings flanked a long corridor that might have been the entrance to this building. The corridor most likely led to a wide courtyard. Each of the wings is a squared-shaped structure comprising several rooms. In the second phase of this building, a southern row of rooms was added to the western wing. The building underwent three destructions and rebuilding phases (phases c–a) until it was finally abandoned at the end of the LBII. During this time (in the LBII), the entire city was abandoned (Heinz 2016, 152–53).

3.3.2.2. Area VI

In the earliest phase (City 1), only the destruction layer of a large building was identified. This building was interpreted as a temple based on cultic activities found in this area in later phases (Heinz 2016, 62–65). The destruction was followed by an abandonment period, followed, in turn, by the first Anomie period. During the first Anomie period, a few installations and walls were built on top

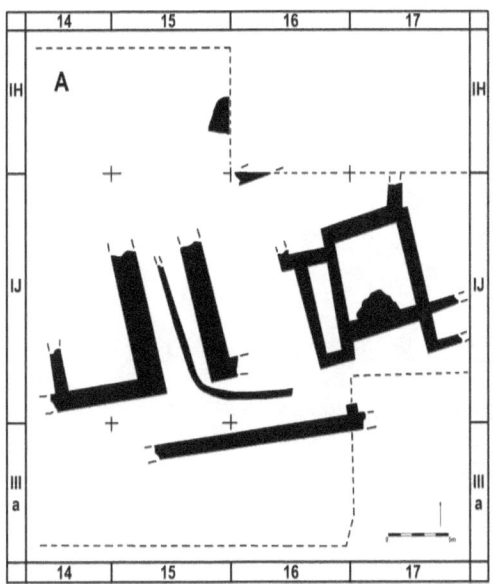

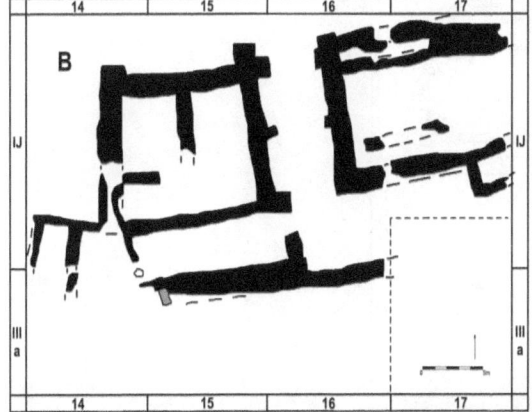

FIGURE 3.11 LBA strata in Kamid el-Loz, Area II, continued—(A) Palace P3, City 3, Phase A (after Heinz 2016, figure 185); (B) Palace P2/P1, City 3, Phase A (after Heinz 2016, figure 187).

of the early temple. After this structure was abandoned, a tomb was built in this area (Heinz 2016, 75–77).

The earliest building found in the revived MBIIc city (City 2) was defined as a house (T5, fig. 3.12: A), only partially uncovered. The excavators identified ten rooms, two courtyards, and several installations. However, because a later LBA temple was identified in the same location, this building was also interpreted as a temple, although no evidence was uncovered indicating a cultic nature.

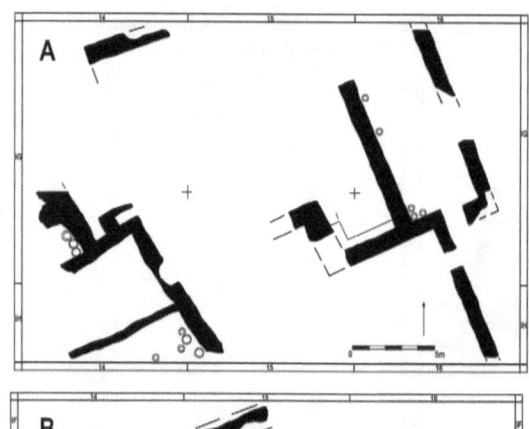
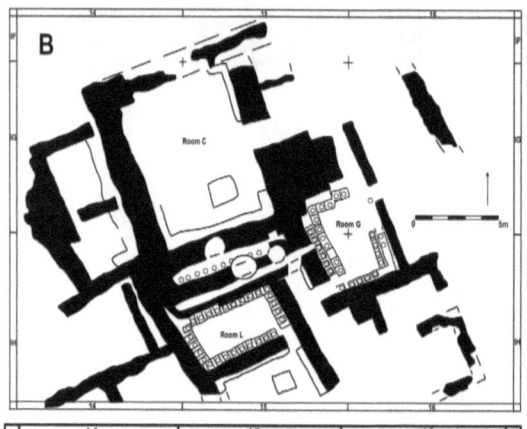
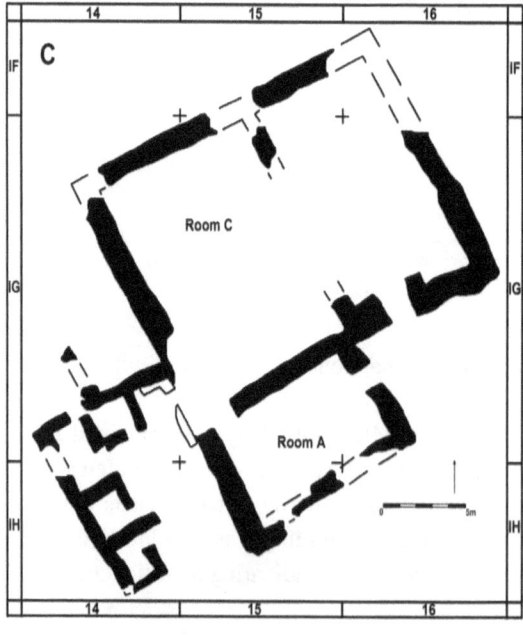

FIGURE 3.12 MBA and LBA strata in Kamid el-Loz, Area VI—(A) Temple T5, City 2 (after Metzger 2012, tf. 46); (B) Temple T4, City 2 (after Metzger 2012, tf. 44); (C) Temple 3, City 3, Phase C (after Heinz 2016, figure 198).

In other words, the building might have functioned as a private residence and not as a temple (Heinz 2016, 90–91).

This building ended in a conflagration, and a new building (T4)—also attributed to City 2—was built on it, using some of its walls (fig. 3.12: B). This large and monumental building has an impressive entrance, benches along some of its walls, and a podium in its main room (Room C). In this room, a row of clay blocks with a depression in their center was found attached to the southern wall. These might be the negatives of large vessels that were stored here. This same feature was discovered along all the walls of the rooms to the south (Room L) and southeast (Room G). Several other rooms and courtyards were found in this building, with cooking installations and other storage facilities in their interior (Heinz 2016, 92–93). This building was abandoned at the end of the MBIIc (Heinz 2016, 95). During the second Anomie phase, Temple T4 was left in ruins, and the inhabitants of the site continued to use the podium in the center of the temple as an installation (Heinz 2016, 120). The cultic area revived together with the city (City 3, dated to the LBA).

Phase C. A new temple was built (T3, fig. 3.12: C) on top of the ruins of the previous MBA temple T4. The new temple differs significantly from the previous temple and includes two large courtyards in the center of the temple and small rooms abutting the western courtyard (C) from the south and west. Benches run alongside the walls of the southern room (A). The courtyard did not lead to the entrances of the rooms but, on the contrary, each room had its own separate entrance. Within the temple and its rooms, several domestic installations were found (such as pits and ovens), together with stone pillar bases and podiums. The temple itself did not change throughout the course of its life, and only the organization of the rooms to its west varied. This temple and the entire complex were destroyed by a large conflagration (Heinz 2016, 159–60).

Phase B. Following the destruction of Temple T3, the area underwent major renovations and a cultic precinct (T2) was built (fig. 3.13: A). Temple T3 was rebuilt, except for its western attached rooms, which were replaced by a vast structure comprising a large central courtyard surrounded by several rooms. The whole complex, termed "the double temple" (Heinz 2016, 161), consisted of two equally sized buildings (the eastern and western temples), each with its own entrance. A large basin was built to the south of the western temple. This double temple, like its predecessors, ended in a violent conflagration (Heinz 2016, 163–64).

Phase A. In this phase, the double temple was rebuilt, termed T1 (fig. 3.13: B). The floors were raised, and minor modifications were made to the earlier Temple T2. The temples were symmetrically enlarged by adding a room to the south (M) of the eastern temple and a room to the north of the western temple (L). At the end of the LBA, the western rooms of the western temple were

FIGURE 3.13 LBA strata in Kamid el-Loz, Area VI, continued—(A) Temple T2, City 3, Phase B (after Heinz 2016, figure 202); (B) Temple T1, City 3 Phase A (after Heinz 2016, figure 207).

burned down while the rest of the building was abandoned but not destroyed (Heinz 2016, 164–65).

3.3.2.3. Area IV

During the first urban period (City 1), both fortifications and residential buildings were identified in Area IV, on the northern slopes of the tel. Two phases were identified during this level (fig. 3.14: A–B). This part of the settlement was not destroyed but rather abandoned at the end of this phase (Heinz 2016, 66–67). In the first period of Anomie this area became a burial ground (Heinz 2016, 74–75).

A new residential space, with two phases, was found in the reurbanized area (City 2). Only a single building (House 1) of the earlier phase has so far been exposed (fig. 3.14: C), consisting of a courtyard surrounded by rooms. A paved pathway was exposed to the south of this building, probably leading from the area of the temple. This house ended in a large fire, and the area on which it was built went out of use. The pathway south of the house also went out of use, and a new domestic building (House 2) was erected in this area in the later phase, using some of the walls of the pathway (fig. 3.15: A). To the east of this building a new casemate fortification system was built. House 2 also ended in a conflagration (Heinz 2016, 97–100).

No remains attributed to the second Anomie period were found in this area. In the LBA (City 3), new residential buildings were erected using none of the earlier structures (fig. 3.15: B). An alley running southeast–northwest and bounded by two structures was identified in this quarter. The structure to its west was interpreted as a metal-processing area, while the structure to its east was interpreted as a temple, based on its stepped façade. However, this façade is not evident from the publications. This latter building was destroyed in a large conflagration at the end of the LBI and remained abandoned until the end of the LBA (Heinz 2016, 172–73, 180).

3.3.2.4. Area III

The earliest remains in Area III[6] are attributed to City 2 (dated to the MBIIc; fig. 3.16: A). Based on a few walls exposed underneath the LBA residential quarter in this area, the excavator suggests a residential area was built in this period to the west of the temple. Similar to other buildings of City 2, this residential area was also abandoned at the end of the MBIIc (Heinz 2016, 96). During the

---

6. This area was excavated only by the renewed excavations and therefore the square numbers that appear on the plans are those of the Freiburg excavation's grid.

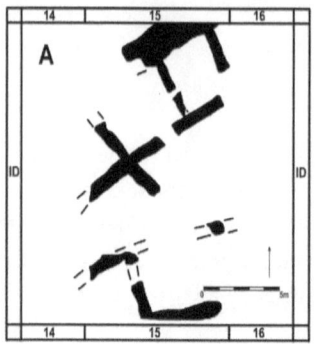
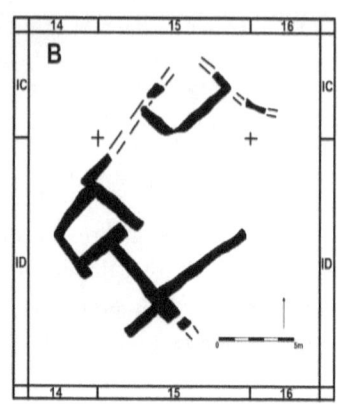
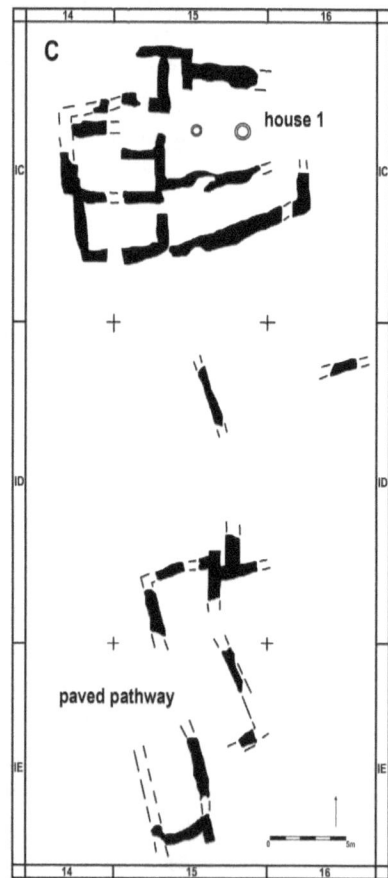

FIGURE 3.14 MBA strata in Kamid el-Loz, Area IV—(A) City 1, Early Phase (after Heinz 2016, figure 73); (B) City 1, Late Phase; (C) City 2 (after Heinz 2016, figure 74).

FIGURE 3.15 MBA and LBA strata in Kamid el-Loz, Area IV, continued—(A) City 2, Late Phase (after Echt 1984, Tf. 15); (B) City 3 (after Heinz 2016, figure 209).

second Anomie period, this area was used as a mass grave where at least ten individuals were buried (Heinz 2016, 120). During the last urban phase of the site, in City 3 (dated to the LBA), a large domestic quarter was found here built next to temples T3–T1 (fig. 3.16: B), with its houses flanking both sides of an alley. Each house shares walls with the neighboring houses. So far, at least nine houses have been excavated, all of them courtyard buildings of similar size and presenting similar building technique (Heinz 2016, 167–68). At the end of Phase C (during the LBI/LBII transition), several houses in this quarter

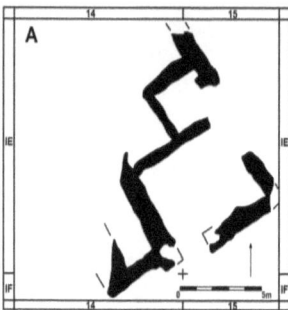

FIGURE 3.16 MBA and LBA strata in Kamid el-Loz, Area III—(A) City 2 (after Heinz 2016, figure 110); (B) City 3 (after Heinz 2016, figure 212).

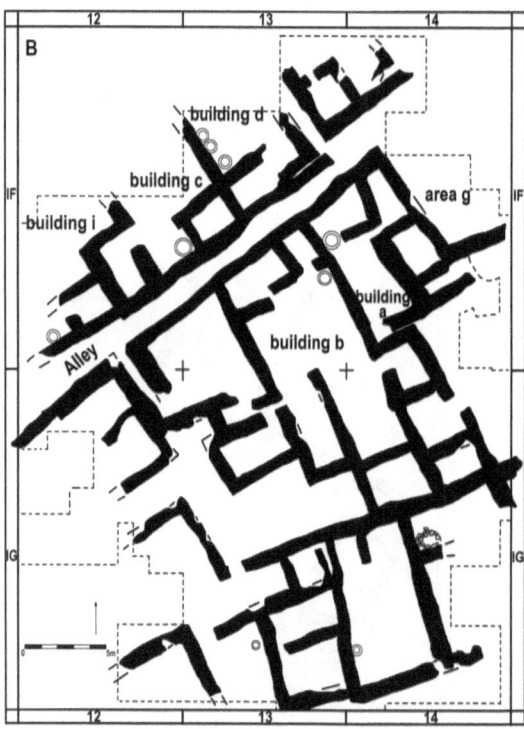

were abandoned (buildings i, c, and d to the north of the alley and buildings a, b, and area g to the south of the alley). The abandoned area was used for household activities such as *tabuns* and hearths. Part of this abandoned area was used to build the western temple of Temple T2. The other houses remained in use until the end of the LBA (Heinz 2016, 170).

3.3.2.5. Area VII

Another residential area was excavated on the east slope of the tel, far from the main buildings described above. Since this quarter was built during the LBII and abandoned at the end of the period (Heinz 2016, 174–75), it does not contribute to the present discussion.

In summary, the most significant changes at Kamid el-Loz occurred between Cities 2 and 3 (between the MBA and the LBA). In certain areas (e.g., Areas III and VI), an evolution is evident in the plan of the buildings between Cities 1 and 2. However, when City 3 is built, a new plan is evident, as seen in area VI (the temple), for example, where the monumental temple of City 2 (T4) is turned into a large building with narrower walls in City 3 (T3) and then into a double temple (T2). Though the orientation of T4 and T3 does not actually differ, the entrance to the temple is moved from the east to the south. In contrast, in the residential areas IV and III, no significant changes were evident between any of the strata. However, no similarities are identified between the strata. In other words, some changes have been detected between each and every two strata. This is perhaps due to the residential nature of the area.

3.3.3. Tell el-Ghassil (Figure 3.17)

Excavations at Tell el-Ghassil were conducted for thirteen seasons by the American University of Beirut between 1956 and 1963, 1968 and 1969, and 1972 and 1974 (Doumet-Serhal 1996, 5).

In the Bronze Age, Tell el-Ghassil was a small village with a few walls, floors and installations found throughout the different strata.

The first settlement at the site is dated to the beginning of the MBIIb and consists only of burials (Strata XI and X).

Stratum IX. In the northeastern part of the excavated area, the southwestern corner of a building was found, formed by two narrow walls (fig. 3.17: A). To the west and south of these walls, a large pavement, a *tabun* and an ash pit were uncovered. This stratum ended in a conflagration evidenced by a 5–12 cm ash layer found throughout the site. This destruction is dated to the MBIIc.

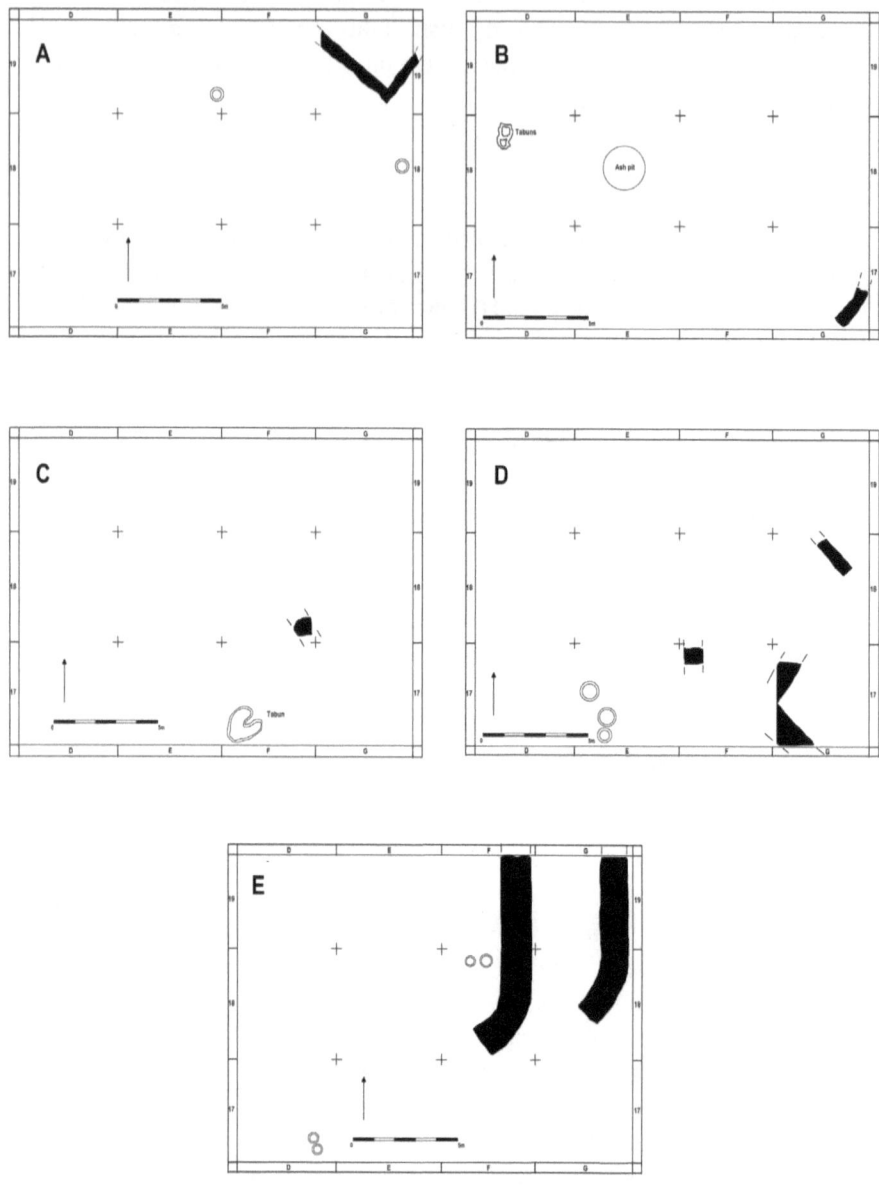

FIGURE 3.17 MBA and LBA strata at Tell el-Ghassil—(A) Stratum IX (after Doumet-Serhal 1996, figure 10); (B) Stratum VIII (after Doumet-Serhal 1996, figure 11); (C) Stratum VII (after Doumet-Serhal 1996, figure 12); (D) Stratum VI (after Doumet-Serhal 1996, figure 13); E. Stratum V (after Doumet-Serhal 1996, figure 14).

Stratum VIII. This stratum, also dated to the MBIIc, includes a narrow wall located in the southeastern part of the excavated area, as well as a floor and two *tabuns* (fig. 3.17: B). In the center of the area a large ash pit was found. This stratum also was destroyed by fire, evidenced by a 6–10 cm ash layer unearthed throughout the area.

Stratum VII. This stratum, dated to the LBI, consists of a narrow fragment of a wall (fig. 3.17: C). A *tabun* and a pavement were found south of this wall. A 5–12 cm ash layer found throughout the area indicates that this stratum was also destroyed by fire.

Stratum VI. This stratum, dated to the LBIIa—the western corner of a building was found in the southeastern part of the area, formed by two relatively wide walls (fig. 3.17: D). A narrow wall with the same orientation was found north of these walls, and west of the wide walls, another wall (of a different orientation), a pavement, and three *tabuns* were discovered.

Stratum V. This stratum, dated to the LBIIa/b, comprises two new large walls bordering a path or a street, with their southwestern end turning west to create a rounded end (fig. 3.17: E). Two *tabuns* were found near the western wall, and two others in the southwestern part of the area (Doumet-Serhal 1996, 12–17).

In summary, Tell el-Ghassil was apparently a small village during the second millennium BCE. The major architectural changes appear to have happened between Stratum VII of the LBI and Stratum VI of the LBIIa. This change is marked by a different building technique seen in its walls: while throughout the MBII and the LBI the walls are narrow, in the LBIIa these are wider and larger and might point to a building of a more public nature.

3.3.4. Tell Arqa (Figures 3.18–3.19 and Photo 3.2)

Tell Arqa has been excavated since 1972 by an expedition from the University of Paris I. Three strata belong to the discussed period: Stratum 13 dated to the MBII, Stratum 12 dated to the LBI and Stratum 11 dated to the LBII (Thalmann 2006a).

Stratum 13 (fig. 3.18: A). A large water reservoir, located in the middle of the area and built already in the MBIIa Stratum 14, continues to be in use throughout Stratum 13, dated to the MBIIb. At the end of Stratum 13, the water reservoir is sealed and a system of terraces is built on top.

The first fortification system at the site is built in this stratum. The system includes a large rampart and two large structures built on top whose western and northwestern parts are eroded. The walls of these structures are relatively wide and are therefore considered by the excavator as monumental in nature. Several tombs were found inside these structures and in the northeastern part of the area, some of them burials of children in storage jars usually characterizing domestic units and not public structures.

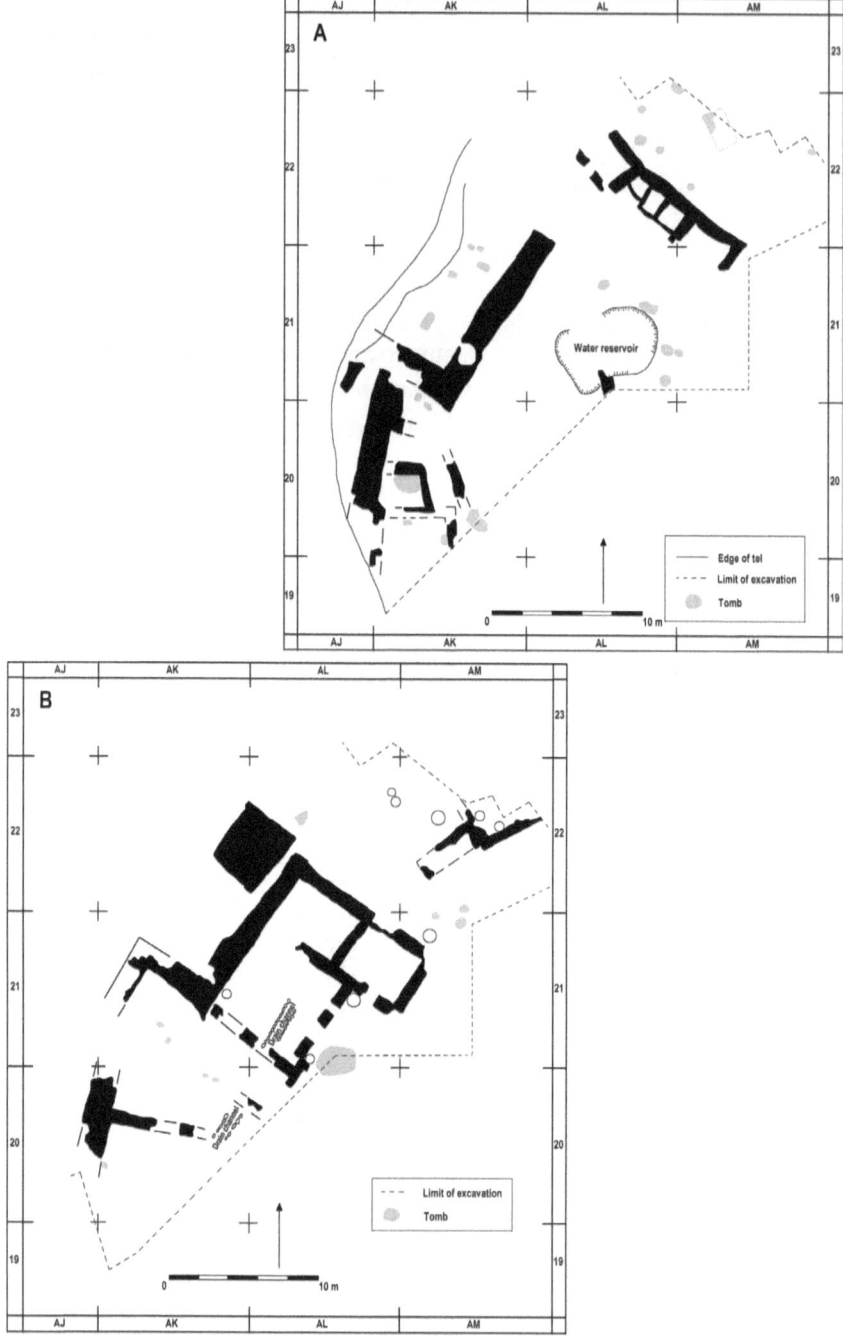

FIGURE 3.18 MBA and LBIa strata in Tel Arqa—(A) Stratum 13 (after Thalmann 2006a, figure 92); (B) Stratum 12, Phases c and b (after Thalmann 2006a, figure 93).

PHOTO 3.2 On the left, terraces of Stratum 12, in the center, terraces of Stratum 13, looking east (from Thalmann 2006b, pl. 32b). Courtesy of the Tell Arqa Excavations Project.

Outside the monumental structures, in the southwestern part of the area, several small walls were found and attributed by the excavator to residential units. Additional residential units were uncovered in the northeastern part of the area, part of a single structure built on the terraces abutting the fortification system. One of the rooms of this structure was divided into three units serving as silos. This structure probably continued to the south where it was cut by later building activities (Thalmann 2006a, 51–57).

Stratum 12. This stratum can be divided into two main phases.[7] In the earlier phase (fig. 3.18: B) a new terrace system was built. The western part of the area is reorganized, with new walls sealing the earlier structures that were probably part of the Stratum 13 fortification system. Based on the similar width of the new walls, Thalmann suggests that these served as part of the new fortification system of the city. The angle that the walls create suggest that the buildings of Stratum 13, which defined the edge of the city, were now replaced by a single wall of an irregular layout.

---

7. Thalmann divides this stratum to three subphases. The difference between subphases 12c and 12b is the raising of the floors and therefore will be discussed as one phase here.

One of these walls continues to the north, using an earlier Stratum 13 wall as foundation, and becoming narrower in this northern part. This wall is part of a new building identified by Thalmann as a courtyard house that underwent several changes, such as the adding of an opening in its southeastern wall and possibly also of a room to the east. To the north of this house, a large courtyard was identified, probably limited in the west by the continuation of the fortification wall. A large depression in this courtyard was identified as a negative of the common pithoi found in this stratum.

A trapezoid space south of the courtyard house probably also functioned as a courtyard. A row of flat stones in the southern part of this courtyard was interpreted as pillar bases, pointing to the existence of a portico at that place. Four burials of children in storage jars were found in the courtyard. In the northeastern corner of the courtyard, an annexed paved room was identified, with two pillar bases in its entrance. However, the passage into this room being very narrow, Thalmann argues that this space is neither practical nor functional, even if these were indeed pillar bases. Based on the high quality of this trapezoid space's construction, he suggests that this structure represents, in fact, a cultic building.

To the west of the fortification wall, a squared building was found, built of worked stones and filled with fieldstones. The excavator suggests that this was a watchtower built next to the fortification system, overlooking the plains in the west and with easy access to the sea.

All the buildings of the earlier phase, apart from the central courtyard house, ended in a conflagration—remains of the destruction are evident in the burnt wooden beams and large amounts of collapsed stones and mudbricks (Thalmann 2006a, 71–76).

The later phase of Stratum 12 (fig. 3.19: A) is attributed to the partial reoccupation of the site following the destruction of the stratum's earlier phase. Settlement remains were identified only in the area of the courtyard house. The floors were raised, and part of the large western wall was sealed. An adult burial, dug into the mudbrick superstructure of this wall, is also attributed to this phase. Several installations and burials were found in the eastern room and the courtyard (Thalmann 2006a, 76).

Stratum 11 (fig. 3.19: B). The nature of the site completely changed after its destruction in Stratum 12. It is now concentrated in the northern and eastern parts of the area and consists of installations including, among other things, silos, pits, and stone basins (Thalmann 2006a, 81–82).

In summary, the settlement evidence at Tell Arqa indicates a clear continuation between Strata 13 and 12. Following the destruction of Stratum 12, a sharp break is seen in the architecture (or rather lack of) at the site.

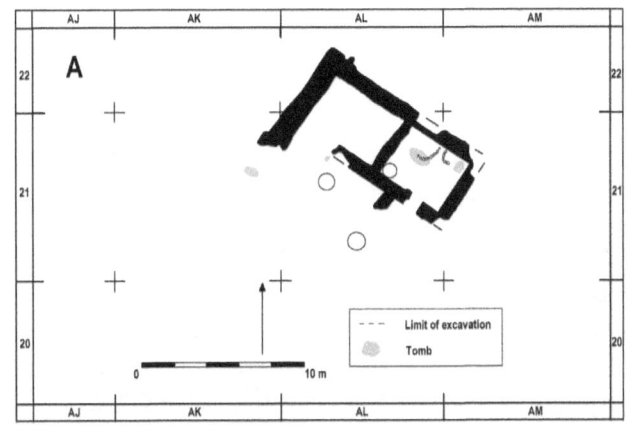

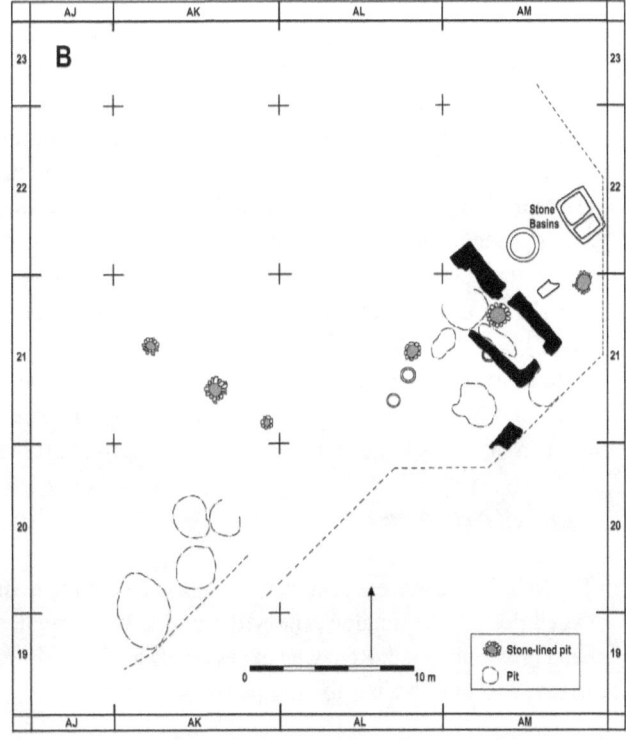

FIGURE 3.19 LBIb and LBII strata in Tel Arqa—(A) Stratum 12, Phase a (after Thalmann 2006a, figure 93); (B) Stratum 11 (after Thalmann 2006a, figure 94).

3.4. Northern Levant: Syria

3.4.1. Tell Sakka

Excavations at Tell Sakka began in 1989 on behalf of the Syrian Directorate-General of Antiquities and Museums (Taraqji 1999, 29), continuing for nine seasons.

Stratum 4. Remains of a large MBA building were found in this stratum, dated to the eighteenth century BCE. This building, interpreted as the palace of an Egyptian official or local governor, had a large hall, probably decorated with wall paintings and surrounded with several smaller rooms. Four basalt pillar bases were discovered in the large hall, while two very large storage vessels were found in one of the smaller rooms, its southern part being seemingly used for storage (Taraqji 1999, 35–37). This stratum was destroyed in a violent conflagration dated to the end of the eighteenth century BCE or the beginning of the seventeenth century BCE, based on the ceramic assemblage (Taraqji 1999, 40).

Stratum 3. Dated to the LBA, this stratum represents a small agricultural village, consisting mainly of small residential units that include a courtyard surrounded by one or two rooms. The courtyards were usually paved. The excavator claims most of these houses are based on the plans of the previous houses, the differences between the two levels being reflected in the interior organization of the rooms, the width of the walls, and the nature of the floors (Taraqji 1999, 32–34).[8] However, no information regarding this earlier level nor a more specific date for either level is supplied by the excavator.

Stratum 3 ended in a large conflagration. Following this destruction, the site was abandoned only to become a burial site in the first millennium CE (Taraqji 1999, 35).

In short, the major changes at Tell Sakka occurred between Stratum 4 of the MBII and Stratum 3 of the LBA, when the site completely changed its nature from an official's large residence to a small agricultural village.

3.4.2. Tell Nebi-Mend

Tell Nebi Mend was excavated in 1921–1922 by a French Mandatory government expedition. Unfortunately, the MBA and LBA excavated levels have not yet been fully published. Renewed excavations by the University of London began in 1975 and have been also only partly published.

---

8. He claims that in the LBA most of the floors were paved but neglects to mention the types of floors in the previous level.

The first fortification system was built at the beginning of the second millennium. This system includes a massive casemate wall and a rampart. Several buildings were found associated with this fortification system. Sometime in the sixteenth century BCE the site was destroyed. Following a short occupation hiatus, the city was rebuilt in the LBA, as evidenced by the presence of several large public buildings of yet unknown function (Parr 1997, 114–15).

The renewed excavations at the site uncovered fragmentary walls and floors revealing two major breaks in the architectural layout. The first occurred between phases G and F. Phase G, dated to the end of the MBA, seventeenth century,[9] ended with a vast destruction. The following Phase F is dated to the LBI, around the sixteenth century. The second architectural break is seen between phases E and D. Phase E is dated to the LBIb, fifteenth century. Phase D is dated to the LBI/LBII transition, at the end of the fifteenth and beginning of the fourteenth centuries (Burke 1993, 158–63). Since only fragmentary walls were found at this site, it cannot be included in the present discussion.

3.4.3. Qatna (Figures 3.20–3.23, Photo 3.3)

Qatna was first excavated between 1924 and 1929 by Count R. Du Mesnil du Buisson, who uncovered parts of what he interpreted as a temple and a palace and several large tombs (Pfälzner 2007, 30–31). Excavations at the site were renewed in 1994 by a Syrian expedition headed by the Syrian General Directorate of Antiquities and Museums, with the University of Udine and the University of Tubingen joining the project in 1999 (Al-Maqdissi et al. 2002, 10–11). MBA and LBA remains were found in several excavation areas.[10]

3.4.3.1. Area J

Located in the center of the acropolis, this area comprises several MBA and LBA occupation phases (J18–J7) consisting of a series of superimposed pottery workshops. The first in this series is dated to the beginning of the MBA and was built together with a monumental building probably used to oversee the work done in the area (fig. 3.20:A). During the late MBA, in Phase J11 (fig. 3.20:B),

---

9. This attribution, as well as all other chronological attributions at this site, are based on the ceramic assemblage (Bourke 1993, 164–89).

10. The chronological division of the MBA and the LBA in the northern Levant is different from that in the Southern Levant and is based on the chronological scheme set in Ebla. Thus, the MBA ends at circa 1600 BCE and is divided into two subphases: MBI and MBII. The LBA is also divided into two subphases, LBI and LBII, separated at circa 1400 BCE. However, recently, Iamoni has suggested adding the MBIII, set at 1600–1500 BCE (Iamoni 2012, 161–72). This suggestion will be further discussed in chapter 4.

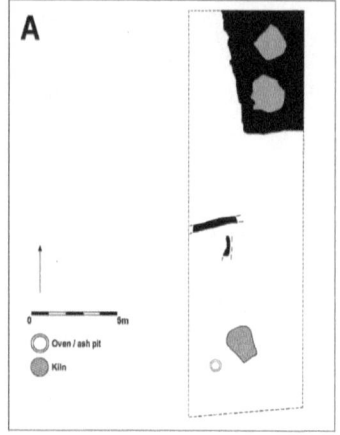
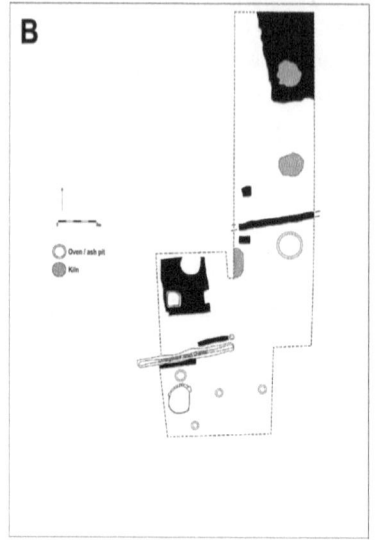
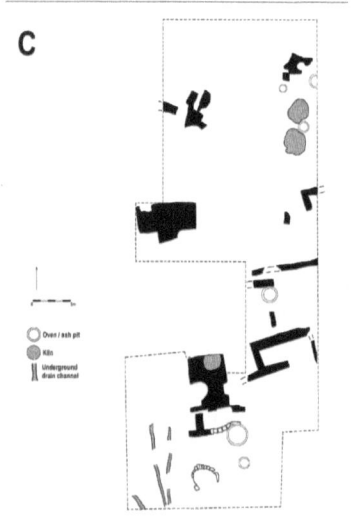
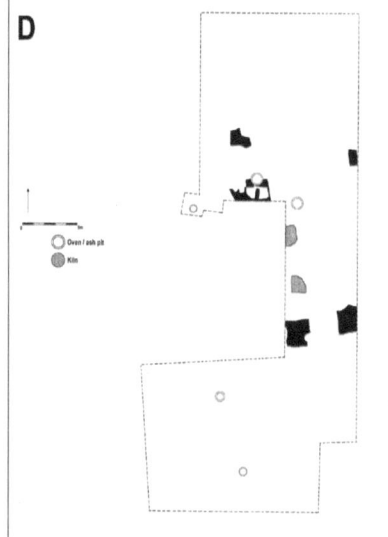

FIGURE 3.20 MBA and LBI strata in Qatna, Area J—(A) Phase J14 (after Morandi Bonacossi 2008, figure 31); (B) Phase J11 (after Morandi Bonacossi 2008, figure 34); (C) Phase J10 (after Morandi Bonacossi 2008, figure 36); (D) Phase J7 (after Morandi Bonacossi 2008, figure 39).

this building no longer served its original function as pottery kilns were dug into its walls. The excavators suggest this building was originally a palace that went out of use after the new Royal Palace in Area G was established (Morandi Bonacossi 2008, 101–7; Iamoni 2012, 70–76).

The area functioned as a ceramic manufacturing workspace also in Stratum J10 (fig. 3.20:C) and continued this function until the LBA Phase J7 (Morandi Bonacossi 2008, 85–92). This continuity in activity consists mainly of the raising of floors and the construction of new kilns and working surfaces. Throughout this time, the area functioned as a specialized area for mass production of ceramic vessels (Morandi Bonacossi 2008, 101–7; Iamoni 2012, 75–76).

At the beginning of the LBA (Phase J7, fig. 3.20:D), only the northern part of the area was used as a pottery workshop. Some of the earlier installations went out of use (such as underground refuse channels). This change is dated by Morandi Bonacossi to the LBI (2008, 112–14) and by Iamoni to the LBII (2012, 73), based on the ceramic assemblages.

The area was not occupied during the LBII and, after a hiatus, its occupation was resumed during the Iron Age II, when pits and graves cut through the LBI remains (Morandi Bonacossi 2002, 125–27; 2008, 114).

3.4.3.2. Area C

This area is located on the eastern slopes of the acropolis. Two strata were dated to the MBA–LBA. In the first stratum, a few walls and several floors belonging to a building of unclear nature (due to the small area of exposure) were uncovered. This stratum has four phases, the first dated to MBIIa/b transition and the last to the LBI. In the second stratum, dated to the LBII–III, a potter's workshop was exposed (Al Maqdissi and Badawi 2002, 37–61; Al-Maqdissi and Morandi Bonacossi 2005, 21).[11]

Another building was exposed in this area, to the south of the Royal Palace. It comprises several rooms built around a hall or courtyard and an additional unit that is not connected to the main building but might have served as a reception suite as suggested by the excavators (Al Maqdissi 2003, 1500–1505). This building has been interpreted as a palace, termed the "Southern Palace," and dated to the LBII (Morandi Bonacossi 2013, 119).

3.4.3.3. Area T

This area is located in the northern part of the acropolis, to the east of the Royal Palace, and is divided into several subareas. The area was excavated by both

---

11. Due to the fact that the plans in Al-Maqdissi and Badawi 2002 do not have square numbers, it is impossible to draw a coherent plan of the remains in this area.

Italian and Syrian teams. An integrated report of their finds has not yet been published, and the data presented here is based on each mission's individually published reports.[12]

Areas T2–T3. In the earliest phase (Phase VII), domestic buildings with many cooking installations were found. A residential quarter also probably occupied this area during Phase VI[13] (Morandi Bonacossi et al. 2009, 63–64; Al-Maqdissi 2009, 1206–1210).

During phase V, the Northern and Southern Buildings were built, most likely concomitantly (fig. 3.21: A). Two entrances to the Southern Building were identified (in Rooms A and C), through Courtyard I, and three buttresses were found in its northern wall. The building remained mostly unchanged throughout its lifespan until it was incorporated into the Eastern Palace in Phase II. In Phase V, the Northern Building had an open space to its west, limited by a wall to its east and north.

This building underwent some changes during phase IV when the exposed walls of the main room were widened (Room G), making this room narrower (fig. 3.21: B). The building was further modified in Phase III when an additional wing was built on its northwestern side, creating a series of small rooms (fig. 3.21: B). These rooms were probably used for storage, except for one that might have been part of a pottery workshop (Iamoni 2015, 454–61; Morandi Bonacossi et al. 2009, 68–69; Kanhoush 2015, 443).

A two-room temple was built east of these buildings. The rooms of the temple are trapezoid in shape. This building was destroyed at the end of the MBII, and a new structure, badly preserved, was built on top (Al-Maqdissi 2009, 1210–1213).

The most significant change in the area occurred in Phase II (fig. 3.22), when the Northern and Southern Buildings united into a single complex termed the Eastern Palace (Morandi Bonacossi et al. 2009, 69; Kanhoush 2015, 444), probably in the MBII (Morandi Bonacossi et al. 2009, 74). A new room (Room E) joined the two structures. This room was built by extending the buttresses of the Southern Building, thus creating the walls of this room (Iamoni 2015, 455). The floors of the other rooms were raised, but the main entrance to the complex was still through one of the rooms of the original Southern Building (Room A) (Morandi Bonacossi et al. 2009, 69). Several rooms and corridors were built in the northeastern part of the palace. In one of the rooms, several figurines were found, as well as a large krater embedded in the room's floor ("Pièce II," being the same as Room M). An even larger krater was set in the floor of one of the palace's corridors (Couloir I). One room (Pièce V) was identified as a storage

---

12. A large domestic building was found in Area T1, dated to the LBIIb and built after 1340 BCE, when the Royal Palace was destroyed (Da Ros 2015), and is thus not part of the present discussion.

13. This phase is not illustrated in any of the cited publications.

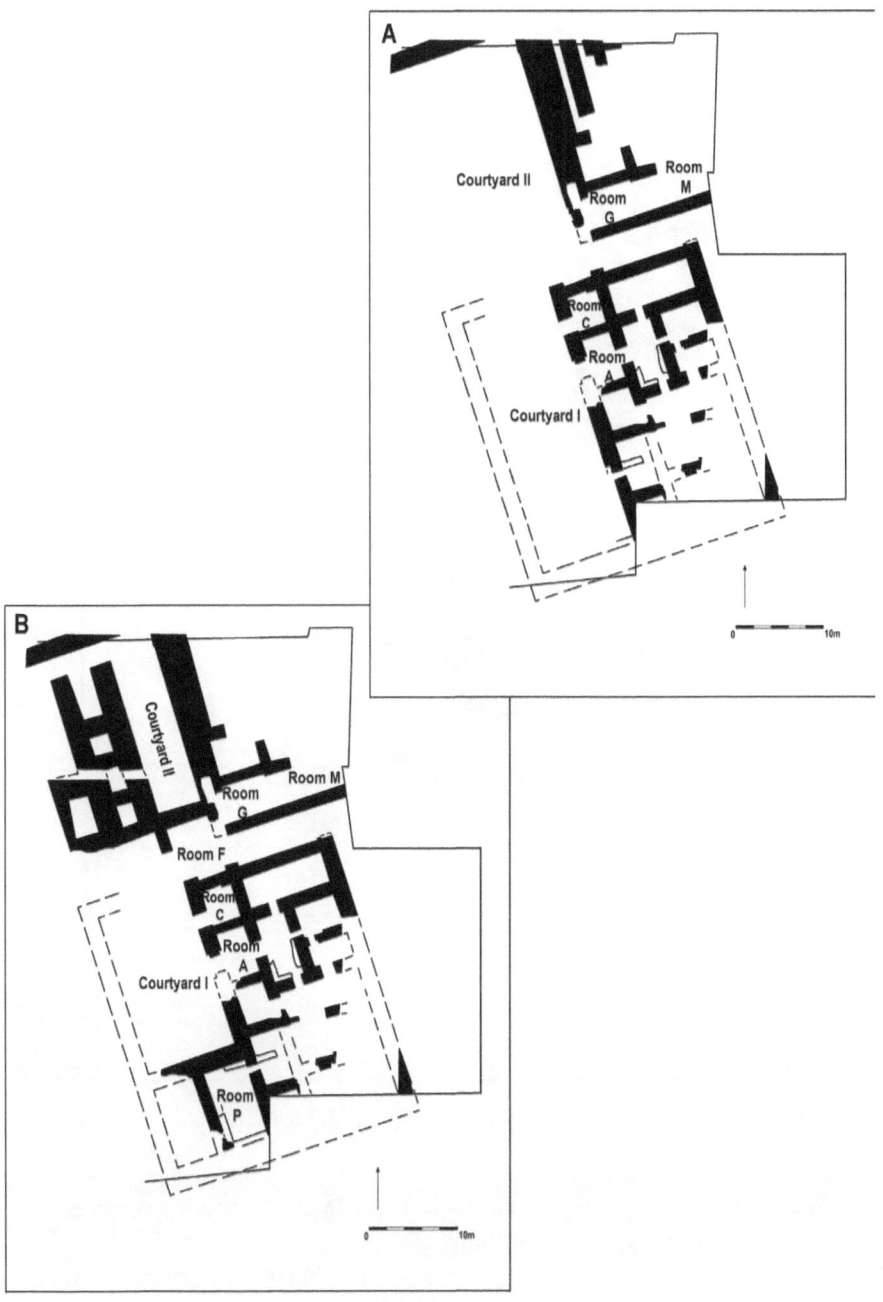

FIGURE 3.21 MBA strata in Qatna, Area T (after Iamoni 2015, figure 5a)—(A) Phase V; (B) B. Phases IV and III.

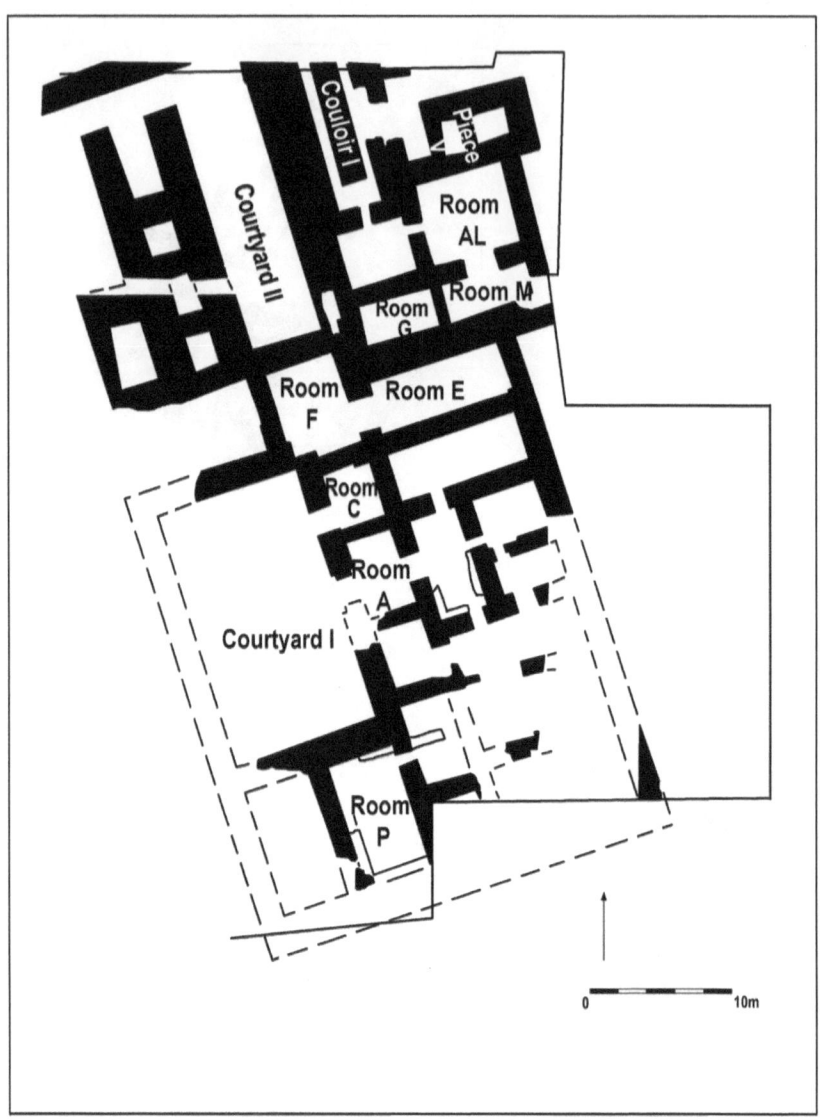

FIGURE 3.22 Qatna, Area T, Phase II (after Iamoni 2015, figure 5a).

room (Kanhoush 2015, 444–48), and two others (Rooms AL and M) were identified as the audience suite (Iamoni 2015, 462).

A staircase leading to an upper floor was found in the northeastern sector of the palace. This sector may have functioned as the private wing of the building, based on parallels from contemporary palaces in the northern Levant (Iamoni 2015, 461, 463). In addition, a new courtyard (Courtyard I) was built west of the palace, and new wings were added on this courtyard's northern and southern sides (Morandi Bonacossi et al. 2009, 69). One of the southern rooms (Room P) might have functioned as a metallurgy workshop (Morandi Bonacossi et al. 2009, 70). A second courtyard (Courtyard II) was built in the northwestern extension of the building, also surrounded by several rooms (Al-Maqdissi 2009, 1216).

The Eastern Palace was probably built in the MBII (Morandi Bonacossi et al. 2009, 74). At the end of the MBA or the beginning of the LBI, the Eastern Palace was abandoned. Eight graves were dug into its remains, most probably during the LBA. Squatter's activities were also detected in some of the rooms of the palace (Morandi Bonacossi et al. 2009, 74–77, 84).

Area T4. At the beginning of the MBA, several storage installations for agricultural produce were constructed in this area. The western wing of the Eastern Palace was built sometime during the MBA. After the Eastern Palace's abandonment and the Royal Palace construction (to the west, also discussed below) at the end of the MBA or the beginning of the LBI, a road was built in this location. In the LBII, the Eastern Palace was completely destroyed by a large pit probably dug to quarry raw material for mudbrick production. This pit was later turned into a refuse dump, also during the LBII (Morandi Bonacossi et al. 2009, 86–90).

Area K. This area is located in the northern part of the lower city, near its Northern Gate. Six building phases were identified in this area, the earliest (termed Building 6) dated to the LBII. Building 6 is a large, monumental residential building, interpreted as a palace and dated to the fifteenth–fourteenth centuries BCE (fig. 3.23: A); it has not yet been fully excavated. It comprises at least thirty-four rooms of different sizes (some only partly excavated) and functions. The only MBA remains in this area are the sherds found both on the surface and in the fills of this building (Luciani 2002, 2003; Iamoni 2012, 76–81; Morandi Bonacossi 2015). Thus, although this palace cannot be fully included in this discussion due to the fact that only MBA sherds were found in this area, it seems that the LBII palace was either built on virgin soil or canceled any building prior to it, perhaps covering it with large fills. Thus, a major change in this area occurred when the palace was built in the LBII.

Areas G, H, and R. These areas represent the "Royal Palace," located on the northern part of the acropolis (fig. 3.23: B, photo 3.3). This palace was first excavated by du Mesnil du Buisson between 1924 and 1929, and then by the three teams present at the site from 1999 to 2006. Contrary to du Mesnil du Buisson's assertion, the palace was not built in two phases but rather represents a single phase (Pfälzner 2007, 36–37).

Prior to the construction of the palace, the area was used as a large cemetery dating from the MBIIa to the beginning of the MBIIb. In the MBIIb, a series of walls and a silo were built (Morandi Bonacossi 2007, 225–28). The Royal Palace

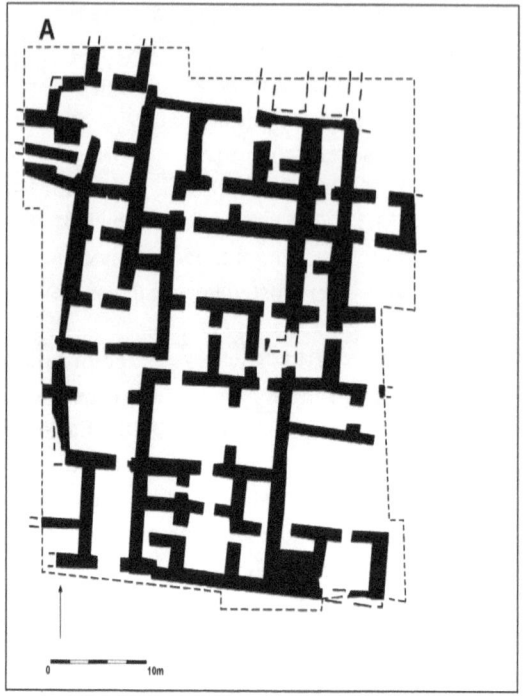

FIGURE 3.23 LBA palaces in Qatna—(A) Area K (after Iamoni 2015, figure 5b); (B) Areas G, H and R—the Royal Palace (after Morandi Bonacossi 2014, figure 7).

PHOTO 3.3 Qatna, the Royal Palace. Courtesy of the Italian Archaeological Mission to Mishrifeh/Qatna.

was subsequently constructed, cutting into some of these walls. The entrance to the palace was from the west, probably accessed by a ramp (Pfälzner 2007, 43–44). The palace included a large ceremonial sector with several halls functioning as reception halls and as the throne room. Parallels to this "reception suite" were found in the Mari Palace of Zimri-Lin (Novak 2004, 305; Pfälzner 2007, 38). Two service wings, one to the north and one to the east of the ceremonial sector, were also found.

The eastern wing included more than thirty-five rooms, most of these probably functioning as storage rooms. In the northeastern part of the palace, a plausible upper story was identified, representing, according to the excavators, the royal living quarters. The northwestern part of the palace probably served as a kitchen area. A large well was dug in Room U of the palace, about twenty meters below the floor level. A royal hypogeum was found underneath the palace and was probably connected to the throne room by an underground passage. The dozens of cuneiform tablets found in the debris that fell into the underground passage suggest that this part of the palace also accommodated a scribal office. Thus, an administrative quarter was also identified in the palace.

A street, whose floor was raised four times, ran along the southern façade of the palace (Morandi Bonacossi 2007, 229–32; Pfälzner 2007, 43–59). The floors of this palace were also raised several times, and numerous renovations were undertaken in the building, though these did not lead to major changes in its layout (Pfälzner 2007, 42).

In a later phase, an annex was added to the southern part of the palace, cutting the street that ran along it. This annex comprised at least ten rooms (Morandi Bonacossi 2007, 230).

Morandi Bonacossi suggested that the Royal Palace was built following the dismantling of the Area J monumental building during the late MBA. He further proposed that the mudbricks of the Area J building were used in the construction of the Royal Palace (Morandi Bonacossi 2007, 227). The Royal Palace's founding date is still being debated and will not be explored here. All three scholars base their dating on the pottery found in the foundation trenches of the palace's walls, Morandi Bonacossi (among others) argues for a date within the transition between the MBA and the LBA or even the LBI as the earliest date for the foundation of the palace (Morandi Bonacossi 2007). Pfälzner suggests an earlier MBIIb date for the foundation although he also claims the building's first use occurred not before the MBIIb/MBIIc transition (Pfälzner 2007, 37–41). Novak maintains a much earlier date for the foundation, during the transition from the MBIIa to the MBIIb (Novak 2004). They all agree that the palace was destroyed around the mid-fourteenth century BCE. In the present study, I concur with Morandi Bonacossi's arguments for the later dating of the foundation of the palace.

In summary, the most significant architectural change in Qatna occurred following the construction of the Royal Palace, which changed the entire layout of the city (Morandi Bonacossi 2013, 115). As noted above the date of the foundation of this building is still in debate.

Although it is not clear why the Eastern Palace was abandoned, its abandonment is contemporary with the construction of both the Royal Palace and the palace in the Lower City (Morandi Bonacossi et al. 2009, 70). It thus seems safe to suggest that these palaces took over the functions of the earlier Eastern Palace. The excavators have also suggested that this replacement might have been due to the Eastern Palace's structural fragility, or that a need for significant changes in the city's layout resulted in a new urban plan being set for it: the Eastern Palace was canceled and the Royal Palace, the palace in the Lower City and the Southern Residence in Area Q in the lower city were built (Morandi Bonacossi et al. 2009, 70–71; Shabo 2015).

Elsewhere, Morandi Bonacossi suggests that the changes were due to a change in tradition. The earlier tradition represents the "nuclear" Mesopotamian model where a single large palace represented all the different functions of power (residential, political and economic). The later tradition is a decentralized pattern where the various functions of power were distributed among several buildings situated in and around the Royal Palace (Morandi Bonacossi 2007, 229).

Based on these changes, it might be suggested that the area of the potters' workshop was also modified during the LBI/LBII transition, being moved from the top of the acropolis to its western slopes.

3.5. Summary and Conclusions

In the previous chapter, it was shown that the most significant architectural changes that occurred at Hazor in the second millennium took place between the LBI (Stratum 2 in the lower city and XV in the acropolis) and the LBII (Stratum 1b in the lower city and XIV on the acropolis). It was shown that Stratum 2/XV should be attributed to the LBIa while stratum 1b/XIV should be attributed to the LBIb–LBIIa. This chapter set out to identify the architectural changes in sites within Hazor's realm and its vicinity. The aim of this chapter was to examine whether the development identified at Hazor is apparent in a specific regional area or a larger region, or if it was specific to Hazor.

In *Tel Qashish*, the major changes are reflected in the cancelation of the site's fortifications between Stratum VIII (dated to the transitional MB/LB phase) and Stratum VII (dated to the LBI). A similar case was observed in *Yoqne'am*, Area A-1, where fortifications or any kind of retaining walls were taken out of use between Stratum XXI (dated to the MBIIc) and Stratum XXb (dated to the transitional MB/LB phase). However, the orientation of the architecture changed between stratum XXa (dated to the LBI) and stratum XIX (dated to the LBII) in areas A-1 and A-4. In the latter, this change occurred after the area was destroyed.

In *Beth-Shean*, the most significant change took place between stratum R-2 (dated to the LBIa) and stratum R-1b (dated to the LBIb). Although the area maintained its cultic nature, the city plan completely changed. In *Sidon*, a continuation is apparent from the MBIIb to the end of the LBA. In *Kamid el-Loz*, the major changes occurred at the beginning of City 3, dated to the LBA. In Area II, where the palaces were uncovered, the major change takes place between Anomie 2 and City 3, when a new palace is built in a somewhat different orientation. Furthermore, the width of some of the walls changes, and the building becomes more monumental. In area VI, where a series of temples was exposed, the most significant change is observed between temples T4 (of City 2) and T3 (of City 3). This change is reflected in the gradual development of the buildings within City 2 (between T5 and T4) until the temple turns into a monumental building. In City 3, the walls of the temple become narrower and the temple is not entered from the east but from the south. This temple (T3) gradually developed into the double temples T2 and T1.

In the residential areas IV and III, no similarities can be seen between any of the phases. Thus, since changes are present in each phase, no continuities throughout the lifespan of the city can be ascertained.

In *Tell el-Ghassil*, the biggest changes came about between Strata VII (dated to the LBI) and VI (dated to the LBIIa). These changes are reflected in the nature of the architecture—that is, from buildings with narrow walls to buildings with wide walls. These changes could, perhaps, also reflect an evolution in the nature of the structures from private to more public buildings.

At *Tell Arqa*, the major changes occurred between Stratum 12b and Stratum 12a, following the destruction of the first. Stratum 12a may represent an apparently unsuccessful attempt to revive the settlement. Both strata are dated to the LBI, and it seems plausible to suggest that the earlier stratum should be dated to the LBIa and the later to the LBIb. This suggestion is strengthened by the destruction level encountered between these two strata, which might have been caused due to Thutmose III's campaign against the city (Charaf 2004, 246).

In *Tell Sakka*, a significant shift took place between Stratum 4 (dated to the MBII), when a large building occupied the site, and Stratum 3 (dated to the LBA) when the site became an agricultural village. A large destruction layer was identified between these two strata.

The major changes in *Qatna*, occurring sometime at the end of the MBA or the beginning of the LBA, included the cancellation of the Area J pottery workshops and the abandonment of this area in the LBII. They also reflect in the abandonment of the MBA Eastern Palace, probably following the construction of the Royal Palace in Areas G, H, and R and the palace of the lower city (in Area K). The latter is dated to the LBII while the former's date is still in debate.

In conclusion, it seems that the development identified at Hazor can be also identified in Beth-Shean, Tell el-Ghassil, Tell Arqa, and Qatna (see map in fig. 3.24). At these sites, the most significant architectural changes occur between the LBI and the LBII. These changes were also observed, to some extent, in Yoqne'am (Area A-4). In Tel Qashish, Kamid el-Loz, and Tel Sakka, the major changes occurred before the LBI (in the transitional MBA/LBA period). However, since the LBA strata in Kamid el-Loz and Tel Sakka were not divided according to the different phases of the LBA, the exact time of change in these sites is difficult to ascertain. The excavated area in Qashish being very small, major conclusions cannot be inferred on its basis.

In most sites, a destruction level was identified, however, not always dated to the end of the MBA. In Yoqne'am, the destruction level was identified in Stratum XIXb of the LBIIa, which is later than the identified significant changes. In Beth Shean, Stratum R-3, dated to the MBIIc was destroyed, though the most significant changes were noted following the next stratum, in the transition between

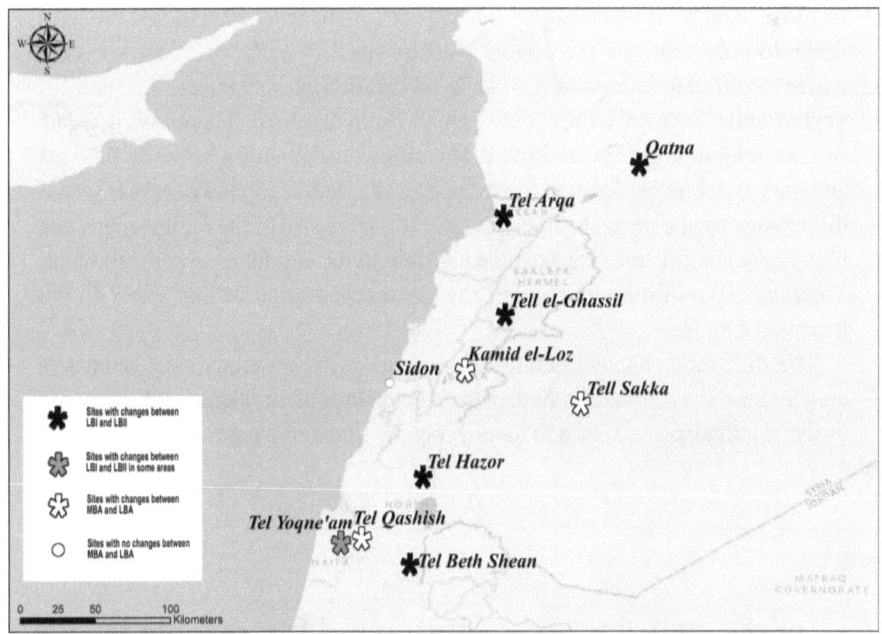

FIGURE 3.24 Map of the Levant with sites mentioned in the study, indicating when major architectural changes occurred.

Strata R-2 and R-1b. In Kamid el-Loz, a destruction level was identified at the end of all City phases, dated to the MBIIb, MBIIc, and the LBA. At Tell Arqa, the destruction of the site (in Stratum 12b) is also the time when major changes were noted (between Strata 12b and 12a). The same was true for Tell Sakka, which was destroyed in Stratum 4, when significant changes were also noted. At Tell el-Ghassil, a destruction level was identified at the end of Stratum IX, dated to the MBIIc, though major changes only occurred between Strata VII and VI.

Thus, it seems that the destruction of some of these sites has nothing to do with internal developments within the cities. In three instances (Yoqne'am, Tell Arqa and Tell Sakka), the destruction level was followed by major architectural changes. In two other sites (Beth-Shean and Tell el-Ghassil), it was not. However, at Tel Qashish, Tel Hazor, and Qatna, no destruction levels were identified. Therefore, it is clear that we cannot automatically attribute destruction levels to major architectural changes or assume that major architectural changes should necessarily occur following the destruction of a site. Although each site has its unique historical record, examining the regional developments can illuminate some geopolitical trends. The overall trend in the geographic framework of this study points to major changes between the LBI and the LBII. Though there are some sites when major changes occur between the MBII and the LBI, these do not constitute the majority of the sites. In addition, these are sites where the differentiation of the strata is not detailed (as in Kamie el-Loz and Tel Sakka) or the excavated area is very small (as in Qashish). Therefore, it seems safe to point to a generalized trend of architectural changes between the LBI and the LBII. I will suggest in the following chapters (especially chapter 5) that this change can be traced back in the geopolitical record of the region and is due to the new administrative system established in the southern Levant following Thutmose III's military campaign and the incorporation of this area into the Egyptian Empire.

The following chapter contains an analysis of the ceramic evidence uncovered in these sites, which strengthen the conclusions of this chapter. The ceramic analysis will also contribute to identifying the time of change.

CHAPTER 4

Pottery Assemblages from the Middle and Late Bronze Ages

4.1. Methodology

This chapter aims at identifying the changes in the ceramic assemblages and traditions during the Middle–Late Bronze Age transition—namely, which changes took place and when. Identifying these changes will facilitate discussing the differences in consumption within both the MBA and the LBA. Only published ceramic assemblages are being examined here, since most of the sites mentioned in the previous chapter, located in Syria and Lebanon, were not accessible to me.

It is well known that publications do not present *entire* assemblages but only representative vessels from the assemblages uncovered at the sites. Since this study is based on published data alone, any future publications of assemblages that are inaccessible or, thus far, unpublished, may change the conclusions of this research. This is a "calculated risk" that must be taken since we are, eventually, dealing with statistics and the excavators' view of what should and should not be published. Not taking this "risk" and not relying on published material for conducting further studies, out of fear of reaching the "wrong" conclusions, will end in our wings being cut off. This wide-scope research relies on the excavators' publications, and we should be wary of unpublished data. Therefore, it should be stated up front that the conclusions rely s*olely* on published material and might be altered in the future when new excavation results are published.

However, there are a few sites for which statistical analysis of the entire assemblages has been published (Tel Qashish, Yoqneʻam, and Beth-Shean). To avoid creating a bias while comparing to other sites, the statistical analysis from these three sites has been analyzed only in regard to general changes in consumption (e.g., changes in consumption of cooking pots and not of cooking pots of type CP3), since some types defined here do not conform to the ones defined in those publications. Therefore, to avoid any possible biases, the statistical analysis of the publication was not applied to the specific types, even when possible, but only to the general families.

The only sherds and vessels taken into account were those originating in "secure" contexts (floors, makeup of floors, and installations but not fills and tombs). This information was available in additional tables from the Tel Qashish and Yoqne'am reports. For Beth-Shean, the excavators merely mention whether the samples came from stratified or unstratified contexts. Obviously, only stratified samples from this site were added to this study (below, I discuss the difficulties of using the Beth-Shean tables). These samples appear in the accompanying tables to graphs 4.48–4.65.

4.1.1. Chronological Framework

The periods examined in this chapter are in line with those of the previous chapter; in other words, only assemblages dating from the MBIIb to the LBIIa were examined. It should be emphasized that, when a single stratum is dated to the LBI, it is currently not possible to suggest whether it should be dated to the LBIa or the LBIb, which is not the case when there are two strata dated to the LBI.

In some cases, assemblages dated to the LBII (e.g., Tell Arqa Stratum 11) were discussed, while in other cases, assemblages dated to the LBIIa–LBIIb (Hazor Stratum 1a; see Ben-Tor and Bechar 2017, 3) were not discussed. The reason for not adding this Hazor stratum 1a to the discussion was based on the aims of this chapter: when does the most significant change take place? When does the material culture of the MBA end and a new material culture begin? Since the material culture of the LBIIa at Hazor represents the "full-blown" LBA material culture, it did not seem necessary to discuss the later ceramic assemblages. Obviously, assemblages that were dated strictly to the LBIIb were not considered in this discussion.

With this, it should be noted that, in some cases, remains dated to the LBIIb were included in the discussion when these contributed to the overall picture (e.g., imported Aegean vessels from Beth-Shean and kraters with a gutter rim from Hazor).

4.1.2. Ceramic Classification

The typological scheme used here is based, at large, on the scheme set in a recent Hazor publication (Bechar 2017), modified and condensed for the purposes of the present discussion. Therefore, types that appear in sites other than Hazor were also added. However, types that do not appear in the southern Levant but only in the northern and central Levant have not been added, since this research focuses on Hazor and the sites in its vicinity and does not aim at creating a comprehensive typological scheme for the entire Levant.

The types defined for this study are general, not specific, based on the macro and not micro differences between the vessels. In other words, the various shapes of the rims, the forms of the bases, and so forth, were usually not taken into account when defining the types. However, there are a few exceptions where the shape of the rim was extremely indicative chronologically. These include the kraters' ridged and y-shaped rims as well as cooking pot rims. In addition, since the fabric and production techniques were also not considered in the framework of this work, the "chaîne opératoire" could not be discussed. These issues have been disregarded due to the inaccessibility of some assemblages.

Since the aim of this study was to keep the number of types to a minimum, only thirty-six types of vessels were defined (including the imported families but not the decorative wares, such as Chocolate-on-White, Eggshell, and *Charom Ware*).

4.1.3. Sites

As with the previous chapters, the analysis here focuses on Hazor. The other sites examined in this chapter have been already discussed in the previous chapters—sites corresponding with the geographical framework of this work, where MBA and LBA occupational levels were identified. However, since some sites discussed in chapter 3 did not have a publication of their ceramic assemblages (e.g., Tell Sakka and Tell el-Ghassil), they could not be included in the present discussion. In some cases, where the sites' architecture did not contribute to the present discussion, their ceramic assemblages were also not considered (e.g., Sidon and Tel Nebi Mend).

Out of the seven remaining sites, the material from Qatna has already been discussed by Iamoni (2012) and will be summarized here. The ceramic assemblages (as well as the architectural finds) from Kamid el-Loz were not assigned to the different phases within the LBA (LBI and LBII) and could therefore not contribute to the present discussion. We are thus left with five sites on which a few remarks should be mentioned here.

Hazor yielded the largest and richest assemblages of the discussed period. A total of 2,517 vessels and sherds were analyzed for the present study, all depicted in the publications, though ninety-six have not been used since they come from insecure contexts resulting from the vast and extensive excavations carried out at Tel Hazor. These excavations were fully published—both Yadin's excavations (Yadin et al. 1958, 1960, 1961; Ben-Tor 1989; Ben-Tor and Bonfil 1997) and the renewed excavations (Ben-Tor et al. 2012 and 2017). To avoid confusion, the discussion of the strata at Hazor is defined by the strata of the lower city (4–1b), even when discussing the strata of the acropolis. The remains from Stratum 2, dated to the LBI, cannot be separated into the LBIa and the LBIb, in contrast to most of the other sites examined here. Thus, the importance of the other sites to the present discussion is immense.

A statistical analysis of the unpublished ceramic evidence could not be carried out. First, the vast amount of the material would add up to thousands of sherds and vessels. Second, the material is scattered all over the country in different warehouses and museums. Third, loci and basket numbers are not always written on the sherds from Yadin's excavations, making it nearly impossible to attribute them to a specific context. Fourth, I consider the publication of Yadin's excavations to be very comprehensive and sufficient. Fifth, I had prepared the statistical analysis of the MBA material, and Zuckerman, in her Ph.D. dissertation, was thought to have prepared one for the LBA (Zuckerman 2003). However, after examining her statistical analysis, it appeared that this only included the published material uncovered in the Ceremonial Precinct and not the remaining sherds and vessels. Since using only the MBA material would undoubtedly create a bias, I decided to use only the published material from Hazor from both periods (including the unpublished material from Area S).

The analyzed vessels and sherds were considered to represent entire assemblages for each stratum, without distinction between the lower city and the acropolis in general or between the different areas. Tombs were included in the analysis only when their stratigraphic context was secure (that is, tombs from Stratum 3 in Area C and tombs from Stratum 1b in Area F). All assemblages from Strata 4–1b were examined.

Tel Qashish yielded a total of 476 sherds and vessels, all of which were analyzed for the present study (including those in the tables, discussed below). This small number should not come as a surprise since the excavations at the site were of a small scale. The LBI was identified in two strata—VIIb dated to the LBIa and VIIa dated to the LBIb.

The major architectural changes at the site were identified between Strata VIII and VII, and thus any correlation or discrepancy with the ceramic assemblage will be of interest. However, the small size of this assemblage should also be taken into consideration, and any conclusions based on this assemblage should be very cautious. All assemblages from Strata IX–VI are examined.

Yoqneʻam yielded a total of 1,004 sherds and vessels, all examined in the present study (including those in the tables, discussed below). Stratum XXb was ascribed to the transitional MBA/LBA phase at the site. The relation of this stratum to the previous MBIIc Stratum XXI and the following LBI Stratum XXa will be of great interest in identifying the changes in the ceramic assemblages. All assemblages from Strata XXII–XIXb were examined.

Beth-Shean includes another relatively large assemblage—a total of 840 sherds and vessels were analyzed, although 172 could not be used in this study as they come from contexts that could not be ascribed to a specific stratum. These assemblages were published by the renewed excavations expedition (volume 2) since the UME had never published the MBA strata and did not excavate the LBI strata (Mazar and Mullins 2007, 12, 17; Maeir 2007, 242).

To these, another 7,038 sherds can be added. These are not depicted in the figures and are only mentioned in the tables accompanying the typological discussions of the publications (Maeir 2007, table 4.1; Mullins 2007, table 5.1).

Since the publication distinguishes between the several MBA strata (R-5–R-3), these were analyzed as separate phases within the MBA. Two strata were ascribed to the LBI: R-2 dated to the LBIa and R-1b dated to the LBIb. It should be stressed that the major architectural differences were identified between these two strata; their corresponding assemblages will, therefore, shed more light on questions concerning the changes in material culture and their relation to historical events.

Tell Arqa is the smallest assemblage in this study. A total of only 310 vessels and sherds were incorporated in the present analysis due to the fact that several types that appear at the site are not part of the southern Levantine assemblages and are, therefore, not included. Vessels and sherds that did not fit the typological scheme presented here were considered when discussing the overall consumption of the different families of vessels.

Since most of the ceramic assemblages published in the Megiddo American excavations reports derive from mortuary contexts, the Megiddo assemblages will not be examined in this discussion (similarly to the architectural remains, which were not analyzed in chapter 3).

4.1.4. Methods of Analysis

"Archaeologists (and others) sometimes are as wary of statistics as school children are of the classroom holding the most imposing disciplinarian among the teachers" (Drennan 2009, vi). As stated above, the analysis presented below relies solely on published material. Consequently, since no information on the exact part of the vessel was available in all excavation reports, both sherds and complete vessels were counted as one vessel (see Zuckerman 2003, 112; contra Mazar and Panitz-Cohen 2001, 12–13; for the difficulties in counting sherds for statistical analysis, see Rice 1987, 290–19).

The publications of the ceramic assemblages examined for the purposes of the present study used different publishing methods, counting systems and typologies (as noted above), posing a challenge in their comparison and raising several difficulties. However, in order to examine the similarities within these sites, for understanding trends in the ceramic consumption and realizing the connections and relationship between the sites, one must take a risk and create a comprehensive and general typology. This is done out of constraint and not by choice.

A total of almost thirteen thousand potsherds and vessels was analyzed for the present study. In many cases, the study of ceramic assemblages has to rely on statistical analysis, due to the enormous number of samples (the sherds and vessels) and, consequently, the numerous data produced by each sample (each sherd or vessel belongs to a certain family, a certain type and occasionally also a type of ware or decoration). In this study, a descriptive statistical analysis was used: graphs and tables were used to depict the data gathered and accumulated, to study the ceramic assemblages and the consumption behaviors in the different strata and sites. These graphs and tables describe the different trends identified within the sites and periods.

The data and material were presented in the most comprehensive (yet concise) and clear manner. Each assemblage was compared with other contemporaneous assemblages from different sites, and with other assemblages from the same site but from different periods of time. Thus, the data were presented in percentages, creating a homogeneous database. However, the real numbers were also considered important, since, without them, minor and major occurrences could be placed on the same level (that is, the same percentages in an assemblage could indicate a single sherd in one assemblage and twenty-five sherds in a different, much larger assemblage). Therefore, real numbers were also added to most graphs and tables (graphs 4.42–71 and tables 4.2–25) to avoid creating a distorted overview of the data.

A method to distinguish a "cut-off" level of occurrence is sometimes used in published reports to identify whether a change is significant or not. However, in the present study, it was practically impossible to set this sort of "cut-off" level (Iamoni 2012, 108–9). Thus, the identification of the significant change in the assemblages was made in comparison to contemporaneous assemblages from other sites and other assemblages from the same site. In other words, in order to distinguish when the major change in shallow bowls occurred at Hazor, the changes in the shallow bowl assemblage was compared to those from other sites and assemblages of other types of bowls at Hazor. No general rule can be used to identify such a change. Let us assume a cut-off level of 10% decline or increase in the appearance of a particular type between two strata. If such a change appears in one stratum and a change of 20% appears in the following stratum, according to the cut-off level of 10%, both would indicate significant changes. On the other hand, there could be, for example, a type of vessel whose occurrence is very constant and then suddenly increases or declines by 5%. Such a decline would represent a significant change in the assemblage, yet with a general rule of >10%, the change would not be considered significant. Therefore, every assemblage had to be examined individually.

Two general rules were created for the discussion of significant changes within the assemblages to avoid any distortions in the analysis. First, the abundance of different types was noted—peaks in the occurrences of each type were considered signs of possible chronological importance (this is also based on the work done by Iamoni 2012). The second rule was exactly the opposite—the disappearance of types from the assemblages was noted as a possible chronological indicator.

In addition to discussing the specific types, a general discussion of the consumption patterns of vessel families (the five families described above) within the strata was also discussed and described for each site.

The statistical analysis, which is the body of data for the ceramic examination, is presented in graphs and tables (graphs 4.1–71), differentiated by the various data they reflect.

Graphs 4.1–4.41 detail the changes in the consumption of each type both within each site and within each period, with the purpose of identifying when a particular type's presence begins or ends. Thus, each graph depicts batches of data—the occurrences of each type in each examined stratum. As noted above, since this is a chronological and not a functional analysis, the statistical analysis in graphs 4.1–4.41 is based on entire (published) assemblages from each stratum in each site, not divided into the different loci or area.

The percentages presented in the graphs reflect the subtype within the type (for example, shallow bowls within the rounded bowls, closed kraters within kraters, pithoi within large storage vessels, and so forth). Graphs 4.1–4.41 are arranged by periods. The MBA strata from the different sites were grouped together, as were the LBI and LBII strata, aiming at giving a general view of the changes in consumption in all the examined sites. The strata groups are, thus, the following:

1. MBII (early):[1] Hazor 4, Tel Qashish IX, Yoqne'am XXII
2. MBII (late): Hazor 3, Tel Qashish VIII, Yoqne'am XXI, Beth-Shean R-5,[2] R-4 and R-3, Tell Arqa 13
3. MB/LB: Yoqne'am XXb
4. LBI and LBIa: Hazor 2, Tel Qashish VIIb, Yoqne'am XXa, Beth-Shean R-2, Tell Arqa 12c–b[3]
5. LBIb: Tel Qashish VIIa, Beth-Shean R-1b, Tell Arqa 12a
6. LBII and LBIIa: Hazor 1b, Tel Qashish VI, Yoqne'am XIXb, Beth-Shean R-1a, Tell Arqa 11

1. MBII early relates to strata dating to the MBIIb, whereas MBII late relates to strata dating to the MBIIb/c transition or the MBIIc.
2. This stratum is dated by Mullins (2002, 26) to the MBIIb/c transition, based on pottery vessels found in infant jar burials that have "MBIIb affinities." Therefore, all MBA strata in Beth-Shean are grouped in the MBA late group.
3. These two strata were grouped together and are referred to as a single stratum, based on the architectural analysis (discussed in chapter 3).

Graphs and tables 4.42–4.71 present the data from each site separately. The tables that accompany these graphs include percentages of the types in each family assemblage, the percentages of each family in the assemblage of the entire stratum, and the real number of samples for each category. In some cases, the additional sherds and vessels—present only in the statistical tables of the various site—were also included (below, I present a full description of these graphs and tables and a discussion of each site).

Tables 4.1–4.25 include both percentages and real numbers of changes in consumption for the different families at each site, for each category.

The typological scheme will be presented first, including several figures with a depicted example of each type, followed by an analysis-based discussion of the finds. Once the typological scheme has been set and discussed, a full discussion of the appearance and consumption trends in each of the sites will be presented.

4.2. Typological Scheme

Following is a description of the different types of vessels analyzed in the present study. In some cases, the contribution of the different subtypes, or the lack thereof, was only noted. However, types that were analyzed and did not contribute to the discussion are also mentioned here, explained, and discussed.

4.2.1. Rounded Bowls

Bowls were divided into three subcategories, based on their depth-to-diameter ratio. Neither the shape of their rims nor their bases or decoration had a significant impact on the typological scheme. This method was also developed from the fact that all the types of rims appear in both shallow and deep bowls (Bechar 2017, 199–203). It should be mentioned that the measurements of the bowls (used to define them as shallow or deep) was only applied when the base of the bowl had been preserved or when its position could easily be assumed, otherwise being defined as open bowls.

Shallow bowls (SB, fig. 4.1:1). These bowls have the highest depth-to-width ratio (>5.00). The analyzed material clearly indicates a decline in the number of shallow bowls, being more common during the MBA, especially the MBIIc (Hazor Stratum 3, Qashish Stratum VIII, and Beth-Shean Stratum R-3), than in the LBA (graph 4.1). Their number declines toward the LBII when they make up very small percentages within the rounded bowl assemblages. In general, the major quantitative difference is seen between the MBA and the LBI strata, with a sharp decline after the last MBA stratum.

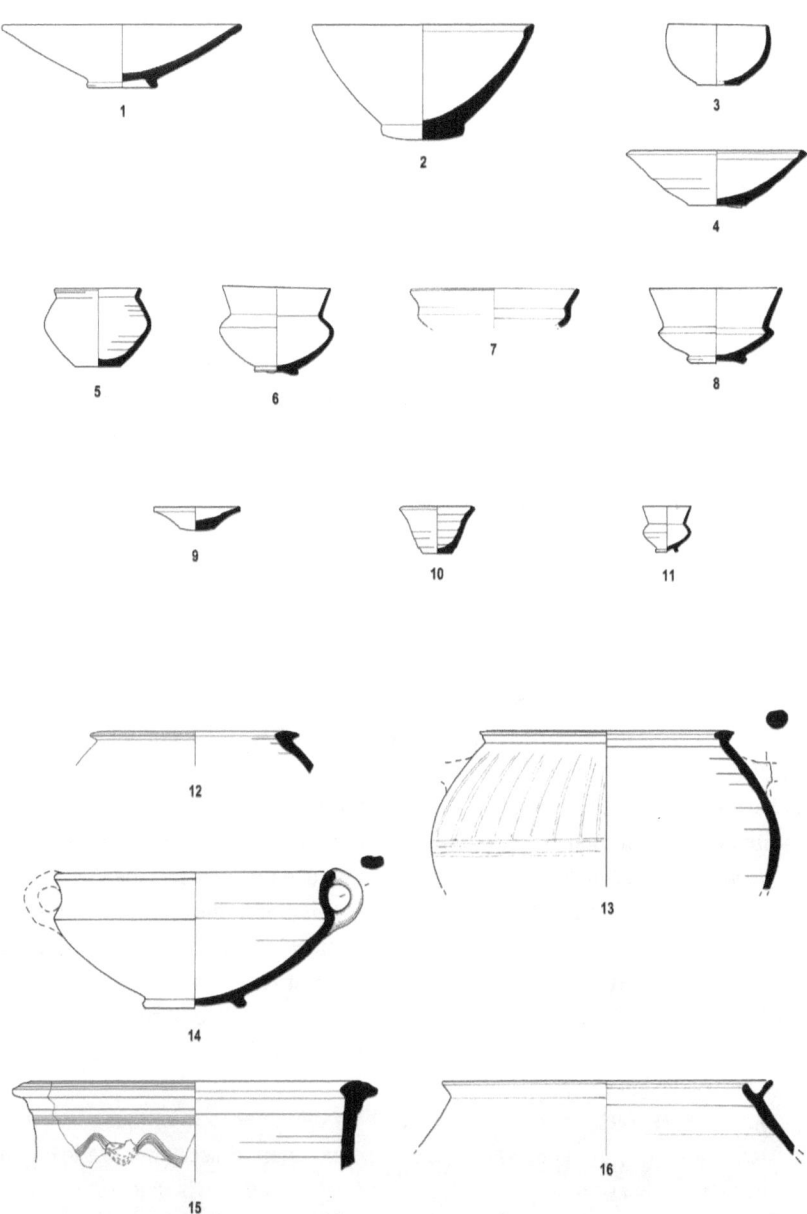

FIGURE 4.1 Bowls and kraters.

No.	Vessel	Type	Reference	No.	Vessel	Type	Reference
1	Bowl	SB	Bechar 2017, figure 7.141: 18	9	Bowl	MV1	Bechar 2017, figure 7.143: 1
2	Bowl	DB	Bechar 2017, figure 7.103: 4	10	Bowl	MV2	Bechar 2017, figure 7.143: 15
3	Bowl	HB	Bechar 2017, figure 129: 1	11	Bowl	MV3	Bechar 2017, figure 7.142: 32
4	Bowl	OB	Bechar 2017, figure 7.141: 9	12	Krater	CK	Bechar forthcoming, figure 3.5: 1
5	Bowl	CB1	Bechar 2017, figure 7.21: 3	13	Krater	CKR	Bechar 2017, figure 7.43: 9
6	Bowl	CB2	Bechar 2017, figure 7.142: 22	14	Krater	NK	Bechar 2017, figure 7.81: 9
7	Bowl	CB3	Bechar 2017, figure 7.76: 18	15	Krater	NKR	Bechar 2017, figure 7.34: 3
8	Bowl	CB4	Bechar 2017, figure 7.134: 2	16	Krater	NKY	Bechar 2017, figure 7.77: 20

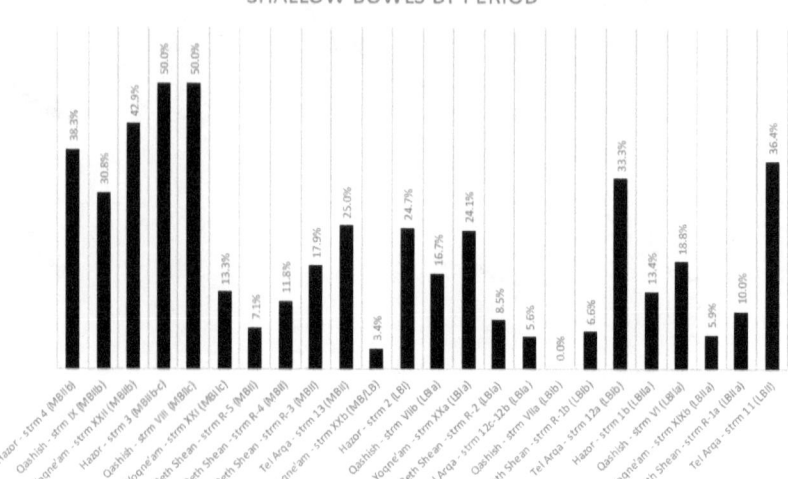

GRAPH 4.1 Shallow bowls (SB), organized by period.

Deep bowls (DB, fig. 4.1:2). These bowls have the lowest depth-to-width ratio (<3.00) and tend to appear in larger percentages in LBA assemblages, although this is not very conspicuous in most sites (graph 4.2). At Hazor and Tel Qashish, an increase in their appearance was noted. In Yoqne'am, however, they appear to constitute a large portion of the assemblage during the MBA, declining in the LBA.

Hemispherical bowls (HB, fig. 4.1:3). These usually have rounded walls and are mostly closed vessels (the largest diameter is not in the rim of the vessel). These are a subtype of the deep bowls. No noticeable trend could be observed for these bowls—they appear in a small amount at Hazor; at Tel Qashish, they appear only in MBA strata, at Beth-Shean only in the LBIb Stratum R-1b, and at Tell Arqa only in the MBA Stratum 13. Thus, they cannot contribute to the present discussion (graph 4.3).

Open bowls (OB, fig. 4.1:4). The depth-to-diameter ratio of these bowls is between 3.01 and 4.99. This type of bowl also includes vessels whose ratio could not be determined (due to the small size of sherds) and bowls that could not be defined as either shallow or deep. Since in many cases the depth of the bowls could not be determined, most bowls can be ascribed to this type. Thus, the distribution of these bowls has no chronological implications (graph 4.4).

4.2.2. Carinated Bowls

These bowls have a soft or sharp carination, usually located in the middle section of their body, although there are examples of carination in the upper third

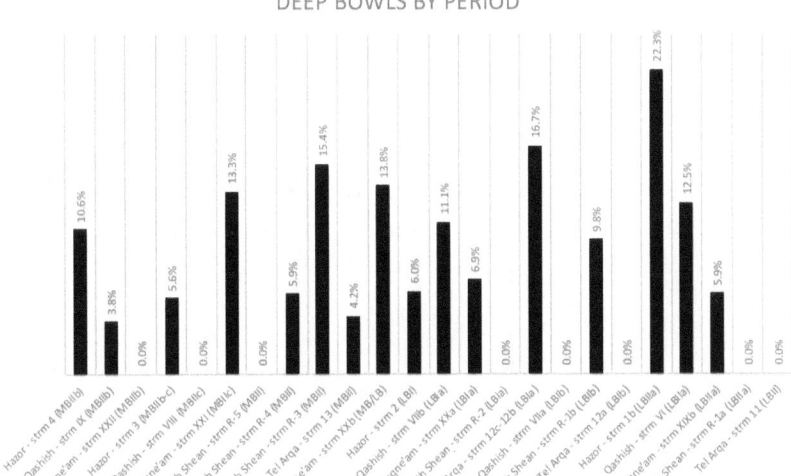

GRAPH 4.2 Deep bowls (DB), organized by period.

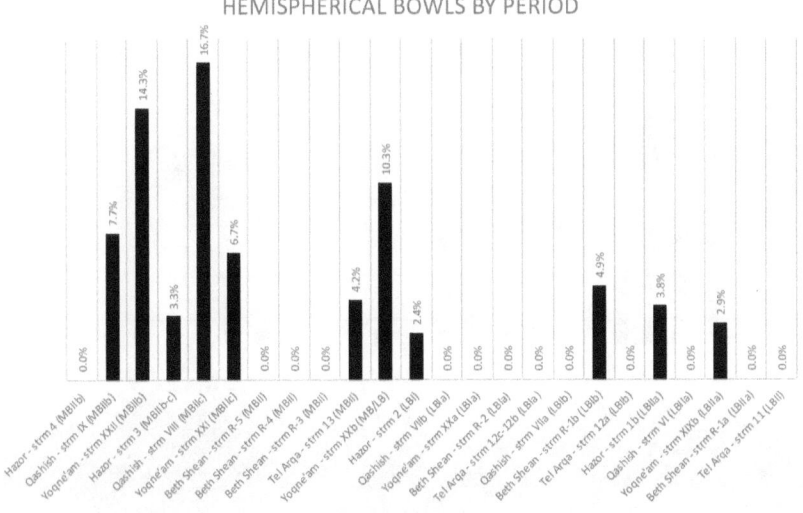

GRAPH 4.3 Hemispherical bowls (HB), organized by period.

of the body. These bowls can be divided into two main types, each further subdivided into two subtypes.

Closed carinated bowls. Unlike most bowls, the largest diameter of these bowls is at the vessel's carination and not on the rim. They can be subdivided into very short-neck (CB1) and long-neck bowls (CB2).

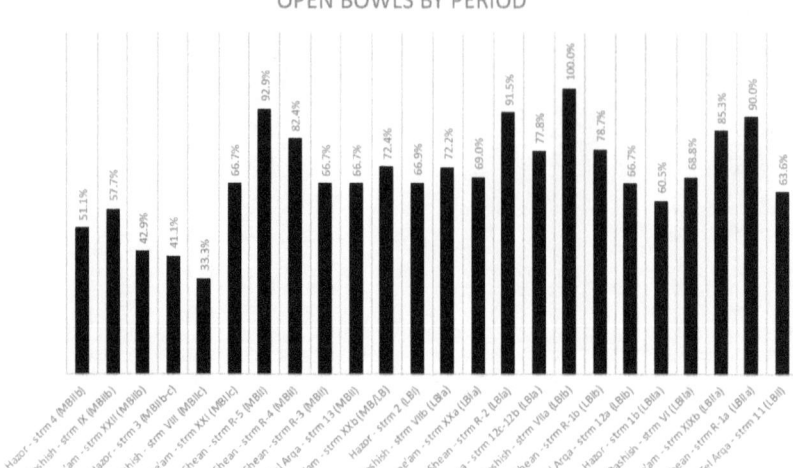

GRAPH 4.4 Open bowls (OB), organized by period.

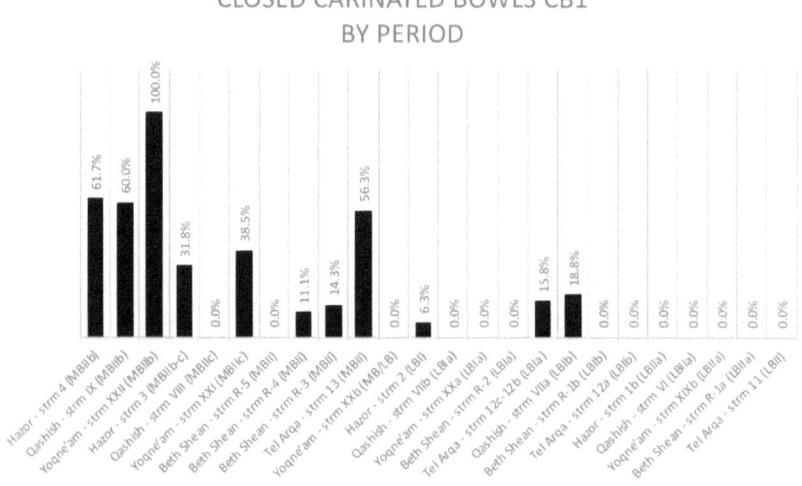

GRAPH 4.5 Closed carinated bowls with low neck (CB1), organized by period.

Bowls belonging to subtype CB1 (fig. 4.1:5, graph 4.5) are more common during the MBA, more so in the MBIIb when they make up a larger share of the carinated bowl assemblage (more than 60% of the carinated bowl assemblage at Hazor and Tel Qashish). However, at Beth-Shean, Stratum R-5, they are completely absent, and only a few samples were found in Strata R-4 and R-3.

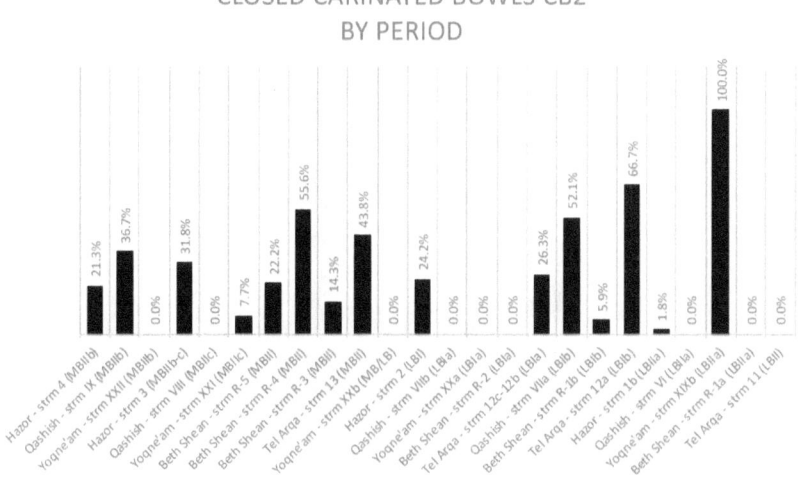

GRAPH 4.6 Closed carinated bowls with high neck (CB2), organized by period.

These bowls make their last appearance in the LBI, in Hazor Stratum 2 and Tell Arqa Strata 12c–12b, where they constitute a smaller portion of the assemblage. Thus, it can be cautiously said that these bowls, which are a hallmark of the MBA (Amiran 1969, 94) continue until the LBIa, and that their most significant consumption-rate change occurs between the LBI and the LBII.

Bowls belonging to subtype CB2 (fig. 4.1:6, graph 4.6) are also more common in the MBA, though they continue well into the LBI. During the MBIIb, they are present in all the sites dealt with in this study (except Yoqne'am Stratum XXII) and constitute 20%–37% of the carinated bowl assemblages. They continue into the MBIIc in large numbers (30%–57% of the carinated bowls), being completely absent, however, from Tel Qashish Stratum VIII and appearing in small percentages in Yoqne'am Stratum XXI (8% of the carinated bowls, making their first appearance at the site in this period).

In the LBI, CB2 appear together with CB1 bowls at Hazor, Beth-Shean, and Tell Arqa. CB2 bowls continue into the LBIb, though in smaller amounts (only 6% at Beth-Shean). At Tell Arqa they constitute a large portion of the assemblage though they amount to only two samples. In the LBII, they almost completely disappear—at Hazor, for example, they amount to only 2% of the carinated bowl assemblage.[4] Thus, it seems that the major change in the CB2 bowls' consumption occurred between the LBI and the LBII.

4. The only carinated bowl found at Yoqne'am, in Stratum XIXb dated to the LBIIa, belongs to this type and cannot, therefore, be taken into account when reaching conclusions in the present discussion.

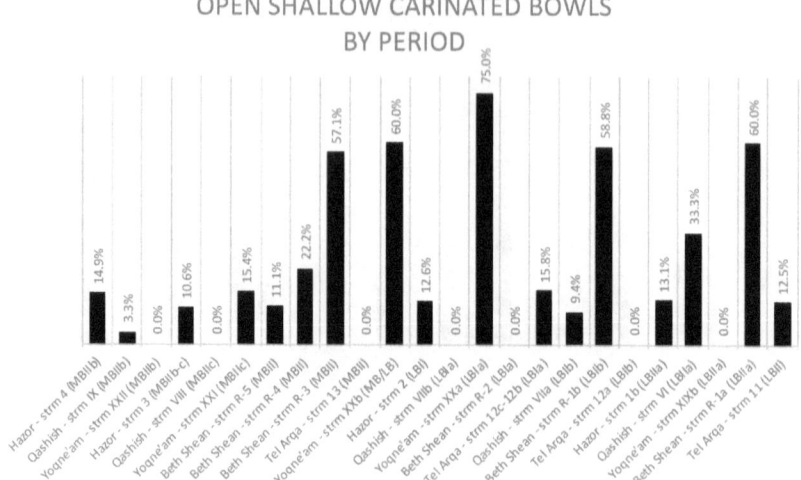

GRAPH 4.7 Open shallow carinated bowls (CB3), organized by period.

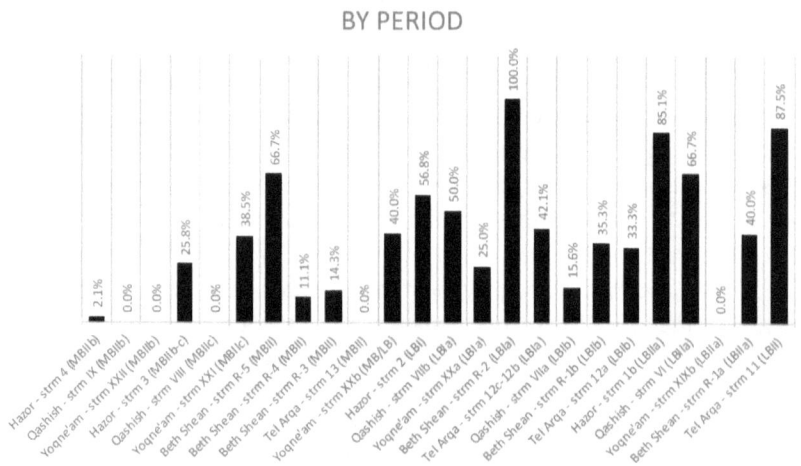

GRAPH 4.8 Open deep carinated bowls (CB4), organized by period.

Open carinated bowls. These are typical open bowls, with their largest diameter at the rim of the vessel. These can also be subdivided into two subtypes—shallow carinated bowls (CB3, fig. 4.1:7, graph 4.7) and deep carinated bowls (CB4 fig. 4.1:8, graph 4.8).

In general, shallow carinated bowls, CB3, seem to be more prevalent in the LBA, as they make up the largest part of the carinated bowl assemblages in Qashish Stratum VIIa (LBIb), Yoqneʻam Stratum XXb (MBA/LBA transition), and Beth-Shean Strata R-3–R-1a (MBII to LBIIa). At Tell Arqa, they only appear in the LBA Strata 12c–b and 11. At Hazor they are most common during the MBA, being subsequently replaced by the deep CB4 carinated bowls. The appearance of the CB4 bowls clearly increases toward the LBII. However, in Beth-Shean and Yoqneʻam, these are most common in the MBA strata (Stratum R-5 in Beth-Shean; Stratum XXI of the MBIIc in Yoqneʻam), after which their appearance declines. Thus, although these were thought to be a hallmark of the LBA, it seems their appearance starts already in the MBIIb/c. Even so, it should be mentioned that, at Hazor and Tell Arqa, the two sites where these are the most common, they also constitute the most dominant type of carinated bowls in the LBII.

4.2.3. Miniature Vessels

These vessels are similar in shape to "regular"-sized vessels of the same type. They can be divided into three types:

- Shallow bowls (MV1, fig. 4.1:9), straight-sided
- Deep bowls (MV2, fig. 4.1:10), also usually straight-sided bowls, although a few examples of rounded bowls are also present
- Closed bowls (MV3, fig. 4.1:11), similar to the carinated closed bowls type CB1 and CB2, but in miniature version

The only site where miniature vessels were found in large numbers is Hazor. In some cases, a single example was found in other sites, in different strata, though in most cases, miniature vessels are completely absent from the assemblages. However, no clear development could be observed within the miniature vessels, even within Hazor's assemblage (graph 4.9, also discussed below).

4.2.4. Kraters

These large vessels were probably used for serving. They can be divided into four types: closed, necked, bowl-like, and pithos-like kraters.

Closed kraters. This category includes holemouth, rounded, kraters, in two variants—simple rim (CK, fig. 4.1:12, graph 4.10) or ridged rim (CKR, fig. 4.1:13, graph 4.11). Except for a single example found in Hazor Stratum 1b (of the LBII), which can be considered a stray example, kraters with a simple rim appear only in MBA and LBIa contexts. In the earlier MBA strata at Hazor, Tel Qashish, and Yoqneʻam, the closed kraters are more common than the necked kraters. Although closed kraters continue into the LBIa, their occurrence declines in this

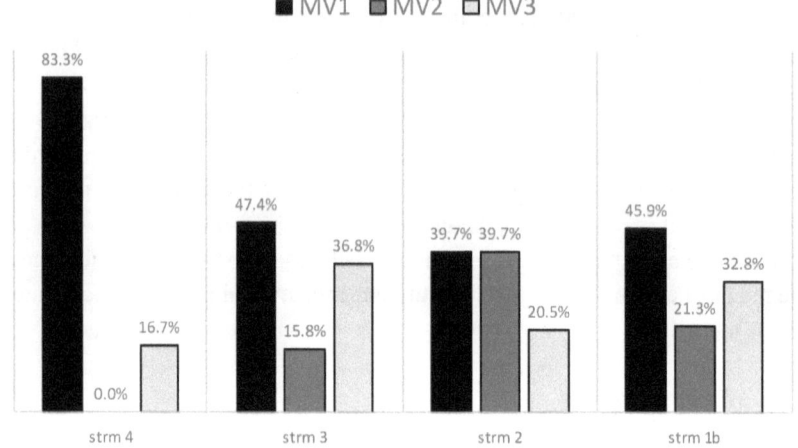

GRAPH 4.9 Miniature bowls from Hazor, by strata.

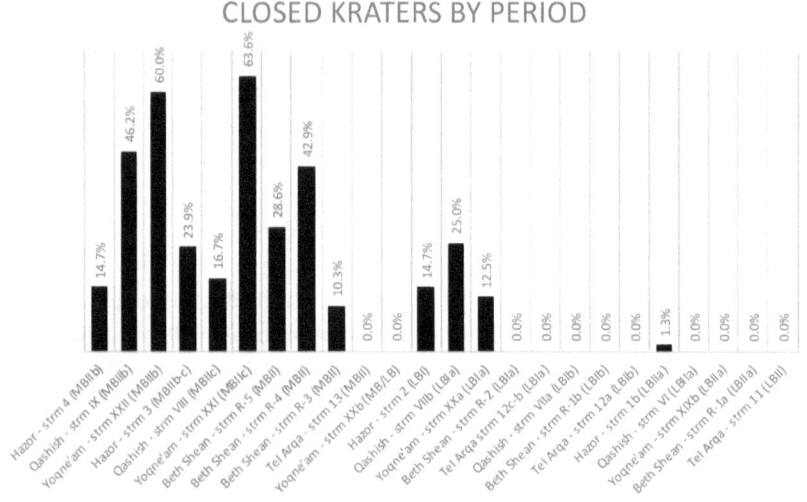

GRAPH 4.10 Closed kraters (CK), organized by period.

period. In the following LBII strata, they disappear altogether from all assemblages. It should be noted that they are absent from the Tell Arqa assemblages in all periods.

Closed kraters with a ridged rim are not common in the assemblages and appear only in MBA contexts, especially in the earlier MBIIb assemblages in Hazor Strata 4 and 3, and in Tel Qashish Stratum IX (graph 4.11)

CLOSED KRATERS WITH RIDGED RIM
BY PERIOD

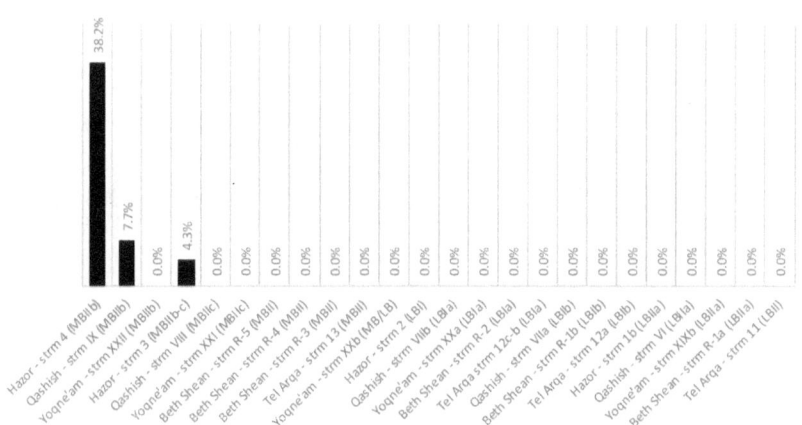

GRAPH 4.11 Closed kraters with ridged rim (CKR), organized by period.

Necked kraters. These are very common kraters and appear in different shapes and sizes. They generally have a soft carination in the middle of their body. The position of their necks, above this carination, sets them apart from the closed kraters. These kraters can be subdivided into the following three subtypes.

Necked kraters with a simple or worked rim (NK, fig. 4.1:14, graph 4.12). These also including kraters with a ledge rim, a triangular rim, a thickened rim and so forth—that is, any necked kraters not belonging to one of the other two subtypes (NKR and NKY, below). Necked kraters are the most common type of krater found in the different assemblages. However, it is only after the beginning of the LBA that they become the dominant type in the assemblages, making up more than 70% of the krater assemblages. It seems that the major difference in their consumption occurs between the MBA and the LBI (in Yoqne'am, Beth-Shean, and Tell Arqa) or between the LBIa and the LBIb (in Tel Qashish). At Hazor, the difference in consumption is seen between the MBIIb Stratum 4 and the MBIIb–c Stratum 3.

Necked kraters with a ridged rim (NKR, fig. 4.1:15, graph 4.13). These have been traditionally dated to the MBA, but even if more common during this period, they continue to appear until the LBI at Hazor, Yoqne'am, and Beth-Shean, pushing their date later.

Necked kraters with a gutter rim (NKY, fig. 4.1:16, graph 4.14). These include kraters with a very pronounced gutter creating a Y-shaped section, sometimes interpreted as a gutter rim used to support a lid or cover. These kraters are very rare and appear in only two contexts—Beth-Shean Stratum R-3

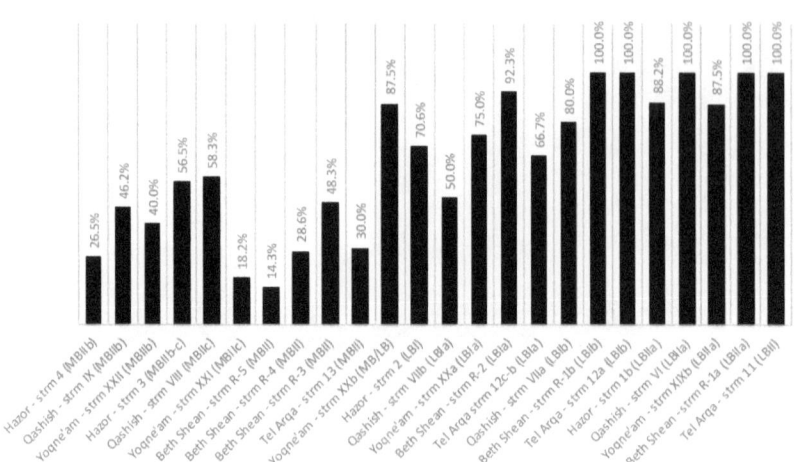

GRAPH 4.12 Necked kraters (NK), organized by period.

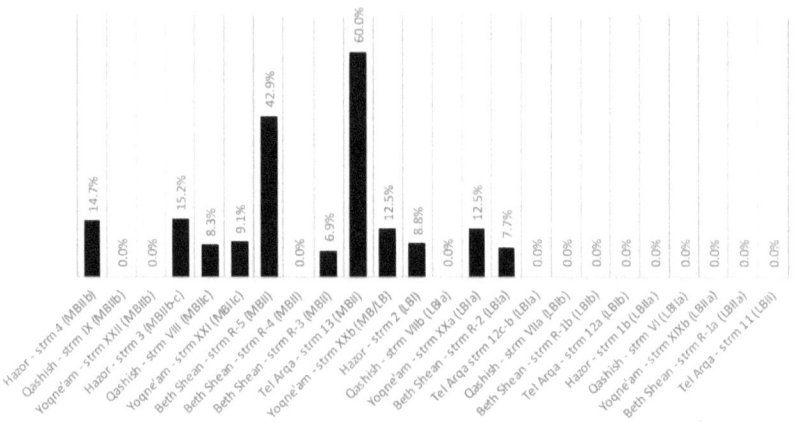

GRAPH 4.13 Necked kraters with ridged rim (NKR), organized by period.

(MBA) and Hazor Stratum 1a (LBIIb). The latter is outside the scope of the present discussion, and therefore it can only be said that these are not exclusive to the MBA.

Bowl-like kraters (K1, fig. 4.2:1, graph 4.15). These kraters are shaped like very large bowls, probably used for serving (unlike regular bowls, which were used for the consumption of food). Only one sample was found in each of

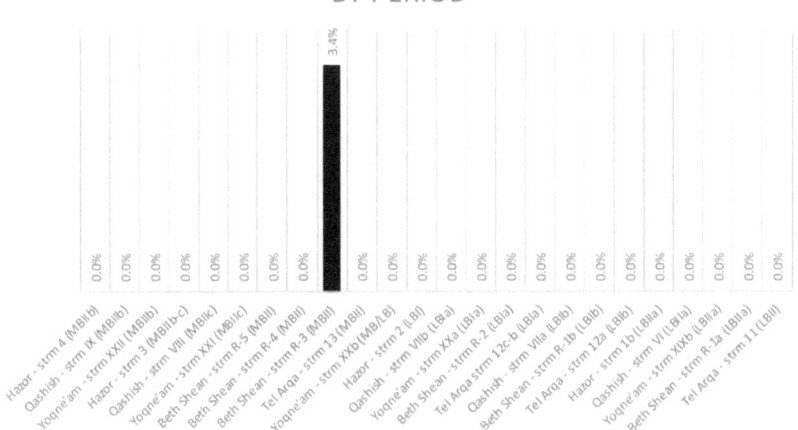

GRAPH 4.14 Necked kraters with Y-shaped or gutter rim (NKY), organized by sites.

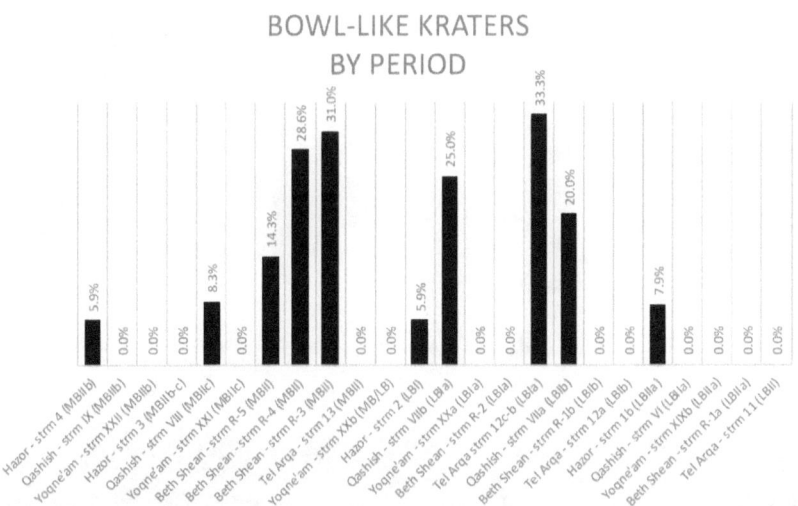

GRAPH 4.15 Bowl-like kraters (KI), organized by period.

the different strata in Tel Qashish (Strata VIII–VIIa). At Hazor, these kraters appear in almost every stratum (except Stratum 3) and gradually become more common. At Beth-Shean, they appear only in the MBA Strata R-5–R-3, where they gradually become more common, completely disappearing in Stratum R-2. Two examples were also found in Strata 12c–b in Tell Arqa. Thus, their appearance has no chronological significance.

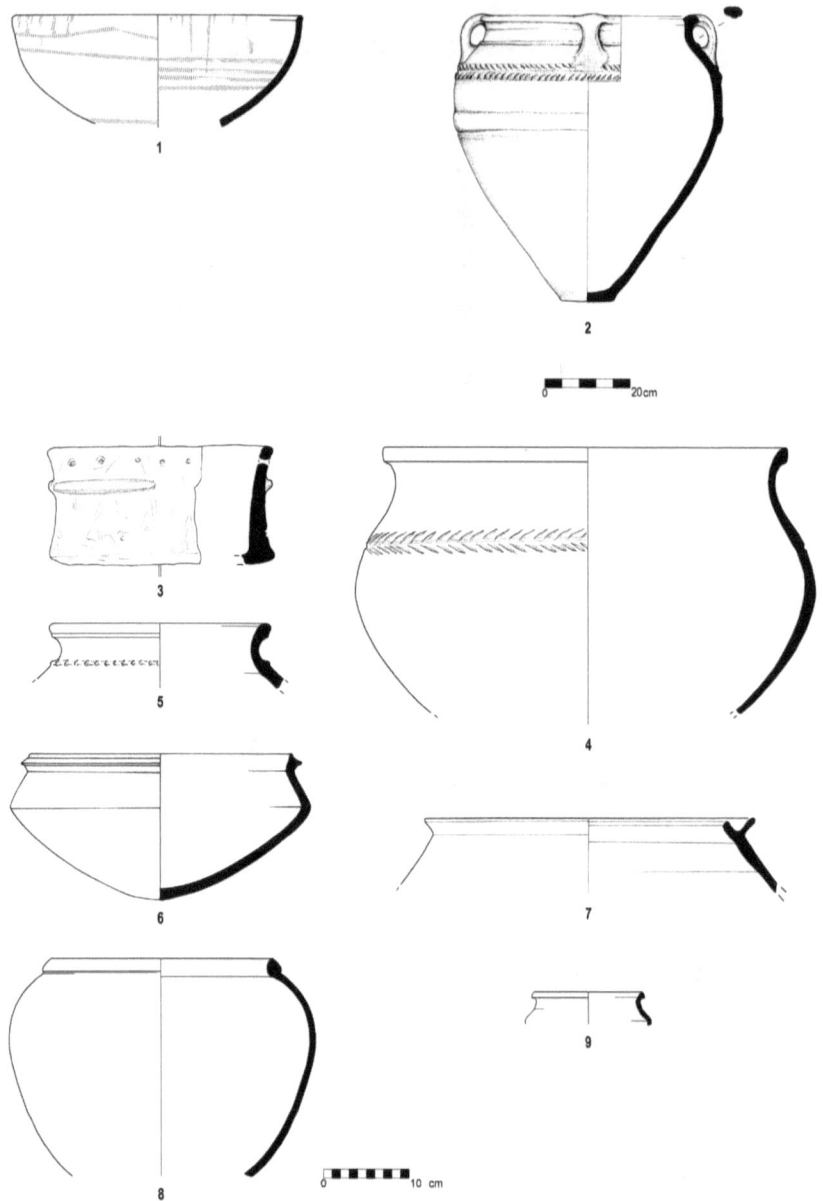

FIGURE 4.2 Kraters and cooking pots.

No.	Vessel	Type	Reference
1	Krater	K1	Bechar 2017, figure 7.129: 9
2	Krater	K2	Bechar 2017, figure 7.95: 1
3	Cooking pot	UCP	Bechar 2017, figure 7.39: 5
4	Cooking pot	CP1	Bechar 2017, figure 7.146: 10
5	Cooking pot	CP2	Bechar forthcoming, figure 3.8: 10

No.	Vessel	Type	Reference
6	Cooking pot	CP3	Bechar 2017, figure 7.75: 8
7	Cooking pot	CP4	Bechar 2017, figure 7.77: 20
8	Cooking pot	HCP	Mullins 2007, plate 22: 6
9	Cooking pot	MCP	Bechar forthcoming, figure 3.8: 20

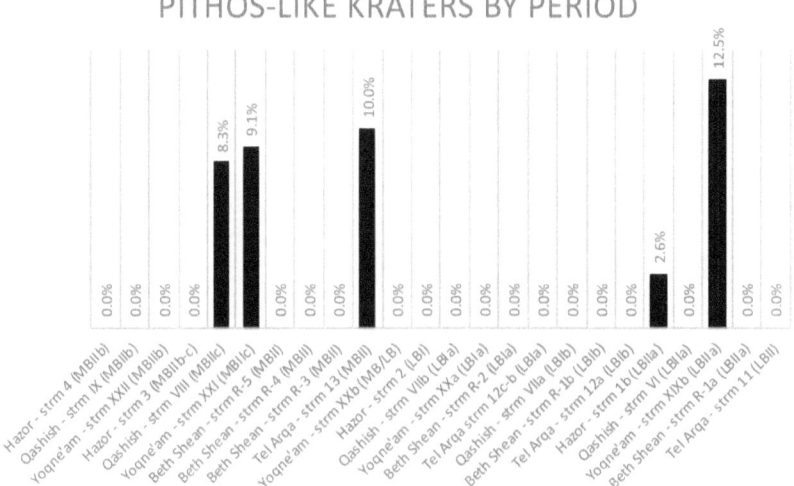

GRAPH 4.16 Pithos-like kraters (K2), organized by period.

Pithos-like kraters (K2, fig. 4.2:2, graph 4.16). These kraters are exceptional in both size and shape. Three examples were found in MBA contexts—in Stratum VIII at Tel Qashish, Stratum XXI at Yoqneʻam, and Stratum 13 at Tell Arqa. Three examples were also found in LBII contexts—in Hazor Stratum 1b and Yoqneʻam Stratum XIXb. These have no chronological significance.

To summarize the use of kraters, the major change in their consumption occurs in the LBII, when kraters of type NK dominate the ceramic assemblages and those of other types disappear from them.

4.2.5. Cooking Pots

Among the cooking vessels known from the Bronze Age, only cooking pots were part of this study. This choice resulted from the fact that cooking jugs and cooking bowls can only be distinguished from "regular" jugs and bowls based on their material, which is not always described in the publications. Cooking pots, on the other hand, are a marked chronological indicator. They can be divided into three subtypes:

Upright cooking pots (UCP, fig. 4.2:3, graph 4.17). These handmade cooking pots with thick walls and a flat base are made of crumbly clay with much organic material. Most of these cooking pots have a ledge below the rim, and sometimes holes or deep circular depressions are also located between ledge and rim. These cooking pots appear only in the MBA and only at Hazor, Tel Qashish, and Beth-Shean. At Hazor and Beth-Shean, they appear in all MBA strata, whereas at Tel

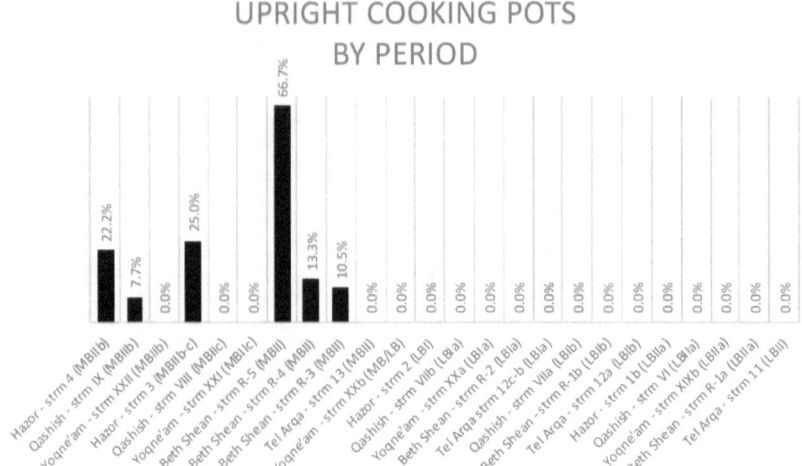

GRAPH 4.17 Upright cooking pots (UCP), organized by period.

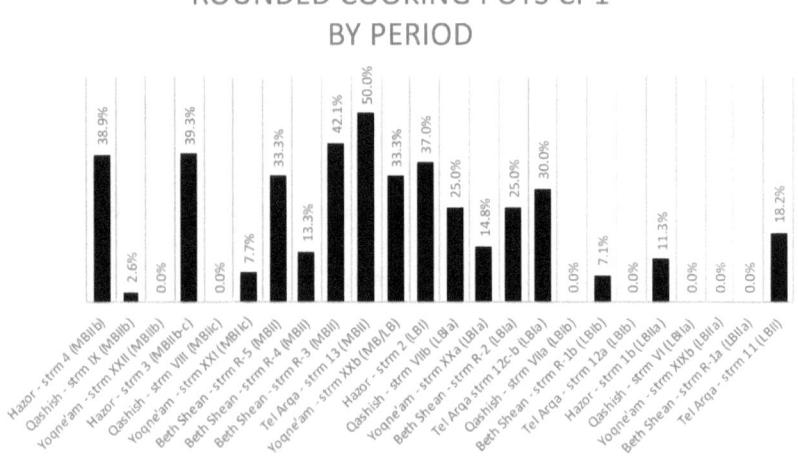

GRAPH 4.18 Rounded cooking pots with a simple rim (CP1), organized by period.

Qashish they were found only in the earlier stratum, Stratum IX (of the MBIIb). At Hazor, they make up a large part of the assemblage in Stratum 3, but not so in Stratum 4, in contrast to Beth-Shean, where they amount to a larger number in Stratum R-5 when compared to the other two MBA strata at the site.

Rounded cooking pots. These vessels have a rounded body, thin walls, and everted rims. Their base is almost always round. They have either simple rims (CP1, fig. 4.2:4, graph 4.18), thickened rims (CP2, fig. 4.2:5, graph 4.19),

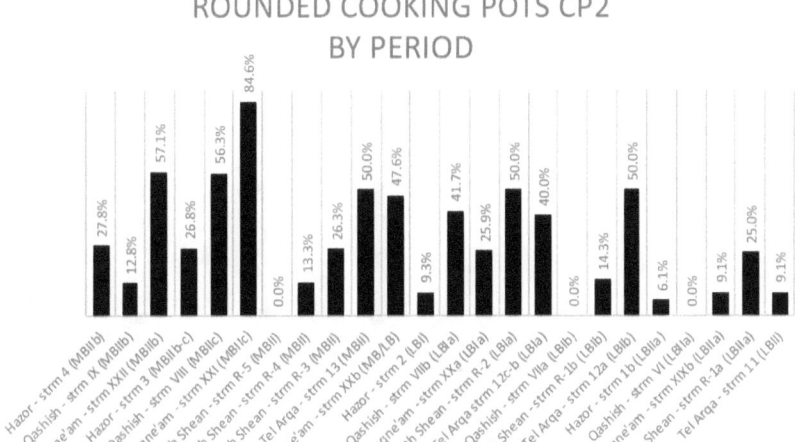

GRAPH 4.19 Rounded cooking pots with a thickend rim (CP2), organized by period.

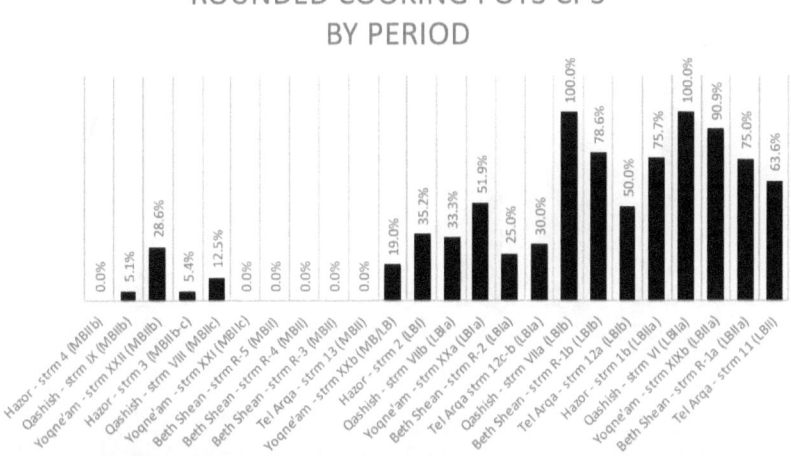

GRAPH 4.20 Rounded cooking pots with a triangular rim (CP3), organized by period.

or triangular rims (CP3, fig. 4.2:6, graph 4.20). The latter is traditionally regarded as the *fossil directeur* of the LBA. Another subtype includes cooking pots with a very pronounced gutter, creating a Y-shaped section of the vessel (CP4, fig. 4.2:7, graph 4.21).

It should not be surprising that cooking pots of types CP1 and CP2 are more common in the MBA and become less common in the LBA when CP3 are the most dominant type. The latter begin to appear already in the MBA (e.g., Hazor

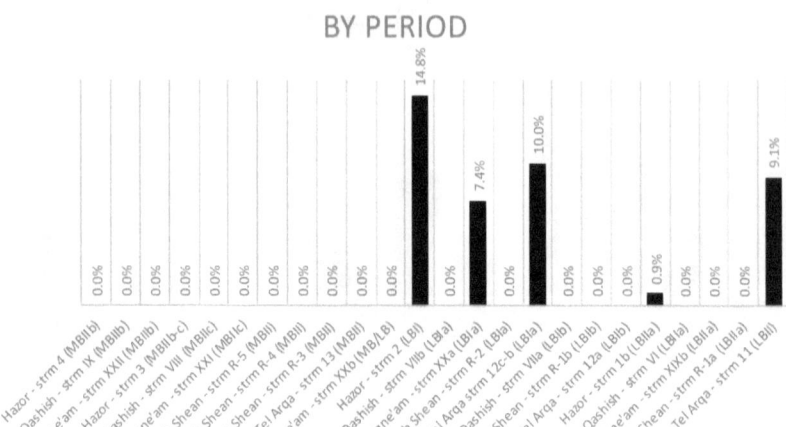

GRAPH 4.21 Rounded cooking pots with a gutter rim (CP4), organized by period.

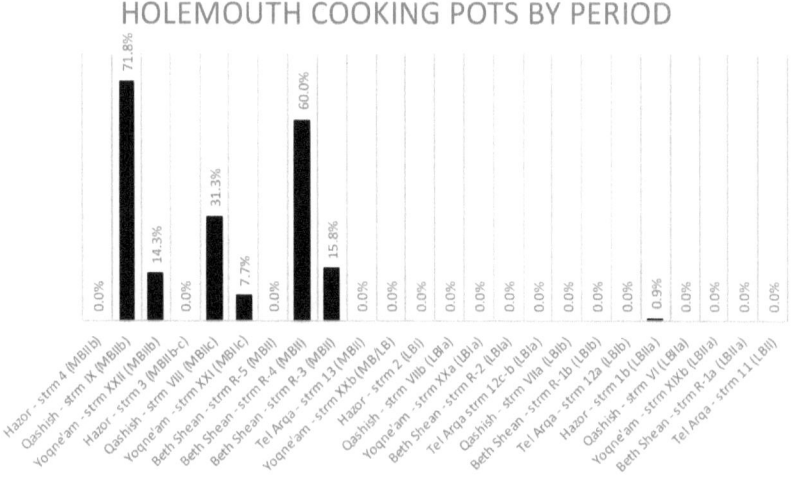

GRAPH 4.22 Holemouth cooking pots (HCP), organized by period.

Stratum 3, Tel Qashish Stratum IX, and Yoqneʻam Stratum XXII), but only in the LBII become the most dominant part of the assemblage (more than 50%), except in Yoqneʻam XXa, where they are already dominant in the LBI.

CP4 cooking pots appear mainly in LBI contexts, though one fragment was found in Hazor Stratum 1b and another in Tell Arqa Stratum 11, both dated to the LBII. Except in Hazor, the CP4 subtype appears in small numbers in the LBI (one sample in Tell Arqa and two in Yoqneʻam). However, since they

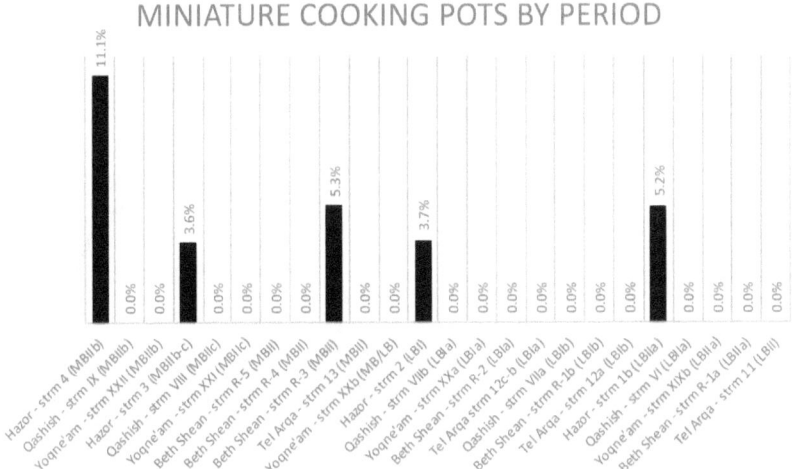

GRAPH 4.23 Miniature cooking pots (MCP): (a) organized by site; (b) organized by period.

are limited to LBI contexts, it seems that they can be considered the cooking pots that characterize this period (Ben-Tor 1989, 236–37; Amiran 1969, 135; contra Charaf forthcoming). It should be noted that the similarly shaped kraters (type NKY, not made of cooking pot material) were only found in Stratum R-3 at Beth-Shean, dated to the MBII, and Stratum 1a at Hazor, dated to the LBIIb.

Holemouth cooking pots (HCP, fig. 4.2:8, graph 4.22). These are closed cooking pots, also with a rounded body, though their walls are not thin. These cooking pots appear mainly in the MBA.

Miniature cooking pots (MCP, fig. 4.2:9, graph 4.23). These show the same rims as the regular-sized cooking pots (CP1–CP4). These miniature vessels are very rare in the assemblages and appear mainly at Hazor. Another single sample comes from Beth-Shean Stratum R-3. The appearance of these has no chronological significance.

4.2.6. Large Storage Vessels

Two types of storage vessels are included in this family.

Pithoi (P, fig. 4.3:1–2, graph 4.24). These are very large vessels. The shape of their body, the openness of their neck, and the shape of their rims differs significantly between the MBA (fig. 4.3:1) and the LBA (fig. 4.3:2). However, these are discussed together in this study to identify differences in consumption. Therefore, neither the shape nor the form of the vessels was considered, only their overall shape (an enormous storage vessel).

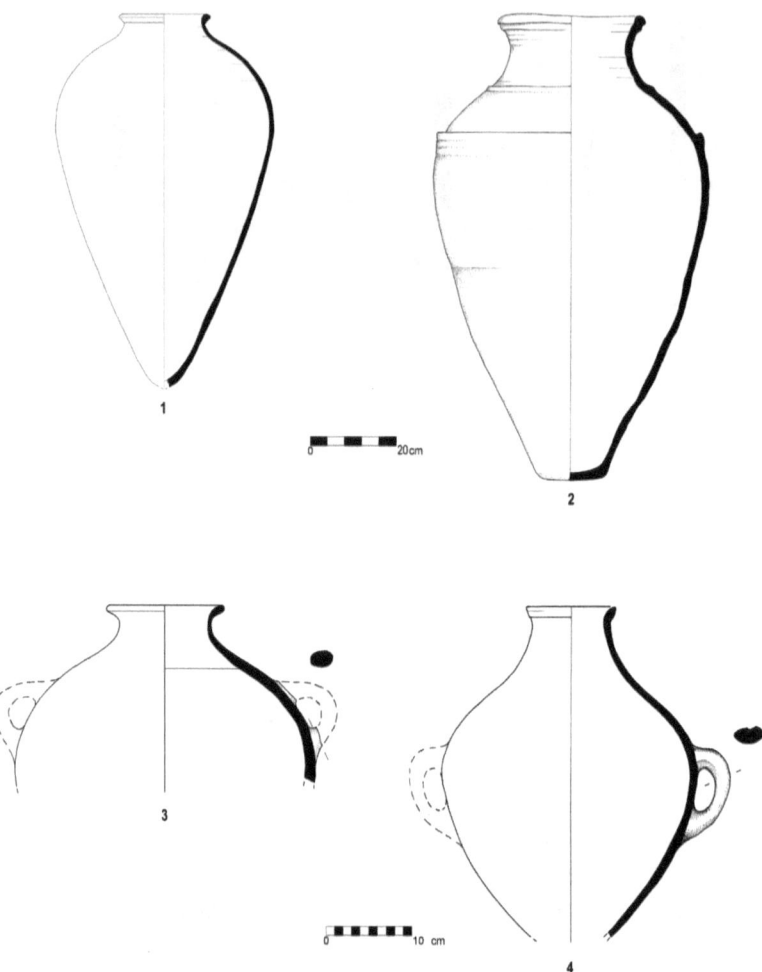

FIGURE 4.3 Large storage vessels.

No.	Vessel	Type	Reference
1	Pithos	P	Bechar 2017, figure 7.35: 2
2	Pithos	P	Bechar 2017, figure 7.91: 1
3	Storage jar	SJ1	Bechar 2017, figure 7.24: 2
4	Storage jar	SJ2	Bechar 2017, figure 7.125: 15

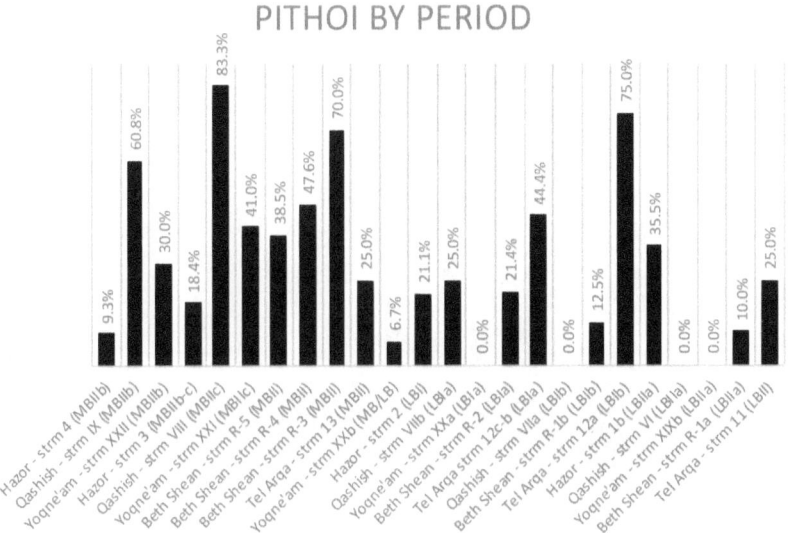

GRAPH 4.24 Pithoi (P), organized by period.

The discussion of the distribution of pithoi should be divided into Hazor and Tell Arqa on the one hand and the remaining sites on the other (graph 4.24), since, at the former, pithoi become more common in the LBA rather than the MBA, while at the latter, pithoi are much more common in the MBA. Pithoi make up an average of 53% of all the large storage vessels in these sites in the MBA, whereas at Hazor and Tell Arqa they make up only 18% of the storage vessels in the MBA strata. In contrast, in the LBA, pithoi constitute an average of 8% at Tel Qashish, Yoqneʿam, and Beth-Shean, and an average of 40% at Hazor and Tell Arqa. This opposite trend in pithoi consumption is further strengthened by the fact that the LBA pithoi found at Tell Arqa are identical to the "Hazor pithoi," known in the southern Levant only from Hazor and Tel Dan (Bechar 2017, 223). However, at Hazor, they are most prevalent in the LBII, whereas at Tell Arqa they only appear in the LBI. It should be remembered that, in the LBI, Hazor was a smaller city, becoming much larger in the LBII. It is precisely in the LBI that Tell Arqa is destroyed, declining in size (in Stratum 12a and furthermore in Stratum 11, also discussed above in chapter 3). Can these pithoi be considered breadcrumbs left on the road home? Can they indicate where the inhabitants of Tell Arqa went when they left? Perhaps they only indicate where the potters from Tell Arqa went? These are probably rash suggestions, but we should keep them in mind.

These pithoi are prevalent in the LBIb stratum at Tell Arqa as well as in Stratum 1b at Hazor, lending further support to the dating of the beginning of Stratum 1b to the LBIb (Ben-Tor and Bechar 2017, 2).

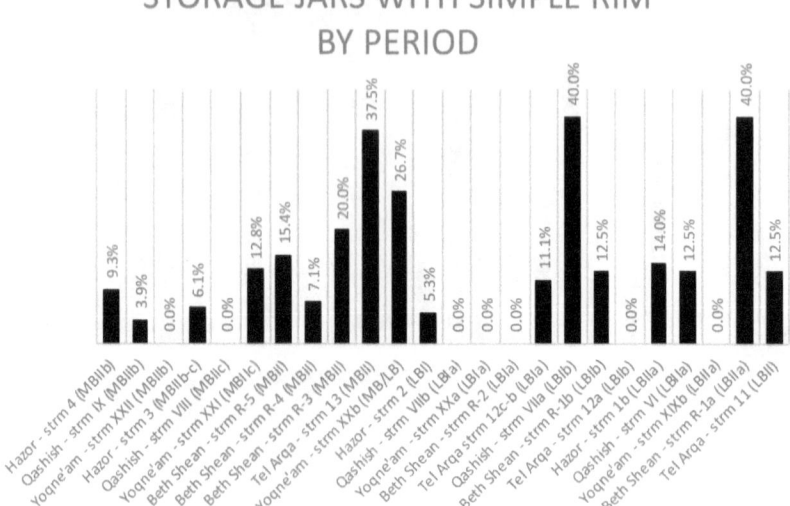

GRAPH 4.25 Storage jars with a simple rim (SJ1), organized by period.

Storage jars. These are traditionally not an indicative chronological marker. They were divided into two main types—storage jars with simple rims (SJ1, fig. 4.3:3, graph 4.25) and storage jars with worked rims (SJ2, fig. 4.3:4, graph 4.26). The worked rims include thickened rims, out-folded rims, ridged rims, wedge-shaped rims, gutter rims, and so forth. Type SJ2 is the most common type of large storage vessel in all periods. Another type of storage jars, the "commercial" storage jars, being defined by the sharp carination of the vessel's shoulder (Amiran 1969, 141), were included only when the vessels were preserved at least from the rim down to the shoulders. Since storage jars do not necessarily preserve very well, this type was rarely identified in the different assemblages (only three were identified in Hazor Stratum 1b, and two in the Stratum XIXa assemblage at Yoqneʻam, which is not discussed here). Thus, in the present discussion, they were included in type SJ2.

The changes in the consumption of storage jars at Hazor and Tell Arqa are contrary to those seen in the other sites, with both storage jar types SJ1 and SJ2 decreasing in the LBA at Hazor and Tell Arqa but increasing in the remaining sites. This picture fits well with the consumption of pithoi in the same period.

It should be noted that several studies have shown that large storage vessels tend to change at a much slower pace than open vessels (Iamoni 2012, 171–72). Therefore, the fact that pithoi disappear in some sites, while they appear in a previously unknown shape in others should be highlighted. Thus, the stark

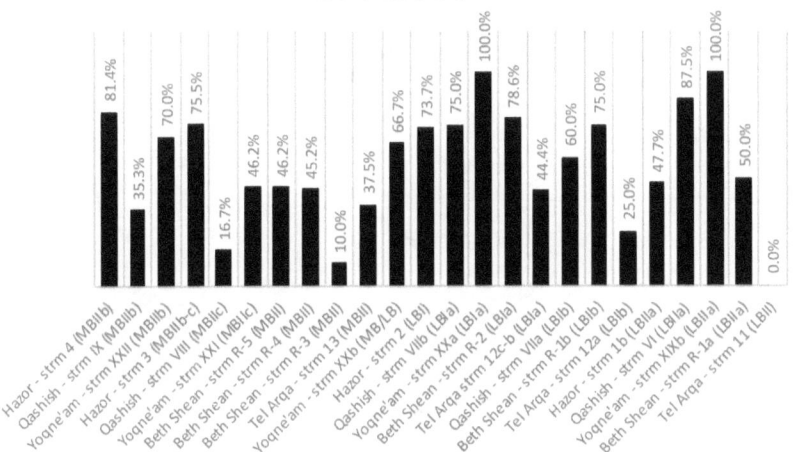

GRAPH 4.26 Storage jars with a worked rim (SJ2), organized by period.

change in the consumption of large storage vessels should be considered one of the most conspicuous changes in the transition from the MBA to the LBA.

4.2.7. Small Storage Vessels

Two types of vessels were included in this family—jugs, and juglets. Four subtypes of jugs can be defined in the framework of this study:

- Jugs with simple rims (J1, fig. 4.4:1, graph 4.27)
- Jugs with worked rims (J2, fig. 4.4:2, graph 4.28), which are similar to storage jars with worked rims and and have the same variety of rims
- Dipper jugs (J3, fig. 4.4:3, graph 4.29)
- Biconical jugs (J4, fig. 4.4:4, graph 4.30)

In almost every assemblage examined in this research, jugs of type J2 were more common than type J1. Thus, it seems that, as in the case of the different rims of storage jars, this fact has no chronological significance. Also, no indicative changes in their consumption were noted between the different periods.

Dipper jugs (J3, fig. 4.4:3, graph 4.29). These have a pinched rim, and their body may be elongated with either a pointy, round, or ring base. No significant differences were noted in this type of jug between the different periods. They are

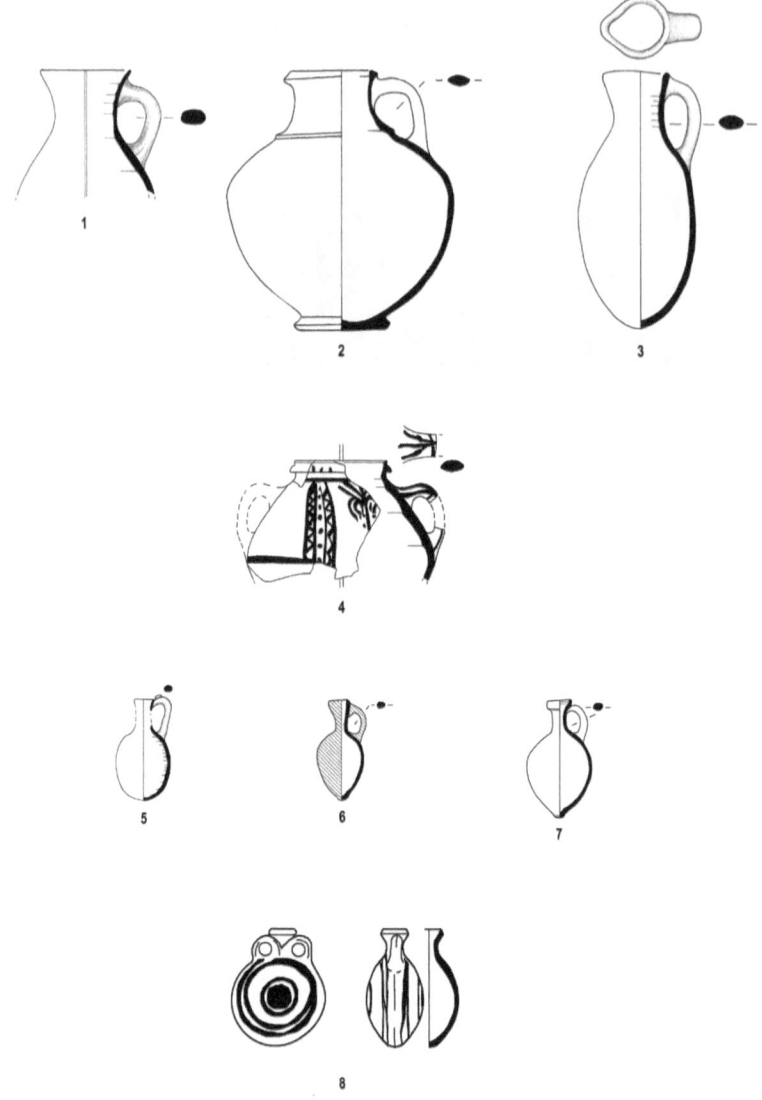

FIGURE 4.4 Small storage vessels.

No.	Vessel	Type	Reference
1	Jug	J1	Bechar 2017, figure 7.35: 2
2	Jug	J2	Bechar 2017, figure 7.91: 1
3	Jug	J3	Bechar 2017, figure 7.24: 2
4	Jug	J4	Bechar 2017, figure 7.125: 15

No.	Vessel	Type	Reference
5	Juglet	JT1	Bechar forthcoming, figure 3.13: 1
6	Juglet	JT2	Bechar 2017, figure 7.21: 14
7	Juglet	JT3	Bechar 2017, figure 7.21: 16
8	Flask	FL	Following Yadin et al. 1960, pl. cxl: 5

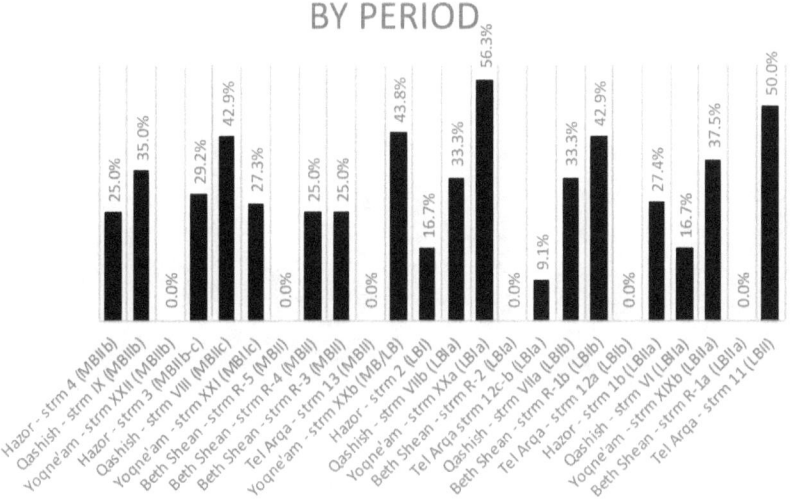

GRAPH 4.27 Jugs with a simple rim (J1), organized by period.

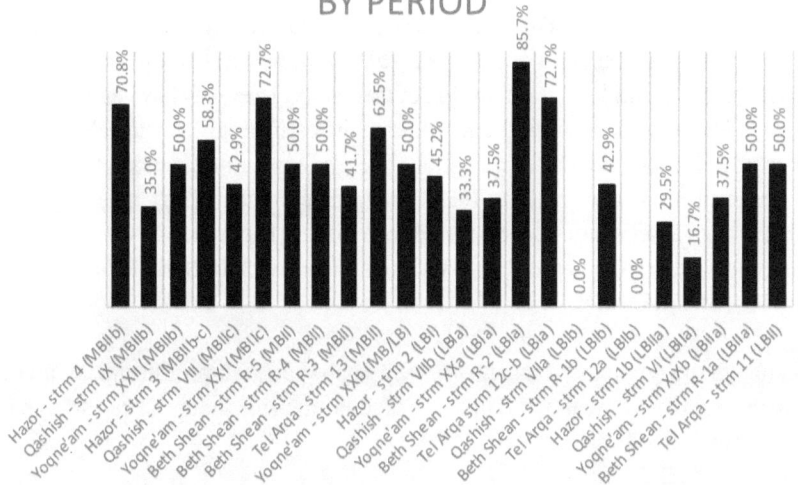

GRAPH 4.28 Jugs with a worked rim (J2), organized by period.

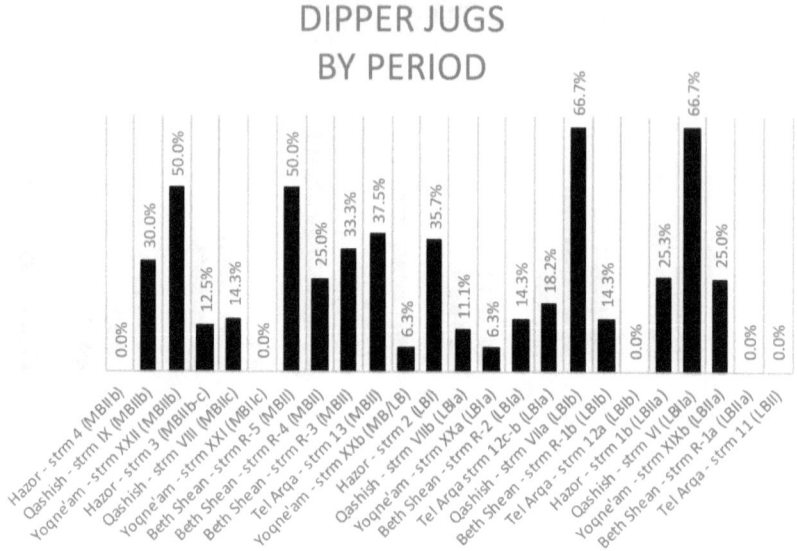

GRAPH 4.29 Dipper jugs (J3), organized by period.

more common in the LBII at Hazor, Tel Qashish, and Yoqneʻam, but they are more common in the MBA at Beth-Shean and Tell Arqa. In the LBIb, they are absent at Tell Arqa, and in the LBII they are absent at both Tell Arqa and Beth-Shean.

Biconical jugs (J4, fig. 4.4:4, graph 4.30). These bear a soft, rounded, or sharp carination in the mid- or lower portion of their body. They may have either one or two handles extending from the shoulder to the carination. They usually have a painted decoration above the carination. Their rims are almost always triangular.

Apart from Stratum VIIb at Tel Qashish (dated to the LBIa), these jugs are absent from assemblages dating earlier than the LBII. They are absent from Tell Arqa altogether. It thus seems that biconical jugs are characteristic of the LBII in the southern Levant.

Although the typology of juglets is usually based on their profile and complete shapes, in this study, the division is based on the rim shape. Three subtypes were thus defined:

- Juglets with simple rims (JT1, fig. 4.4:5, graph 4.31)
- Dipper juglets with pinched rims (JT2, fig. 4.4:6, graph 4.32), similar to the dipper jugs
- Juglets with worked rims (JT3, fig. 4.4:7, graph 4.33), similar to the jugs with worked rims, though in the juglets' case most of the worked rims are, in fact, ring or thickened rims

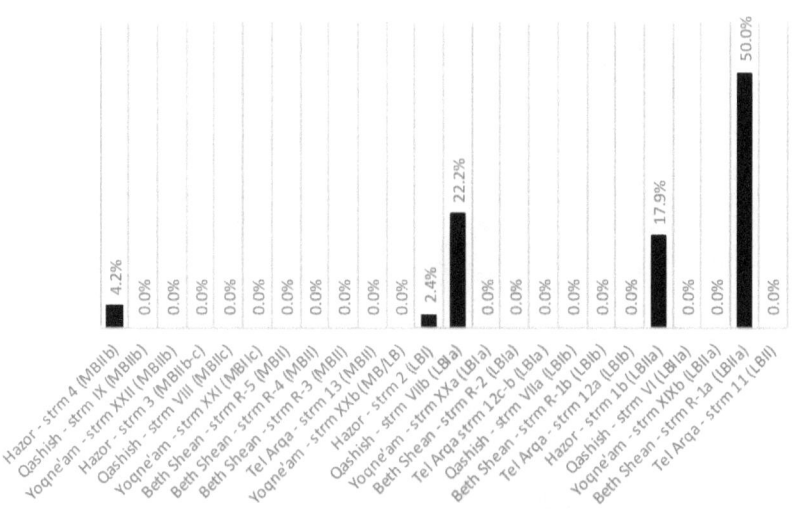

GRAPH 4.30 Biconical jugs (J4), organized by period.

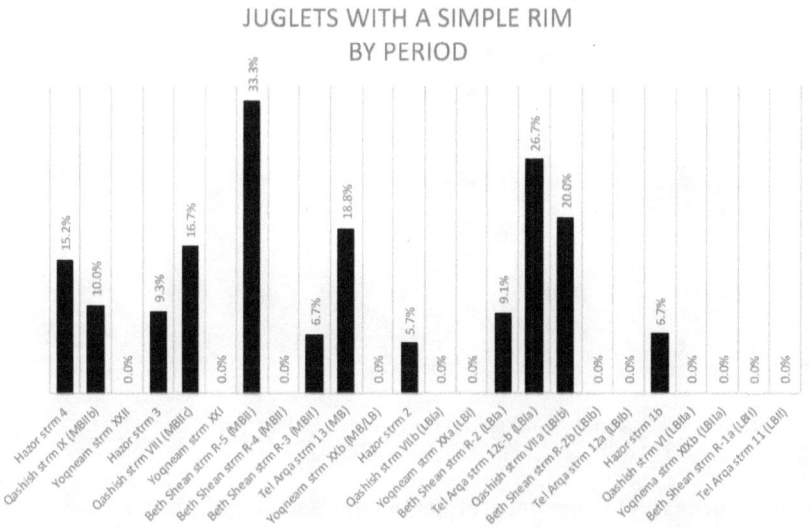

GRAPH 4.31 Juglets with a simple rim (JT1), organized by period.

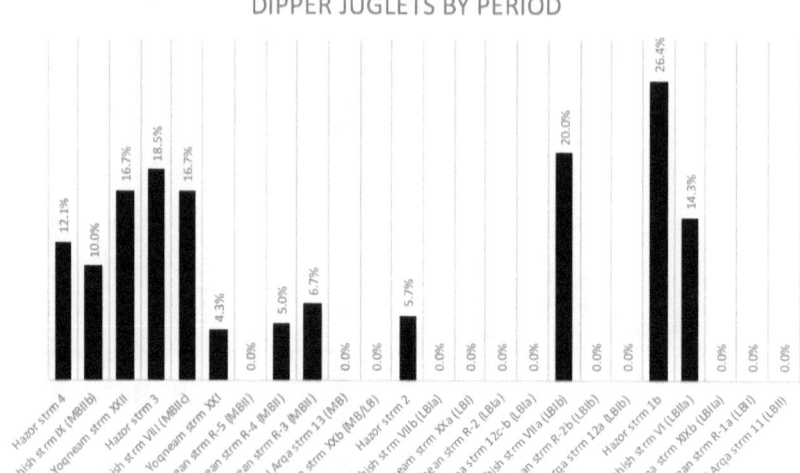

GRAPH 4.32 Dipper juglets (JT2), organized by period.

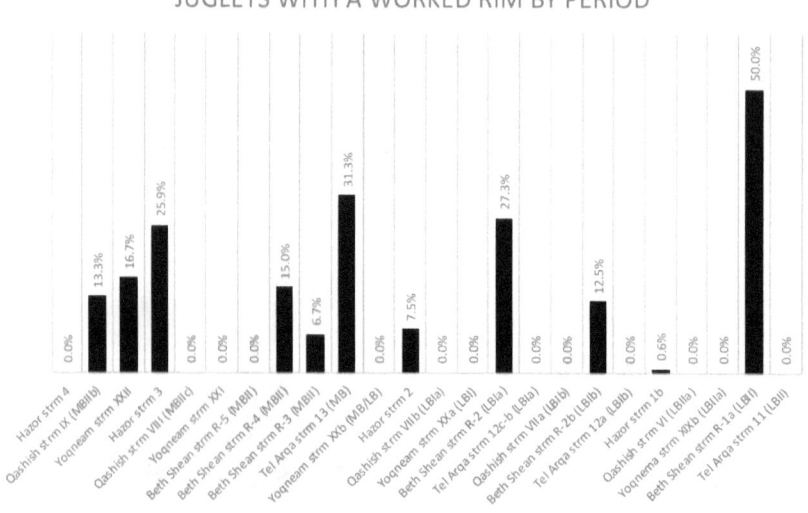

GRAPH 4.33 Juglets with a worked rim (JT3), organized by period.

In general, juglets are not prevalent in the assemblages, being more common in the MBA than in the LBA. No significant difference in their percentage was discerned within the three types. It is interesting to note, when considering small storage vessels, that juglets always make up a smaller portion of the assemblages, in all strata and all sites.

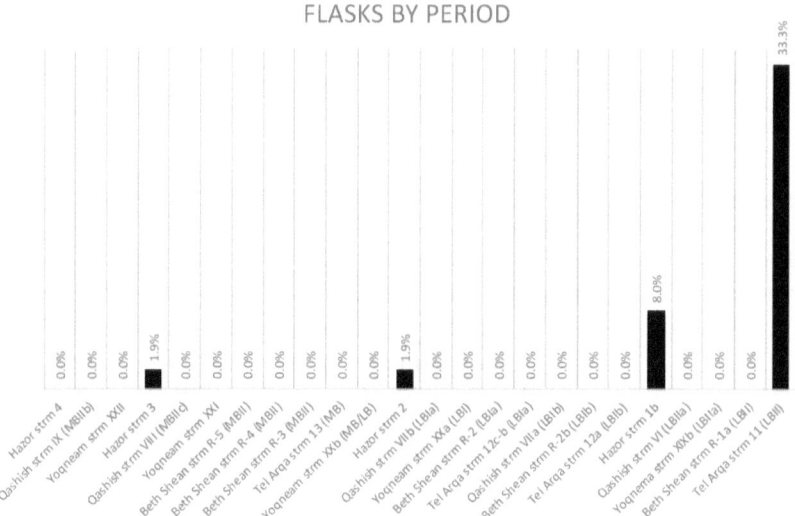

GRAPH 4.34 Flasks (FL), organized by period.

Flasks (FL, fig. 4.4:8, graph 4.34). These are round jugs, sometimes with a flattened section, with two handles usually extending from the neck of the vessel to the shoulder. These are rare in all assemblages. However, they are more common in the LBII at Hazor, Yoqneʻam, and Tell Arqa. A few examples were also found in Strata 3 (of the MBIIb–c) and 2 (of the LBI) at Hazor, but these make up only 2% of the small storage vessel assemblage.

In conclusion, small storage vessels are not a common component in the different examined assemblages. They are more common in the earlier strata; however, this does not have any chronological implications.

4.2.8. Varia

Cup and saucer. These are vessels made of a small and almost V-shaped bowl set inside a larger rounded bowl. The V-shaped bowl is usually pierced on its side. These are very rare in the examined assemblages. Two of these appear in the MBA Strata R-4 and R-3 at Beth-Shean (one in each stratum), and four appear in the LBA strata at Hazor (three in Stratum 1b and one in Stratum 1a). Thus, the distribution and consumption of these vessels do not add to the current discussion.

Chalices. These are shallow open bowls set on a foot. Since it is impossible to identify them when the foot of the bowls did not survive, they were not taken into consideration in the present analysis.

Goblets. These are deep bowls set on a foot. They are among the most varied families and are usually decorated. These were also not taken into consideration in the present study.

4.2.9. "Special" Local Wares

The following families were termed "special" local wares to avoid the discussion of whether they should be considered luxurious or imported wares. These are important and intriguing questions that are beyond the scope of the present study.

Chocolate on White. This family is characterized by vessels with a very thick "creamy" white slip and a yellowish-brown to dark brown painted lines and waves. This family has been traditionally dated to the MBIIc and LBI (Amiran 1969, 159), though Maeir has dated the beginning of their appearance to the MBIIb/c transition based on the Beth-Shean's Stratum R-5 assemblage (Maeir 2007, 287–88).

The present study strengthens Maeir's conclusions to date these vessels from the MBIIb onward, continuing up to the LBI, when these vessels are the most common (graph 4.35), although they also appear in small amounts in later assemblages (Hazor 1b, Yoqne'am XIXb, and Beth-Shean R-1b). However, these few later examples do not indicate that their date should be pushed into the LBII.

Red, White, and Blue Ware. This family is characterized by a painted decoration in red and blue on a white-slipped surface. It is traditionally dated to the MBIIa–MBIIb and appears mainly in southern coastal sites (Maeir 2007, 286).

In the present study, vessels of this family were found mainly in Beth-Shean's MBA strata, and two sherds were also found at Hazor, Stratum 3 (graph 4.36). These finds strengthen Maeir's dating of this family (the entire span of the MBA).

Eggshell Ware. Vessels belonging to this family have very thin walls and are usually made of light clay, although there are a few examples made of a somewhat darker clay (pinkish orange or brownish pink). The bowls and goblets belonging to this family usually have a ring base or raised "trumpet base." The date of this family is still in debate. It has been dated to the MBIIb–c (Dever 1974, 45; Maeir 2007, 250) but also to MBIIc–LBI (Bonfil 2003, 280)—the later date also suggested by their MBIIc–LBI contexts at Dan (Ilan 1996, 218, figs. 4.95:12, 4.99:10, 16). The recent Hazor publications strengthen the later MBIIc–LBI date (Bechar 2017, 236–37).

Vessels of this family are not very common in the studied assemblages (graph 4.37) and are most common in the MBII and LBI. They appear in all strata at Hazor, reaching their peak in Stratum 2, when they make up 4% of the

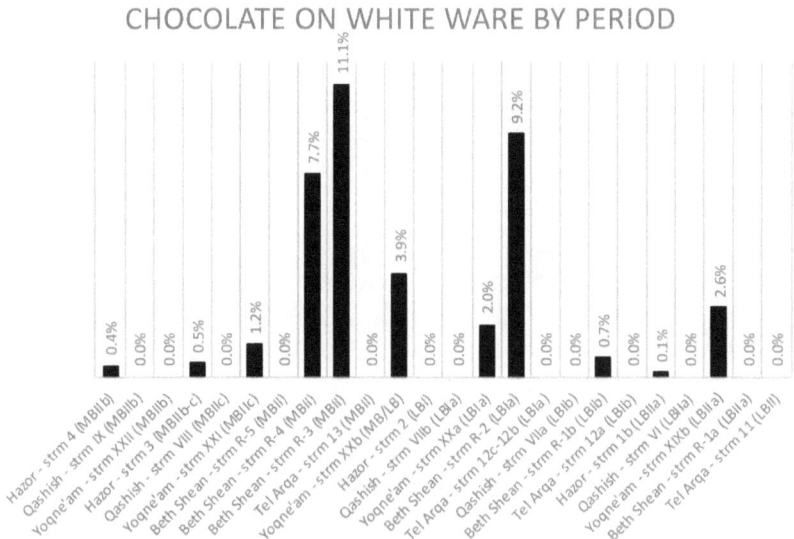

GRAPH 4.35 Chocolate on white, organized by period.

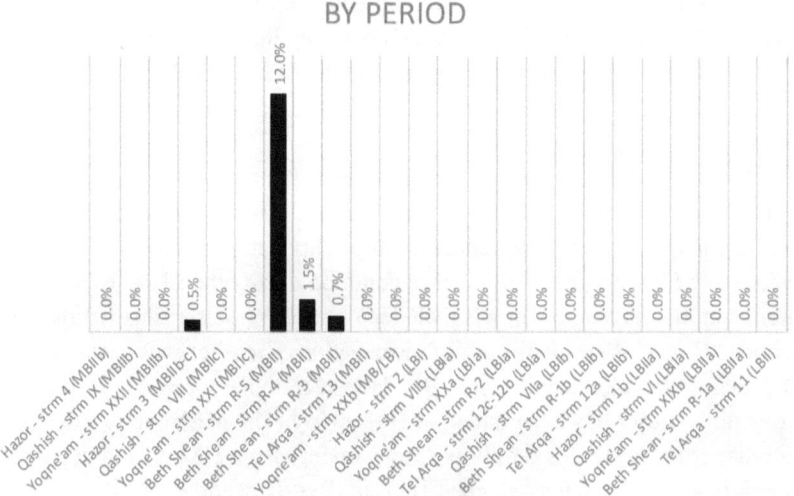

GRAPH 4.36 Red, White, and Blue Ware, organized by period.

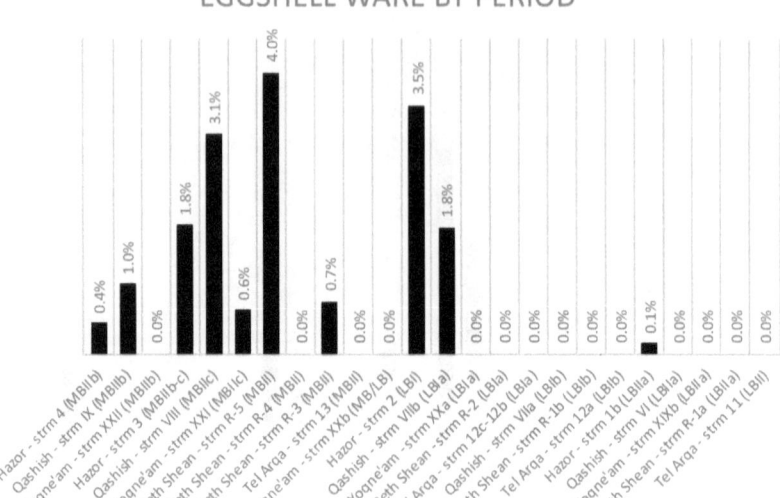

GRAPH 4.37 Eggshell Ware, organized by period.

assemblage.[5] At Tel Qashish, they appear in Strata IX–VIIb, reaching their peak in Stratum VIII when they make up 3% of the assemblage. In Yoqneʻam a single sample appears in Stratum XXI of the MBII, making up 1% of the assemblage. At Beth-Shean, they occur in Strata R-5 (making up 4% of the assemblage) and R-3 (1% of the assemblage). They are absent from the Tell Arqa assemblage.

Thus, it seems that this family appears in the MBA and disappears after the LBI, allowing the suggestion that this family should be regarded as an anchor for this transitional period.

Charom *Ware*. This ware is characterized by an orange slip (varying from light orange to dark reddish orange) and burnish, this decoration being usually applied on bowls. The dark, reddish-orange slip is more typical of the MBA, whereas the light orange slip is more common during the LBII. This ware is more common in shallow bowls than deep bowls. Vessels of this family were termed "Orange Ware" in the Yadin's excavations (Ben-Tor 1989, 250–52, 268) and are traditionally dated to the LBA. However, in the recent Hazor publications, this family has been dated, at Hazor, from the MBIIb–c to the LBIIa (Bechar 2017, 237). This family is known mainly from Hazor, although a few sherds have also been uncovered at Tel Dan (Ben-Dov 2011, 205).

From this present study, these are particularly prevalent in Hazor Stratum 1b, dated to the LBIIa, being more common in the LBA strata in general (graph 4.38).

5. In Stratum 1b, they made up only 0.1% of the assemblage.

CHAROM WARE AT HAZOR

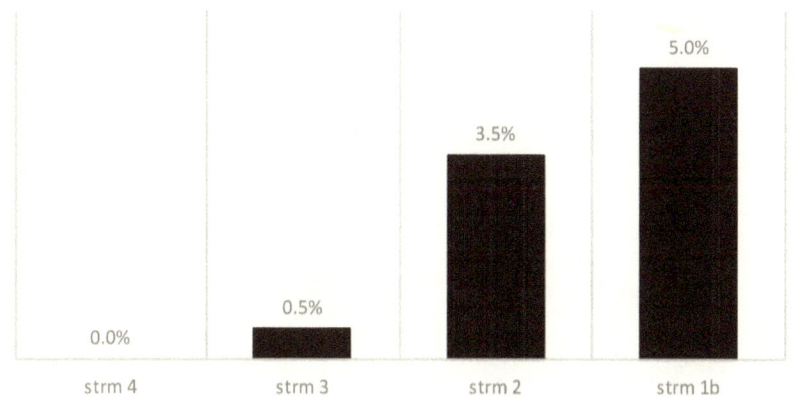

GRAPH 4.38 *Charom* Ware from Hazor, by strata.

4.2.10. Imported Vessels

Cypriot Bichrome Ware (graph 4.39). This family is characterized by a specific type of red and black painted decoration on a light surface, usually found on jugs, juglets, kraters, jars, and bowls. The vessels are usually well burnished. The decorative motifs comprise representations of animals (such as fish, birds, and bulls), trees, and geometric motifs (such as wheels, Maltese crosses, and ladders).

Traditionally, Cypriot Bichrome Ware has been dated from the MBIIc onward, with its peak in the LBI. It continues in small numbers into the LBIIa (Amiran 1969, 152–54, plate 48; Epstein 1966, 2–5, 22–87).

The present study indicates that although these appear already in Stratum 4 at Hazor and Stratum IX at Tel Qashish (both dated to the MBIIb), this is not a widespread phenomenon. In most sites, they appear mainly in the LBI strata. Single samples were also found in LBII contexts in Hazor Stratum 1b (0.1% of the assemblage), and Tell Arqa Stratum 11 (1% of the assemblage), though these might be stray sherds. It is interesting to note that these are absent in the assemblages from Area R in Beth-Shean.

Mycenaean imports (graph 4.40). These imported vessels are considered the hallmark of the LBII in the southern Levant (Amrian 1969, 179–81). These include mainly closed vessels made of well-levigated clay, decorated in red or black and very well-burnished.

These are absent in Tel Qashish and are very rare in Beth-Shean (discussed further below). They appear already in small amounts in Yoqneʿam Stratum XXb

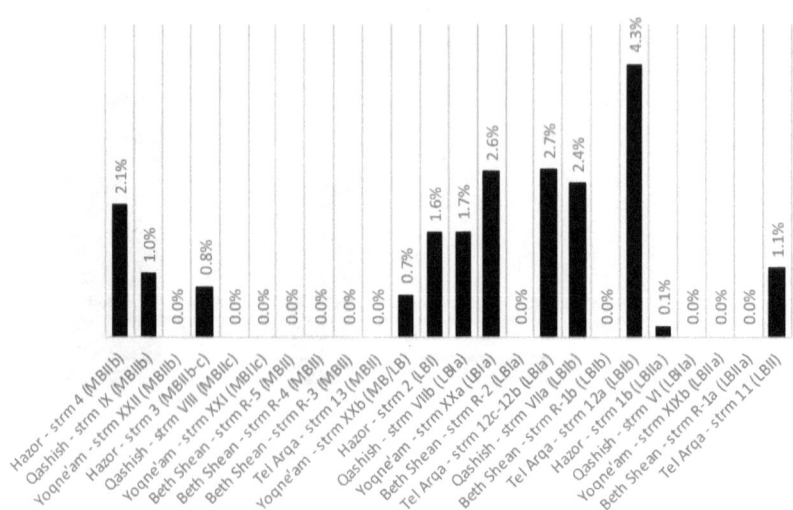

GRAPH 4.39 Cypriot Bichrome Ware, organized by period.

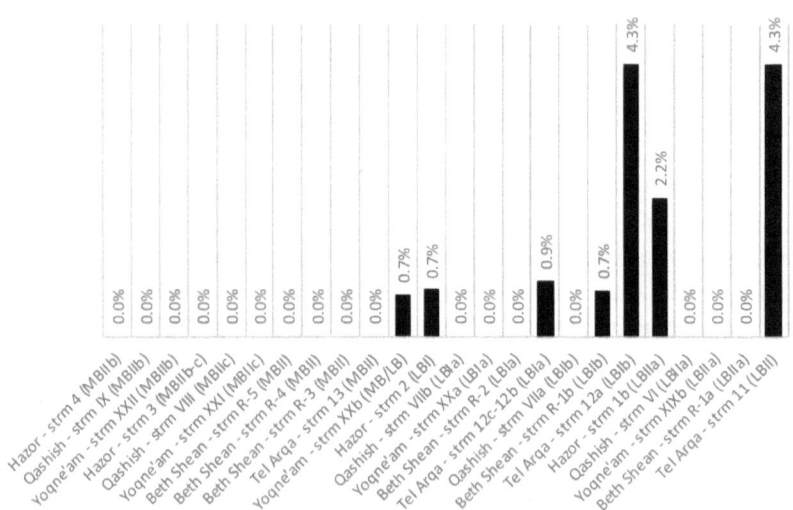

GRAPH 4.40 Mycenaean imports, organized by period.

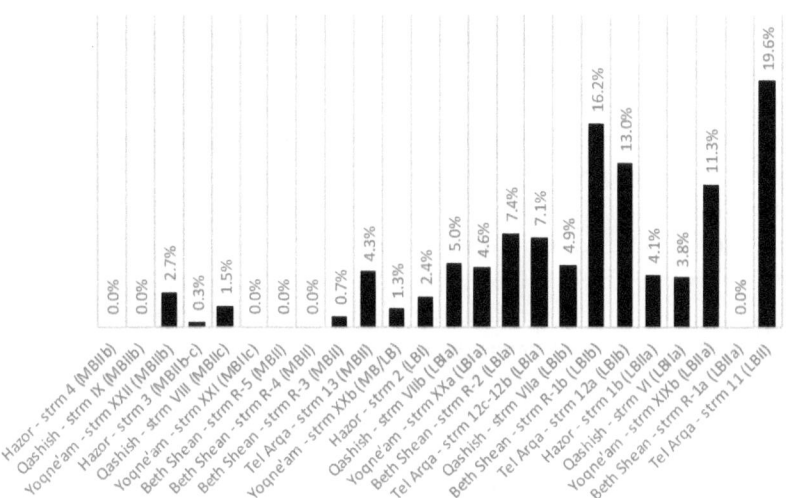

GRAPH 4.41 Cypriot imports, organized by period.

(dated to the transitional MBA/LBA) and in some earlier LBI strata (Hazor Stratum 2, Tell Arqa Strata 12c–b), making up a maximum of 1% of the assemblages. However, it is in the LBII (as well as in the LBIb Tell Arqa Stratum 12a) that these make up a larger part of the assemblages, between 2% and 4%. It is interesting to note that, in Hazor Stratum 1a, a decline was noted in their consumption.

Cypriot imports (graph 4.41). This family of imported vessels includes a variety of shapes and decorations. The vessels were not separated into different families (e.g., white slipped, base ring, and so forth) but were all rather treated as a group, these being the most common type of ware imported to the southern Levant.

The earliest appearance of imported Cypriot vessels (which are not the Bichrome Ware) was noted in the MBII in Qashish Stratum VIII (making up 1% of the assemblage), Yoqne'am Stratum XXII (3%), Beth-Shean Stratum R-3 (2%), and Tell Arqa Stratum 13 (4%). The peak of these imported vessels, in most sites, occurs during the LBII: in Hazor Stratum 1b (when they make up 4% of the assemblage), Yoqne'am Stratum XIXb (11%), and Tell Arqa Stratum 11 (20%). At Tel Qashish, they are a bit more common in the LBIa and LBIb strata (5% in each) in comparison to the LBII stratum (4%). At Beth-Shean, they are most common in the LBIb Stratum R-1b (16.2%). Only a single example was found in Stratum R-1a.[6]

---

6. It should be emphasized that the assemblages from Strata VIII–VI of the University of Pennsylvania excavations were not considered here, as they are beyond the chronological framework of this study.

4.3. Discussion by Site

The following discussion will present the distribution of the families presented above within the different sites. The families of vessels (bowls, kraters, cooking pots, large storage vessels, and small storage vessels) will be discussed by site. The discussion deals with each type in reference to its assemblage. This refers to the family assemblage (as noted above) within the specific stratum of each site unless otherwise stated. In some cases, the assemblage of the entire stratum will also be discussed, and this will be noted.

Two types of graphs and tables accompany this discussion. The first, graphs 4.42–4.71, depicts the percentages of the types in each stratum in every site discussed. The tables accompanying the graphs include the percentages and the number of vessels and sherds analyzed for this research. The second are tables recording the percentages of each family in the different strata (tables 4.2–4.25). These tables include the number of vessels and sherds analyzed for this research and, in some cases, also the number of vessels and sherds that only appeared in the statistical tables of the publications. Table 4.1 presents the average consumption of vessels in all the sites that were examined in this study. Unstratified finds were not included in this study.

4.3.1. Hazor

4.3.1.1. Bowls (Graph 4.42, Table 4.2)

Shallow bowls appear throughout the MBA and the LBA, though it is clear that their distribution declines between Strata 3 and 2, from 50% of the assemblage of rounded bowls (29% of all bowls) to about 25% (16% of all bowls). In stratum 1b, they make up about 13% of the rounded bowls assemblage (9% of all bowls). Thus, the decline continues from the LBI to the LBIIa.

The deep bowls appear in relatively small numbers in Strata 4–2 (6%–11% of the rounded bowls and 3%–5% of all bowls). The major difference in the consumption of these bowls occurs between Strata 2 and 1b, when their appearance increases from 6% of the rounded bowls (4% of all bowls) to about 22% (16% of all bowls).

TABLE 4.1 Average of the Consumption of Vessels in All Examined Sites

	Bowls	Kraters	Cooking Pots	Large Storage Vessels	Small Storage Vessels
% of all sites	39.2%	7.3%	12.8%	14.1%	12.8%

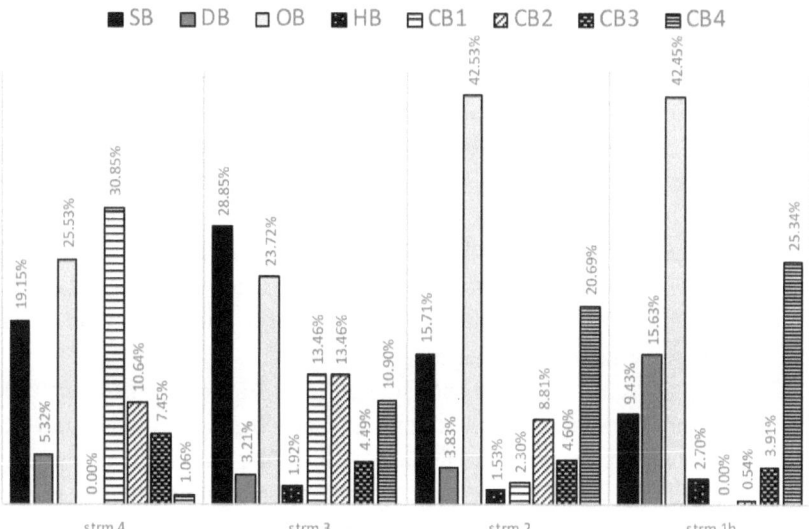

GRAPH 4.42 Hazor, Bowls

	SB	DB	OB	HB	CB1	CB2	CB3	CB4	Total	Of stratum
Stratum 4 N =	19.1% 18	5.3% 5	25.5% 24	0.0% 0	30.9% 29	10.6% 10	7.4% 7	1.1% 1	94	39.3%
Stratum 3 N =	28.8% 45	3.2% 5	23.7% 37	1.9% 3	13.5% 21	13.5% 21	4.5% 7	10.9% 17	156	40.6%
Stratum 2 N =	15.7% 41	3.8% 10	42.5% 111	1.5% 4	2.3% 6	8.8% 23	4.6% 12	20.7% 54	261	48.4%
Stratum 1b N =	9.4% 70	15.6% 116	42.5% 315	2.7% 20	0.0% 0	0.5% 4	3.9% 29	25.3% 188	742	54.8%

TABLE 4.2 Consumption of Bowls at Hazor

	Stratum 4	Stratum 3	Stratum 2	Stratum 1b
N =	94	156	261	742
% of stratum	39.3%	40.6%	48.4%	54.8%

Carinated bowls of type CB1 appear in large numbers in Stratum 4 and decline in Stratum 2, disappearing from the assemblage afterward. They make up the largest part of the assemblage of bowls in Stratum 4 (31%).

Carinated bowls of type CB2 reflect the same trend, appearing in relatively large amounts in Strata 4–2, and peaking in Stratum 3 (making up 32% of all carinated bowls and 14% of all bowls). The major difference occurs between Stratum 2 (where they amount to 24% of the carinated bowls and 9% of all bowls) and Stratum 1b (where they make up 2% of the carinated bowls and 0.5% of all bowls).

Shallow carinated bowls (CB3) are a consistent percentage of the assemblage of carinated bowls (averaging 12% in each stratum). On the other hand, deep carinated bowls (CB4) become more common in the LBA. They are very rare in Stratum 4 (making up 2% of the carinated bowls and 1% of all bowls) and become more common in Stratum 3 (amounting to 25% of the carinated bowls and 11% of all bowls). However, it is only in Stratum 2 that they become the most common type of carinated bowls, making up 57% of the assemblage of carinated bowls (and 21% of all bowls). They make up an even larger part of the assemblages in Stratum 1b, where carinated bowls of type CB1 disappear (CB4 are 85% of the carinated bowls and 25% of all bowls).

Thus, the major difference in carinated bowls at Hazor, in general, can be identified between Stratum 2 and Stratum 1b. Until Stratum 2, all the types of carinated bowls appear in the assemblages, while after this stratum, bowls of type CB1 and then also CB2 disappear from the assemblages. At this point, in Stratum 1b bowls of type CB4 become the most common type of carinated bowls at Hazor, slowly replacing the other types of carinated bowls. In general, bowls are the major part of all the strata's assemblages. They make up 55% in Stratum 1b (table 4.2).

This is the place to discuss the appearance of miniature vessels at Hazor, quite marked when compared to other sites where these are very rare. It should be noted that the miniature vessels were not limited to areas of a cultic nature (that is, they were also found in Areas S and C of the MBA) and at times were not found at all in cultic areas (e.g., they were not found in the area F temples). It is also interesting to note that none were found in funerary contexts at Hazor. Further questions regarding the consumption of miniature vessels at Hazor are not within the scope of this research and should be dealt with elsewhere.

4.3.1.2. Kraters (Graph 4.43, Table 4.3)

As in all the other sites (also discussed below), closed kraters appear only in the earliest strata at Hazor (Strata 4–2), disappearing afterward (though a single example was found in Stratum 1b). Closed kraters of the CKR type are common only in MBA strata, more in Stratum 4 than Stratum 3, reflecting a sharp decline in the consumption of these kraters. They disappear after Stratum 3.

Kraters of the NK type are the most common kraters in Strata 3–1b, their distribution gradually increasing and reaching its peak in Stratum 1b when it makes up 88% of the kraters. Type NKR is common at Hazor in Strata 4–2, making up 9%–15% of the krater assemblages and disappearing from the ceramic assemblage afterward.

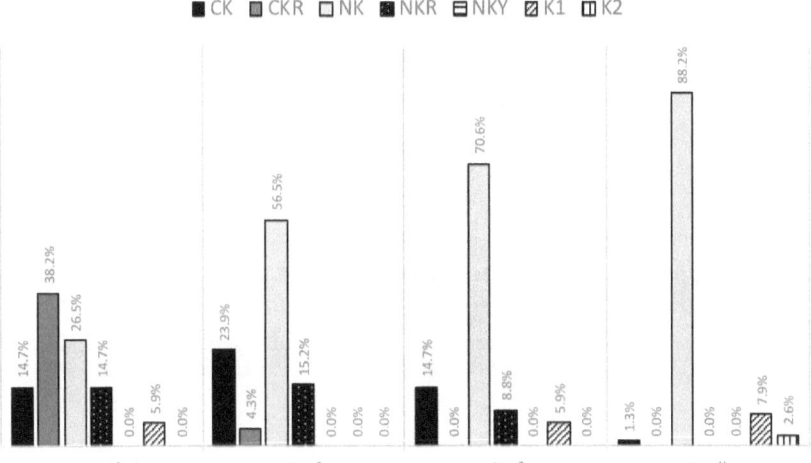

GRAPH 4.43 Hazor, Kraters

	CK	CKR	NK	NKR	NKY	K1	K2	Total	Of stratum
Stratum 4	14.7%	38.2%	26.5%	14.7%	0.0%	5.9%	0.0%	34	14.2%
N =	5	13	9	5	0	2	0		
Stratum 3	23.9%	4.3%	56.5%	15.2%	0.0%	0.0%	0.0%	46	12.0%
N =	11	2	26	7	0	0	0		
Stratum 2	14.7%	0.0%	70.6%	8.8%	0.0%	5.9%	0.0%	34	6.3%
N =	5	0	24	3	0	2	0		
Stratum 1b	1.3%	0.0%	88.2%	0.0%	0.0%	7.9%	2.6%	76	5.6%
N =	1	0	67	0	0	6	2		

TABLE 4.3 Consumption of Kraters at Hazor

	Stratum 4	Stratum 3	Stratum 2	Stratum 1b
N =	34	46	34	76
% of stratum	14.2%	12.0%	6.3%	5.6%

Pithos-kraters (K2) appear only in the LBA Stratum 1b, making up 3% of the krater assemblages. This allows suggesting an LBII date for these vessels, based on their later appearance in LBIIb contexts.

The most significant change in the consumption of kraters at Hazor seems to occur between Strata 2 and 1b. Up to Stratum 2, various types of kraters are present (CK, CKR, NKR, and NK). Following this stratum, only kraters of the NK type continue to appear in the ceramic assemblages of Hazor, in addition to kraters of type K2, which do not appear before Stratum 1b. Nevertheless, it should also be noted that kraters make up a larger part of the Strata 4 and 3 assemblages (see table 4.3) and a relatively smaller portion of the remaining strata. However, these differences in consumption are not significant enough to mark a sharp discrepancy between these strata, the major change occurring between Strata 2 and 1b, as noted above.

4.3.1.3. Cooking Pots (Graph 4.44, Table 4.4)

Handmade cooking pots of the UCP type are common at Hazor in both MBA strata, disappearing from the assemblages afterward. It is surprising that, in contrast to other sites, these cooking pots become more common in the MBA Stratum 3, when they make up 25% of the cooking pot assemblage, compared to 22% of the earlier Stratum 4.

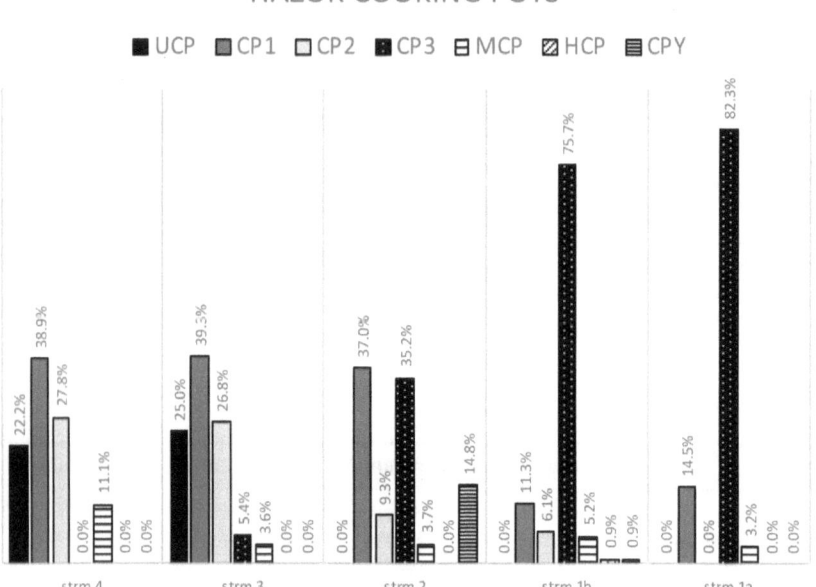

GRAPH 4.44 Hazor, Cooking Pots

	UCP	CP1	CP2	CP3	MCP	HCP	CPY	Total	Of stratum
Stratum 4	22.2%	38.9%	27.8%	0.0%	11.1%	0.0%	0.0%	18	7.5%
N =	4	7	5	0	2	0	0		
Stratum 3	25.0%	39.3%	26.8%	5.4%	3.6%	0.0%	0.0%	56	14.6%
N =	14	22	15	3	2	0	0		
Stratum 2	0.0%	37.0%	9.3%	35.2%	3.7%	0.0%	14.8%	54	10.0%
N =	0	20	5	19	2	0	8		
Stratum 1b	0.0%	11.3%	6.1%	75.7%	5.2%	0.9%	0.9%	115	8.5%
N =	0	13	7	87	6	1	1		

TABLE 4.4 Consumption of Cooking Pots at Hazor

	Stratum 4	Stratum 3	Stratum 2	Stratum 1b
N =	18	56	54	115
% of stratum	7.5%	14.6%	10.0%	8.5%

Wheel-made cooking pots of the CP1 type make up almost 40% of the assemblage in Strata 4–2 (39% in Strata 4 and 3, and 37% in Stratum 2) and make up only 11% in the following Stratum 1b. It is precisely during Stratum 1b that cooking pots of type CP3 begin to be the most dominant in the assemblage (76% in Stratum 1b), thus the decline in consumption of cooking pots of type CP1 fits well with this observation. Cooking pots of type CP3 begin to appear already in Stratum 3 (when they make up 5% of the assemblage), and their occurrence increases in Stratum 2 (35% of the assemblage).

Cooking pots of the CP2 type were very common during Strata 4–3 (when they made up 28% and 27% of the assemblages, respectively). Their appearance declines in Stratum 2 (amounting to only 9% of the assemblage) and continues to decline in Stratum 1b.

In general, the major difference in the consumption of cooking pots at Hazor is seen between Strata 2 and 1b. This case is similar to that of the kraters—it is between these two strata that the assemblage of cooking pots becomes less varied and dominated by a single type (CP3). Although other types appear in Stratum 1b as well, the dominance of CP3 type is the most conspicuous aspect of the assemblage.

Overall, apart from Stratum 3, when cooking pots make up 15% of the assemblage, their consumption is more or less stable throughout all the strata, 8%–10%, a little less than the average of 14% for all sites and strata. The high precentage of cooking pots in Stratum 3 might be due to their high distribution in the Complex of Standing Stones on the acropolis (see Bechar 2017, 240).

4.3.1.4. Large Storage Vessels (Graph 4.45, Table 4.5)

In contrast to most MBA sites in the southern Levant, pithoi are rare in the strata of this period at Hazor, making up only 9% in Stratum 4 and 18% in Stratum 3. They become more common in the LBI (when they make up 21% of the assemblage), making up a much larger part of the assemblages during the LBII (36% in Stratum 1b).

Storage jars of the SJ1 type are the most uncommon type of large storage vessels at Hazor. Apart from Stratum 1b, where they make up 14% of the assemblage, they amount to less than 10% of the assemblages in the different strata.

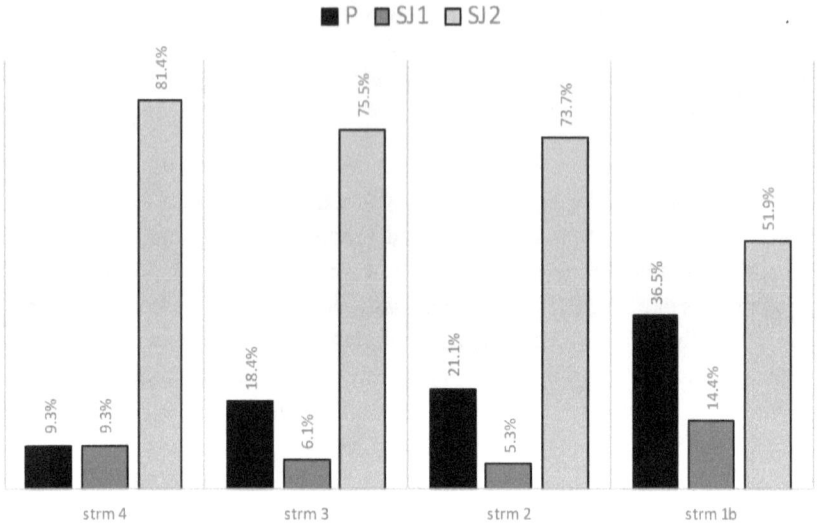

GRAPH 4.45 Hazor, Large Storage Vessels

	P	SJ1	SJ2	Total	Of stratum
Stratum 4	9.3%	9.3%	81.4%	43	18.0%
N =	4	4	35		
Stratum 3	18.4%	6.1%	75.5%	49	12.8%
N =	9	3	37		
Stratum 2	21.1%	5.3%	73.7%	38	7.1%
N =	8	2	28		
Stratum 1b	36.5%	14.4%	51.9%	107	7.9%
N =	38	15	54		

TABLE 4.5 Consumption of Large Storage Vessels at Hazor

	Stratum 4	Stratum 3	Stratum 2	Stratum 1b
N =	43	49	38	107
% of stratum	18.0%	12.8%	7.1%	7.9%

On the other hand, storage jars of type SJ2 are the most common type of large storage vessels. They make up an exceptionally large part of the Stratum 4 assemblage (81%), their appearance in the assemblages declining following this stratum. However, even in Stratum 1b, when they make up the smallest part of the assemblage compared to other strata, they still make up 52% of the assemblage.

At Hazor, the major distinction in the consumption of large storage vessels is seen between Strata 2 and 1b. Before Stratum 1b, pithoi make up, on average,

16% of the assemblages. In Strata 1b, however, the consumption of pithoi increases, making up 36% of the assemblage. As pithoi make up a larger part of the assemblage, the consumption of storage jars declines respectively in this stratum. Consequently, storage jars are the most dominant type of large storage vessels of the earlier strata, especially type SJ2.

It should also be noted that large storage vessels make up a larger part of the Strata 4 and 3 assemblages (18% and 13%, respectively) and a relatively smaller part of the following strata (7% of Stratum 2 and 8% of Stratum 1b), compared to the 15% average in all other sites (see table 4.5). This might be explained by the fact that pithoi become more common in the LBA, and thus, storage at Hazor was achieved using large, immobile vessels. Therefore, the use of many smaller storage jars becomes redundant in the LBII.

4.3.1.5. Small Storage Vessels (Graph 4.46, Table 4.6)

Overall, small storage vessels appear in larger numbers in Stratum 1b of the LBII than in earlier strata. However, they make up almost the same part of the strata's entire assemblages (between 10% in Stratum 2 and 14% in Strata 4 and 3). Except for Stratum 3, where juglets are more dominant than jugs, the latter are the more dominant components of the strata's assemblages.

In general, it seems that the most significant difference in the consumption of small storage vessels at Hazor could be pointed to between Stratum 4 and Stratum 3, when more types of vessels are introduced into the assemblage. In addition, in Stratum 4, jugs of type J2 make up the dominant part of the assemblage, and, consequently, the other types that appear in this stratum amount to a small part of the assemblage.

Overall, the consumption of small storage vessels is essentially consistent within the different strata, making up between 10% and 14% of the entire assemblages (see table 4.6).

4.3.1.6. Varia (Graph 4.47)

Eggshell Ware begins to appear at Hazor in the earliest MBA stratum, Stratum 4. Its appearance gradually increases and reaches its peak in the Stratum 2 assemblage of the LBI, after which a stark decline was noted. Chocolate-on-White Ware is very rare in the Hazor assemblage (as is the Red, White, and Blue Ware).

Imported Bichrome Ware appears already in the earliest MBA stratum at Hazor and continues to appear until the LBI, basically disappearing from the assemblage afterward, especially compared to other Aegean imports. This ware reaches its peak at Hazor during the LBI, in terms of total numbers and not in their relative quantity.

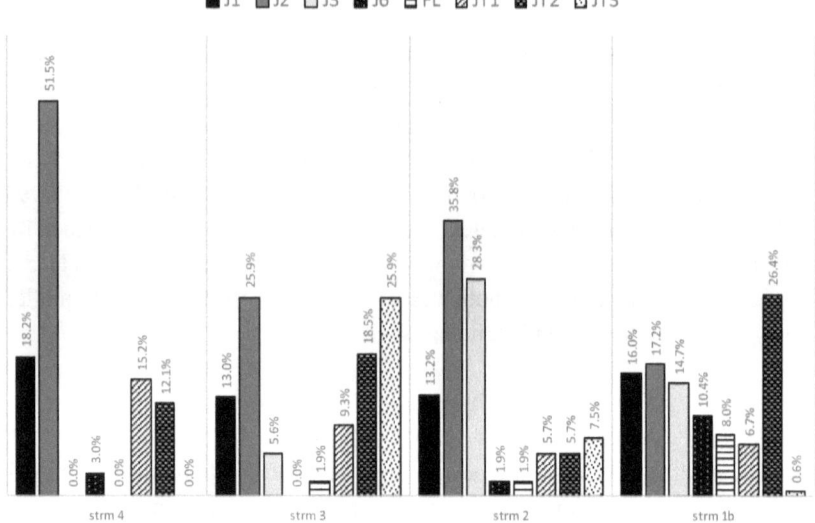

GRAPH 4.46 Hazor, Small Storage Vessels

	J1	J2	J3	J6	FL	JT1	JT2	JT3	Total	Of stratum
Stratum 4	18.2%	51.5%	0.0%	3.0%	0.0%	15.2%	12.1%	0.0%	33	13.8%
N =	6	17	0	1	0	5	4	0		
Stratum 3	13.0%	25.9%	5.6%	0.0%	1.9%	9.3%	18.5%	25.9%	54	14.1%
N =	7	14	3	0	1	5	10	14		
Stratum 2	13.2%	35.8%	28.3%	1.9%	1.9%	5.7%	5.7%	7.5%	53	9.8%
N =	7	19	15	1	1	3	3	4		
Stratum 1b	16.0%	17.2%	14.7%	10.4%	8.0%	6.7%	26.4%	0.6%	163	12.0%
N =	26	28	24	17	13	11	43	1		

TABLE 4.6 Consumption of Small Storage Vessels at Hazor

	Stratum 4	Stratum 3	Stratum 2	Stratum 1b
N =	33	54	53	163
% of stratum	13.8%	14.1%	9.8%	12.0%

Other Cypriot importation appears at Hazor beginning in Stratum 3 of the MBIIb–c; however, this includes a single example. In the LBA strata, Cypriot imports make up a much larger part of the assemblage, reaching its peak in Stratum 1b (when these make up 4% of the stratum's assemblage). It is also in this stratum that Mycenaean ware is most abundant, making up 2% of the entire assemblage; it is completely absent in the MBA assemblages, with only a few examples from Stratum 2, making up 1% of the stratum's assemblage.

Pottery Assemblages from the Middle and Late Bronze Ages 175

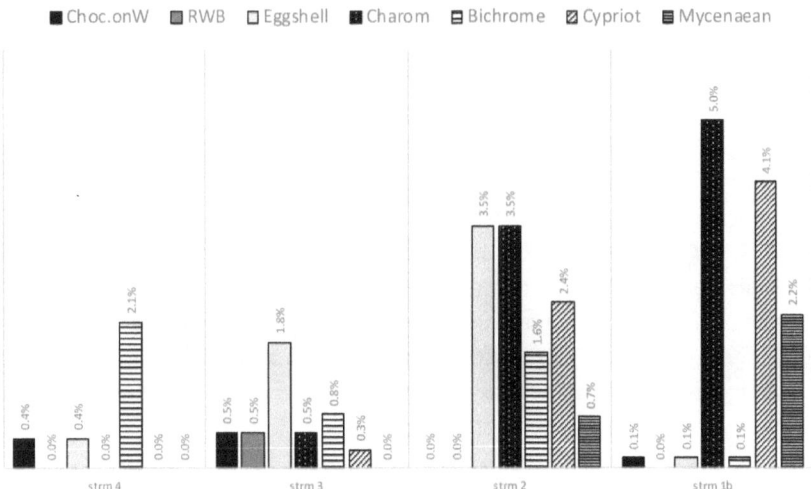

GRAPH 4.47 Hazor, Miscellaneous Families

	Chocolate on White Ware	Red, White, and Blue Ware	Eggshell Ware	*Charom* Ware	Cypriot Bichrome Ware	Cypriot Imports	Mycenaean Imports
Stratum 4	0.4%	0.0%	0.4%	0.0%	2.1%	0.0%	0.0%
N =	1	0	1	0	5	0	0
Stratum 3	0.5%	0.5%	1.8%	0.5%	0.8%	0.3%	0.0%
N =	2	2	7	2	3	1	0
Stratum 2	0.0%	0.0%	3.5%	3.5%	1.6%	2.4%	0.7%
N =	0	0	19	19	9	13	4
Stratum 1b	0.1%	0.0%	0.1%	5.0%	0.1%	4.1%	2.2%
N =	2	0	2	68	2	56	30

Overall, the change in consumption of the "special" wares at Hazor seems to take place in Stratum 1b. If we disregard the Chocolate-on-White and the Red, White, and Blue Wares (which are very rare at Hazor), five families remain—three imported Aegean wares and two local "special" wares. In Stratum 1b, the imported Aegean ware (Mycenaean and Cypriot) are more common in the assemblage than the local "special" wares (Eggshell and *Charom* Wares), this trend continuing in Stratum 1a. In addition, and consequently, far fewer types of "special" wares appear in this stratum.

4.3.1.7. Hazor's Assemblages: Summary

Overall, it seems that the major changes in consumption at Hazor occurred between Strata 2 and 1b. This is marked by the dominance of certain types over the assemblages and, thus, the disappearance of other types. This was noted in the carinated bowls when CB4 becomes the dominant type, in kraters when NK become the dominant type, in cooking pots when CP3 become the dominant type, and in large storage vessels when the consumption of pithoi increases. This was also observed in the "special" and imported wares when the local "special" wares decline and the imported ware incline and are the most dominant component in this category.

Even in terms of specific types within the families, there are several types for which major changes in their consumption were noted between Strata 2 and 1b: DB, CB1, CB2, CK, NKR, K2, and CP1. Nevertheless, in a few types, the changes were noted between Strata 3 and 2 (SB, CB4, UCP, CP2, and JT3), and some fewer types whose major change was seen between Strata 4 and 3 (CB3, CKR, NK, and MCP). Consequently, at Hazor, the changes in consumption of ceramic vessels concurs with the changes in architecture noted in chapter 2. Both occur between Stratum 2 and Stratum 1b.

4.3.2. Tel Qashish

The publication of the ceramic assemblages from Tel Qashish also includes a statistical analysis. Although most of the typological scheme adheres to the one defined here (including CB1, CB2, CB4, CK, NKR, UCP, and P), sherds found in "clean" contexts (floors and make-up of floors) and not depicted in the figures were not considered for the present study.[7] Using them would have created a bias—for example, the typology of Tel Qashish does not include a type that is parallel to bowls of type CB3, and thus, adding bowls of the remaining types would distort the overall consumption picture of carinated bowls. Therefore, all the additional vessels and sherds were considered under their general family, within the overall consumption trends (tables 4.7–4.11). After examining the illustrated figures (all of them taken into consideration), the additional vessels were added in the varia column.

4.3.2.1. Bowls (Graph 4.48, Table 4.7)

The shallow bowls appear in almost every stratum, except Stratum VIIa, dated to the LBIb. However, since these bowls make up approximately the same part of the rounded bowls in the LBIa and the LBII, and since only open bowls were identified in Stratum VIIa, it is reasonable to assume that the LBIb rounded bowls were not preserved well enough to determine their specific subtype.

The large decline in the appearance of these bowls occurs between Stratum VIII (making up 50% of the rounded bowls and 46% of all bowls) and

---

7. These were considered in the overall consumption but not in regards to specific types, as was noted in the introduction to this chapter.

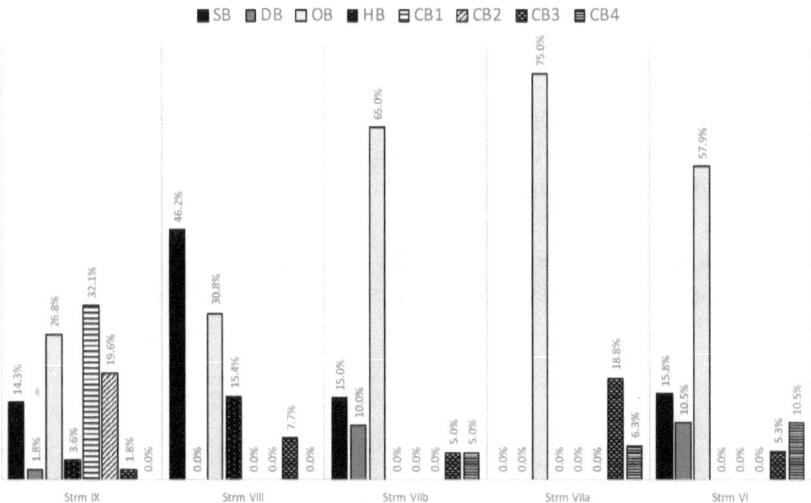

GRAPH 4.48 Tel Qashish, Bowls

	SB	DB	OB	HB	CB1	CB2	CB3	CB4	Varia[a]	Total	Of stratum
Stratum IX N =	14.3% 8	1.8% 1	26.8% 17	3.6% 2	32.1% 21	19.6% 11	1.8% 1	0.0% 0	2	63	29.4%
Stratum VIII N =	46.2% 6	0.0% 0	30.8% 4	15.4% 2	0.0% 0	0.0% 0	7.7% 1	0.0% 0	4	17	23.6%
Stratum VIIb N =	15.0% 3	10.0% 2	65.0% 13	0.0% 0	0.0% 0	0.0% 0	5.0% 1	5.0% 1	10	30	39.0%
Stratum VIIa N =	0.0% 0	0.0% 0	75.0% 12	0.0% 0	0.0% 0	0.0% 0	18.8% 3	6.3% 1	0	16	35.6%
Stratum VI N =	15.8% 3	10.5% 2	57.9% 11	0.0% 0	0.0% 0	0.0% 0	5.3% 1	10.5% 2	5	24	40.7%

[a]Not in figures (Bonfil 2003, table 20).

TABLE 4.7 Consumption of Bowls at Tel Qashish

	Stratum IX	Stratum VIII	Stratum VIIb	Stratum VIIa	Stratum VI
N =	63	17	30	16	24
% of stratum	29.4%	23.6%	39.0%	35.6%	40.7%
N (in figures)	61	13	20	16	19

Stratum VIIb (making up about 17% of the rounded bowls and 15% of all bowls), in other words, between the MBIIc and the LBIa.

Deep bowls are absent in the assemblage of rounded bowls of Strata VIII (MBIIc) and VIIa (LBIb). Within the other strata, an increase can be observed— from about 4% in stratum IX to 11% in Stratum VIIb and 13% in Stratum VI of the rounded bowls, and from 2% to 10% and 11%, respectively, of all bowls in each stratum.

Closed carinated bowls appear only in Stratum IX of the MBIIb at Tel Qashish, disappearing afterward. This is surprising since they make up much of the assemblage of bowls (CB1 make up 32% of all bowls and CB2 amount to 20% of all bowls).

Carinated bowls of types CB3 and CB4 are not common in the ceramic assemblages at Tel Qashish. In fact, after Stratum IX, these appear in very small

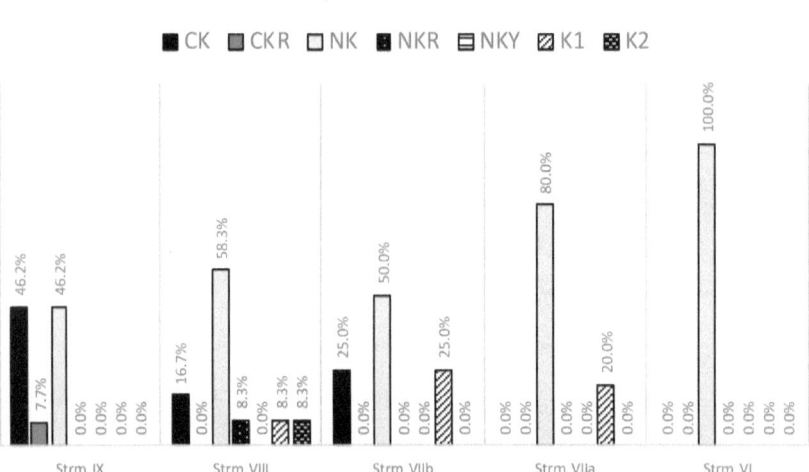

GRAPH 4.49 Tel Qashish, Kraters

	CK	CKR	NK	NKR	NKY	K1	K2	Varia[a]	Total	Of stratum
Stratum IX N =	46.2% 6	7.7% 1	46.2% 6	0.0% 0	0.0% 0	0.0% 0	0.0% 0	0	13	6.1%
Stratum VIII N =	16.7% 2	0.0% 0	58.3% 7	8.3% 1	0.0% 0	8.3% 1	8.3% 1	0	12	16.7%
Stratum VIIb N =	25.0% 1	0.0% 0	50.0% 2	0.0% 0	0.0% 0	25.0% 1	0.0% 0	0	4	5.2%
Stratum VIIa N =	0.0% 0	0.0% 0	80.0% 4	0.0% 0	0.0% 0	20.0% 1	0.0% 0	0	5	11.1%
Stratum VI N =	0.0% 0	0.0% 0	100.0% 1	0.0% 0	0.0% 0	0.0% 0	0.0% 0	1	2	3.4%

[a] Not in figures (Bonfil 2003, table 21).

numbers—for example, only one carinated bowl was found in Stratum VIII and only two in Stratum VIIb. Thus, a full discussion on the distribution of these bowls is not possible. However, the fact that the change in consumption of carinated bowls occurs after Stratum IX is noteworthy.

In general, bowls at Tel Qashish also always make up a smaller part of the assemblage than the average 42% in all sites (see table 4.7). Though bowls are the most prominent part of the assemblages at Tel Qashish, they are not the dominant component as seen in Hazor, Beth-Shean, and Tell Arqa, where they make up more than 40% of most of the assemblages. Only in Stratum VI (LBIIa) do they exceed this percentage (41% of the stratum's assemblage). However, the overall trend of consumption of bowls is similar to that at Hazor and Beth-Shean, their consumption intensifying from the MBA to the LBA.

4.3.2.2. Kraters (Graph 4.49, Table 4.8)

Closed kraters appear only in Strata IX–VIIb. In Stratum IX, closed kraters of type CK and CKR make up 54% of all kraters. This is also the only stratum where kraters of type CKR appear. Kraters of type NKR appear only in Stratum VIII, as a single example. Kraters of type NKY are absent in the Tel Qashish ceramic assemblage. Kraters of type NK make up the largest portion of the krater assemblage from Stratum VIII (dated to the MBIIc) onward until they make up the entire assemblage of kraters in Stratum VI (dated to the LBII, granted this is only one example).

It appears that the assemblage of kraters is more varied in the MBA Strata IX and VIII, its variability reducing in the following strata. It is also interesting to note that the number of kraters is also reduced following Stratum VIII. Thus, in general, both the variability and the quantity of kraters is reduced following Stratum VIII (MBIIc) at Tel Qashish.

The changes in consumption of kraters at Tel Qashish, in general, does not indicate a certain trend (see table 4.8). Kraters are almost always the least consumed vessel in the assemblages (except Stratum VIII, where small storage vessels make up a smaller part of the assemblage).

TABLE 4.8 Consumption of Kraters at Tel Qashish

	Stratum IX	Stratum VIII	Stratum VIIb	Stratum VIIa	Stratum VI
N =	13	12	4	5	2
% of stratum	6.1%	16.7%	5.2%	11.1%	3.4%
N (in figures)	13	12	4	5	1

4.3.2.3. Cooking Pots (Graph 4.50, Table 4.9)

Cooking pots of the UCP type were only found in the MBA Stratum IX. Wheel-made cooking pots of type CP1 are not common at Tel Qashish. They appear only in Strata IX and VIIb, making up 3% and 25% of the cooking pot assemblages in each stratum, respectively. Cooking pots of type CP2 are more common and appear in Strata IX–VIIb, reaching their peak in Stratum VIII (when they make up 56% of the cooking pot assemblage). The most common type of cooking pots is type CP3, which appears in all strata. Their occurrence is very low in Stratum IX (5% of the assemblage), but they become more prevalent until they make up 100% of the cooking pots in Strata VIIa and VI of the LBII.

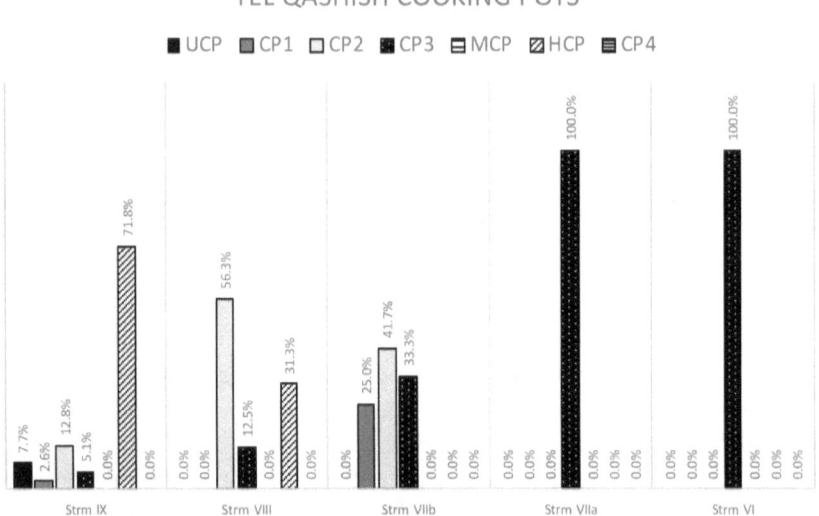

GRAPH 4.50 Tel Qashish, Cooking Pots

	UCP	CP1	CP2	CP3	MCP	HCP	CPY	Varia[a]	Total	Of stratum
Stratum IX	7.7%	2.6%	12.8%	5.1%	0.0%	71.8%	0.0%	8	48	22.4%
N =	3	1	5	2	0	29	0			
Stratum VIII	0.0%	0.0%	56.3%	12.5%	0.0%	31.3%	0.0%	2	18	25.0%
N =	0	0	9	2	0	5	0			
Stratum VIIb	0.0%	25.0%	41.7%	33.3%	0.0%	0.0%	0.0%	6	18	23.4%
N =	0	3	5	4	0	0	0			
Stratum VIIa	0.0%	0.0%	0.0%	100.0%	0.0%	0.0%	0.0%	4	10	22.2%
N =	0	0	0	6	0	0	0			
Stratum VI	0.0%	0.0%	0.0%	100.0%	0.0%	0.0%	0.0%	3	16	27.1%
N =	0	0	0	13	0	0	0			

[a]Not in figures (Bonfil 2003, table 23).

TABLE 4.9 Consumption of Cooking Pots at Tel Qashish

	Stratum IX	Stratum VIII	Stratum VIIb	Stratum VIIa	Stratum VI
N =	48	18	18	10	16
% of stratum	22.4%	25.0%	23.4%	22.2%	27.1%
N (in figures)	40	16	12	6	13

Holemouth cooking pots (HCP) are the most common type of cooking pots in the MBA Stratum IX (making up 72% of the assemblage) and continue to appear in Stratum VIII (when they make up 31% of the assemblage), disappearing after this.

Cooking pots of types CP4 and MCP are absent from the Tel Qashish assemblages. The most significant change in the cooking pot assemblages of Tel Qashish occurs between Stratum VIIb (LBIa) and VIIa (LBIb) when the assemblage is limited to type CP3. Before Stratum VIIa, the cooking pot assemblages were much more varied and comprised at least three types.

Overall, cooking pots are a prominent part of the Tel Qashish assemblage (see table 4.9). They always make up at least 22% of the assemblage, which stands out compared to the other sites, exceeding the average 14% consumption of cooking pots.

4.3.2.4. Large Storage Vessels (Graph 4.51, Table 4.10)

Pithoi are only common in Strata IX–VIIb at Tel Qashish, more so in Strata IX (61%) and VIII (83%). They are completely absent in the later LBIb–LBII strata (VIIa–VI).

Storage jars of type SJ1 are very rare at Tel Qashish. As in all other sites, storage jars of type SJ2 are the most common type of large storage vessels at Tel Qashish. However, it is only in Stratum VIIb that type SJ2 becomes the most dominant type of large storage vessels at the site, making up 75% of the large storage vessel assemblage.

It is difficult to draw the discrepancy line in the assemblages of large storage jars at Tel Qashish. Nevertheless, this can be drawn at three different points, depending on the element being considered. The earliest is between Strata IX and VIII. In Stratum IX, a numerous amount of large storage vessels was recovered (a total of 58) compared to the later strata, where an average of sixteen storage vessels was found in each stratum.

The second line can be drawn between Stratum VIII and Stratum VIIb. Although the same types of storage vessels are found within these strata, their occurrence is reversed—in Stratum VIII, pithoi make up 83% of the assemblage and storage jars of type SJ2 make up 13%; in Stratum VIIb, pithoi are 25% of the assemblage and SJ2 are 75% of the assemblage.

The third line can be drawn between Stratum VIIb and Stratum VIIa. In Stratum VIIa, pithoi disappear from the assemblages of Tel Qashish. The latter

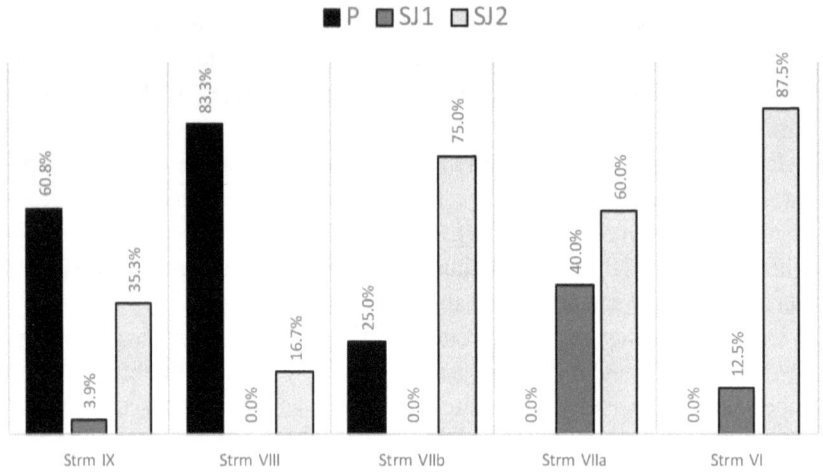

GRAPH 4.51 Tel Qashish, Large Storage Vessels

	P	SJ1	SJ2	Varia[a]	Total	Of stratum
Stratum IX N =	60.8% 32	3.9% 2	35.3% 23	1	58	27.1%
Stratum VIII N =	83.3% 10	0.0% 0	16.7% 2	2	14	19.4%
Stratum VIIb N =	25.0% 2	0.0% 0	75.0% 6	5	13	16.9%
Stratum VIIa N =	0.0% 0	40.0% 2	60.0% 3	1	6	13.3%
Stratum VI N =	0.0% 0	12.5% 1	87.5% 7	0	8	13.6%

[a] Not in figures (Bonfil 2003, table 24).

TABLE 4.10 Consumption of Large Storage Vessels at Tel Qashish

	Stratum IX	Stratum VIII	Stratum VIIb	Stratum VIIa	Stratum VI
N =	58	14	13	6	8
% of stratum	27.1%	19.4%	16.9%	13.3%	13.6%
N (in figures)	57	12	8	5	8

Pottery Assemblages from the Middle and Late Bronze Ages 183

seems to be the most convincing argument since this indicates a change in the consumption habits concerning large storage vessels and the lack of the need to store goods in immobile, massive vessels.

4.3.2.5. Small Storage Vessels (Graph 4.52, Table 4.11)

Small storage vessels make up a roughly constant part of the assemblages of the various strata (between 13% and 16%; see table 4.11).

Jugs of type J1 and J2 show the same shift in consumption—their consumption reaches its peak in Stratum VIII and then slowly declines (type J2 is absent from Stratum VIIa). Dipper jugs of type J3 are the dominant component in the Strata VIIa–VI assemblages of small storage vessels (making up 40% and 57%, respectively). Jugs of type J4 appear only in Stratum VIIb, which differs from other sites.

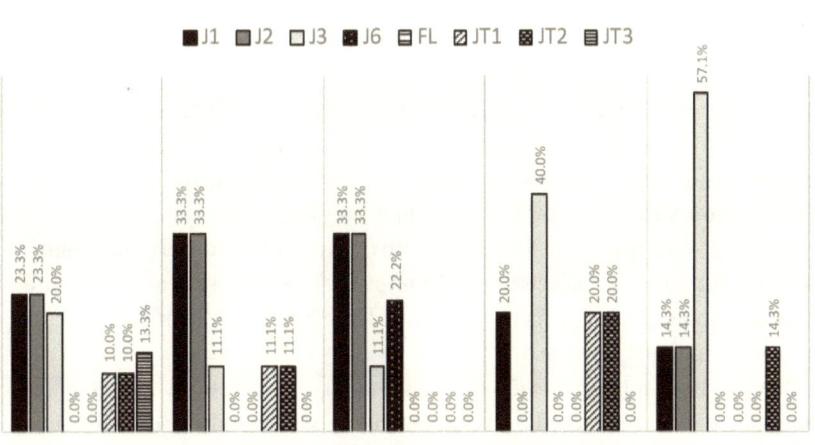

GRAPH 4.52 Tel Qashish, Small Storage Vessels

	J1	J2	J3	J6	FL	JT1	JT2	JT3	Varia[a]	Total	Of stratum
Stratum IX N =	23.3% 7	23.3% 7	20.0% 6	0.0% 0	0.0% 0	10.0% 3	10.0% 3	13.3% 4	1	31	14.5%
Stratum VIII N =	33.3% 3	33.3% 3	11.1% 1	0.0% 0	0.0% 0	11.1% 1	11.1% 1	0.0% 0	0	9	12.5%
Stratum VIIb N =	33.3% 3	33.3% 3	11.1% 1	22.2% 2	0.0% 0	0.0% 0	0.0% 0	0.0% 0	0	9	11.7%
Stratum VIIa N =	20.0% 1	0.0% 0	40.0% 2	0.0% 0	0.0% 0	20.0% 1	20.0% 1	0.0% 0	1	6	13.3%
Stratum VI N =	14.3% 1	14.3% 1	57.1% 4	0.0% 0	0.0% 0	0.0% 0	14.3% 1	0.0% 0	0	7	11.9%

[a]Not in figures (Bonfil 2003, table 23).

TABLE 4.11 Consumption of Small Storage Vessels at Tel Qashish

	Stratum IX	Stratum VIII	Stratum VIIb	Stratum VIIa	Stratum VI
N =	31	9	9	6	7
% of stratum	14.5%	12.5%	11.7%	13.3%	11.9%
N (in figures)	30	9	9	5	7

Juglets are not very common in the Tel Qashish assemblages, and they are absent from the Stratum VIIb assemblage. Flasks are absent from all the Tel Qashish assemblages.

The major difference in consumption of small storage vessels at Tel Qashish was noted between Stratum VIIb (LBIa) and VIIa (LBIb). This is due to the fact that, at this stage, jugs of type J3 are the most dominant component in the assemblages, while in previous phases, the distribution of the different types is more balanced.

4.3.2.6. Varia (Graph 4.53)

Sherds and vessels of the Chocolate-on-White, the Red, White, and Blue, and *Charom* Wares, as well as Mycenaean imports, are absent in the Tel Qashish assemblages. It is quite surprising that no Mycenaean imports were found at the site, as these appear in almost every site in the region.

Eggshell Ware appears in Strata IX–VIIb (MBIIb–LBIa) in very small numbers (1–2 examples in each stratum). Cypriot Bichrome Ware is also very rare in the assemblage and appears from Stratum IX to Stratum VIIa of the LBIb, its appearance inclining in time.

Other Cypriot imports are the most common type of "special" wares at Tel Qashish. However, it should be noted that, even as "the most common type," their appearance is still insubstantial (1–3 examples in each stratum). They appear from Stratum VIII to Stratum VI. They reach their peak in Stratum VIIb (making up 5% of the assemblage). Thus, it is difficult to draw a discrepancy line for the "special" wares, since these are so few.

4.3.2.7. Tel Qashish's Assemblages: Summary

The overall picture from the Tel Qashish assemblages is that the most significant changes in the consumption of ceramic vessels occurred between Strata VIIb and VIIa, that is, between the LBIa and the LBIb. This is evident in the consumption of cooking pots (when cooking pots of type CP3 become dominant), large storage vessels (when pithoi disappear, indicating a change in storage methods), and

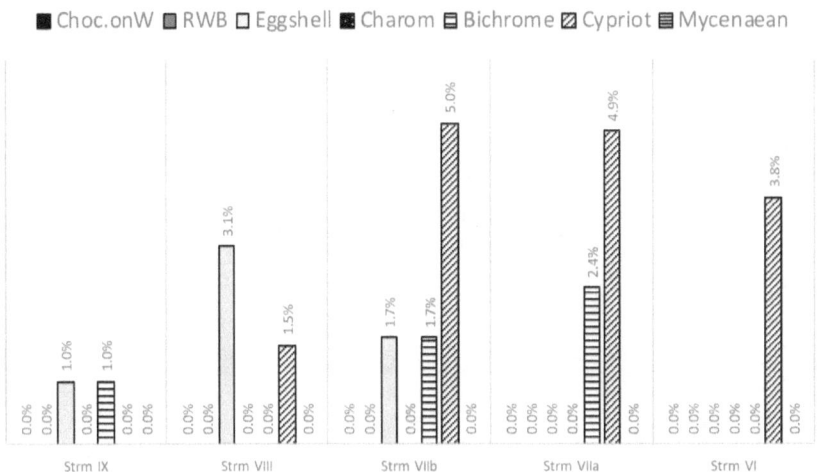

GRAPH 4.53 Tel Qashish, Miscellaneous Families

	Chocolate on White Ware	Red, White, and Blue Ware	Eggshell Ware	Charom Ware	Cypriot Bichrome Ware	Cypriot Imports	Mycenaean Imports
Stratum IX	0.0%	0.0%	1.0%	0.0%	1.0%	0.0%	0.0%
N =	0	0	2	0	2	0	0
Stratum VIII	0.0%	0.0%	3.1%	0.0%	0.0%	1.5%	0.0%
N =	0	0	2	0	0	1	0
Stratum VIIb	0.0%	0.0%	1.7%	0.0%	1.7%	5.0%	0.0%
N =	0	0	1	0	1	3	0
Stratum VIIa	0.0%	0.0%	0.0%	0.0%	2.4%	4.9%	0.0%
N =	0	0	0	0	1	2	0
Stratum VI	0.0%	0.0%	0.0%	0.0%	0.0%	3.8%	0.0%
N =	0	0	0	0	0	2	0

small storage vessels (when jugs of type J3 become dominant). Consequently, and more specifically, these changes appear in types CK, CP2, CP3, P, and J3.

Nevertheless, changes in specific types were observed between Strata IX and VIII (CB1, CB2, and NK) and between Strata VIII and VIIb (SB, HB, HCP, and SJ2). The changes in pottery consumption do not line up with the architectural changes noted in chapter 2, identified between Strata VIII and VIIb when the site is no longer fortified.

4.3.3. Yoqne'am

The publication of the ceramic assemblages from Yoqne'am also includes a statistical analysis. Since most of the types defined in the Yoqne'am publications did not always fit their definition in the present analysis, they were not considered for this study.[8] I excluded them because using them would have created a bias (for example, the different types of jugs and juglets were defined not based on the rims but on the body shape). Thus, all the additional vessels and sherds, which appear in the tables accompanying Yoqneʻam's publication, were added to their general family and with regard to the general consumption trends (tables 4.11–4.15). After examining the illustrated figures (all of them taken into consideration, as long as they were attributed to a specific stratum, regardless of context), the additional vessels were added to the varia column (not depicted in the graphs).

4.3.3.1. Bowls (Graph 4.54, Table 4.12)

Shallow bowls appear in large percentages in both the MBIIb Stratum XXII and the LBI Stratum XXa, the major difference in their appearance occurring between Stratum XXII (where they make up about 43% of the rounded bowls and 33% of all bowls) and Stratum XXI dated to the MBIIc (where they make up about 13% of the rounded bowls and 10% of all bowls).

Deep bowls appear in almost every stratum at Yoqneʻam, except the earliest Stratum XXII. In contrast to Hazor and Tel Qashish, at Yoqneʻam the trend is inverted—their appearance declines from the MBA to the LBA, as in Tell Arqa. Although this is a gradual decline, it can be noted that the major differences are seen between Stratum XXB, of the transitional MB/LB (where they make up about 14% of the rounded bowl assemblage and 12% of all bowls) and Stratum XXa of the LBIa (where they make up about 7% of the rounded bowl assemblage and 7% of all bowls).

The only carinated bowls found in Stratum XXII are of type CB1; however, these add up to two examples. Carinated bowls of type CB1 begin to appear in Stratum XXII (MBIIb) and continue into Stratum XXI (MBIIc, making up 39% of the carinated bowls and 9% of the entire assemblage of bowls), disappearing afterward at Yoqneʻam. Carinated bowls of type CB2 appear only in Stratum XXI (MBIIc) amounting to 8% of the carinated bowls and 2% of all bowls. Shallow carinated bowls (CB3) are not common in the Yoqneʻam assemblage. Deep carinated bowls (CB4) appear in Strata XXI—XXa and, surprisingly, are absent in Stratum XIXb of the LBIIa when they are usually most common (as at Hazor and Tell Arqa). In general, Stratum XXI (MBIIc) stands out in its relatively large quantities of carinated bowls. Since carinated bowls make up a small portion of the assemblages of the remaining strata, a full discussion on the

---

8. These were considered in the overall consumption but not in regard to specific types, as was noted in the introduction to this chapter.

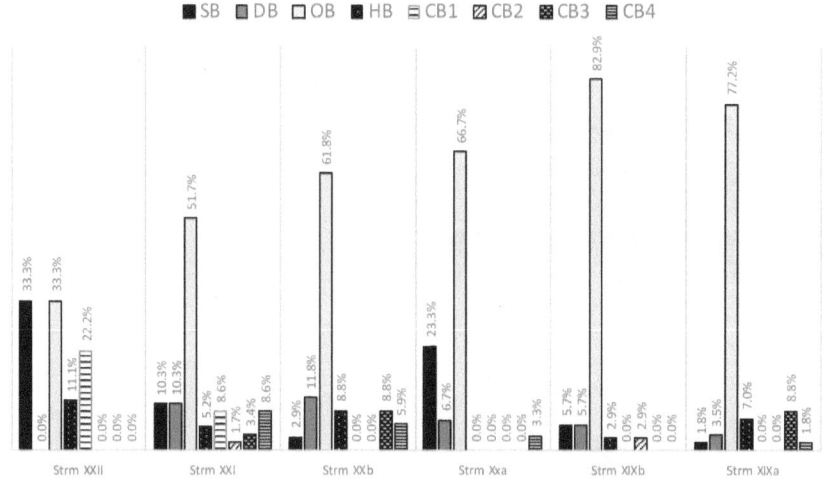

GRAPH 4.54 Yoqne'am, Bowls

	SB	DB	OB	HB	CB1	CB2	CB3	CB4	Varia[a]	Total	Of stratum
Stratum XXII	33.3%	0.0%	33.3%	11.1%	22.2%	0.0%	0.0%	0.0%	4	13	17.3%
N =	3	0	3	1	2	0	0	0			
Stratum 3=XXI	10.3%	10.3%	51.7%	5.2%	8.6%	1.7%	3.4%	8.6%	2	60	36.6%
N =	6	6	30	3	5	1	2	5			
Stratum XXb	2.9%	11.8%	61.8%	8.8%	0.0%	0.0%	8.8%	5.9%	21	55	35.9%
N =	1	4	21	3	0	0	3	2			
Stratum XXa	23.3%	6.7%	66.7%	0.0%	0.0%	0.0%	0.0%	3.3%	33	63	41.4%
N =	7	2	20	0	0	0	0	1			
Stratum XIXb	5.7%	5.7%	82.9%	2.9%	0.0%	2.9%	0.0%	0.0%	55	90	39.1%
N =	2	2	29	1	0	1	0	0			

[a] Not in figures (Ben-Ami and Livneh 2005, tables IV.14-15).

TABLE 4.12 Consumption of Bowls at Yoqne'am

	Stratum XXII	Stratum XXI	Stratum XXb	Stratum XXa	Stratum XIXb	Stratum XIXa
N =	13	60	55	63	90	102
% of stratum	17.3%	36.6%	35.9%	41.4%	39.1%	40.2%
N (in figures)	9	58	34	30	35	57

distribution of these bowls at Yoqne'am is not possible, and thus, they cannot contribute to the discussion concerning the transition from the MBA to the LBA.

The consumption of bowls at Yoqne'am is similar to that observed at Tel Qashish and Hazor—they are the most common component in the assemblage and their consumption inclines in time (see table 4.12). The consumption of bowls at Yoqne'am can be divided into three periods. The first corresponds with Stratum XXII when the consumption of bowls is 17%, the lowest in all the assemblages of all the other examined sites. The second corresponds with Strata XXI–XXb, when the consumption is higher, but still not dominant, making up 35%–36% of the entire assemblage. The last one corresponds with Strata XXa–XIXb when the bowls are the dominant component in the assemblages, making up 39%–41% of the assemblage.

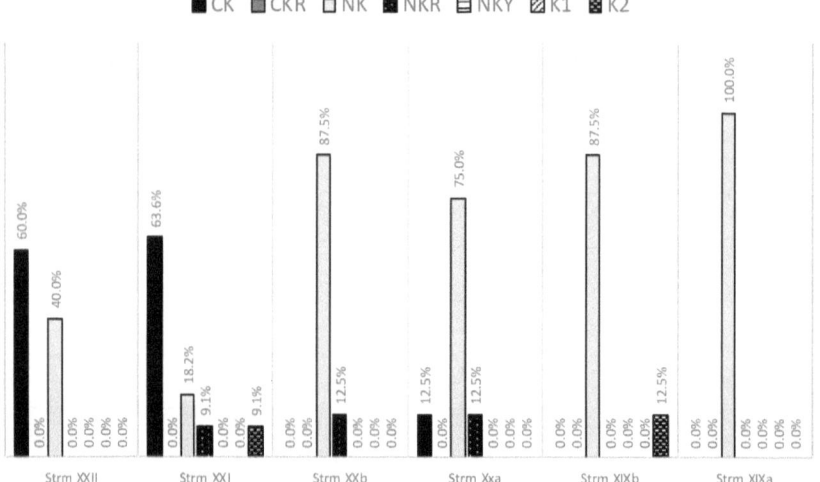

GRAPH 4.55 Yoqne'am, Kraters

	CK	CKR	NK	NKR	NKY	K1	K2	Varia[a]	Total	Of stratum
Stratum XXII	60.0%	0.0%	40.0%	0.0%	0.0%	0.0%	0.0%	0	5	6.7%
N =	3	0	2	0	0	0	0			
Stratum XXI	63.6%	0.0%	18.2%	9.1%	0.0%	0.0%	9.1%	0	11	6.7%
N =	7	0	2	1	0	0	1			
Stratum XXb	0.0%	0.0%	87.5%	12.5%	0.0%	0.0%	0.0%	2	10	6.5%
N =	0	0	7	1	0	0	0			
Stratum XXa	12.5%	0.0%	75.0%	12.5%	0.0%	0.0%	0.0%	1	9	5.9%
N =	1	0	6	1	0	0	0			
Stratum XIXb	0.0%	0.0%	87.5%	0.0%	0.0%	0.0%	12.5%	4	12	5.2%
N =	0	0	7	0	0	0	1			

[a]Not in figures (Ben-Ami and Livneh 2005, tables IV.16, IV.18).

TABLE 4.13 Consumption of Kraters at Yoqneʻam

	Stratum XXII	Stratum XXI	Stratum XXb	Stratum XXa	Stratum XIXb	Stratum XIXa
N =	5	11	10	9	12	16
% of stratum	6.7%	6.7%	6.5%	5.9%	5.2%	6.3%
N (in figures)	5	11	8	8	8	15

4.3.3.2. Kraters (Graph 4.55, Table 4.13)

Closed kraters appear in Strata XXII–XXI,[9] and thus, the most significant change in their consumption is between Stratum XXI (MBIIc) and Stratum XXb (dated to the transitional MB/LB). Closed kraters of type CKR, kraters of type NKY, and bowl-like kraters (K1) are all absent in the Yoqneʻam assemblage.

Kraters of type NKR appear in Strata XXI–XXa, one example in each stratum. Kraters of type NK appear in every stratum, but they become more dominant from Stratum XXb (MB/LB) onward. Pithos-like kraters (K2) appear in both Stratum XXI (MBIIc) and Stratum XIXb (LBIIa), one example in each stratum, and thus cannot contribute to the discussion. As a whole, it is possible to mark the changes in the consumption of kraters to the transition from Stratum XXI (MBIIc) to Stratum XXb (MB/LB), when kraters of type NK become the dominant component of the assemblage, replacing type CK.

In general, kraters are not very common in the Yoqneʻam assemblages (see table 4.13). Their consumption is almost identical in all strata (between 5% and 7%).

4.3.3.3. Cooking Pots (Graph 4.56, Table 4.14)

Cooking pots of type CP1 appear only in Strata XXII–XXa, reaching their peak in Stratum XXb (when they make up 33% of the cooking pots). Type CP2 is the most common type of cooking pot. Its peak is in stratum XXII (making up 85% of the cooking pots assemblage), and its occurrence gradually declines (amounting to 9% of the Stratum XIXb cooking pots assemblage). Cooking pots of type CP3 appear in every stratum except Stratum XXI. Their first occurrence is in Stratum XXII (29% of the assemblage), dated to the MBIIb. They are a smaller portion of the Stratum XXb assemblage (making up 19% of the assemblage), but their distribution gradually rises until they make up 91% in Stratum XIXb.

Holemouth cooking pots appear only in the MBA Strata XXII and XXI, though they are not common in either assemblage. Cooking pots of types UCP and MCP are absent from the Yoqneʻam assemblages.

9. A single example in Stratum XXa (LBI) is probably a stray example.

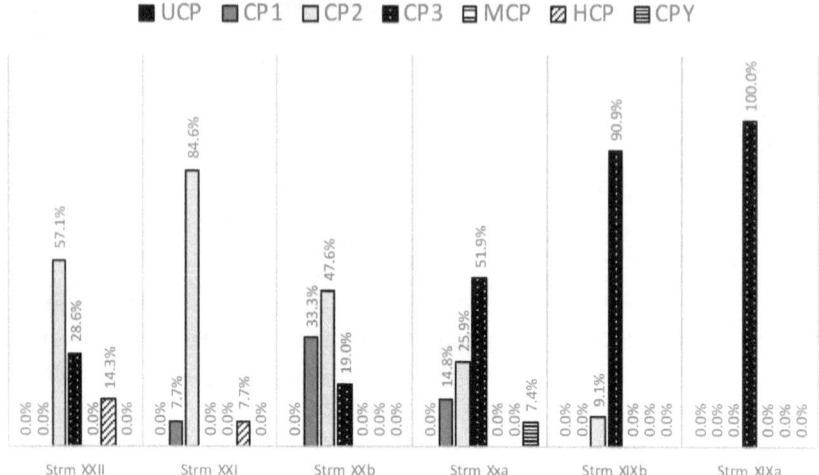

GRAPH 4.56 Yoqne'am, Cooking Pots

	UCP	CP1	CP2	CP3	MCP	HCP	CPY	Varia[a]	Total	Of stratum
Stratum XXII N =	0.0% 0	0.0% 0	57.1% 4	28.6% 2	0.0% 0	14.3% 1	0.0% 0	1	8	10.7%
Stratum 3=XXI N =	0.0% 0	7.7% 1	84.6% 11	0.0% 0	0.0% 0	7.7% 1	0.0% 0	1	14	8.5%
Stratum XXb N =	0.0% 0	33.3% 7	47.6% 10	19.0% 4	0.0% 0	0.0% 0	0.0% 0	5	26	17.0%
Stratum XXa N =	0.0% 0	14.8% 4	25.9% 7	51.9% 14	0.0% 0	0.0% 0	7.4% 2	9	36	23.7%
Stratum XIXb N =	0.0% 0	0.0% 0	9.1% 1	90.9% 10	0.0% 0	0.0% 0	0.0% 0	25	36	15.7%

[a] Not in figures (Ben-Ami and Livneh 2005, table IV.19).

TABLE 4.14 Consumption of Cooking Pots at Yoqne'am

	Stratum XXII	Stratum XXI	Stratum XXb	Stratum XXa	Stratum XIXb	Stratum XIXa
N =	8	14	26	36	36	38
% of stratum	10.7%	8.5%	17.0%	23.7%	15.7%	15.0%
N (in figures)	7	13	21	27	11	23

The most significant change in the assemblages of cooking pots in Yoqne'am occurs in the transition from Stratum XXa (LBI) to Stratum XIXb (LBIIa). Similarly to other sites, the major difference is seen in the variety of cooking pots (or rather the lack of it in Stratum XIXb) and the dominance of type CP3.

Although this type is already dominant in Stratum XXa (making up 52% of the assemblage), cooking pots of other types (CP1, CP2, and CP4) make up a large portion of the assemblage. In contrast, in Stratum XIXb, type CP3 makes up 91% of the assemblage.

No trend in the consumption of cooking pots was observed at Yoqne'am, as their appearance is unsteady through time (see table 4.14). However, they make up an extremely large part of the Stratum XXa assemblage (24%), well above the average of 14% of all the sites, their appearance declining afterward.

4.3.3.4. Large Storage Vessels (Graph 4.57, Table 4.15)

Pithoi appear in Yoqne'am only in Strata XXII–XXb, reaching their peak in Stratum XXI, when they make up 41% of the assemblage. In Stratum XXb, they

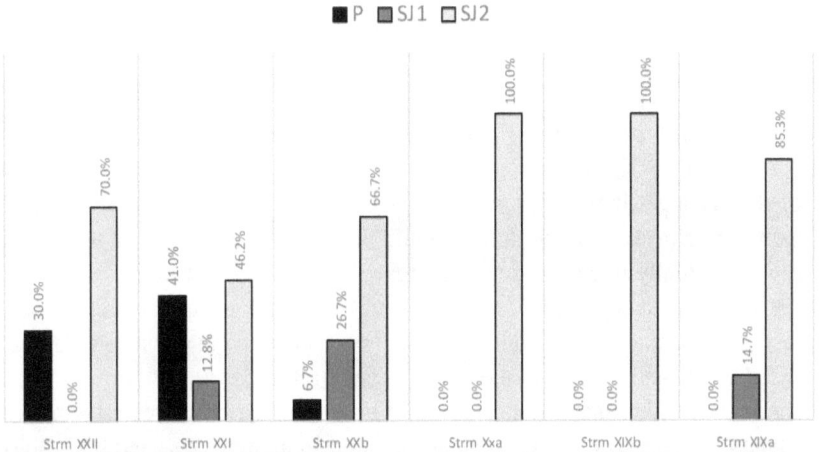

GRAPH 4.57 Yoqne'am, Large Storage Vessels

	P	SJ1	SJ2	Varia[a]	Total	Of stratum
Stratum XXII N =	30.0% 3	0.0% 0	70.0% 7	1	11	14.7%
Stratum 3=XXI N =	41.0% 16	12.8% 5	46.2% 18	14	53	32.3%
Stratum XXb N =	6.7% 1	26.7% 4	66.7% 10	4	19	12.4%
Stratum XXa N =	0.0% 0	0.0% 0	100.0% 11	0	11	7.2%
Stratum XIXb N =	0.0% 0	0.0% 0	100.0% 22	15	37	16.1%

[a]Not in figures (Ben-Ami and Livneh 2005, tables IV.20–21).

TABLE 4.15 Consumption of Large Storage Vessels at Yoqne'am

	Stratum XXII	Stratum XXI	Stratum XXb	Stratum XXa	Stratum XIXb	Stratum XIXa
N =	11	53	19	11	37	42
% of stratum	14.7%	32.3%	12.4%	7.2%	16.1%	16.5%
N (in figures)	10	39	15	11	22	34

represent a small part of the assemblage (7%, only one example), disappearing from the ceramic assemblages afterward.

Storage jars of type SJ1 are not common at Yoqne'am. They appear in small numbers in Strata XXI–XXb. Storage jars of type SJ2 are the most prevalent. They make up the entire assemblages of large storage vessels in Strata XXa and XIXb. Thus, the major difference in consumption of large storage vessels at Yoqne'am is seen between Strata XXb and XXa, when pithoi are no longer consumed and only one type of storage jar is in use. No trend was noted in the overall consumption of large storage vessels within the entire assemblages (see table 4.15).

4.3.3.5. Small Storage Vessels (Graph 4.58, Table 4.16)

No clear changes in the consumption of small storage vessels was remarked at Yoqne'am. However, a few things should be noted. The occurrence of jugs of type J1 gradually increases until they reach their peak in Stratum XXa, when they are the most dominant part of the assemblage (making up 56% of the small storage vessels). The dominance of type J1 was not noted in any assemblage at any other site and is thus unique to Yoqne'am Stratum XXa.

As in most other sites, the most common type of small storage vessels is the jug of type J2. These jugs are the dominant component in Strata XXI and XXb. Juglets are very rare in the Yoqne'am assemblage and only appear in Strata XXII and XXI.[10] Last, jugs of type J4 and flasks are absent from the Yoqne'am assemblage.

As for the overall consumption of small storage vessels at Yoqne'am, in most strata the consumption is between 10% and 15%, the average of all the sites being 14% (see table 4.16). Two strata stand in stark contrast with this trend: Stratum XXb, when the small storage vessels make up 22% of the assemblage, and Stratum XXII, when they make up 48% (!) of the assemblage. These high

---

10. These juglets were identified in the tables accompanying the typological scheme of Yoqne'am (Ben-Ami and Livneh 2005), but, as noted above, it was not possible to integrate them in this discussion, due to their typological division.

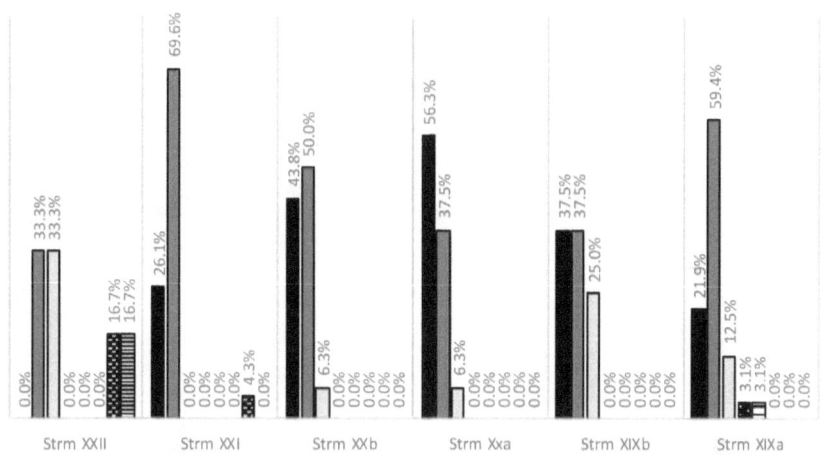

GRAPH 4.58 Yoqne'am, Small Storage Vessels

	J1	J2	J3	J6	FL	JT1	JT2	JT3	Varia[a]	Total	Of stratum
Stratum XXII	0.0%	33.3%	33.3%	0.0%	0.0%	0.0%	16.7%	16.7%	30	36	48.0%
N =	0	2	2	0	0	0	1	1			
Stratum 3=XXI	26.1%	69.6%	0.0%	0.0%	0.0%	0.0%	4.3%	0.0%	0	23	14.0%
N =	6	16	0	0	0	0	1	0			
Stratum XXb	43.8%	50.0%	6.3%	0.0%	0.0%	0.0%	0.0%	0.0%	17	33	21.6%
N =	7	8	1	0	0	0	0	0			
Stratum XXa	56.3%	37.5%	6.3%	0.0%	0.0%	0.0%	0.0%	0.0%	3	19	12.5%
N =	9	6	1	0	0	0	0	0			
Stratum XIXb	37.5%	37.5%	25.0%	0.0%	0.0%	0.0%	0.0%	0.0%	15	23	10.0%
N =	3	3	2	0	0	0	0	0			

TABLE 4.16 Consumption of Small Storage Vessels at Yoqne'am

	Stratum XXII	Stratum XXI	Stratum XXb	Stratum XXa	Stratum XIXb	Stratum XIXa
N =	36	23	33	19	23	37
% of stratum	48.0%	14.0%	21.6%	12.5%	10.0%	14.6%
N (in figures)	6	23	16	16	8	32

percentages are unique to Yoqneʿam and deserve a separate discussion, which is beyond of the scope of this study.

4.3.3.6. Varia (Graph 4.59)

Chocolate-on-White Ware appears at Yoqneʿam from Stratum XXb to Stratum XIXb, making up between 1% and 3% of the assemblages. Eggshell Ware appears only in Stratum XXI of the MBIIc, makng up 1% of the assemblage, but this includes a single sample. Red, White, and Blue Ware, as well as *Charom* Ware, are absent in the Yoqneʿam assemblages. Cypriot Bichrome Ware appears in Strata XXb and XXa, making up 1% and 3%, respectively, replaced by the other imported ware afterward.

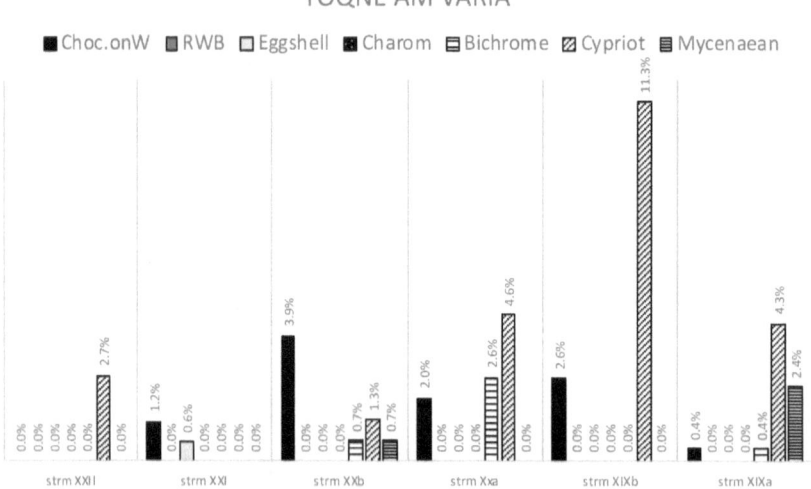

GRAPH 4.59 Yoqneʿam, Miscellaneous Families[a]

	Chocolate on White Ware	Red, White, and Blue Ware	Eggshell |Ware	*Charom* Ware	Cypriot Bichrome Ware	Cypriot Imports	Mycenaean Imports
Stratum XXII	0.0%	0.0%	0.0%	0.0%	0.0%	2.7%	0.0%
N =	0	0	0	0	0	0	0
Stratum 3=XXI	1.2%	0.0%	0.6%	0.0%	0.0%	0.0%	0.0%
N =	2	0	1	0	0	0	0
Stratum XXb	3.9%	0.0%	0.0%	0.0%	0.7%	1.3%	0.7%
N =	6	0	0	0	1	2	1
Stratum XXa	2.0%	0.0%	0.0%	0.0%	2.6%	4.6%	0.0%
N =	3	0	0	0	4	7	0
Stratum XIXb	2.6%	0.0%	0.0%	0.0%	0.0%	11.3%	0.0%
N =	6	0	0	0	0	26	0

[a]Some of the data presented in this table is extracted from Ben-Ami and Livneh 2005, table IV.24.

Mycenaean imports make a very early appearance in Yoqne'am, in Stratum XXb (transitional MBA/LBA), making up 1% of the assemblage (a single sherd). This is one of the earliest examples within all the sites examined. These imports are absent from later assemblages but appear in the last, LBIIb Stratum XIXa. This is a different trend from the one observed in other sites, where Mycenaean imports increase through time, but then declines in the last LBA stratum.

Imported Cypriot vessels appear already in Stratum XXII of the MBIIb, making up 3% of the assemblage. This is the earliest appearance of these imported vessels within all the examined sites. They do not appear in Stratum XXI but appear again from Stratum XXb to Stratum XIXb, reaching their peak in Stratum XIXb of the LBIIa, when they make up 11% of the entire assemblage.

If we overlook the two imported pieces from Stratum XXII, it seems that the major change in the consumption of "special" wares occurs in Stratum XIXb. It is at this time that Cypriot imports make up a large part of the entire assemblage, more than all the kraters or all the small storage vessels. It should be noted that the assemblage of imported wares in Stratum XXa is also relatively large (7% of the entire assemblage), which is more than the percentage of kraters in this stratum's assemblage and almost as high as that of the large storage vessels. However, the large amounts of imported ware in Stratum XIXb make it stand out more than Stratum XXa.

It is interesting to note that in Stratum XIXa (dated to the LBIIb and thus not in the scope of this discussion), local "special" wares practically disappear from the assemblage, this being also when Mycenaean imports appear at the site. In other words, the addition of the imported Aegean ware to the ceramic assemblages influenced the consumption of local "special" ware.

4.3.3.7. Yoqne'am's Assemblages: Summary

Examining the overall trends and the specific types of vessels and their changes over time, it seems that the major changes in consumption in Yoqne'am took place between Strata XXb (transitional MB/LB) and XXa (LBI). At this time, bowls become a more dominant component in the assemblages, while pithoi disappear from them. Changes in consumption of cooking pots were also noted in these two strata—cooking pots of type CP2, which were previously the dominant type at Yoqne'am, are replaced by type CP3 in Stratum XXa.

Regarding kraters of type NK, these become the dominant type of kraters in the transition between Strata XXI and XXb, replacing type CK, which were the dominant kraters prior to that. As for specific types, major changes occurred in types CB1, CK, and HCP, which disappear at this time (in the transition between Strata XXI and XXb).

However, although changes in the consumption of the "special" local and imported wares also occur between Strata XXb and XXa, the most significant change occurs between Stratum XXa and Stratum XIXb, when imported vessels make up a large part of the assemblage.

As at Tel Qashish, the changes in the consumption of pottery at Yoqne'am are not contemporary with the major architectural changes (presented in chapter 3) that took place between Stratum XXa and Stratum XIXb, which is, interestingly, consistent with the appearance of the imported Aegean ware at the site.

4.3.4. Beth-Shean

As noted above, the material used here from Beth-Shean derives from only one report—that of the renewed excavations (Mazar and Mullins 2007). Other reports of the renewed excavations (Mazar 2006, Panitz-Cohen and Mazar 2009) and the University Museum Excavations' (UME) publication (James and McGovern 1993) include only LBIIb material, which is beyond the scope of this discussion.

The Beth-Shean report also includes a detailed statistical analysis of the distribution of types within the different strata. As noted above, the statistical analysis I carried out included counting the samples within the published plates and subtracting these from the tables, showing the sum of all vessels found in the strata. There are two sets of tables in the report, one compiling all the vessels found in the different strata, by families (Maeir 2007, table 4.1; Mullins 2007, table 5.1) and the second compiling the different types. Maeir's types tables do not always conform to those of the different families. For example, in Maier 2007, table 4.1, he lists 190 bowls in Stratum R-5, while in table 4.2, which presents the distribution of bowls by strata, he lists a total of 169 bowls from this stratum. It should be noted that such a problem was not noted in Mullins's tables. In addition, all the statistical tables (of both Maeir and Mullins) do not show the stratigraphic context of the finds, apart from the stratum, contrasting with the statistical analysis published by the Tel Qashish and Yoqne'am excavations.

Another problem encountered was the fact that the published data are insignificant in number compared to the unpublished data. For example, there are a total of 1,884 bowls in Stratum R-1b, but only seventy-eight of them were illustrated in the plates, this being the case for every family of vessels in every stratum.[11] This posed a dilemma—should the unpublished data be used in the analysis of the different types or the families, or should they be disregarded

---

11. This problem is not unique to Beth-Shean and is the common method of publishing representative ceramic assemblages of most sites. The unique feature in the publication of Beth-Shean is

since the exact location of the sherds cannot be established (fills or floors)? Note also the various challenges regarding the "special" wares presented below.

It was decided to use the statistical analysis with this caveat, and only when discussing changes in consumption of the different families and not the different types as done in the other sites (Tel Qashish and Yoqne'am). The problem this might create was taken into consideration (no exact stratigraphic context and an abundance of unpublished data making the published data, at times, almost insignificant). However, the advantages overtake the disadvantages.

Since only the statistical data presented in the Beth-Shean publication was used for discussing the overall consumption of the different families, not the changes of consumption of the different types, the study was based on the general tables (Maeir 2007, table 4.1; Mullins 2007, table 5.1) and not the type-distribution tables. The fact that the stratigraphic context of the finds could not be examined has limited the conclusions drawn on general consumption trends.

4.3.4.1. Bowls (Graph 4.60, Table 4.17)

The peak appearance of shallow bowls at Beth-Shean was identified in Stratum R-3, where they make up about 18% of the assemblage of rounded bowls and 15% of all bowls. The major difference is seen between Stratum R-3 of the MBII and Stratum R-2 of the LBIa (when they make up about 9% of the assemblage of rounded bowls and 6% of all bowls).

Deep bowls are absent in the assemblages of Strata R-5 (MBII), R-2 (LBIa), and R-1a (LBIIa). Thus, the contribution of their general presence at the site is minimal.

Hemispherical bowls appear only in the LBA Strata R-1b and VII (making up 4% and 6%, respectively, of all the bowls' assemblage of these strata), indicating these bowls are common, in the LBA, at Beth-Shean.

Carinated bowls of type CB1 appear only in Strata R-4 and R-3, making up 11% and 14% of the assemblage of carinated bowls and 6% and 2% of all bowls, respectively. Carinated bowls of type CB2 are much more prevalent at the site. They start appearing in Stratum R-5 and reach their peak in Stratum R-4 (making up 56% of the carinated bowls and 29% of all bowls). A major decline in their appearance was noted in the following Stratum R-3, when they make up 14% of the assemblage of carinated bowls and 2% of all bowls. After this, they disappear from the assemblage.[12]

---

that the authors noted the quantity of pottery sherds not depicted in the illustrations and also noted to which family these sherds belonged.

12. Apart from a single example found in Stratum R-1b, though this might be a stray piece.

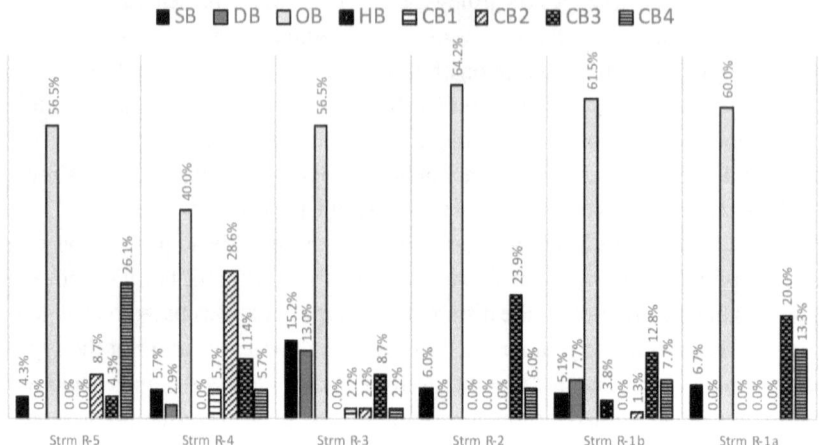

GRAPH 4.60 Beth Shean, Bowls

	SB	DB	OB	HB	CB1	CB2	CB3	CB4	Varia[a]	Total	Of stratum
Stratum R-5	4.3%	0.0%	56.5%	0.0%	0.0%	8.7%	4.3%	26.1%	167	190	42.8%
N =	1	0	13	0	0	2	1	6			
Stratum R-4	5.7%	2.9%	40.0%	0.0%	5.7%	28.6%	11.4%	5.7%	389	424	37.5%
N =	2	1	14	0	2	10	4	2			
Stratum R-3	15.2%	13.0%	56.5%	0.0%	2.2%	2.2%	8.7%	2.2%	528	574	49.9%
N =	7	6	26	0	1	1	4	1			
Stratum R-2	6.0%	0.0%	64.2%	0.0%	0.0%	0.0%	23.9%	6.0%	1215	1282	63.4%
N =	4	0	43	0	0	0	16	4			
Stratum R-1b	5.1%	7.7%	61.5%	3.8%	0.0%	1.3%	12.8%	7.7%	1806	1884	69.7%
N =	4	6	48	3	0	1	10	6			
Stratum R-1a	6.7%	0.0%	60.0%	0.0%	0.0%	0.0%	20.0%	13.3%	264	279	65.5%
N =	1	0	9	0	0	0	3	2			

[a]Not in figures (Maeir 2007, table 4.1; Mullins 2007, table 5.1).

TABLE 4.17 Consumption of Bowls at Beth Shean

	Stratum R-5	Stratum R-4	Stratum R-3	Stratum R-2	Stratum R-1b	Stratum R-1a
N =	190	424	574	1282	1884	279
% of stratum	42.8%	37.5%	49.9%	63.4%	69.7%	65.5%
N (in figures)	23	35	46	67	78	15

Shallow carinated bowls (CB3) appear in all strata at Beth-Shean, and their occurrence reaches its peak in Stratum R-2 (LBIa), when they make up 80% of the carinated bowls and 24% of all bowls. The major difference in their distribution is seen between Strata R-4 and R-3.

The major difference in the distribution of the deep carinated bowls (CB4) occurs between Stratum R-5 (when they make up 67% of the carinated bowls and 26% of all bowls) and Stratum R-4 (when the bowls only make up 11% of the carinated bowls and 6% of all bowls of the ceramic assemblages of this stratum). Following Stratum R-4, there is a clear incline in the bowls' appearance until Stratum R-1a, when they make up 13% of the bowls (and 40% of the carinated bowls). It seems that, although these bowls are more common in LBA strata at most sites, at Beth-Shean they are also very common in the MBA.

The consumption of bowls at Beth-Shean, in general, reflects the two trends observed in the other sites: Bowls are the most dominant component in all the assemblages, making up at least 40% of the assemblage (38% in Stratum R-4), like at the sites of Hazor and Tell Arqa; and similarly to Hazor, and in contrast with Tell Arqa, the consumption of bowls intensifies over time, peaking in Stratum R-1b, when they make up 70% (!) of the assemblage, well above the average 42% of all sites (see table 4.17).

4.3.4.2. Kraters (Graph 4.61, Table 4.18)

Only closed kraters of type CK were found in Beth-Shean. These reach their peak in Stratum R-4, making up 43% of the krater assemblage. Their distribution sharply declines in Stratum R-3, when they make up only 10% of the krater assemblage, after which they completely disappear from the ceramic assemblage of Beth-Shean.

Kraters of type NKR are very common in Stratum R-5 (making up 43% of the krater assemblage), their distribution subsequently declining from Stratum R-3 onward until they completely disappear in Stratum R-1b. Only one example of NKY-type kraters was found in Beth-Shean, in Stratum R-3 (dated to the MBA). Kraters of type NK appear in all strata at Beth-Shean, though they are less prevalent in Strata R-5–R-3 and become a dominant part of the assemblages starting in Stratum R-2 (when they make up 92% of the kraters' assemblage) up to Strata R-1b and R-1a.

Bowl-like kraters (K1) appear only in the MBA Strata R-5–R-3. Their distribution inclines (14% in Stratum R-5, 29% in R-4 and 31% in R-3), disappearing from the ceramic assemblages afterward. Pithos-like kraters (K2) appear only in LBIIb contexts and are therefore beyond the scope of this discussion.

Overall, the krater assemblages from Beth-Shean are more varied in the MBA Strata R-5–R-3, when they mainly comprise types CK, NK, NKR, and K1. In the LBIb and LBIIa strata, kraters of type NK make up 100% of the krater assemblage. Thus, the main difference in consumption of kraters in Beth-Shean is seen between Strata R-3 and R-2.

The consumption of kraters at Beth-Shean reaches its peak in Strata R-4 and R-3, when they make up 11% of the assemblages, declining after this (see table

BETH-SHEAN KRATERS

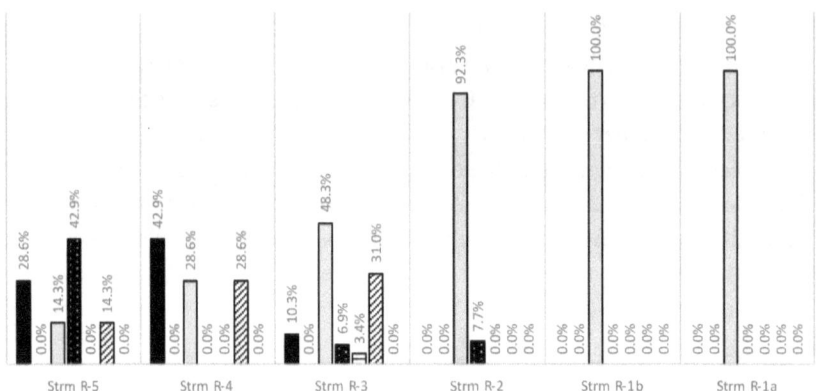

GRAPH 4.61 Beth Shean, Kraters

	CK	CKR	NK	NKR	NKY	K1	K2	Varia[a]	Total	Of stratum
Stratum R-5 N =	28.6% 2	0.0% 0	14.3% 1	42.9% 3	0.0% 0	14.3% 1	0.0% 0	36	43	9.7%
Stratum R-4 N =	42.9% 6	0.0% 0	28.6% 4	0.0% 0	0.0% 0	28.6% 4	0.0% 0	115	129	11.4%
Stratum R-3 N =	10.3% 3	0.0% 0	48.3% 14	6.9% 2	3.4% 1	31.0% 9	0.0% 0	102	131	11.4%
Stratum R-2 N =	0.0% 0	0.0% 0	92.3% 12	7.7% 1	0.0% 0	0.0% 0	0.0% 0	121	134	6.6%
Stratum R-1b N =	0.0% 0	0.0% 0	100.0% 11	0.0% 0	0.0% 0	0.0% 0	0.0% 0	97	108	4.0%
Stratum R-1a N =	0.0% 0	0.0% 0	100.0% 6	0.0% 0	0.0% 0	0.0% 0	0.0% 0	7	13	3.1%

[a]Not in figures (Maeir 2007, table 4.1; Mullins 2007, table 5.1).

TABLE 4.18 Consumption of Kraters at Beth Shean

	Stratum R-5	Stratum R-4	Stratum R-3	Stratum R-2	Stratum R-1b	Stratum R-1a
N =	43	129	131	134	108	13
% of stratum	9.7%	11.4%	11.4%	6.6%	4.0%	3.1%
N (in figures)	7	14	29	13	11	6

4.18). Kraters are least common in Strata R-1b and R-1a, when they make up 4% and 3%, respectively, of the assemblages, much lower than the average 8% of all sites.

4.3.4.3. Cooking Pots (Graph 4.62, Table 4.19)

Handmade cooking pots of type UCP were found in all three MBA strata. They make up a relatively large part of the Stratum R-5 assemblage (67% of the cooking pots) compared to the other two strata (13% in Stratum R-4 and 11% in Stratum R-3).

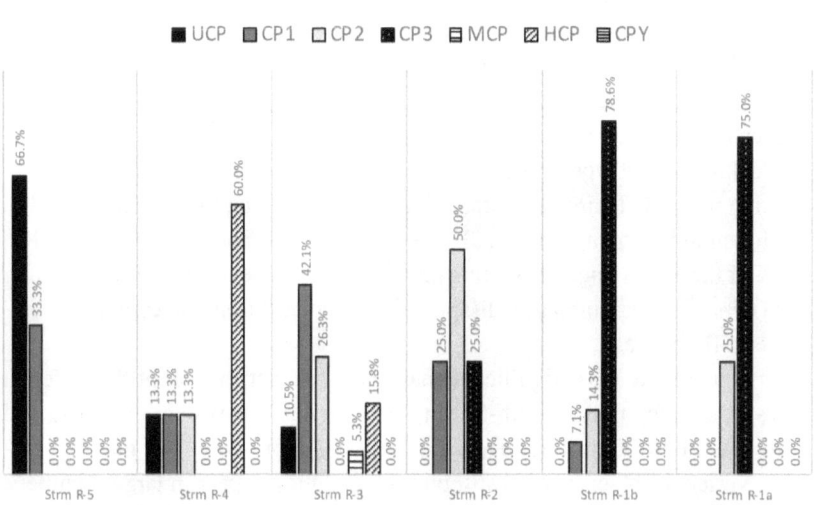

GRAPH 4.62 Beth Shean, Cooking Pots

	UCP	CP1	CP2	CP3	MCP	HCP	CPY	Varia[a]	Total	Of stratum
Stratum R-5 N =	66.7% 2	33.3% 1	0.0% 0	0.0% 0	0.0% 0	0.0% 0	0.0% 0	45	48	10.8%
Stratum R-4 N =	13.3% 2	13.3% 2	13.3% 2	0.0% 0	0.0% 0	60.0% 9	0.0% 0	118	133	11.8%
Stratum R-3 N =	10.5% 2	42.1% 8	26.3% 5	0.0% 0	5.3% 1	15.8% 3	0.0% 0	110	129	11.2%
Stratum R-2 N =	0.0% 0	25.0% 2	50.0% 4	25.0% 2	0.0% 0	0.0% 0	0.0% 0	163	171	8.5%
Stratum R-1b N =	0.0% 0	7.1% 1	14.3% 2	78.6% 11	0.0% 0	0.0% 0	0.0% 0	198	212	7.8%
Stratum R-1a N =	0.0% 0	0.0% 0	25.0% 1	75.0% 3	0.0% 0	0.0% 0	0.0% 0	24	28	6.6%

[a]Not in figures (Maeir 2007, table 4.1; Mullins 2007, table 5.1).

TABLE 4.19 Consumption of Cooking Pots at Beth Shean

	Stratum R-5	Stratum R-4	Stratum R-3	Stratum R-2	Stratum R-1b	Stratum R-1a
N =	48	133	129	171	212	28
% of stratum	10.8%	11.8%	11.2%	8.5%	7.8%	6.6%
N (in figures)	3	15	19	8	14	4

Wheel-made cooking pots of type CP1 appear in all strata at Beth-Shean, except Stratum R-1a. They are most common in Stratum R-3 (when they make up 42% of the assemblage), their occurrence declining in the subsequent Strata R-2 and R-1b (25% and 7% respectively). Cooking pots of type CP2 appear in all strata beginning in Stratum R-4. Their number reaches their peak in Stratum R-2, amounting to 50% of the assemblage.

Cooking pots of type CP3 appear in Strata R-2 to R-1a. They make up the dominant part of the Strata R-1b and R-1a assemblages (at least 75% in each), as seen also in other sites.

Cooking pots of type CP4 are absent in the Beth-Shean assemblage. Miniature cooking pots (MCP) are very rare, a single example being found in Stratum R-3.

Holemouth cooking pots (HCP) are the most common type in Stratum R-4 (60% of the assemblage of cooking pots). Their occurrence declines in Stratum R-3 (16% of the assemblage), disappearing afterward from the ceramic assemblage of Beth-Shean.

In general, the most significant changes in the distribution of the different types of cooking pots at Beth-Shean seems to occur between Strata R-2 and R-1b. Before Stratum R-1b, even if one type is more dominant than the others, a variety of other types is still present, and they appear in larger numbers. In contrast, in Strata R-1b and R-1a, cooking pots of type CP3 are dominant, and cooking pots of other types appear in very small numbers, if at all.

As for the general consumption of cooking pots at Beth-Shean, this is mostly constant throughout the strata within each period (MBA or LBA), and no stark change is seen between these periods (see table 4.19). Cooking pots appear in almost the same percentages in the MBA Strata R-5–R-3 (12%–11%), followed by a decline in the consumption of cooking pots in the LBA Strata R-2–R-1a when they make up between 7% and 9%.

4.3.4.4. Large Storage Vessels (Graph 4.63, Table 4.20)

In contrast to most other sites, pithoi appear in every stratum at Beth-Shean, as in Hazor. However, they are much more common in the earlier MBA Strata

BETH-SHEAN LARGE STORAGE VESSELS

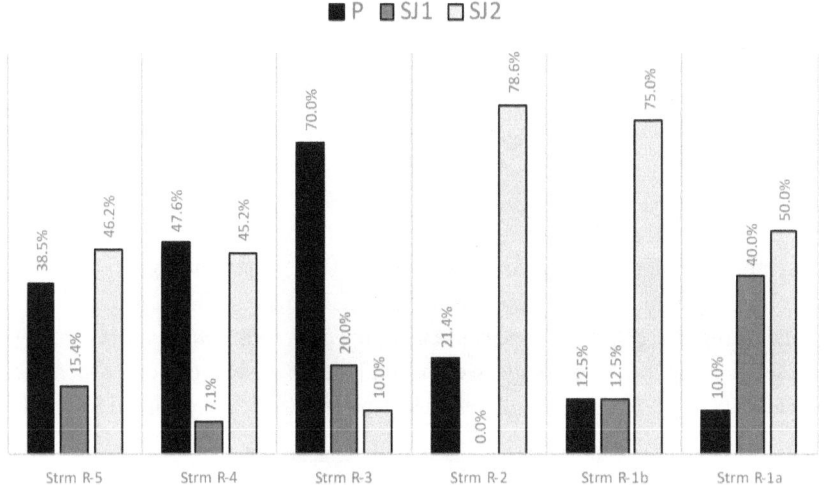

GRAPH 4.63 Beth Shean, Large Storage Vessels

	P	SJ1	SJ2	Varia[a]	Total	Of stratum
Stratum R-5	38.5%	15.4%	46.2%	111	124	27.9%
N =	5	2	6			
Stratum R-4	47.6%	7.1%	45.2%	304	346	30.6%
N =	20	3	19			
Stratum R-3	70.0%	20.0%	10.0%	205	225	19.5%
N =	14	4	2			
Stratum R-2	21.4%	0.0%	78.6%	83	97	4.8%
N =	3	0	11			
Stratum R-1b	12.5%	12.5%	75.0%	133	149	5.5%
N =	2	2	12			
Stratum R-1a	10.0%	40.0%	50.0%	23	33	7.7%
N =	1	4	5			

[a]Not in figures (Maeir 2007, table 4.1; Mullins 2007, table 5.1).

R–5–R-3, especially in Stratum R-3, when they make up 70% of the assemblages. Consequently, the consumption of storage jars, in direct opposite relation to the consumption of pithoi in these periods, is not as high in these strata as in the subsequent strata.

As in other sites, storage jars of type SJ2 are more common than those of type SJ1. This is especially prominent in Strata R-2 and R-1b, when they make up 79% and 75% of the assemblages, respectively.

Thus, the major differences in consumption of large storage vessels at Beth-Shean can be identified between Strata R-3 and R-2. At this time, the consumption of pithoi declines and, accordingly, storage jars become a larger part of the

TABLE 4.20 Consumption of Large Storage Vessels at Beth Shean

	Stratum R-5	Stratum R-4	Stratum R-3	Stratum R-2	Stratum R-1b	Stratum R-1a
N =	124	346	225	97	149	33
% of stratum	27.9%	30.6%	19.5%	4.8%	5.5%	7.7%
N (in figures)	13	42	20	14	16	10

assemblages. Since storage jars of type SJ2 are the most common type of storage jars, these make the greater part of the assemblages. The consumption of large storage vessels at Beth-Shean reaches its peak in Stratum R-4, when they make up 31% of the assemblage, well beyond the 15% average in other sites (see table 4.20). A stark decline follows in Stratum R-2, when they amount to only 5% of the assemblage.

4.3.4.5. Small Storage Vessels (Graph 4.64, Table 4.21)

The the assemblage of small storage vessels also shows a major change between the MBA and the LBA strata. In the MBA they make up 6%–9% of the entire assemblage, while in the LBA their consumption is almost doubled, amounting to 12%–17% of the assemblage (see table 4.21). However, since most of these vessels have not been published, no clear trends were noted. Nonetheless, some issues could still be addressed.[13]

First, as in other sites, jugs of type J2 are the most common type of jugs. Second, the occurrence of jugs of type J3 declines in time. Third, although juglets are not common in the Beth-Shean assemblages, they appear in every stratum. They make up at least 20% of the assemblage of small storage vessels, except in Stratum R-1b. Finally, flasks are present only in Stratum R-1a, as in Yoqne'am and Tell Arqa.

4.3.4.6. Varia (Graph 4.65)

The statistical tables of Beth-Shean include no data on the "special" local ware, only the imported ware. In the text, the authors sometimes specify how many sherds of a specific family were found, but not in all cases. For example, Maeir noted that seven sherds of the Chocolate-on-White Ware were retrieved from Stratum R-5, and that they become "progressively more common in strata R-4

---

13. It should be noted that Stratum R-5 was not taken into consideration, since it includes only three vessels and thus may create a biased analysis.

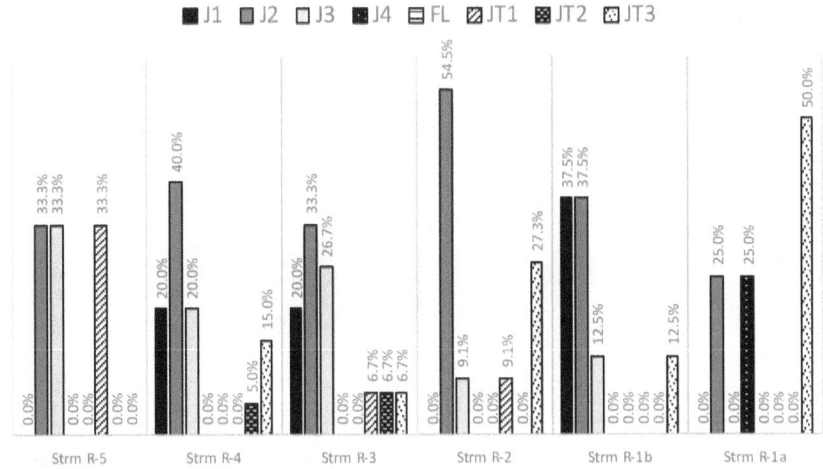

GRAPH 4.64 Beth Shean, Small Storage Vessels

	J1	J2	J3	J6	FL	JT1	JT2	JT3	Varia[a]	Total	Of stratum
Stratum R-5	0.0%	33.3%	33.3%	0.0%	0.0%	33.3%	0.0%	0.0%	35	38	8.6%
N =	0	1	1	0	0	1	0	0			
Stratum R-4	20.0%	40.0%	20.0%	0.0%	0.0%	0.0%	5.0%	15.0%	73	93	8.2%
N =	4	8	4	0	0	0	1	3			
Stratum R-3	20.0%	33.3%	26.7%	0.0%	0.0%	6.7%	6.7%	6.7%	58	73	6.3%
N =	3	5	4	0	0	1	1	1			
Stratum R-2	0.0%	54.5%	9.1%	0.0%	0.0%	9.1%	0.0%	27.3%	307	318	15.7%
N =	0	6	1	0	0	1	0	3			
Stratum R-1b	37.5%	37.5%	12.5%	0.0%	0.0%	0.0%	0.0%	12.5%	323	331	12.2%
N =	3	3	1	0	0	0	0	1			
Stratum R-1a	0.0%	25.0%	0.0%	25.0%	0.0%	0.0%	0.0%	50.0%	68	72	16.9%
N =	0	1	0	1	0	0	0	2			

[a]Not in figures (Maeir 2007, table 4.1; Mullins 2007, table 5.1).

TABLE 4.21 Consumption of Bowls at Beth Shean

	Stratum R-5	Stratum R-4	Stratum R-3	Stratum R-2	Stratum R-1b	Stratum R-1a
N =	38	93	73	318	331	72
% of stratum	8.6%	8.2%	6.3%	15.7%	12.2%	16.9%
N (in figures)	3	20	15	11	8	4

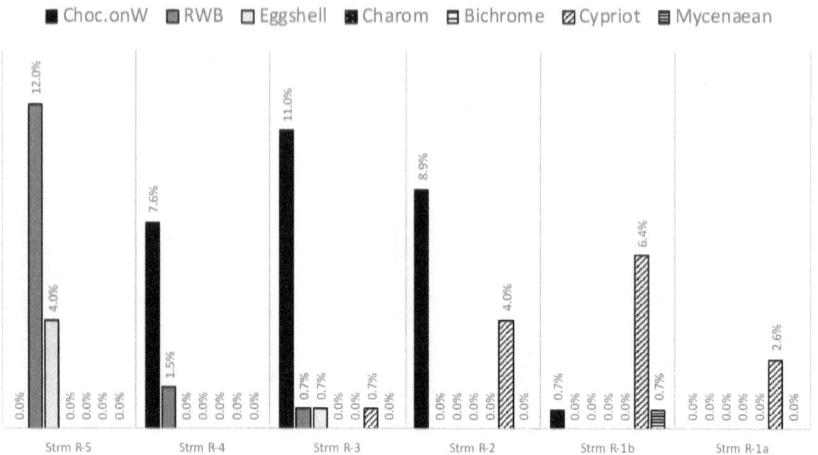

GRAPH 4.65 Beth Shean, Miscellaneous Families

	Chocolate on White Ware[a]		Red, White, and Blue Ware		Eggshell Ware		Charom Ware	Cypriot Bichrome Ware	Cypriot Imports		Mycenaean Imports	
Stratum R-5	0.0%		12.0%	0.7%	4.0%	0.2%	0.0%	0.0%	0.0%		0.0%	
N =	0		3		1		0	0	0		0	
Stratum R-4	7.6%	0.4%	1.5%	0.1%	0.0%		0.0%	0.0%	0.0%		0.0%	
N =	5		1		0		0	0	0		0	
Stratum R-3	11.0%	0.4%	0.7%	0.1%	0.7%	0.1%	0.0%	0.0%	0.7%	0.1%	0.0%	
N =	15		1		1		0	0	1		0	
Stratum R-2	8.9%	0.5%	0.0%		0.0%		0.0%	0.0%	4.0%	0.5%	0.0%	
N =	11		0		0		0	0	10		0	
Stratum R-1b	0.7%	0.04%	0.0%		0.0%		0.0%	0.0%	6.4%	0.7%	0.7%	0.04%
N =	1		0		0		0	0	18		1	
Stratum R-1a	0.0%		0.0%		0.0%		0.0%	0.0%	2.6%	0.2%	0.0%	
N =	0		0		0		0	0	1		0	

[a]Percentages in the right column represent the relative appearance in the entire assemblage, including the data included only in tables; percentages on the left column represent the relative appearance out of the assemblages depicted in the figures, presented here in the graph (discussion appears in text).

and R-3," but he does not mention how many were found in those strata (2007, 287–88). This turned the statistical analysis into quite a difficult task. While the enormous quantity of data included in this publication is better not being disregarded, the lack of information regarding the "special" wares would distort part of the picture. However, since imported wares were only noted in the LBA strata and were incorporated in the statistical analysis of those strata (Mullins 2007, table 5.1), and that the number of sherds of "special" wares is very small compared to the other families, I decided that the statistical data should be used in the present study. However, the percentages presented in graph 4.65 of this study derive from the assemblages depicted in the plates and not from the entire assemblages, as was done in other sites. The reason for this choice is that, if the latter had been applied, the representation of the "special" and imported wares would have become insignificant, most of them making up less than 0.5% of the assemblage (these percentages were added to the table accompanying the graph in a separate column).

Chocolate-on-White Ware appears in Beth-Shean from Stratum R-5 onward, according to the excavators (Maeir 2007, 287–88, not shown in figures) and become more common between Strata R-4 and R-2, practically disappearing afterward. Red, White, and Blue Ware appears in all MBA strata, but they are most common in Stratum R-5.

Eggshell Ware is very rare in the Beth-Shean assemblage (only two were depicted in the figures, in Strata R-5 and R-3), and these are not present in Maier's discussion. The Cypriot Bichrome Ware is absent in the Beth-Shean assemblages. The excavators suggest that this can probably be explained by the large amount of Chocolate-on-White Ware, which, as they suggest, met the needs that both families fulfilled. Mycenaean Ware is also very rare—a single example was unearthed in Stratum R-1b.

Imported Cypriot vessels first appear in Stratum R-3 (a single example) and become more common in Strata R-2 and R-1b. In Stratum R-1b, these are the most prevalent within the "special" and imported wares. However, it is interesting to note that although imported Aegean vessels are very rare in the LBIIa at Beth-Shean, they were very common in the UME LBIIb strata (Strata VIII–VII), outnumbering the Egyptian-style vessels (James and McGovern 1993, 238). However, imported Aegean ware was very rare in the renewed excavations' LBIIb strata (Mazar 2011, 173).

4.3.4.7. Beth-Shean's Assemblages: Summary

The major changes in consumption of pottery vessels at Beth-Shean seem to have occurred between Stratum R-3 and R-2. This is not only true for the general consumption trends but also for specific types.

These general trends were observed in the consumption of kraters and large storage vessels. The change within the kraters is reflected in many types disappearing after Stratum R-3, while kraters of type NK becoming the dominant component of the assemblage. In Strata R-1b and R-1a, NK type kraters become the sole type in the assemblages. As for large storage vessels, the consumption of pithoi declines dramatically between Strata R-3 and R-2, storage jars becoming, consequently, much more common from Stratum R-2 onward.

Several of the specific types disappear following Stratum R-3: CB1, CB2, CK, K1, UCP, and HCP. Significant changes in the consumption of cooking pots were noted between Stratum R-2 and R-1b, when the cooking pots of type CP3 become the dominant component in the assemblages, with no variation being noted within the assemblages.

As already stated above, this lack of variation from Strata R-2 to R-1b does not entirely fit with the architectural changes identified at the site between these strata (based on a new city plan). However, changes were also noted between Strata R-3 and R-2 in the nature of the area, changing from a residential to a cultic area.

4.3.5. Tell Arqa

The assemblage of Tell Arqa is the smallest assemblage examined and does not include statistical data. Therefore, until a comprehensive publication of the assemblages is published, the conclusions on this site are only tentative (see also the opening remarks to this chapter).[14]

4.3.5.1. Bowls (Graph 4.66, Table 4.22)

In contrast to the other sites, in Tell Arqa the shallow bowls make up very small percentages of the MBA assemblage, their appearance increasing in the LBA when they make up at least 30% of the rounded bowl assemblages (and at least 17% of all bowls) in Strata 12a and 11.

Deep bowls appear in Tell Arqa only in Strata 13 (MB) and 12c–12b (LBI), contrasting, again, with other sites. Their presence increases in the assemblage of rounded bowls from Stratum 13 (making up 2% of all bowls) to Strata 12c–b (making up 8% of all bowls).

Hemispherical bowls appear only in Stratum 13 when they make up 2% of all bowls found in this stratum. The appearance of carinated bowls at Tell Arqa reflects a similar trend to that observed in most of the southern Levantine sites discussed above. Carinated bowls of type CB1 appear only in Strata 13–12c–b, their appearance declining between these two strata, disappearing from the assemblages of Tell Arqa afterward. Carinated bowls of type CB2 also appear mainly in Strata 13–12c–b, though two examples were also found in Stratum 12a. Their appearance declines from Stratum 13 to Strata 12c–b. Bowls of type CB3 are more common in Stratum 12c–b, though they are still uncommon at Tell Arqa. A single example of this type was found in Stratum 11. Bowls of type CB4 appear in all strata beginning in Stratum 12c–b. They appear in relatively large amounts in Strata 12c–b and 11 (only one example in Stratum 12a). Thus,

---

14. Since no statistical data are published from Tell Arqa, and since the publications of the site are considered to be "preliminary," it should be emphasized that all conclusions of this research are based on the published material alone and are therefore a rough estimation of occurrences in assemblages.

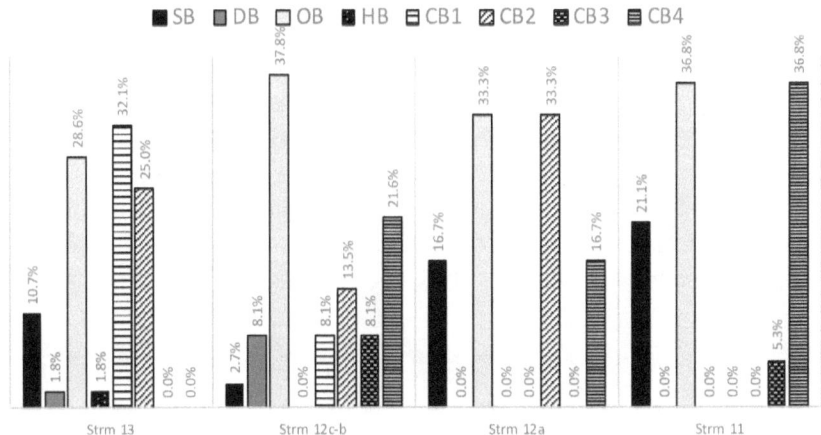

GRAPH 4.66 Tel Arqa, Bowls

	SB	DB	OB	HB	CB1	CB2	CB3	CB4	Varia	Total	Of stratum
Stratum 13 N =	10.7% 6	1.8% 1	28.6% 16	1.8% 1	32.1% 18	25.0% 14	0.0% 0	0.0% 0	0	56	50.9%
Stratum 12c-b N =	2.7% 1 a	8.1% 3	37.8% 14	0.0% 0	8.1% 3	13.5% 5	8.1% 3	21.6% 8	9	46	45.1%
Stratum 12a N =	16.7% 1	0.0% 0	33.3% 2	0.0% 0	0.0% 0	33.3% 2	0.0% 0	16.7% 1	2	8	42.1%
Stratum 11 N =	21.1% 4	0.0% 0	36.8% 7	0.0% 0	0.0% 0	0.0% 0	5.3% 1	36.8% 7	3	22	29.3%

TABLE 4.22 Consumption of Bowls at Tel Arqa

	Stratum 13	Stratum 12c-b	Stratum 12a	Stratum 11
N =	56	46	8	22
% of stratum	50.9%	45.1%	42.1%	29.3%

the first appearance of these bowls (CB4), in Stratum 12c–b, marks the major change in consumption of carinated bowls.

As in all other sites, bowls are the most dominant component in all assemblages at Tell Arqa. This trend is similar to that noticed at Hazor and Beth-Shean. However, in contrast to all the other sites, the consumption of bowls gradually declines at Tell Arqa, reaching only 29% in Stratum 11 (well below the 42% average of other sites), while at the other sites the consumption of bowls intensifies toward the end of the LBA (see table 4.22).

4.3.5.2. Kraters (Graph 4.67, Table 4.23)

Closed kraters are absent in the ceramic assemblages of Tell Arqa, as are kraters of type NKY and K2. Kraters of type NKR are the most common kraters in Stratum 13, making up 60% of the assemblage, disappearing afterward. Two examples of kraters of type K1 were identified in Strata 12c–b. From Stratum 12a onward, kraters of type NK make up the entire krater assemblages.

Although the Tell Arqa assemblage is very small and unvaried, it still validates the trend identified at the other examined sites—that is, the LBA assemblages are dominated by kraters of type NK.

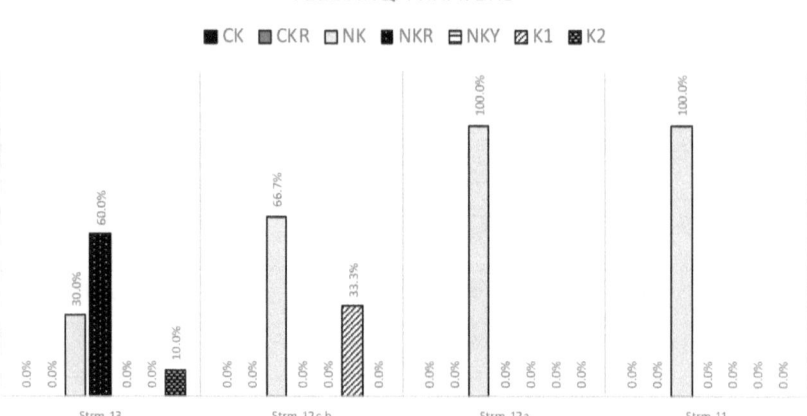

GRAPH 4.67 Tel Arqa, Kraters

	CK	CKR	NK	NKR	NKY	K1	K2	Total	Of stratum
Stratum 13	0.0%	0.0%	30.0%	60.0%	0.0%	0.0%	10.0%	10	9.1%
N =	0	0	3	6	0	0	1		
Stratum 12c-b	0.0%	0.0%	66.7%	0.0%	0.0%	33.3%	0.0%	6	5.9%
N =	0	0	4	0	0	2	0		
Stratum 12a	0.0%	0.0%	100.0%	0.0%	0.0%	0.0%	0.0%	1	5.3%
N =	0	0	1	0	0	0	0		
Stratum 11	0.0%	0.0%	100.0%	0.0%	0.0%	0.0%	0.0%	8	10.7%
N =	0	0	8	0	0	0	0		

TABLE 4.23 Consumption of Kraters at Tel Arqa

	Stratum 13	Stratum 12c-b	Stratum 12a	Stratum 11
N =	10	6	1	8
% of stratum	9.1%	5.9%	5.3%	10.7%

A difference in consumption of kraters at Tell Arqa was noted between Stratum 12a and 11 when, after a gradual decline in their consumption, kraters become a large component of the assemblage (see table 4.23). This is surprising since at the other sites kraters do not make up a large part of the assemblage and especially not at the end of the LBA. The major difference in consumption is seen, nonetheless, between Strata 12c–b and 12a, due to the dominance of type NK in the latter.

4.3.5.3. Cooking Pots (Graph 4.68, Table 4.24)

The discussion of the assemblage of cooking pots from Tell Arqa is quite difficult due to its small size. Only two examples of cooking pots belonging to the types defined here were found in both Strata 13 and 12a. Thus, any analysis regarding these strata, compared to the other strata or to corresponding strata at other sites, would be biased (see table 4.24). However, a few issues could be

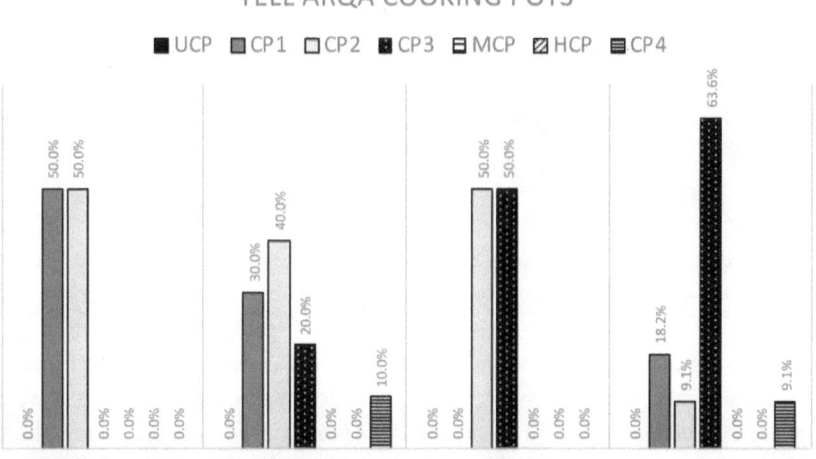

GRAPH 4.68 Tel Arqa, Cooking Pots

	UCP	CP1	CP2	CP3	MCP	HCP	CPY	Varia	Total	Of stratum
Stratum 13	0.0%	50.0%	50.0%	0.0%	0.0%	0.0%	0.0%	4	6	5.5%
N =	0	1	1	0	0	0	0			
Stratum 12c-b	0.0%	30.0%	40.0%	20.0%	0.0%	0.0%	10.0%	0	10	9.8%
N =	0	3	4	2	0	0	1			
Stratum 12a	0.0%	0.0%	50.0%	50.0%	0.0%	0.0%	0.0%	0	1	5.3%
N =	0	0	1	1	0	0	0			
Stratum 11	0.0%	18.2%	9.1%	63.6%	0.0%	0.0%	9.1%	0	11	14.7%
N =	0	2	1	7	0	0	1			

TABLE 4.24 Consumption of Cooking Pots at Tel Arqa

	Stratum 13	Stratum 12c–b	Stratum 12a	Stratum 11
N =	6	10	2	11
% of stratum	5.5%	9.8%	10.5%	14.7%

noted. First, upright cooking pots (UCP), miniature cooking pots (MCP), and holemouth cooking pots (HCP) are absent in the Tell Arqa assemblage. Second, the consumption of cooking pots at Tell Arqa intensifies in Strata 12c–b, and it is only after Stratum 13 that cooking pots of type CP3 appear.

4.3.5.4. Large Storage Vessels (Graph 4.69, Table 4.25)

Pithoi appear in all strata at Tell Arqa. It is interesting to note, once again, that the pithoi that appear in Strata 13–11 are similar, if not identical, to those found at Hazor in Strata 1b–1a.

Although the Tell Arqa assemblage is very small, a discrepancy line can still be drawn between Strata 12a and 11, when the consumption of the storage vessels that are not pithoi, in general, and of storage jars that are not similar to those of the southern Levantine types, in particular, increases.

4.3.5.5. Small Storage Vessels (Graph 4.70)

The assemblage of small storage vessels at Tell Arqa is not very diverse. However, the major changes occur between Strata 12c–b and 12a, the latter having no small storage vessels. Small storage vessels also make up a large part of the entire assemblage in Strata 13 and 12c–b (21% and 18% respectively, the highest percentage compared to those in the assemblages of all the other sites, and well above the average of 14% in all sites, and see table 4.25). The total consumption of small storage vessels at Tell Arqa declines in Stratum 11 (when they make up only 5% of the entire assemblage of the stratum).

Jugs of type J2 are the most common type of jugs, similarly to most other sites. They are the dominant type of small storage vessel in Stratum 12c–b (making up 44% of the small storage vessel assemblage). Juglets are also more common in Strata 13 and 12c–b, making up 39% of the assemblage of small storage vessels in both earlier strata. In contrast, no juglets were found either in Strata 12a or 11.

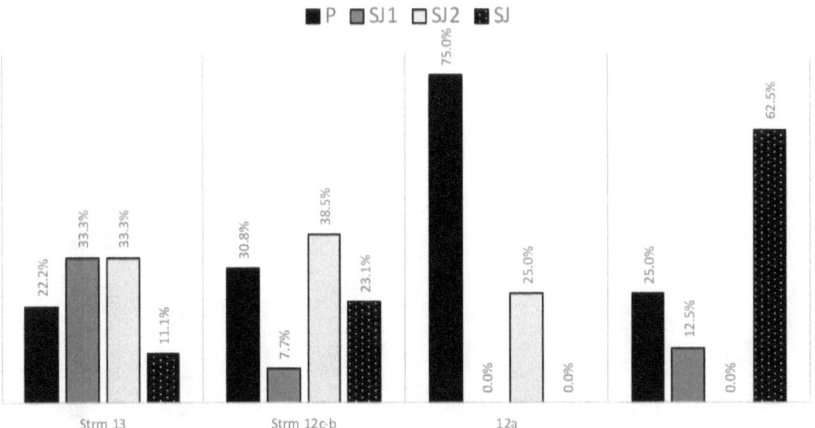

GRAPH 4.69 Tel Arqa, Large Storage Vessels

	P	SJ1	SJ2	SJ varia	Total	Of stratum
Stratum 13	22.2%	33.3%	33.3%	11.1%	9	8.2%
N =	2	3	3	1		
Stratum 12c-b	30.8%	7.7%	38.5%	23.1%	13	12.7%
N =	4	1	5	3		
Stratum 12a	75.0%	0.0%	25.0%	0.0%	4	21.1%
N =	3	0	1	0		
Stratum 11	25.0%	12.5%	0.0%	62.5%	8	10.7%
N =	2	1	0	5		

TABLE 4.25 Consumption of Large Storage Vessels at Tel Arqa

	Stratum 13	Stratum 12c-b	Stratum 12a	Stratum 11
N =	9	13	4	8
% of stratum	8.2%	12.7%	21.1%	10.7%

4.3.5.6. Varia (Graph 4.71)

Imported Aegean and Cypriot vessels are the only family of this category at Tell Arqa. Bichrome Cypriot imports appear at Tell Arqa in all strata except Stratum 13. Their number reaches its peak in Stratum 12a, though they are rare.

Cypriot imports appear in all strata, and their consumption increases until it reaches its peak in Stratum 11, making up 20% of the assemblage. This is

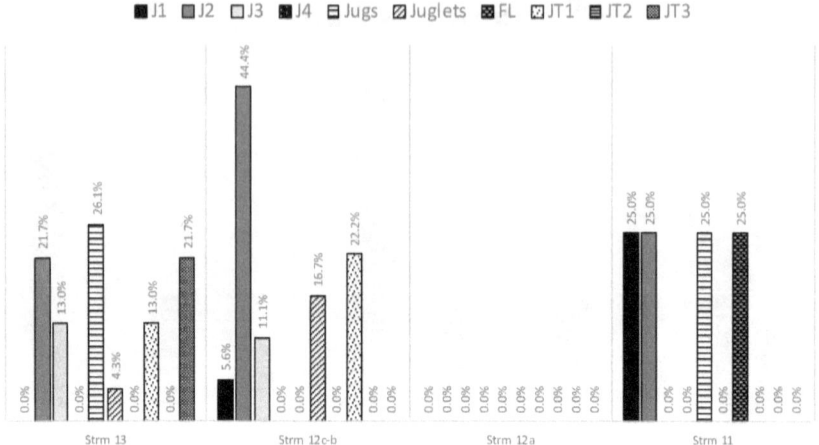

GRAPH 4.70 Tel Arqa, Small Storage Vessels

	J1	J2	J3	J4	FL	JT1	JT2	JT3	Varia	Total	Of stratum
Stratum 13	0.0%	21.7%	13.0%	0.0%	0.0%	13.0%	0.0%	21.7%	7	23	20.9%
N =	0	5	3	0	0	3	0	5			
Stratum 12c-b	5.6%	44.4%	11.1%	0.0%	0.0%	22.2%	0.0%	0.0%	3	18	17.6%
N =	1	8	2	0	0	4	0	0			
Stratum 12a	0.0%	0.0%	0.0%	0.0%	0.0%	0.0%	0.0%	0.0%	0	0	0.0%
N =	0	0	0	0	0	0	0	0			
Stratum 11	25.0%	25.0%	0.0%	0.0%	25.0%	0.0%	0.0%	0.0%	1	0	0.0%
N =	1	1	0	0	1	0	0	0			

the highest percentage of these vessels in all the sites and might be due to Tell Arqa's proximity to the coast.

Mycenaean imports appear in all strata except Stratum 13, though they are very rare.

4.3.5.7. Tell Arqa's Assemblage: Summary

The changes in Tell Arqa's assemblage could not be pinpointed to one transition period, though most of the changes occurred between Strata 12c–b and 12a, including the changes in consumption of deep bowls and carinated bowls of type CB1, both disappearing in Stratum 12a. It also includes changes in kraters, with type NK becoming the dominant component of the assemblage. In addition, juglets also disappear in Stratum 12a and, in general, there is a sharp decline in consumption of small storage vessels in this stratum. Between Strata 13 and 12c–b, changes were noted in the consumption of cooking pots—their consumption increases, and cooking pots of type CP3 appear in the assemblage, becoming dominant in

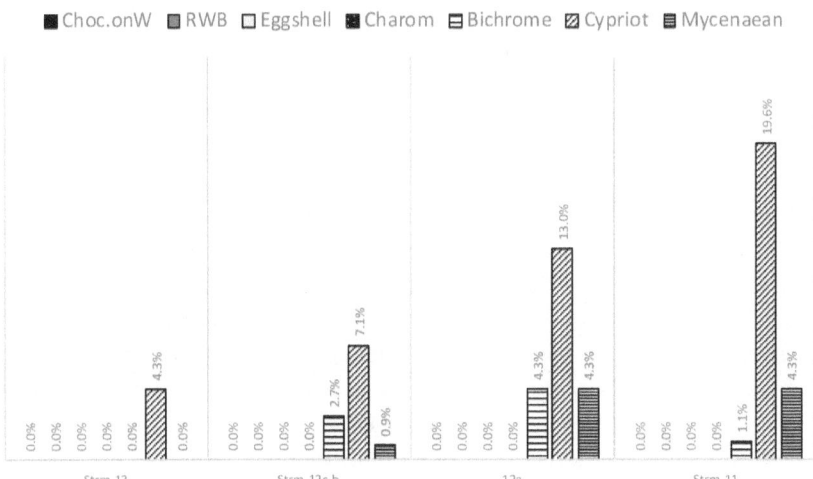

GRAPH 4.71 Tel Arqa, Miscellaneous Families

	Chocolate on White Ware	Red, White, and Blue Ware	Eggshell Ware	*Charom* Ware	Cypriot Bichrome Ware	Cypriot Imports	Mycenaean Imports
Stratum 13	0.0%	0.0%	0.0%	0.0%	0.0%	4.3%	0.0%
N =	0	0	0	0	0	5	0
Stratum 12c-b	0.0%	0.0%	0.0%	0.0%	2.7%	7.1%	1
N =	0	0	0	0	3	8	0.9%
Stratum 12a	0.0%	0.0%	0.0%	0.0%	4.3%	13.0%	4.3%
N =	0	0	0	0	1	3	1
Stratum 11	0.0%	0.0%	0.0%	0.0%	1.1%	19.6%	4.3%
N =	0	0	0	0	1	18	4

Stratum 12a. Carinated bowls of type CB4 also appear in Stratum 12c–b. On the other hand, kraters of type NKR appear only in Stratum 13 and disappear in Stratum 12c–b. Several changes were also noted between Strata 12a and 11, such as in the consumption of kraters (following a decline in consumption between Stratum 13 and Stratum 12a, there is an increase in Stratum 11) and in larger storage vessels (when the consumption of pithoi sharply declines and that of storage jars increases, especially storage jars of types not known in the southern Levant).

In terms of architecture, the major changes were noted between Strata 12c–b and 12a. As most of the changes noted above occur between these strata, it seems that, similarly to Hazor, the architectural and ceramic changes are more or less contemporary. It is possible to suggest that the architectural and ceramic changes can support placing Strata 12c–b in the LBIa and Stratum 12c in the LBIb, even though the excavators did not make this distinction.

4.3.6. Qatna

Changes in the ceramic horizons of the MBA and the LBA at Qatna were previously studied by Marco Iamoni, who excavated at the site and had full access to all its assemblages. Since I had no access to this material, any attempt to challenge Iamoni's study would be presumptuous. Therefore, a brief summary of Iamoni's study will be presented here, followed by a brief discussion on the differences between Iamoni's study and method and this study.

Iamoni's research focused on Qatna and its surrounding sites. His comprehensive study has shown that there is no sudden change between the MBA and the LBA forms and fabrics but rather a "normal development of features … which were already visible in the final MBA" (Iamoni 2012, 140–43). Iamoni infers many chronological implications from this, which I discuss further in chapter 5.

In addition, also relevant to the present discussion, he notes that the assemblages from the southern Levant are too distinct and different from those of the northern Levant. For example, one of the most common types of bowls—the carinated bowls that are the hallmark of the MBA in central-western Syria (shallow bowls with a very sharp carination in the middle of the body and an outturned rim)—are absent in southern Levantine assemblages (Iamoni 2012, 142 and n. 349). This is a crucial point in the discussion. Only a few types of the southern Levant appear in the Qatna assemblage, similar to those defined in the framework of the present study. These are:[15]

- CB1: Parallel to type C7D in Qatna; this type is typical of the MBIIa. It appears in Phase J-15, though in very small numbers (Iamoni 2012, 113 and fig. v-17).
- CB2: Parallel to types C10C and C11C in Qatna, typical of the MBII. The former was found in Phase T-12, and the latter was in the Eastern Palace's phases. Both disappear in the LBA (Iamoni 2012, 114 and fig. v-17).
- CB4: Only one example of this type was found, not defined as a type in Iamoni's typological scheme (Iamoni 2012, plate 40:14). This bowl was found in Phase J-7, dated to the LBI.
- CK: Parallel to type GJ20 in Qatna, typical of the MBII, these kraters were found only in Phase T-16 of the Eastern Palace. They continue into the LBA in Phases T-9 and J7 though in small numbers. Iamoni notes that these probably represent influences from the southern Levant, as they are not common in western central Syria and most parallels come from Cisjordan (Iamoni 2012, 117, 131 and figs. v-19 and v-31).

---

15. Since no complete bowls were illustrated in the Qatna publications, a discussion of the round bowls could not be carried out, as almost all the bowls would fall under type OB.

NK: Although similar to Qatna types GJ4, GJ5, GJ6, they are not exact matches. These are dated to the late MBA and continue into the LBA (Iamoni 2012, 116, 130).

NKR: Parallel to types GJ1 and GJ2 in Qatna; the former is typical of the MBA (Iamoni 2012, 116) but also appears in the LBII (Iamoni 2012, 175), and the latter is typical of the LBI (Iamoni 2012, 130–31). Similar kraters, types K1 and K2, are both typical of the MBII, but the latter also continues into the LBII (Iamoni 2012, 120 and 133–34).

Though this was not discussed in the typological scheme above, it is interesting to note that the typical decoration of many of the MBA kraters (incised, combed decoration of lines and waves) also appears on the MBA kraters from Qatna (e.g., Iamoni 2012, plates 16:12, 20:7, and 27:6), though in some cases, the shape of the vessel is not similar to that found in the southern Levant. This decoration continues into the LBI (Iamoni 2012, plate 65:1, 7–8, 11, Phase J7), and a single sherd was also found in the LBII assemblage (Iamoni 2012, plate 65:18), though this might be a residual appearance.

Cooking pots. The cooking pots found in Qatna are in no way similar to those of the southern Levant. In the MBA, cooking pots with an outturned squared rim are the most common type (Iamoni 2012, 119, table iv-2), similar, but not *identical*, to the triangular rim cooking pots (CP3) of the LBA. Comparably to the Tell Arqa pithoi of the LBI, it is possible to suggest that the overall shape and form of cooking pots of type CP3 were influenced by those of the central Levant (interestingly, the central Levantine type does not appear at Tell Arqa). It is also noteworthy that both of these influences occur during the LBII.

SJ1/J1. Only one type of storage jar, NJ12, was identified as similar to storage jars of type SJ1 and jugs of type J1, typical of the southern Levant. Type NJ12 starts to appear in Qatna in the MBII and continues to the LBII (Iamoni 2012, 132).

SJ2/J2. Most of the jars found at Qatna could fit into this type. These include NJ2, NJ3, NJ5, NJ6, NJ8, NJ10, NJ14, and NJ15, which appear in the MBA and the LBA (Iamoni 2012, 117–18 and 131–33).

Several families of vessels found in Qatna are not similar to vessels from the southern Levant. These include, among others, the pithoi and the short necked storage vessels.

In summary, out of the 229 types defined in the Qatna assemblage (Iamoni 2012, tables iv-1 and iv-2), only twenty types are similar to the ones defined in the present study. Most of these are typical only of the MBA while some begin to appear in the MBA and continue to the LBA. In other words, it seems that the MBA assemblages of Qatna are more similar to those of the other sites discussed above than its LBA assemblages.

Following the description of the various types of vessels and their occurrences within the different periods, Iamoni states that the most significant changes in the ceramic horizon occur in the LBIIa when twenty-three new types appear in the assemblage (compared to an average of fifteen new types in other periods). In general, the LBII assemblages are more varied than those of other periods, comprising 203 types, compared to 155 types in the LBI, 122 in the MBIIc, 126 in the MBIIb and 109 in the MBIIa. According to him, the fact that a higher number of types appear in the LBI indicates that the variation began probably a short time before the LBIIa (Iamoni 2012, 178).

It is interesting to note, on the contrary, that in the present study the significant changes occurring in the LBII were exactly the opposite—less variation in types and a dominant type in most families of vessels. However, it should be stressed that Iamoni examined specific types based on rims, necks, and carination of vessels, while in the present study these were usually not considered. The differences in the number of types (Iamoni's 229 types versus 36 in this study) practically speak for themselves.

4.4. Discussion and Summary

This chapter dealt with the ceramic assemblages at five sites whose architecture was discussed in the previous chapters. The pottery vessels were first discussed by their form (families, types, and subtypes) for identifying their starting and ending point of appearance. The ceramic assemblages of the different sites were subsequently discussed: in each site, every family was discussed, examining the consumption of the different types and the general consumption of each family within the entire assemblage of each stratum. Last, the ceramic assemblage of Qatna, a site also discussed in the previous chapter and previously studied by Iamoni, was presented.

4.4.1. Changes in Ceramic Traditions and Consumption: Previous Studies

Several studies have been conducted for assessing and understanding the homogeneity of the LBA assemblages and the ceramic changes that took place between the MBA and the LBA. These studies have led to different opinions on the methods of production, distribution, and consumption of ceramic assemblages in the different sites. Some scholars also used the ceramic assemblages to suggest a historical reconstruction of the MBA and the LBA. Below are some relevant studies.

Wood noted the changes in pottery production between the two periods—MBA pottery was produced using the fast wheel, while in the LBA, a slow wheel or coils were used (1990, 18–25). He stated that the most dominant mode of pottery production system in the urban periods of the third to first millennia BCE in the southern Levant were the "village industry" or "urban industry" modes. These production modes are characterized by a high output volume and relatively standardized products in both quality and shape, resulting in mass-produced vessels. These industries are sometimes made up of several pottery workshops that clustered together for reasons of availability of raw material, market opportunities, and demand. The clustered workshops could be located either within or outside the potters' homes, in an industrial complex. They had to be located near an adequate market to make the production profitable, and thus, were most likely situated in large urban centers (Wood 1990, 38–41, 49–50).

In addition, he notes that the literary (and the archaeological) evidence indicates that LBA potters worked in guilds under the central control of the city—either administrative rulers or religious institutions. The texts indicate that artisans who were working under royal service were provided with raw material, were paid in kind or in silver and received land. These artisans were dependents of the royal administration, but not slaves, enjoying the same status as other groups under the royal service, such as administrative, military and religious officials (Wood 1990, 48–49).

In other words, Wood attributes the changes in the ceramic assemblages to both technological and organizational changes in production. He suggests that potters were attached specialists to the palace or temple and that the pottery was distributed in a market economy.

Panitz-Cohen examined the changes in the material culture of Tel Batash from the MBIIb to the early Iron Age, analyzing the technological aspects of the assemblages—the *"chaîne opératoire"* and the fabric groups. She noted that, in the MBIIb, the vessels are made up of three major fabric groups, all found in the vicinity of the site. She also observed that almost all the MBA vessels are wheel-turned and standardized. In the LBA, the production technique changed. The vessels were no longer wheel-turned but rather wheel-finished on a slow wheel and, sometimes, vessels of the same type were made using different techniques (coiling, molding, turning, etc.). Besides the three fabric groups identified in the MBA, four new fabric groups were used in the LBA, all seven local. Panitz-Cohen concluded that the shift from a few fabrics in the MBA to several more fabrics in the LBA is due to changes in the production methods. In the MBA, production was centralized, conducted by specialized potters linked to the ruling elites, while in the LBA it was mainly conducted in household workshops. These potters were independent specialists, and, in her opinion, probably worked seasonally. Therefore, pottery production in the MBA was on a larger scale than in the LBA. However, she also suggests that some ceramic types (cooking pots and storage jars) were indeed produced by specialists in community-centralized workshops and not in the households. This is based on both the standardization of these types and the location of workshops—attached to temples (such as the one in Hazor Area C, though see above, chapter 2)—this being the exception to the rule in LBA production. Panitz-Cohen posits that neither the Egyptian rulers nor the local Canaanite rulers had any interest in controlling the production and distribution of plain pottery. That being said, it is interesting to note that the majority of the fabric groups of the LBA assemblages from Tel Batash originate in the area of the kingdom of Gezer, and very few ceramic vessels produced outside of this kingdom reached the site of Tel Batash in this period.

Her research continues to the early Iron Age when a new fabric group is introduced in the Tel Batash assemblage. This fabric group originates outside of the kingdom of Gezer, probably in Gath or Lachish. In other words, vessels were being imported to the site from other regions. Panitz-Cohen suggests that this is due to the strong Egyptian presence during the 19th and 20th dynasties, which weakened the autonomy and control of the city-states, allowing free exchange of more commodities and goods (Panitz-Cohen 2009, 186–88, 191–92).

Zuckerman examined the LBA assemblage of plain ware from Building 7050 at Hazor. She argued that the standardization of the vessels found in this building shows these were created by specialists, attached to the ruling elites, and were meant to serve in cultic rituals and feasts. However, according to her, the vessels found in the Area C and Area H temples are not as standardized as those found in the Area A temple (Building 7050), and, therefore, the former temples seem to have not been exclusive to the elites, as the Area A temple was. She sees in the uniformity of the vessels a social message of abundance. The consumption of simple vessels in the temples was used to emphasize the value of their contents. She agrees with Panitz-Cohen regarding the lack of interest of the Canaanite elite in controlling the production and distribution of the plain vessels (which stands in contrast to her claim that bowls and other pottery found in Building 7050 were produced by attached specialists; see Zuckerman 2015, 147). She argues that these household workshops were probably expected to provide their products to the local elites, leading to the use of this plain ware by all segments of society and thus creating a "Canaanite identity" through the vessels (Zuckerman 2015, 147–49).

In other words, Zuckerman seems to suggest a middle ground between the independent household potters and the attached potters, though this is not very convincing. In addition, Earle has noted that pottery production has an "economy of scale"—the cost declines as the produced number of vessels increases. According to him, households do not usually produce their own pottery vessels, as this would be uneconomical (Earle 2002, 133). The standardization of the

LBII pottery, together with the abundance that Zuckerman relies on, supports the claim that LBII potters were independent rather than attached specialists.

Killebrew conducted a comprehensive study of the thirteenth–twelfth centuries BCE ceramic assemblages of four sites (Deir el-Balah, Tel Miqne/Ekron, Beth-Shean, and Giloh), and of their implications on the ethnicity of their consumers. The petrographic studies she conducted indicate that most of the major centers produced their own pottery vessels. She also noted that, in most cases, the only plain vessels imported to the site were storage jars or other closed vessels, imported for their contents and not for the vessel itself. She concluded that each major center produced its own ceramic vessels for the consumption of its inhabitants and periphery, with little evidence for interregional trade. According to her, these were produced by a professional workshop-level industry. Furthermore, the fact that the Egyptian-style vessels remain unchanged over a period of several hundred years indicates that the production was regulated and under Egyptian control (Killebrew 1998, 255–56, 274; 2005, 137–38). These conclusions fit well with Panitz-Cohen's study, except for the production level (Panitz-Cohen maintains that pottery was produced in household workshops in the LBA).

Iamoni noted rapid changes in the ceramic assemblages at Qatna in both the MBA and the LBA. He suggested that it was the rise of the Mitannian Kingdom that most influenced these changes. According to him, even though we know so little of the Mitannian activity in the region, it is possible that their presence in western Syria and the intense commercial and diplomatic contacts within their kingdom are behind the changes in Qatna's material culture. The fact that Qatna was under Mitannian rule allowed more interconnections and influences within the different regions of northern and eastern Mesopotamia. Iamoni believes that the Hittite or the Egyptian military campaigns in northern Syria had only minor or no influence on Qatna (Iamoni 2012, 186–88).

Iamoni stated that, at the end of the MBA or the beginning of the LBI, demand for vessels decreased, leading to the termination of the Qatna's pottery workshops (Iamoni 2012, 187; also discussed in chapter 3). Iamoni agrees with Mazzoni that the decrease in pottery production was due to the fall of the Amorite kingdoms in Mari and Aleppo and the decline of centralized urban centers. Mazzoni posits that this led not only to a less strict control of the administrative centers over the production of pottery but also to a reduction in ceramic-forms innovation, a simplification or standardization of forms, and, thus, to a poorer ceramic horizon (Mazzoni 2000, 145). Mazzoni claims the LBIb witnesses an increase in the production and circulation of pottery. She suggested that the influx of Aegean pottery in the LBII led to an increase also in local production (Mazzoni 2000, 145–46). It is my belief that northern Canaan reflects the same trends suggested by Mazzoni, though Iamoni argues against this.

4.4.2. Ceramic Assemblages: Conclusions

The following conclusions can be drawn from the present study, deriving from the five examined sites. First, in most sites, the major changes seem to occur between the LBI and the LBII or between the LBIa and the LBIb, except in Yoqneʻam, where the major changes occur between Stratum XXb, dated to the transitional MB/LB, and Stratum XXa, dated to the LBI.

Second, what marks these changes is the lack of variability within the assemblages—that is, they become less varied. Certain types become dominant in the assemblages, first and foremost the cooking pot with the triangular rim (CP3), which is the *fossil directeur* of the LBII. Another type of vessel that becomes dominant in its family is the necked krater (NK), eliminating all the other types of kraters. Finally, the open, deep carinated bowls (CB4) become the most dominant type of carinated bowls in the LBII. As for the large storage vessels, at Hazor and Tell Arqa, pithoi (P) become dominant in the later part of the LBA, while at the remaining sites, these disappear in the LBA and the storage jars become more common.

The third conclusion is that the assemblages examined in the present study, which show a decline in their variability, stand in contrast to the increase in variability in the assemblages from the northern Levant. Iamoni argued that in the transition from the LBI to the LBII the assemblage becomes more varied (Iamoni 2012, 140–43). Iamoni and Mazzoni argue that, in the MBA, the region has "steady borders," or, in other words, the material culture has clear and defined limits that result from workshops performing under close administrative control. On the other hand, in the LBA, the "paradigm of expanded borders" comes into play. In this scenario, the large-scale interconnections between different regions is strongly influential (Iamoni 2012, 186; Mazzoni 2000, 144–46). This fits well with the finds from Qatna, but not with the ceramic evidence from sites to its south, as described above.

The historical, political and economic implications of these conclusions will be discussed in the next chapter.

CHAPTER 5

Discussion and Conclusions

> Our clock strikes when there is a change from hour to hour; but no hammer in the horologe of Time peals through the universe when there is a change from Era to Era. Men understand not what is among their hands; as calmness is the characteristic of strength, so the weightiest causes may be most silent. It is, in no case, the real historical Transaction, but only some more or less plausible scheme and theory of the Transaction, or the harmonized result of many such schemes, each varying from the other and all varying from truth, that we can ever hope to behold.
>
> —Thomas Carlyle (*On History*)

5.1. Introduction and Summary of Previous Chapters

The previous chapters examined the changes in the material culture, both architecture and ceramic assemblages, in several sites. In chapter 2, it was shown that major architectural changes took place at Hazor between the LBI and the LBII, in every excavation area. These conclusions were further examined in chapter 3, pertaining to other sites in Hazor's vicinity. It was concluded that the major architectural changes in Yoqne'am, Beth-Shean, Tel el-Ghassul, Tell Arqa, and Qatna also took place mostly between the LBI and the LBII, or sometimes between the LBIa and the LBIb. However, since in most sites there is only one stratum dated to the LBI, it is practically impossible to distinguish between the LBIa and the LBIb. Consequently, I suggest here that the general date of transition—that is, when the most significant changes in the material culture occur—is between the LBI and the LBII.

Following these conclusions, in chapter 4, the ceramic development of sites whose MBA and LBA pottery assemblages had been published were examined:

Hazor, Tel Qashish, Yoqne'am, Beth-Shean, and Tell Arqa. The results pointed to major ceramic changes also occurring between the LBI and the LBII in all sites, except Yoqne'am (where the major changes took place between the transitional MBA/LBA and the LBI strata). Examination of the pottery types also brought to light the lack of variety within the LBII types, where, in almost every family, a single type was seemingly dominant, contrasting with the previous periods, where several types were common in each assemblage. In other words, chapters 2–4 answered the main research question (When did the most significant changes in the material culture occur?), clarifying that these changes took place in the transition from the LBI to the LBII.

As stated in chapter 1, the prevailing notion among archaeologists up to the present is that the LBI and the LBII belong to a single cultural horizon. However, the present study has shown that the LBI, especially the LBIa, is, in fact, similar to the MBA cultural horizon. Thus, grouping the LBIa with the LBII, in fact, distorts our understanding of the political and social aspects of the LBA. However, considering the LBIa as part of the MBA and regarding it as the final decline of the MBA heydays will have a significant impact on our understanding of the construction of the LBA political and economic systems.

This chapter explores the role of the Egyptian Empire in the transformation of the urban landscape and the ceramic production and distribution systems in northern Canaan, with its implications on our understanding of the current historical view of the fifteenth century BCE.

5.2. Historical Implications

The MBA–LBA transition is the first archaeological period based on historical events rather than changes in the material culture. This transition was, consequently, characterized by its continuity. The event used to define this transition was the expulsion of the Hyksos from Egypt. As I noted in chapter 1, the banishment of the Hyksos from Egypt also resulted in Egyptian attacks on Canaanite sites in the southern Levant (Weinstein 1981, 1, 10). However, the material evidence presented here does not support this transition date, as the changes between the MBA and the LBI are not significant enough to mark a new *archaeological* period, at least not in northern Canaan.

Although this conclusion was already suggested by other scholars (Finkelstein 1996, 116–17; Bonfil 2003, 2012; A. Ben-Tor and Ben-Ami 2005; D. Ben-Tor 2011), who attributed the transition between the MBA and the LBA to Thutmose III's military campaign and his conquest of the southern Levant in 1457/6 BCE, the present study innovates in its incorporation of architectural and ceramic evidence from several sites spreading in a broader region—from Qatna to Beth-Shean. The typological scheme used here—that is, macrotypology—is also rarely used and stands in sharp contrast to the very popular microtypology used today by scholars (e.g., Karasik and Smilansky 2008). As was noted in chapter 1, macrotypology was applied here to show broader changes in the production and consumption of pottery vessels and not specific, minute changes. This study indicates that a much more significant change in the material culture occurred following Thutmose III's conquest. This conclusion also fits well with the overall historical reconstruction presented below. The study also examines the economic implications of this transition, showing, for the first time, that the LBI, and specifically the LBIa, actually represents a period of decline. It shifts the attention away from the Hyksos and the internal turmoil in Egypt and focuses it back on the local developments in northern Canaan.

Thus, I suggest here that the Egyptian conquest and consequent control over the Canaanite cities had a much deeper and resilient impact on local political, social, and economic systems than the expulsion of the Hyksos. The latter event might have affected cities in southern Canaan, but its impact did not reach northern Canaan in such a way as to affect or change the material culture. One possibility is that the removal of the Hyksos rule in Egypt was the catalyst to the economic decline. Though it is commonly agreed that the Hyksos had some type of relationship with the inhabitants of the Canaanite city-states during the MBA, it is not clear whether these were blood ties, trade relationships, or marital associations (Redford 1992, 119–22; Bietak 2010; D. Ben-Tor 2011). We do know that during its ruling days in Lower Egypt, Avaris imported large amounts of pottery vessels, some probably containing liquids from the central and the southern Levant (Beitak 1991; Maeir 2010, 113; D. Ben-Tor 2018, 46). Following the end of the settlement at Avaris, even if large amounts of liquids were still imported into Lower Egypt, it was not on the same scale as before (Broodbank 2013, 385–87) and this undoubtedly hurt the local economy of the southern Levant (Ilan 1995, 314–15).

Langgut et al. (2013) have engaged in a high-resolution pollen analysis from a core drilled in the Sea of Galilee. They identified olive trees at the Intermediate Bronze Age and the beginning of the MBA, concluding that they only served for local consumption. In the MBIIb and MBIIc, the percentages of olive trees in the core decreased sharply, while those of other Mediterranean trees increased. This increase continued in the LBA, until about 1250 BCE, when it dropped sharply, a period when a dry age was also recognized by the authors. They identified a decrease in the horticulture of olive trees in the MBIIb–c and maintained that this reduction was not based on climate changes but rather caused by changes in economic strategies (Langgut et al. 2013, 159–60). Though this cannot be pinpointed to a specific time within this long period (for C14, see Date 2 in Langgut et al. 2013, table 2), it is tempting to suggest this should be connected to the end of trade relations with Egypt following the expulsion of the Hyksos, or to the changes in trade relationship with Syrian cities following the Mitannian and Hittite battles. Therefore, acknowledging the Egyptian conquest as the definitive boundary between an era of independent city-states and an era of enslaved Canaanite vassal cities would better articulate the archaeological evidence and Levantine history.

5.2.1. Egyptian Presence in the Southern Levant

The period termed the LBIa, the time following the banishment of the Hyksos from Egypt and preceding the conquest of Canaan by Thutmose III, is still very ambiguous and elusive. The present study has shown that the material culture attributed to this period, and the changes seen in the material culture between the sixteenth and the fourteenth centuries BCE, indicate a period of decline and crisis during the LBIa. These conclusions raise some questions. Did the southern Levant come under Egyptian control immediately after the Hyksos expulsion, or were there about seventy-five years (approximately between 1530 and 1457 BCE) of tranquility? If so, how does this fit with the changes in material culture presented here?

One should be reminded that during these seventy-five years, Egypt was not so interested in Canaan and most of the Egyptian efforts were focused toward recolonizing Nubia. Egypt was interested in reestablishing its hegemony over its southern region and dismantling the Kushite kingdom, which developed during the Second Intermediate Period. The local population of Nubia being tribal, a colonial model of control by the Egyptians was required there (Redford 1992, 149, 192; Hoffmeier 2004, 126–27). According to Steinmetz, *colonialism* is the conquest by a foreign people after which an organization controlled by the foreign entity is created and used to rule the indigenous population of the conquered territory (Steinmentz 2014, 79).

In contrast, the population of the Levant was more urbanized and centralized, more socially stratified, with a functioning administrative system, evident by the cuneiform tablets found in several sites. Therefore, Egypt did not need to colonize the region but instead used an Imperial mode of control. Steinmentz defines *Imperial* as "a strategy of political control over foreign lands that does not necessarily involve conquest, occupation, and durable rule by outside invaders" (Steinmentz 2014, 79). The Imperial system in the Levant relied on local princes to keep Egypt's interest. This mode of control was more cost-effective than the colonization mode of control. It has also been suggested that Nubia's gold was one of the reasons for Egypt's colonization of that region (Redford 1992, 192–93; Hoffmeier 2004, 127–28). In other words, the effective administration of the MBA city-states is actually the reason Egypt could turn its focus away from this area and concentrate on colonizing Nubia, gaining its economic interests back. It should also be noted that, following the conquest, mass deportations are recorded from the central hill area and the Shephelah, establishing the Eighteenth Dynasty as the first documented Imperial power in the Levant.[1]

Concerning the few questions raised above on the state of northern Canaan during the seventy-five years between the removal of the Hyksos from their rule of Lower Egypt and the Egyptian Empire's conquest of Canaan, I believe that the lack of Egyptian interest in the southern Levant during these seventy-five years resulted in a faux-tranquility. Even though there were no battles between the Canaanites and the Egyptians, the fact that there was also less trade between the two sides had immense effects on the local economy, especially evident at Hazor and Beth-Shean. Both of these cities would only revive in the LBIb–LBIIa, following the Egyptian conquest. Since both were located on major crossroads, it is tempting to suggest that their revival could only have taken place after the advent of peace and resumed trade between Egypt and northern Syria. According to Egyptian records, it was only after Thutmose III's eighth campaign against Mitanni, during his 33rd year of rule, that Egypt began receiving gifts from rulers in Syria and Mesopotamia (Redford 2003, 250–51). However, it was only during the days of Thutmose IV that peace between the two powers was finally achieved, which also included the marriage of this Pharaoh to the daughter of Artatama I, the king of Mitanni (Redford 1992, 165; Kahn 2011, 138–39). Therefore, *if* these two sites (Hazor and Beth-Shean) were indeed revived after peace between Egypt and northern Syria was established, then Thutmose IV's marriage, dated to sometime in the second half of the fifteenth century BCE (Redford 1992, 165), could be the *terminus post quem* for this revival.

If we accept a period of faux-tranquility during the LBIa, we should also ask whether the Egyptian control of the southern Levant materialized through a long process or was caused by a single event. Obviously, the control of northern Canaan did not take place after many battles fought between the Egyptians and Canaanites, as was the case in southern Canaan. The question is whether internal events in northern Canaan could be viewed as part of a long process that led to the conquest by the Egyptians or if the Battle of Megiddo is to be considered as the single event that accomplished that. In the following section, it will

---

1. For a comprehensive study of Egypt's foreign policy changes in the Levant see Hoffmeier 2004; for Nubia, see Smith 1995. For a full analysis of the Egyptian Empire in Canaan, see Koch 2015.

be shown that the former case-scenario is actually true and that these internal events are, in fact, an economic decline of the local population.

5.2.2. Crisis Architecture at Hazor and Its Vicinity

As already shown in chapter 2, it seems that at the end of Stratum XV on the acropolis, and Stratum 2 in the lower city, both dated to the LBI, Hazor was experiencing a crisis. The city was partially abandoned, built spaces were replaced with open courtyards, some built architecture was reduced, monumental architecture decreased in size (Area F) or was completely abandoned (Area A), and the route entering the acropolis changed (Area M). In Area F, installations were built inside the monumental structure, and entrances were sealed, indicating perhaps a change in its function.

In addition, during the LBII, the city almost entirely changed its urban plan. A lack of continuation or a complete break were noted in almost all excavation areas (apart from Area H). These should be viewed in light of the historical events described above and more specifically in chapter 1, notably, the appointment of new vassal kings and assignment of new dynasties in the different cities by Thutmose III. It can be suggested that the comprehensive and wide-range changes at Hazor in the LBII were due to the ruling of a new dynasty. However, as yet, we have no evidence to support this suggestion, other than the architectural changes and the Egyptian texts mentioning this method.

Surveys conducted around Hazor and small salvage excavations in its vicinity have indicated that, while in the MBA several installations and villages are present in Hazor's surroundings, in the LBA this completely changes. In his survey of Hazor's vicinity, Stepansky identified several sites that date to the MBA, even suggesting an assigned function for them in relation to Hazor. However, in the LBA, only one site was identified in Hazor's vicinity, which fits (though to an extremity) the overall settlement distribution in the country during this time (Stepansky 1999, 92–95; Bunimovitz 1989; Knapp 1992, 93–94). Wachtel has recently conducted a comprehensive survey in the Upper Galilee where a similar picture arises, indicating that during the LBII settlement was very sparse (Wachtel, 2018 and forthcoming). Only a few rural sites around Hazor have been excavated, as yet, in very small salvage excavations. These include installations and quarries dated to the MBA (none were dated to the LBA; see Amos and Getzov 2011).

It appears, therefore, that during the LBI, a decline is seen in the size of the settlement at Hazor while in the LBII, the settlement increased in size and in population together with an abandoning of its hinterland. In other words, if any mass relocation occurred in the Galilee, it happened at the beginning of the LBI, prior to the conquest, and not following it. This is not to suggest a forced mass relocation in the LBI, but rather one caused by life circumstances (e.g., the population's need to find new sources of income). This is further strengthened by the changes in the architectural fabric of the city of Hazor discussed in chapter 2. In the MBA and the LBI public architecture is more prevalent at the site, whereas in the LBII domestic architecture is more common.

This conclusion may have vast implications on our understanding of the LBA. First, it strengthens the suggestion noted above that the LBI was a period of decline, triggered by the Hyksos expulsion and the lack of trade relationship with Egypt.

Second, it brings to mind Na'aman's suggestion regarding the end of the LBA at Hazor. Na'aman maintained that the destruction was caused by an economic depression in the city due to the costly building activities of the city's rulers focused mainly on cultic structures, and the vast amounts of resources probably also invested in cultic activities and their maintenance (Na'aman 2012, 337–39). It is suggested here that this economic depression, which was caused due to the high taxation on Hazor's subjects, is in fact the reason for these costly building activities. The rulers of Hazor wanted to portray themselves as those ruling a thriving economy and a flourishing urban center ("the head of all those kingdoms," Josh 10:11), when in fact, Hazor was already in an economic depression, as it had to build an entire new city in Stratum 1b. However, this idea is beyond the scope of the current research and will be dealt with elsewhere.

Returning to Na'aman's theory, according to him, due to this economic depression, when the city needed its inhabitants to protect itself from external enemies, there was no one to turn to (Na'aman 2012, 337). This suggestion is comparable to the one raised above, that the partial abandonment of the city in the LBI (probably due to the economic decline at this time) allowed the Egyptian forces to conquer the area, and, when the city of Hazor needed its inhabitants and the residents of its hinterland to protect itself from the Egyptian enemy, there was no one to whom it could turn.

Third, this conclusion sheds new light on Hazor's role in the textile industry. In the MBA, Hazor's role is evident both in documents from Hazor itself (Horowitz and Oshima 2006, 83–86, Hazor 12 and Hazor 14) and in documents from Mari naming clothes, carpets, covers for chariots or carriages and even leather and linen products that were sent to Mari from Hazor (Malmat 2006, 353). In the LBA, two Amarna letters (EA 22 and EA 25) testify that Hazor was still known for its textile industry (Horowitz and Oshima 2006, 83; Moran 1992).[2] A recent study by Marom et al. (2014) sheds light on Hazor's sheep consumption during the MBA and materializes the textual evidence on Hazor's role in the textile industry. The

---

2. In contrast, it is interesting to note that Egypt did not receive sheep in the taxes collected from its conquered lands in the Levant (Redford 2003, 248).

study suggests an intensification of wool production in the MBA at Hazor, based on the presence of more sheep than goats in the faunal assemblage. On the other hand, at Kabri, the faunal assemblage is dominated mainly by goats. Also, the Hazor assemblage mainly comprised younger males while at Kabri it consisted of older females. Marom and his colleagues suggest that the rulers of Hazor relied on the rural settlements for wool and meat, a demand met by increasing the number of sheep in the herds (Marom et a. 2014, 75–79). In a different study, Marom and Zuckerman have shown that in the LBA faunal assemblages of Area S (located in the lower city of Hazor), goats are more numerous than sheep (Marom and Zuckerman 2012, 578), similarly to Kabri in the MBA (Marom et al. 2014, 75). Kabri, a large MBA settlement located to the west of Hazor, fell in the MBIIb–MBIIc transition (dated to approximately 1700 BCE by C14, see Höflmayer et al. 2016). This is contemporary to the vacating of the Galilee and the economic decline noted at Hazor, at the end of the MBIIc. In addition, sometime toward the end of the MBIIb or the beginning of the MBIIc, Mari was destroyed by Hammurabi and Yamhad, Ebla, and probably also Babylon were later attacked and some destroyed by the Hittites around 1650–1600 BCE (Klengel 2014, 91). Ebla, for example, never revived from this destruction, with only squatters' activity identified in the LBA (Pinnock 2014). The destruction of these Syrian cities must have resulted in a decline in textile demand from Hazor. It is also during this time that the faunal assemblage from Hazor is no longer dominated by sheep, as was the case in the MBA, but that for the first time in the second millennium, goats are more numerous than sheep (Marom and Zuckerman 2012), perhaps indicating a decline in the need for sheep's wool. Therefore, it is suggested here that the economic decline noted at Hazor should be viewed in light of the Syrian events, focusing again on the local politics of Hazor and turning away from the end of the Hyksos rule.

Fourth, the economic decline suggested for the LBI reinforces the claim above that the transition from the MBA to the LBA was, in fact, not caused by a single event but was a process spanning seventy-five years—beginning with the expulsion of the Hyksos and ending in the establishment of a new administrative system in the southern Levant, following the Egyptian conquest.

It is important to note that, based on the changes in the political, economic and social conditions following the Egyptian conquest and subsequent control of the southern Levant, a single "Bronze Age economic model" seems not convincing and cannot be discussed. In contrast, the economic model of the MBA–LBI (preconquest, when northern Canaan was part of the Syrian world) differs from that of the LBII (postconquest, after northern Canaan came under Egyptian control). Thus, it is my belief that Earle's Political Model (defined in chapter 1) could best explain these changes and the economic circumstances of the transition from the LBI to the LBII. This point will be further examined following the discussion of the ceramic production and distribution.

5.3. Changes in Ceramic Traditions and Consumption

5.3.1. The Aegean and Cypriot Pottery and Their Influence

As implied in chapter 4, the introduction of the Aegean and Cypriot pottery into the local assemblages is believed to have affected the simplification of the local shapes. It is suggested here that the influx in trade of these vessels, considered luxurious ware by most scholars, not only affected the social stratification of the Canaanite culture but also led to a decline in the variety of shapes and decorations in the local assemblages.

Aegean pottery first appeared on a very small scale, in the southern Levant in the MBA, known as the Minoan pottery—Kamares Ware. This appearance was limited to large urban centers, mainly in the northern and central Levant (only a few sherds were found in the southern Levant, e.g., Dothan et al. 2000). This trend continued in the LBI with the Bichrome Ware, imported from Cyprus. However, this ware was found in much larger quantities and, as a consequence, excluded the Aegean zone from this trading network. It is only with the introduction of the Mycenaean pottery (also known as LHIIIA–B pottery) into the Levant that an influx is seen in the Aegean pottery and, consequently, in the Cypriot pottery as well (Steel 2002, 30; Leonard 1994). Aegean-type vessels included mainly closed vessels (which might have been imported mainly for their contents), but also open vessels, imported for their own value (van Wijngaarden 2002). Scholars have already noted that this influx resulted in a change in the organization of large-scale, long-distance trade in the Mediterranean (to name a few, see Sherratt and Sherratt 1991; Steel 2002; van Wijngaarden 2002), and in changes in the pottery production in the Aegean area itself, namely the Levanto-Mycenaean ware (Furumark 1941, 9–10; van Wijngaarden 2002, 10–11).

As for the Levant, the Mycenaean pottery (and most likely the Cypriot pottery as well) and its long-distance trade was part of the Bronze Age palatial economy. These vessels were added-value commodities, their value not being measured by their raw material but rather by their manufacture techniques and as socially appropriated to the elites (Sherratt and Sherratt 1991, 359; van Wijngaarden 2002, 26–28; contra Stockhammer 2012).

As this pottery affected pottery manufacture in the Aegean and Cyprus, it should not come as a surprise that it might have also affected pottery manufacture at its receiving end, more specifically in the southern Levant. It is suggested here that this imported pottery was one of the causes that led to the simplification of the local Canaanite ware, and that the intensification of Mycenaean and Cypriot imports to the southern Levantine sites, and possibly also to coastal Lebanese and Syrian sites, resulted in a decline in innovation and variation in the local ware. Van Wijngaarden has shown that the Mycenaean and Cypriot imports he examined in different regions (the Levant, Cyprus, and Italy) stood in stark difference to the local pottery. The imported pottery showed a much higher firing quality, and greater variation in decoration and shape (van Wijngaarden 2002, 271–72). I would like to propose that the high quality of these vessels, together with the increased burden of taxes levied on the local population, led the local potters to realize their inability to compete for the demand of luxury ceramic vessels. Thus, the potters adhered to specific, regular forms of vessels (the vessels are not identical but there is a decline in the variety of forms), leading to the simplification of the assemblages. This does not imply an industry that is controlled from above. It should be noted, however, that imported Aegean pottery is not abundant in Qatna (Iamoni 2012, 139), perhaps due to its relative distance from the coast. The paucity of imported Aegean pottery at Qatna fits well with the increased variation within the LBA assemblages at the site, in contrast to the conclusions reached after having examined southern and coastal Levantine sites in the present study.

5.3.2. Interpreting Ceramic Changes

As has been shown in chapter 4 and noted above, the major change seen in the ceramic assemblages is the lack of variety in the LBA assemblages, especially in the LBII assemblages, compared to those of the MBA. It is proposed here that the MBA pottery production was based on attached specialists, who were less efficient and invested vast energy and resources in producing the vessels, while the LBA production was based on independent specialists, who promoted efficiency and standardization. The independent specialists of the LBA could control all systems of manufacture and distribution due to the lack of interest of the elites in this system of production and the shift of their focus to luxury goods, which were also used to maintain social differences.

The prevailing notion regarding LBII assemblages is that they have a *standardized nature*. As already stated above, this study did not include technological aspects and, therefore, the *chaîne opératoire*, which in many cases contributes to the study of standardization, was of no help here. However, it is believed that the mere examination of the shapes and forms of the vessels can contribute to this discussion. The standardization discussed here is not one that creates a homogeneous assemblage in all families; in other words, not all kraters look exactly alike, but they all share similar features (i.e., large open vessels with a raised neck), and all cooking pots *do* have similar shapes (carinated closed vessels with a triangular rim), but their sizes vary. Rice has argued that specialization in craft production may result in either standardization or simplification in many aspects of pottery production, including shapes, sizes and the decorative style of the vessels (Rice 1984, 47–48). She further suggests that such specialization may be due to mass production of bulks of identical objects and can also be reflected in high-proficiency forming or decorating of certain vessels (Rice 1984, 48). Others have also suggested that ceramic standardization and simplification are promoted by mass production (Rathje 1975, 430; Wood 1999, 58). Therefore, the fact that the LBA assemblages are simplified (with less variety than earlier assemblages) does not necessarily mean that these were part of a nonspecialized industry, but rather that these were mass produced by specialized potters, most probably in a standardized fashion.

Mazar has suggested that the Egyptian domination and exploitation of the population and the city-states in LBA Canaan resulted in the Canaanite culture being deteriorated (Mazar 1992, 232). One could argue that the simplification of shapes and decorations in LBA ceramic assemblages strengthens this notion. Although it could also be argued that the LBA ceramic assemblages actually show an enhancement in Canaanite material culture, as now the assemblages are standardized, in contrast to the MBA assemblages that were much more varied. Mazar's claim is accepted here.

Adams noted that although political and ideological changes do not always lead to changes in ceramic traditions, immediate changes were noted in the ceramic traditions when Nubia became annexed to the Ottoman Empire. This change was due to a *technological* shift—the end of use of the wheel. Although we do not know what brought about the changes in Nubia, Adams suggests that a tax on the potters' wheels or pottery trade is to blame, which are both consistent with Ottoman policy (Adams 1979, 732). The similarities to the changes from the MBA to the LBA are striking (for the end of use of the potters' wheels in the LBA, see above, chapter 4, discussion and summary). At present, we have no information on the policy of the local Canaanite rulers regarding taxes in general and taxes on pottery trade in particular. We also have no records of such taxes raised by the Egyptians (and see above, in chapter 1: Na'aman 1981). Nevertheless, it is suggested here that the changes in the pottery manufacture and organization of production were affected by the increase in taxes (see below).

Regarding the *type of specialization* applied in the MBA and the LBA, it is concluded here that the relatively large variety in shapes, decorations and finishing of the vessels' surface (burnished and/or slipped vessels during the MBA compared to those of the LBII, which are none of the above) all suggest that significant energy was invested in the manufacture of the MBA vessels. The lack of standardization results in an inefficient production system, which is indicative of attached specialists (see chapter 1). In contrast, the LBII vessels show a decline in the variety of shapes, decorations, and finishing of the vessels' surface, resulting in simplification, and, thus, more regular-shaped vessels, suggesting the potters of the LBII were independent specialists.

Regarding the *political model*, Schloen already maintained that the elites of the LBA had control over the production and distribution of luxury goods.[3] It is suggested here that this control over luxury goods is precisely what allowed the rulers and elites to secede their control of the plain, common ware. In other words, the elites were not interested in having strict control over pottery manufacture and distribution systems. Therefore, under the new administrative system, following the Egyptian conquest, the local potters were no longer attached specialists but independent specialists, controlling the production, distribution, and, consequently, the consumption systems.

Iamoni suggested that it was the *Mitannian influence* on Qatna that led to the changes in the material culture there. This Mitannian influence could also be associated with changes in material culture in northern Canaan. As far as we know, Mitanni had some influence on the local kings, attested in Egyptian records (Redford 1992, 151–56). This influence most probably ended with the new Egyptian control over Canaan, which began in the fifteenth century BCE. It could be suggested that the end of this influence affected the material culture. However, since we know practically nothing about the Mitanni Kingdom, this suggestion is difficult to examine. Nevertheless, the fact that pottery shapes in Tell Arqa, during the LBII, become less similar to those in the southern Levant and more similar to those of the northern Levant, might also point to changes in the political division of the region.

5.4. Final Conclusions—From a Super Power in the MBA to a Great Vassal in the LBA

One of the leading research questions of this study was the degree to which political events affected material culture. Based on the gathered data, I believe that the evidence presented here clearly indicates that political events *do* affect the material culture. As was already proposed above, the major event that led to the changes in the material culture was the conquest of the southern Levant by the Egyptian Empire, following Thutmose III's campaign. Since the material culture illustrates a time of decline during the LBI (especially at Hazor), it might even be suggested that one of the reasons for the Egyptian conquest was the fact that the local population was already in a state of economic decline. The decline was probably caused by the fall of the Syrian cities and the temporary break in trade relations between Egypt and the southern Levant. This conclusion may explain the establishment of the first Egyptian Empire in the Levant in a

---

3. This point is accepted by most scholars and Schloen is quoted here as he conducted a comprehensive discussion and analysis this type of control during the LBA.

different light. In view of this conclusion, it may be suggested that the Egyptian Empire in the second millennium was materialized with the "aid" of the economic crisis suffered by northern Canaan and not only to Thutmose III's brilliant military tactics (Redford 2003), not lessened here whatsoever.

This conquest led to major administrative changes in the Canaanite city-states, whose rulers now had to raise taxes for the Egyptian Empire, taxes that were perhaps paid as a tribute and not actual levies (Na'aman 1981; Redford 2003, 245–49). Following this battle, during the days of Amenophis II and his son Thutmose IV, the records mention mass deportation, especially from the hill country and the Shephelah. Since this is a time of peace between northern Syria and Egypt, it is possible that these mass deportations were a preventative measure. Though we have no records of such mass deportation from the Galilee during this time, the archaeological evidence indicates that, at the very least, people left the hinterland of Hazor of their own will at the end of the MBA or the beginning of the LBI. Sometime after Thutmose III's campaign, the new city of Hazor was built, but, in some areas, monumental and public architecture was replaced by domestic buildings. Therefore, it seems reasonable to suggest that the remaining rural population of Hazor's hinterland relocated to the lower city. These people most likely continued to work the fields and the orchards within Hazor's vicinity (which fits well with Schloen's reconstruction of the population of Ugarit in the LBA, see Schloen 2001). Some of these people were probably also potters.

The LBA possible mass deportations and the extensive decrease in population size, resulted in less demand for pottery. Perhaps this drove the urban administrative centers to forsake their interest in strict control over pottery production, the rulers of these centers being now mainly interested in controlling the production of luxury products such as ivories, faience, metal industry and so forth, as already suggested by Schloen. The lack of interest in controlling pottery production has already been suggested by Iamoni and Mazzoni for LBA Qatna due to the decline in the number of centralized sites in LBIa northeastern Syria.

That Canaan was under the control of the Egyptian Empire also meant that cities had to raise taxes from the local population for the Egyptian Empire. Obviously, taxes were also collected during the MBA, but the cities were at that time independent city-states and taxes were most probably allocated directly to the rulers of the cities. In the LBII, however, taxes had to be higher, since the rulers of the cities had to accumulate more revenue in order to both keep their status and control and pay the Egyptian kingdom. These rulers wanted to keep as many people as possible under their control to raise enough revenue for the Egyptians. As established above, fewer people populated the hinterland of Hazor during the LBA, more people relocating to the city itself, where they were better protected in times of danger but, at the same time, came under more tightened control by the king of Hazor. It is reasonable to assume that these people chose to relocate to Hazor, where they could find a source of income, their relocation also being in the king's interest, as suggested above. This may explain why one of the monumental buildings in the city (Area F) was forsaken and replaced by domestic buildings.

It is also suggested here that the generated vacuum over the control of pottery production and distribution by the city was filled by the local potters—independent specialists probably working in large workshops in a regular and organized manner. Since it is our understanding that the MBA potters were attached specialists, they probably paid little or no taxes to the king who received the final goods and controlled their distribution. Since in the LBA potters were independent specialists, they must have paid taxes to the king. It is thus possible to suggest that this burden also contributed to the specialized, regular and efficient ceramic production, resulting in "mass produced" pottery vessels, with fewer decorations and unfinished surfaces (i.e., not well slipped and burnished), which would use time and energy consuming methods, and shapes with little or no variation. In addition, the vessels' final shape can at times be considered sloppy—the rims of bowls and storage jars are distorted, the bodies of storage jars are warped, and the painted decorations are not precise, in contrast to the precise execution in the MBA, in the shapes and decorations of vessels.

In sum, the fact that Canaan was under Egyptian rule led to a complete change in the methods of pottery production, which resulted in a more "mass-produced" final product; the largest urban center in northern Canaan, Hazor, completely changed its layout and plan and was now more densely populated than before. Therefore, in conclusion, the answer to our main question is yes—political events did indeed result in changes in the material culture. In the transition from the MBA to the LBA, this political event is not the Hyksos expulsion, as far as northern Canaan is concerned, but rather the new Egyptian control that materialized after Thutmose III's military campaign.

5.4.1. Future Research

As with many studies, answering a few research questions leads to several new ones. This study is no different. Some of these new questions derive from the conclusions of the present study and are in fact suggestions for further examining these conclusions in the future.

First, it would be extremely interesting and important to test the conclusions of this research for southern and central Canaan as well. Would architectural and ceramic assemblages "behave" in the same manner identified for northern Canaan? As was noted in chapter 1, the last MBA levels in southern Canaan are characterized by destruction layers, unlike northern Canaan, where sites show little or no evidence for a destruction. Therefore, it would be intriguing to examine whether the changes in the ceramic assemblages are chronologically parallel to the architectural changes in those sites.

Second, as was established above, the changes in pottery production are mainly reflected in the transition from attached to independent specialists' production. It is possible to suggest that in the LBA, when pottery was "mass produced," the workshops were larger than those of the MBA, as it would be more efficient to have one large workshop than several small ones. This suggestion could be easily assessed through petrographic and technological studies of individual assemblages. This technological study would examine the *"chaîne opératoire"* of the production process, identifying a single manufacturing technique that could indicate production by a single or a few workshops, thus strengthening the conclusions of this study. In contrast, identifying different manufacturing techniques for the same type of vessels at the same site would indicate several workshops and would force us to revise some of our present conclusions.

Third, concerning the changes in the built environment of the city (domestic architecture replacing public architecture), an examination of the phenomenon noted at Hazor could also be executed in sites of the southern Levant where MBA monumental architecture was found (a comparison that cannot be made with Yoqne'am and Tel Qashish). For example, though not thoroughly studied here, it seems that the circumstances at Tell Arqa are similar to those at Hazor.

Fourth, the LBII economic system should also be further examined. Excavations at Hazor have uncovered numerous examples of the secondary use of architectural elements in LBII monumental buildings. This includes removing large limestone ashlars from the Southern Temple in Area A and placing them in the construction of the altar in the center of the courtyard of Building 7050, removal of orthostats from MBA buildings and using them in the construction of Building 7050 itself, and many other examples. In my opinion, this also testifies to the inability of Hazor's ruler to quarry and work these stones from scratch, resulting in the recycling of older elements. This phenomenon should be examined at other sites to identify whether or not this is restricted to Hazor. The implications would be significant either way.

Finally, a study of the changes in the consumption of cattle was carried out at Megiddo (Finkelstein et al. 2017). This study showed that this consumption changed in the transition from the LBI to the LBIIa. In the LBI, cattle were used mainly for consumption of meat, while in the LBII and LBIII they served mainly agricultural needs. In addition, it is likely that zebu cattle were imported to Canaan in the LBA, as these animals are strong and well adapted to hot and dry climate conditions. The authors suggest that together with other evidence, this may point to the rise in the importance of dry farming in LBII Megiddo and its vicinity, especially in view of the dry event of the LBA that caused an agricultural crisis in the Levant.[4] The authors propose that this was due to Egyptian political and economic strategies in the Levant and their interests in Anatolia; the Egyptian Empire tried to manage the crisis of the LBA dry event and stabilize agriculture and farming in the Levant. Their aim was to supply the needs of the northern Levant and Anatolia. In other words, it seems that Egypt was invested and involved in the local economies during the LBA, beginning in its conquest of the southern Levant in the days of Thutmose III.

Following the conclusions of the present research, it would be extremely interesting to examine the changes in zooarchaeological remains between the MBA and the LBA at sites examined under the present study. Egypt's involvement in the local economy and production systems still lies in the dark. The study by Finkelstein et al. (2017) sheds some light on their involvement, and it is hoped that future studies will further carry out such examination.

5.4.2. Contributions of the Present Research

The final conclusions of this research—namely, that the transition from the MBA to the LBA should be marked by Thutmose III's campaign—make an immense contribution to our understanding of the LBA. It shifts our attention away from the Hyksos and back to the local population. At present, we have no evidence of the nature of the relationship between the Hyksos and the local population (was it based on marriage? Bloodline? Trade?). Thus, placing such a weight on their banishment from Egypt would not reflect the reality of northern Canaan. The LBI is still an elusive period, but the present study was able to shed more light on it, showing that this was a time of economic decline, perhaps ignited by the end of the Hyksos rule in Lower Egypt, although the political changes in the northern Levant most probably also had an impact on this decline. It has also been shown that, from a cultural perspective, the LBI was in fact still part of the MBA cultural horizon and not of the LBII. This conclusion also has extensive implications on the study of the LBA, as it indicates that it is explained by Egyptian control, influence, and involvement in the local administrative systems.

The results of this study also point to the reasons behind the specific characteristics of the LBA ceramic assemblages. Previous scholars have noted the standardized nature of the LBA ceramic assemblages. However, this applies, in fact, to the nature of the LBII assemblages and not to the LBI. It was suggested here that this standardized nature was caused both by changes in the

---

4. This dry era, dated to the end of the LBA (1250–1150 BCE), was beyond the scope of our study (Langut et al. 2013).

production and distribution of pottery and by the influx of Aegean and Cypriot imports. Potters of the LBII were independent specialists, producing pottery in a "mass production" system and unable to compete with the luxurious Aegean and Cypriot pottery. Since the local rulers had little interest in having strict control over the ceramic production, both the production and the distribution systems of local pottery were controlled by independent specialists, whose finished goods were less varied, with less energy being invested in their production.

In other words, no single factor could be held responsible for the change in material culture. It was the combination of several factors that led to an economic decline at the beginning of the LBA. Malmat (1960) argued that the Hazor referred to as "the head of all those kingdoms" (Josh. 11:10) actually was Hazor of the MBA. Not only do the results of this research support these claims but also offer several reasons for the changes that took place. In fact, the present study suggests that Canaan's heyday was during the MBA when cities were independent city-states. The LBI was the swan song of this zenith, characterized by a yet unrecognized economic decline. This was to be followed by the fallout of the Bronze Age, when LBII cities became vassals of the Egyptian Empire until their final demise.

BIBLIOGRAPHY

Abrams, E. M. 1989. "Architecture and Energy: An Evolutionary Perspective." *Archaeological Method and Theory* 1:47–87.
Adams, W. Y. 1979. "On the Argument from Ceramics to History: A Challenge Based on Evidence from Medieval Nubia [and Comments and Reply]." *Current Anthropology* 20.4:727–44.
Ahituv, S. 1978. "Economic Factors in the Egyptian Conquest of Canaan." *Israel Exploration Journal* 28.1:93–105.
Akkermans, P. M. M. G, and G. M. Schwartz. 2003. *The Archaeology of Syria: From Complex Hunter-Gatherers to Early Urban Societies (c.16,000–300 BC)*. Cambridge: Cambridge University Press.
Albright, W. F. 1920. "A Revision of Early Hebrew Chronology." *Journal of the Palestine Oriental Society* 1:48–79.
———. 1949. *The Archaeology of Palestine*. Harmondsworth, UK: Pelican.
Al-Maqdissi, M. 2003. "Recherches Archéologiques Syriennes à Mishirfeh-Qatna au nord-est de Homs (Émèse)." *Comptes Rendus des Séances de l'Académie des Inscriptions et Belles-Lettres* 147.4:1487–515.
———. 2009. "Recherches Archéologiques Syriennes à Mishirfeh-Qatna au nord-est de Homs-Émèse (2004–2009)." *Comptes Rendus des Séances de l'Académie des Inscriptions et Belles-Lettres* 153.3:1201–43.
Al-Maqdissi, M., and M. Badawi. 2002. "Rapport Preliminaire Sur La Sixieme Campagne Des Fouilles Syrienne à Mishrifeh/Qatna." Pages 25–63 in *Excavating Qatna*. Edited by M. Al-Maqdissi, M. Luciani, D. Moranci Bonacossi, M. Novak, and P. Pfälzner. Damascus: Direction Générale des Antiquités et des Musées de la République Arabe Syrienne; Udine: University of Udine Press; Tübingen : University of Tübingen Press.
Al-Maqdissi, M., Y. Kanhoush, M. Cremaschi, and Morandi Bonacossi, D. 2009. "Présentation Sommaire Des Travaux Archéologiques de la Mission Syro-Italienne: Les Fouilles Archéologiques à Mishirfeh—Qatna et la Prospection de la Palmyrène Occidentale." *Studia Orontica* 1:5–20.
Al-Maqdissi, M., M. Luciani, D. Moranci Bonacossi, M. Novak, and P. Pfälzner. 2002. "Introduction." Pages 7–16 in *Excavating Qatna*. Edited by M. Al-Maqdissi, M. Luciani, D. Moranci Bonacossi, M. Novak, and P. Pfälzner. Damascus:

Direction Générale des Antiquités et des Musées de la République Arabe Syrienne; Udine: University of Udine Press; Tübingen : University of Tübingen Press.

Al-Maqdissi, M., and D. Moranci Bonacossi. 2005. *The Metropolis of the Orontes: Art and Archaeology from the Ancient Kingdom of Qatna*. Damascus.

Amiran, R. 1969. *Ancient Pottery of the Holy Land*. Jerusalem.

Amos, E., and N. Getzov. 2011. "The Rural Hinterland West of Tel Hazor." *'Atiqot* 67:27–39.

Arnold, D. E. 2000. "Does the Standardization of Ceramic Pastes Really Mean Specialization?" *Journal of Archaeological Method and Theory* 7.4:333–75.

Bard, K. A. 2008. *An Introduction to the Archaeology of Ancient Egypt*. Malden, MA: Wiley-Blackwell.

Bechar, S. 2017. "The Middle and Late Bronze Age Pottery." Pages 199–467 in *Hazor VII: The 1990–2012 Excavations—The Bronze Age*. Edited by A. Ben-Tor, S. Zuckerman, S. Bechar, and D. Sandhaus. Jerusalem: Israel Exploration Society.

———. Forthcoming. "The Middle and Late Bronze Age Pottery." In *The Rise and Decline of a Canaanite Kingdom: A View from the Lower City—An Account of the 2008–2010 Excavation Seasons of Area S*. Edited by S. Zuckerman, I. Wachtel, and S. Bechar. Jerusalem: Qedem Reports.

Bechar, S., A. Ben-Tor, I. Wachtel, D. Ben-Tor, E. Boaretto, and P. W. Stockhammer. 2021. "The Destruction of Late Bronze Age Hazor." *Agypten und Levante* 31:45–73.

Ben-Ami, D. 2005. "The Architecture and Stratigraphy of the Late Bronze Age." Pages 141–64 in *Yoqne'am III: The Middle and Late Bronze Ages*. Edited by A. Ben-Tor, D. Ben-Ami, and A. Livneh. Jerusalem: Qedem Reports.

Ben-Ami, D., and A. Livneh. 2005. "The Typological Analysis of the Pottery of the Middle and Late Bronze Ages." Pages 247–348 in *Yoqne'am III: The Middle and Late Bronze Ages*. Edited by A. Ben-Tor, D. Ben-Ami, and A. Livneh. Qedem Reports 7. Jerusalem: Qedem Reports.

Ben-Dov, R. 2011. *Dan III: Avraham Biran Excavations (1966–1999); The Late Bronze Age*. Jerusalem: Nelson Glueck School of Biblical Archaeology, Hebrew Union College–Jewish Institute of Religion.

Ben-Tor, A., ed. 1989. *Hazor III–IV: An Account of the Third and Fourth Seasons of Excavation, 1957–1958. Text*. Jerusalem: Israel Exploration Society.

———. 1996. "Introduction." Pages 1–2 in *Yoqne'am I: The Late Periods*. Edited by A. Ben-Tor, M. Avissar, and Y. Portugali. Qedem Reports 3. Jerusalem: Qedem Reports.

———. 2005. "Hazor and Chronology." *Agypten und Levante* 14:45–67.

———. 2015. *Hazor: Canaanite Metropolis, Israelite City*. Jerusalem: Israel Exploration Society.

———. 2020. "Building 7050 at the Acropolis of Late Bronze Age Hazor: A Palace After All." *Tel Aviv* 47:173–92.

Ben-Tor, A., and S. Bechar. 2017. "Introduction." Pages 1–3 in *Hazor VII: The 1990–2012 Excavations—The Bronze Age*. Edited by A. Ben-Tor, S. Zuckerman, S. Bechar, and D. Sandhaus. Jerusalem: Israel Exploration Society.

Ben-Tor, A., and D. Ben-Ami. 2005. "The Late Bronze Age Strata at Yoqne'am: Terminology, Chronology and Historical Background." Pages 241–43 in *Yoqne'am III: The Middle and Late Bronze Ages*. Edited by A. Ben-Tor, D. Ben-Ami, and A. Livneh. Qedem Reports 7. Jerusalem: Qedem Reports.

Ben-Tor, A., D. Ben-Ami, and D. Sandhaus, eds. 2012. *Hazor VI: The 1990–2009 Excavations, the Iron Age.* Jerusalem: Israel Exploration Society.

Ben-Tor, A., and R. Bonfil, eds. 1997. *Hazor V: An Account of the Fifth Season of Excavations, 1968: Text and Illustrations.* Jerusalem: Qedem Reports.

———. 2003. "The Stratigraphy and Pottery Assemblage of the Middle and Late Bronze Ages in Area A." Pages 185–276 in *Tel Qashish: A Village in the Jezreel Valley.* Edited by A. Ben-Tor, R. Bonfil, and S. Zuckerman. Qedem Reports 5. Jerusalem: Qedem Reports.

Ben-Tor, A., R. Bonfil, and S. Zuckerman, eds. 2003. *Tel Qashish: A Village in the Jezreel Valley.* Qedem Reports 5. Jerusalem: Qedem Reports.

Ben-Tor, A., S. Zuckerman, S. Bechar, R. Bonfil, D. Weinblatt, and D. Sandhaus. 2017b. "The Late Bronze Age." Pages 66–141 in *Hazor VII: The 1990–2012 Excavations—The Bronze Age.* Edited by A. Ben-Tor, S. Zuckerman, S. Bechar, and D. Sandhaus. Jerusalem: Israel Exploration Society.

Ben-Tor, A., S. Zuckerman, S. Bechar, and D. Weinblatt. 2017a. "The Middle Bronze Age." Pages 20–65 in *Hazor VII: The 1990–2012 Excavations—The Bronze Age.* Edited by A. Ben-Tor, S. Zuckerman, S. Bechar, and D. Sandhaus. Jerusalem: Israel Exploration Society.

Ben-Tor, D. 2009. "Can Scarabs Argue for the Origin of the Hyksos?" *Journal of Ancient Egyptian Interconnections* 1.1:1–7.

———. 2011. "Egyptian-Canaanite Relations in the Middle and Late Bronze Ages as Reflected by Scarabs." Pages 23–43 in *Egypt, Canaan and Israel: History, Imperialism, Ideology and Literature Proceedings of a Conference at the University of Haifa, 3–7 May 2009.* Edited by S. Bar, D. Kahn, and J. J. Shirley. Leiden: Brill.

———. 2018. "Evidence for Middle Bronze Age Chronology and Synchronisms in the Levant: A Response to Höflmayer et al. 2016." *Bulletin of the American School of Oriental Research* 379:43–54.

Bienkowski, P. 1989. "Prosperity and Decline in LBA Canaan: A Reply to Liebowitz and Knapp." *Bulletin of the American Schools of Oriental Research* 275:59–63.

Bietak, M. 1991. "Egypt and Canaan During the Middle Bronze Age." *Bulletin of the American Schools of Oriental Research* 281:27–72.

———. 2010. "From Where Came the Hyksos and Where Did They Go?" Pages 139–81 in *The Second Intermediate Period (Thirteenth–Seventeenth Dynasties).* Edited by M. Maree. Leuven: Peeters.

———. 2013. "Antagonisms in Historical and Radiocarbon Chronology." Pages 76–109 in *Radiocarbon and the Chronologies of Ancient Egypt.* Edited by C. Bronk Ramsey and A. J. Shortland. Oxford: Oxbow.

Binford, L. R. 1962. "Archaeology as Anthropology." *American Antiquity* 28.2:217–25.

Bonfil, R. 1997. "Area A." Pages 15–176 in *Hazor V: An Account of the Fifth Season of Excavations, 1968.* Edited by A. Ben-Tor and R. Bonfil. Jerusalem: Israel Exploration Society.

———. 2003. "Changes in the Material Culture at Tel Qashish Over Time in Comparison with Other Sites in the Jezreel Valley." Pages 319–26 in *Tel Qashish: A Village in the Jezreel Valley.* Edited by A. Ben-Tor, R. Bonfil, and S. Zuckerman. Qedem Reports 5. Jerusalem: Qedem Reports.

———. 2012. "Did Thutmose III's Troops Encounter Megiddo X?" Pages 129–55 in *All the Wisdom of the East: Studies in Near Eastern Archaeology and History in Honor of Eliezer D. Oren*. Edited by M. Gruber, S. Aḥituv, G. Lehmann, and Z. Talshir. Fribourg: Academic Press.

Bourriau, J. 2003. "The Second Intermediate Period." Pages 172–206 in *The Oxford History of Ancient Egypt*. Edited by I. Shaw. Oxford: Oxford University Press.

Bronk Ramsey, C., M. W. Dee, J. M. Rowland, T. F. G. Higham, S. A. Harris, F. Brock, A. Quiles, E. M. Wild, E. S. Marcus, and A. J. Shortland. 2010. "Radiocarbon-Based Chronology for Dynastic Egypt." *Science* 328:1554–57.

Broodbank, C. 2013. *The Making of the Middle Sea: A History of the Mediterranean from the Beginning to the Emergence of the Classical World*. London: Oxford University Press.

Brumfiel, E. M., and T. K. Earle. 1987. "Specialization, Exchange, and Complex Societies: An Introduction." Pages 1–10 in *Specialization, Exchange, and Complex Societies*. Edited by E. M. Brumfiel and T. K. Earle. Cambridge: Cambridge University Press.

Bryan, B. M. 2003. "The 18th Dynasty Before the Amarna Period (c.1550–1352 B.C.)." Pages 207–64 in *The Oxford History of Ancient Egypt*. Edited by I. Shaw. Oxford: Oxford University Press.

Bunimovitz, S. 1989. "The Land of Israel in the Late Bronze Age: A Case Study of Socio-Cultural Change in a Complex Society." Ph.D. diss., Tel Aviv University.

———. 1995. "On the Edge of Empires—Late Bronze Age (1500–1200 BCE)." Pages 3120–3331 in *The Archaeology of Society in the Holy Land*. Edited by T. E. Levy. New York: Continuum.

———. 1996. "The Problem of Human Resources in Late Bronze Age Palestine and Its Socio-Economic Implications." *Eretz-Israel* 25:45–54.

Burke, A. A. 2007. "Magdalūma, Migdālîm, Magdoloi, and Majādīl: The Historical Geography and Archaeology of the Magdalu (Migdāl)." *Bulletin of the American School of Oriental Research* 346:29–57.

———. 2008. *"Walled Up to Heaven": The Evolution of Middle Bronze Age Fortification Strategies in the Levant*. Winona Lake, IN: Eisenbrauns.

———. 2014. "Introduction to the Levant During the Middle Bronze Age." Pages 403–13 in *The Oxford Handbook of the Archaeology of the Levant, c. 8000–332 BCE*. Edited by M. L. Steiner and A. E. Kilbrew. Oxford: Oxford University Press.

Burke, A. A., M. Peilstöcker, A. Karoll, G. A. Pierce, K. Kowalski, Ben-Marzouk N., J. C. Damm, A. J. Danielson, H. D. Fessler, and B. Kaufman. 2017. "Excavations of the New Kingdom Fortress in Jaffa, 2011–2014: Traces of Resistance to Egyptian Rule in Canaan." *American Journal of Archaeology* 121.1:85–133.

Burke, S. J. 1993. "The Transition from the Middle to the Late Bronze Age in Syria: The Evidence from Tell Nebi Mend." *Levant* 25:155–95.

Carlyle, T. n.d. "On History." Blupete.com. http://www.blupete.com/Literature/Essays/Best/CarlyleHistory.htm.

Charaf, H. 2004. "An Assessment of the Continuity and Change in the LBI Pottery at Tell Arqa, Lebanon." *Ägypten und Levante* 14:231–48.

———. 2014. "The Northern Levant (Lebanon) During the Middle Bronze Age." Pages 434–50 in *The Oxford Handbook of the Archaeology of the Levant, c. 8000–332 BCE*. Edited by M. L. Steiner and A. E. Kilbrew. Oxford: Oxford University Press.

———. Forthcoming. "Ceramic Manufacture Traditions at Tell Arqa, Lebanon During the Late Bronze Age: From Traditionalism to Regionalism." In *Ceramic Identities* at the Edges of Empires: The Regional Dimension of Pottery Production in Late Bronze Age Northern Syria and Anatolia; Acts of the International Symposium, Florence January 14–17, 2015.

Cohen, S. L. 2002. *Canaanites, Chronoloies, and Connections: The Relationship of Middle Bronze Age IIa Canaan to Middle Kingdom Egypt*. Winona Lake, IN: Eisenbrauns.

———. 2015. "Periphery and Core: The Relationship Between the Southern Levant and Egypt in the Early Middle Bronze Age (MB I)." Pages 245–64 in *There and Back Again: The Crossroads II; Proceedings of an International Conference Held in Prague, September 15–18, 2014*. Edited by J. Mynářová, P. Onderka, and P. Pavúk. Prague: Czech Institute of Egyptology.

Collingwood, R. G. 1927. "Oswald Spengler and the Theory of Historical Cycles." *Antiquity* 1:311–25.

Collins, S. 2006. "A Monumental Building at Sidon: Room 3, Context 971." *Archaeology and History in the Lebanon* 24:106–13.

Costin, C. L. 1991. "Craft Specialization: Issues in Defining, Documenting, and Explaining the Organization of Production." *Archaeological Method and Theory* 3:1–56.

Cryer, F. H. 1995. "Chronology: Issues and Problems." Pages 651–64 in volume 4 of *Civilizations of the Ancient Near East*. Edited by J. M. Sasson, J. Baines, G. M. Beckman, and K. S. Rubinson. New York: Scribners.

Da Ros, M. 2015. "An Example of Late Bronze Age II Residential Architecture in Area T1 at Mishrifeh." Pages 415–21 in *Qatna and the Networks of Bronze Age Globalism (Proceedings of an International Conference in Stuttgart and Tubingen in October 2009)*. Edited by P. Pfälzner and M. Al-Maqdissi. Weisbaden: Harrassowitz.

Dever, W. G. 1974. "The MB IIC Stratification in the Northwest Gate Area at Shechem." *Bulletin of the American School of Oriental Research* 216:31–52.

———. 1980. "New Vistas on the EB IV ('MB I') Horizon in Syria-Palestine." *Bulletin of the American Schools of Oriental Research* 237:35–64.

———. 1987. "Archaeological Sources for the History of Palestine: The Middle Bronze Age: The Zenith of the Urban Canaanite Era." *The Biblical Archaeologist* 50.3:149–77.

———. 1992. "The Chronology of Syria-Palestine in the Second Millennium BCE: A Review of Current Issues." *Bulletin of the American Schools of Oriental Research* 288:1–25.

Dijk, J. van. 2003. "The Amarna Period and the Later New Kingdom (c.1352–1069 BC)." Pages 265–307 in *The Oxford History of Ancient Egypt*. Edited by I. Shaw. Oxford: Oxford University Press.

Dothan, T., S. Zuckerman, and Y. Goren. 2000. "Kamares Ware at Hazor." *Israel Exploration Journal* 50:1–15.

Doumet-Serhal, C. 1996. *Les Fouilles de Tell El-Ghassil de 1972 à 1974: Étude Du Matériel*. Beirut: IFPO.

———. 2002. "Fourth Season of Excavation at Sidon Preliminary Report." *Bulletin d'Archéologie et d'Architecture Linanaises* 6:179–210.

———. 2004. "Sixth and Seventh Seasons of Excavations at Sidon Preliminary Report." *Bulletin d'Archéologie et d'Architecture Linanaises* 8:47–82.

———. 2006. "Eighth and Ninth Season of Excavation (2006–2007) at Sidon: Preliminary Report." *Bulletin d'Archéologie et d'Architecture Linanaises* 10:131–65.

---. 2009a. "Second Millennium BC Levantine Ceremonial Feasts: Sidon a Case Study." *Bulletin d'Archéologie et d'Architecture Linanaises*, n.s. 6:229–42.
---. 2009b. "Tenth, Eleventh and Twelfth Season of Excavation (2008–2010) at Sidon." *Bulletin d'Archéologie et d'Architecture Linanaises* 13:7–69.
Drennan, R. D. 2010. *Statistics for Archaeologists*. New York: Springer.
Driessen, J. 1995. "'Crisis Architecture'? Some Observations on Architectural Adaptations as Immediate Responses to Changing Socio-Cultural Conditions." *Topoi* 5.1:63–88.
---. 2003. "Towards an Archaeology of Crisis: Defining the Long-Term Impact of the Bronze Age Santorini Eruption." Pages 250–63 in *Natural Disasters and Cultural Change*. Edited by R. Torrence and J. Grattan. London: Routledge.
Dunayevsky, I., and Kempinski A. 1973. "The Megiddo Temples." *Zeitschrift Des Deutschen Palästina-Vereins* 89.2:161–87.
Earle, T. K. 2002. *Bronze Age Economics: The Beginnings of Political Economies*. Boulder, CO: Routledge.
Echt, R. 1984. *Kamid El-Loz 5: Die Stratigraphie*. Bonn: Habelt.
Engles, F. 1972. *The Origin of the Family, Private Property, and the State*. New York: International Publishers.
Epstein, C. 1965. "An Interpretation of the Megiddo Sacred Area During Middle Bronze II." *Israel Exploration Journal* 15.4:204–21.
---. 1966. *Palestinian Bichrome Ware*. Leiden: Brill.
Fink, A. S. 2010. *Late Bronze Age Tell Atchana (Alalakh): Stratigraphy, Chronology, History*. Oxford: Archaeopress.
Finkelstein, I. 1996. "Towards a New Periodization and Nomenclature of the Archaeology of the Southern Levant." Pages 103–24 in *The Study of the Ancient Near East in the Twenty-First Century: The William Foxwell Albright Centennial Conference*. Edited by J. S Cooper and G. M. Schwartz. Winona Lake, IN: Eisenbrauns.
---. 2013. "Area M: Part III: Another Interpretation of the Remains—The Nordburg and Chamber F." Pages 228–46 in *Megiddo V: The 2004–2008 Seasons*. Edited by I. Finkelstein, D. Ussishkin, and E. H. Cline. Tel Aviv: Institute of Archaeology of Tel Aviv University.
---. 2016. "To Date or Not to Date: Radiocarbon and the Arrival of the Philistines." *Agypten und Levante* 26:285–84.
Finkelstein, I., D. Langgut, M. Meiri, and L. Sapir-Hen. 2017. "Egyptian Imperial Economy in Canaan: Reaction to the Climate Crisis at the End of the Late Bronze Age." *Agypten und Levante* 27:249–59.
Finkelstein, I., D. Ussishkin, and B. Halpern. 2000. "Introduction: The Megiddo Expedition." Pages 1–13 in *Megiddo III: The 1992–1996 Seasons*. Edited by I. Finkelstein, D. Ussishkin, and B. Halpern. Tel Aviv: Institute of Archaeology of Tel Aviv University.
---. 2006. "Introduction: The 1998–2002 Season." Pages 1–18 in *Megiddo IV: The 1998–2002 Seasons*. Edited by I. Finkelstein, D. Ussishkin, and B. Halpern. Tel Aviv: Institute of Archaeology of Tel Aviv University.
Franklin, N. 2013. "Area M: Part I: The Excavation." Pages 178–214 in *Megiddo V: The 2004–2008 Seasons*. Edited by I. Finkelstein, D. Ussishkin, and E. H. Cline. Tel Aviv: Institute of Archaeology of Tel Aviv University.
Furumark, A. 1941. *The Mycenaean Pottery: Analysis and Classification*. Stockholm: Kungl. Vitterhets Historie och Antikvitets Adademien.

Gadot, Y. 2010. "The Late Bronze Egyptian Estate at Aphek." *Tel Aviv* 37.1:48–66.
Garstang, J., L. Vincent, W. F. Albright, and W. J. Phythian-Adams. 1922. "A New Chronological Classification of Palestinian Archaeology." *Bulletin of the American Schools of Oriental Research* 7:9.
Gonen, R. 1984. "Urban Canaan in the Late Bronze Period." *Bulletin of the American Schools of Oriental Research* 253:61–73.
Greenberg, R. 2002. *Early Urbanizations in the Levant: A Regional Narrative.* London: Leicester University Press.
Heinz, M. 2016. *Kamid El-Loz: 4000 Years and More of Rural and Urban Lebanese Beqa'a Plain.* Beirut: Beyrouth.
Higginbotham, C. R. 2000. *Egyptianization and Elite Emulation in Ramesside Palestine: Governance and Accommodation on the Imperial Periphery.* Leiden: Brill.
Hoffmeier, J. K. 2004. "Aspects of Egyptian Foreign Policy in the 18th Dynasty in Western Asia and Nubia." Pages 121–41 in *Egypt, Israel, and the Ancient Mediterranean World: Studies in Honor of Donald B. Redford.* Edited by G. N. Knoppers and A. Hirsch. Boston: Brill.
Höflmayer, F. 2017. "A Radiocarbon Chronology for the Middle Bronze Age Southern Levant." *Journal of Ancient Egyptian Interconnections* 13:20–33.
Höflmayer, F., and S. L. Cohen. 2017. "Chronological Conundrums: Egypt and the Middle Bronze Age Southern Levant." *Journal of Ancient Egyptian Interconnections* 13:1–6.
Höflmayer, F., J. Kamlah, H. Sader, M. W. Dee, W. Kutschera, W. M. Wild, and S. Riehl. 2016. "New Evidence for Middle Bronze Age Chronology and Synchronisms in the Levant: Radiocarbon Dates from Tell El-Burak, Tell el-Dab'a, and Tell Ifshar Compared." *Bulletin of the American School of Oriental Research* 375:53–76.
Höflmayer, F., A. Yasur-Landau, E. H. Cline, M. W. Dee, B. Lorentzen, and S. Riehl. 2016. "New Radiocarbon Dates from Tel Kabri Support a High Middle Bronze Age Chronology." *Radiocarbon* 58.3:599–613.
Horowitz, W., and T. Oshima. 2006. *Cuneiform in Canaan: Cuneiform Sources from the Land of Israel in Ancient Times.* Jerusalem: Israel Exploration Society.
Iamoni, M. 2012. *The Late MBA and LBA Pottery Horizons at Qatna: Innovation and Conservation in the Ceramic Tradition of a Regional Capital and the Implications for Second Millennium Syrian Chronology.* Udine: Forum.
———. 2014. "Transitions in Ceramics, a Critical Account and Suggested Approach: Case-Study Through Comparison of the EBA–MBA and MBA–LBA Horizons at Qatna." *Levant* 46.1:4–26.
———. 2015. "Pottery Production During the Third and Second Millennium B.C. in Western Syria: The Development of Ceramic Technology as a Result of the Rise of Qatna as a Regional Capital." Pages 183–206 in *The Transmission of Technical Knowledge in the Production of Ancient Mediterranean Pottery: Proceedings of the International Conference at the Austrian Archaeological Institute at Athens 23rd–25th November 2012.* Edited by W. Gauss, G. Klebinder-Gauss, and C. von Rüden. Vienna: Österreichisches Archäologisches Institut.
Ilan, D. 1995. "The Dawn of Internationalism: The Middle Bronze Age." Pages 297–319 in *The Archaeology of Society in the Holy Land.* Edited by T. E. Levy. New York: Continuum.
———. 1996. "The Middle Bronze Age Tombs." Pages 161–329 in *Dan I: A Chronicle of the Excavations, the Pottery Neolithic, the Early Bronze Age and the Middle*

Bronze Age Tombs. Edited by A. Biran, D. Ilan, and R. Greenberg. Jerusalem: Nelson Glueck School of Biblical Archaeology, Hebrew Union College–Jewish Institute of Religion.

———. 2003. "The Middle Bronze Age (circa 2000–1500 B.C.E.)." Pages 331–42 in *Near Eastern Archaeology: A Reader*. Edited by S. Richard. Winona Lake, IN: Eisenbrauns.

Ilan, D., N. Franklin, and R. S. Hallote. 2000. "Area F." Pages 75–103 in *Megiddo III: The 1992–1996 Seasons*. Edited by I. Finkelstein, D. Ussishkin, and B. Halpern. Tel Aviv: Institute of Archaeology of Tel Aviv University.

Josephus, Flavius. 2007. *Against Apion*. Translated by J. M. G Barclay. Leiden: Brill.

Kahn, D. 2011. "One Step Forward, Two Steps Backwards: The Relationship Between Amenhotep III, King of Egypt and Tushratta, King of Mitanni." Pages 136–54 in *Egypt, Canaan and Israel: History, Imperialism, Ideology and Literature Proceedings of a Conference at the University of Haifa, 3–7 May 2009*. Edited by S. Bar, D. Kahn, and J. J. Shirley. Leiden: Brill.

Kanhoush, Y. 2015. "Rapport Préliminaire Des Résultats Des Campagnes de Fouilles Syrriennes 2006–2009. Le 'Palais Est' Du Chantier T Sur l'Acropole de Mishrifeh-Qatna." Pages 441–49 in *Qatna and the Networks of Bronze Age Globalism (Proceedings of an International Conference in Stuttgart and Tubingen in October 2009)*. Edited by P. Pfälzner and M. Al-Maqdissi. Weisbaden: Harrassowitz.

Karasik, A., and U. Smilansky. 2008. "3D Scanning Technology as a Standard Archaeological Tool for Pottery Analysis: Practice and Theory." *Journal of Archaeological Science* 35.5:1148–68.

Kassis, H. E. 1964. "The Ceramic Chronology of the Late Bronze Age in Palestine: Phase I: 1525–1450 B.C." Ph.D. diss., Harvard University.

Kenyon, K. M. 1969. "The Middle and Late Bronze Age Strata at Megiddo." *Levant* 1.1:25–60.

Killebrew, A. E. 1998. "Ceramic Craft and Technology During the Late Bronze and Early Iron Ages: The Relationship Between Pottery Technology, Style and Cultural Diversity." Ph.D. diss., The Hebrew University of Jerusalem.

———. 2005. *Biblical Peoples and Ethnicity: An Archaeological Study of Egyptians, Canaanites, Philistines, and Early Israel, 1300–1100 BCE*. Atlanta: SBL.

Kitchen, K. 2000. "The Historical Chronology of Ancient Egypt, a Current Assessment." Pages 40–52 in *The Synchronisation of Civilisations in the Eastern Mediterranean in the Second Millennium B.C*. Edited by M. Bietak. Vienna: Verlag der Osterreichischen Akademie der Wissenschaften.

Klengel, H. 2014. "Anatolia (Hittites) and the Levant." Pages 90–97 in *The Oxford Handbook of the Archaeology of the Levant, c.8000–332 BCE*. Edited by M. L. Steiner and A. E. Killebrew. Oxford: Oxford Uniersity Press.

Knapp, A. B. 1987. "Pots, PIXE, and Data Processing at Pella in Jorda." *Bulletin of the American Schools of Oriental Research* 266:1–30.

———. 1992. "Independence and Imperialism: Politico-Economic Structures in the Bronze Age Levant." Pages 83–98 in *Archaeology, Annales and Ethnohistory*. Edited by A. B. Knapp. Cambridge: Cambridge University Press.

Koch, I. 2014. "Goose Keeping, Elite Emulation and Egyptianized Feasting at Late Bronze Lachish." *Tel Aviv* 41:161–79.

———. 2015. "Southwestern Canaan During the Late Bronze Age and the Early Iron Age: Empire, Elites and Colonial Encounters." Ph.D. diss., Tel Aviv University.

Krauss, R., and D. A. Warburton. 2009. "The Basis for the Egyptian Dates." Pages 125–44 in *Time's Up! Dating the Minoan Eruption of Santorini: Acts of the Minoan Eruption Chronology Workshop, Sandbjerg November 2007, Initiated by Jan Heinemeier and Walter L. Friedrich*. Edited by D. A. Warburton, J. Heinemeier, and W. L. Friedrich. Athens: Danish Institute at Athens.

Kutschera, W., M. Bietak, E. M. Wild, B. C. Ramsey, M. Dee, R. Golser, K. Kopetzky, P. Stadler, P. Steier, and U. Thanheiser. 2012. "The Chronology of Tell el-Daba: A Crucial Meeting Point of 14C Dating, Archaeology, and Egyptology in the 2nd Millennium BC." *Radiocarbon* 54.3–4:407–22.

Langgut, D., I. Finkelstein, and T. Litt. 2013. "Climate and the Late Bronze Collapse: New Evidence from the Southern Levant." *Tel Aviv* 40.2:149–75.

Leonard, A. 1989. "Archaeological Sources for the History of Palestine: The Late Bronze Age." *The Biblical Archaeologist* 52.1:4–39.

———. 1994. *An Index to the Late Bronze Age Aegean Pottery from Syria-Palestine*. Jonsered: Astroms.

———. 2003. "The Late Bronze Age." Pages 349–56 in *Near Eastern Archaeology: A Reader*. Edited by S. Richard. Winona Lake, IN: Eisenbrauns.

Liebmann, M., T. J. Ferguson, and R. W. Preucel. 2005. "Pueblo Settlement, Architecture, and Social Change in the Pueblo Revolt Era, AD 1680 to 1696." *Journal of Field Archaeology* 30.1:45–60.

Liebowitz, H. 1987. "Late Bronze II Ivory Work in Palestine: Evidence of a Cultural Highpoint." *Bulletin of the American Schools of Oriental Research* 265:3–24.

Liverani, M. 2001. *International Relations in the Ancient Near East, 1600–1100 BC*. Basingstoke, UK: Palgrave.

Livneh, A., and Ben-Tor A. 2005. "The Architecture and Stratigraphy of the Middle Bronze Age." Pages 11–39 in *Yoqne'am III: The Middle and Late Bronze Ages*. Edited A. Ben-Tor, D. Ben-Ami, and A. Livneh. Qedem Reports 7. Jerusalem: Qedem Reports.

Loud, G. 1948a. *Megiddo II: Seasons of 1935–39—Plates*. Chicago: University of Chicago Press.

———. 1948b. *Megiddo II: Seasons of 1935–39—Text*. Chicago: University of Chicago Press.

Luciani, M. 2002. "Operation K." Pages 145–68 in *Excavating Qatna*. Edited by M. Al-Maqdissi, M. Luciani, D. Moranci Bonacossi, M. Novak, and P. Pfälzner. Damascus: Direction Générale des Antiquités et des Musées de la République Arabe Syrienne; Udine: University of Udine Press; Tübingen: University of Tübingen Press.

———. 2003. "The Lower City of Qatna in the Late Bronze Age and Iron Ages: Operation K." *Akkadica* 124:144–63.

———. 2014. "The Northern Levant (Syria) During the Late Bronze Age." Pages 509–23 in *The Oxford Handbook of the Archaeology of the Levant, c. 8000–332 BCE*. Edited by M. L. Steiner and A. E. Kilbrew. Oxford: Oxford University Press.

Maeir, A. M. 1997. "The Material Culture of the Central Jordan Valley During the Middle Bronze II Period: Pottery and Settlement Pattern." Ph.D. diss., Hebrew University of Jerusalem.

———. 2000. "The Political and Economic Status of MB II Hazor and MB II Trade: An Inter- and Intraregional View." *Palestine Exploration Quarterly* 132.1:37–58.

———. 2007. "The Middle Bronze Age II Pottery." Pages 242–389 in *Excavations at Tel Beth-Shean, 1989–1996*, volume 4: *The 4th and 3rd Millennia BCE*. Edited by A. Mazar and R. Mullins. Jerusalem: Israel Exploration Society.

———. 2010. *"In the Midst of the Jordan": The Jordan Valley During the Middle Bronze Age (Circa 2000–1500 BCE)*. Vienna: Verlag der Osterreichischen Akademie der Wissenschaften.

Malamat, A. 1960. "Hazor 'The Head of All Those Kingdoms.'" *Journal of Biblical Literature* 79.1:12–19.

———. 2006. "Trade Relations Between Mari and Hazor (State of Research, 2002)." Pages 351–55 in *Confronting the Past: Archaeological and Historical Essays on Ancient Israel in Honor of William G. Dever*. Edited by S. Gitin, J. E. Wright, and J. P. Dessel. Winona Lake, IN: Eisenbrauns.

Manning, S. W., C. B. Griggs, B. Lorentzen, G. Barjamovic, C. Bronk Ramsey, B. Kromer, and E. M. Wild. 2016. "Integrated Tree-Ring-Radiocarbon High-Resolution Timeframe to Resolve Earlier Second Millennium BCE Mesopotamian Chronology." *PLoS ONE* 11.7:1–27.

Manning, S. W., C. B. Griggs, B. Lorentzena, C. Bronk Ramsey, D. Chivall, T. Jull, and T. E. Lange. 2018. "Fluctuating Radiocarbon Offsets Observed in the Southern Levant and Implications for Archaeological Chronology Debates." *Proceedings of the National Academy of Sciences of the United States of America* 115.24:6141–46.

Maran, J. 2006. "Mycenaean Citadels as Performative Space." Pages 75–92 in *Constructing Power: Architecture, Ideology and Social Practice*. Edited by J. Maran, J. Carsten, H. Schwengel, and U. Thaler. Hamburg: Lit Verlag.

Marée, M. 2017. "A Fragment of the Statue of an Egyptian Official." Pages 578–83 in *Hazor VII: The 1990–2012 Excavations—The Bronze Age*. Edited by A. Ben-Tor, S. Zuckerman, S. Bechar, and D. Sandhaus. Jerusalem: Israel Exploration Society.

Marom, N., A. Yasur-Landau, S. Zuckerman, E. H. Cline, A. Ben-Tor, and G. Bar-Oz. 2014. "Shepherd Kings? A Zooarchaeological Investigation of Elite Precincts in Middle Bronze Age Tel Hazor and Tel Kabri." *Bulletin of the American School of Oriental Research* 371:59–82.

Marom, N., and S. Zuckerman. 2012. "The Zooarchaeology of Exclusion and Expropriation: Looking Up from the Lower City in Late Bronze Age Hazor." *Journal of Anthropological Archaeology* 31:573–85.

Martin, M. A. S. 2011. *Egyptian-Type Pottery in the Late Bronze Age Southern Levant*. Wien: Verlag der Osterreichischen Akademie der Wissenschaften.

Matthiae, P. 2009. "Crisis and Collapse: Similarity and Diversity in the Three Destructions of Ebla from EB IVa to MB II." *Scienze Dell'Antichità* 15:43–83.

Mazar, A. 1992. *Archaeology of the Land of the Bible: 10,000–586 B.C.E.* New York: Doubleday.

———. 1997. "Area P." Pages 353–84 in *Hazor V: An Account of the Fifth Season of Excavation, 1968*. Edited by A. Ben-Tor and R. Bonfil. Jerusalem: Israel Exploration Society.

———, ed. 2006. *Excavations at Tel Beth-Shean, 1989–1996*, volume 1: *From the Late Bronze Age IIb to the Medieval Period*. Jerusalem: Israel Exploration Society.

———. 2011. "The Egyptian Garrison Town at Beth-Shean." Pages 155–89 in *Egypt, Canaan and Israel: History, Imperialism, Ideology and Literature*. Edited by A. Bar, D. Kahn, and J. J. Shirley. Leiden: Brill.

Mazar, A., and R. Mullins. 2007. "Introduction and Overview." Pages 1–22 in *Excavations at Tel Beth-Shean, 1989–1996*, volume 2: *The Middle and Late Bronze Age Strata in Area R*. Edited by A. Mazar and R. Mullins. Jerusalem: Israel Exploration Society.

Mazar, A., and N. Panitz-Cohen. 2001. *Timnah (Tel Batash) II: The Finds from the First Millenium BCE*. Qedem 42. Jerusalem: Institute of Archaeology, the Hebrew University of Jerusalem.

Mazar, B. 1968. "The Middle Bronze Age in Palestine." *Israel Exploration Journal* 18.2:65–97.

Mazzoni, S. 2000. "Pots, People and Cultural Borders in Syria." Pages 139–52 in *Landscapes, Territories, Frontiers and Horizons in the Ancient Near East*. Edited by L. Milano, S. de Martino, F. M. Fales, and G. B. Lanfranchi. Padova: Sargon.

Mettinger, T. N. D. 1995. *No Graven Image? Israelite Aniconism in Its Ancient Near Eastern Context*. Stockholm: Almqvist & Wiksell.

Metzger, M. 2012. *Kamid El-Loz 17: Die Mittlebronzezeitlichen Templeanlangen T4 und T5*. Saarbrücker Beiträge zur Altertumskunde 71. Bonn: Habelt.

Moran, W. L. 1992. *The Amarna Letters*. Baltimore: Johns Hopkins University Press.

Morandi Bonacossi, D. 2002. "Operation J." Pages 123–44 in *Excavating Qatna*. Edited by M. Al-Maqdissi, M. Luciani, D. Moranci Bonacossi, M. Novak, and P. Pfälzner. Damascus: Direction Générale des Antiquités et des Musées de la République Arabe Syrienne; Udine: University of Udine Press; Tübingen: University of Tübingen Press.

———. 2007. "The Chronology of the Royal Palace of Qatna Revisited: A Reply to a Paper by Mirko Novak, Egypt and the Levant 14, 2004." *Agypten und Levante* 27:221–40.

———. 2008. "Excavations on the Acropolis of Mishrifeh: A New Early Bronze Age III—Iron Age III Sequence for Central Inner Syria. Part 1: Stratigraphy, Chronology and Architecture." *Akkadica* 129.1:55–127.

———. 2013. "The Crisis of Qatna at the Beginning of Late Bronze Age II and the Iron Age II Settlement Revival: A Regional Trajectory Towards the Collapse of the Late Bronze Age Palace System in the Northern Levant." Pages 113–46 in *Across the Border: Late Bronze-Iron Age Relations Between Syria and Anatolia*. Edited by K. A. Yener. Leuven: Peeters.

———. 2014. "The Northern Levant (Syria) During the Middle Bronze Age." Pages 414–33 in *The Oxford Handbook of the Archaeology of the Levant, c. 8000–332 BCE*. Edited by M. L. Steiner and A. E. Kilbrew. Oxford: Oxford University Press.

———. 2015. "The Lower City Palace at Qatna." Pages 359–75 in *Qatna and the Networks of Bronze Age Globalism (Proceedings of an International Conference in Stuttgart and Tubingen in October 2009)*. Edited by P. Pfälzner and M. Al-Maqdissi. Weisbaden: Harrassowitz.

Morandi Bonacossi, D., M. Da Ros, G. Garna, M. Iamoni, and M. Merlino. 2009. "The 'Eastern Palace' and the Residential Architecture of Area T at Mishrifeh/Qatna." *Mesopotamia* 44:61–113.

Morris, E. F. 2005. *The Architecture of Imperialism: Military Bases and the Evolution of Foreign Policy in Egypt's New Kingdom*. Leiden: Brill.

Mullins, R. 2002. "Beth-Shean During the Eighteenth Dynasty: From Canaanite Settlement to Egyptian Garrison." Ph.D. diss., Hebrew University of Jerusalem.

———. 2007. "The Late Bronze Age Pottery." Pages 390–547 in *Excavations at Tel Beth-Shean, 1989–1996*, volume 4: *The 4th and 3rd Millennia BCE*. Edited by A. Mazar and R. Mullins. Jerusalem: Israel Exploration Society.

Mullins, R., and A. Mazar. 2007. "Area R: The Stratigraphy and Architecture of the Middle and Late Bronze Ages: Strata R-5–R-1." Pages 39–241 in *Excavations at Tel Beth-Shean, 1989–1996*, volume 2: *The Middle and Late Bronze Age Strata in Area R*. Edited by A. Mazar and R. Mullins. Jerusalem: Israel Exploration Society.

Na'aman, N. 1976. "A New Look at the Chronology of Alalakh Level VII." *Anatolian Studies* 26:129–43.

———. 1979. "The Chronology of Alalakh Level VII Once Again." *Anatolian Studies* 29:103–13.

———. 1981. "Economic Aspects of the Egyptian Occupation of Canaan." *Israel Exploration Journal* 31.3–4:172–85.

———. 1982. "Eretz-Israel in the Canaanite Period: The Middle Bronze Age and the Late Bronze Age (2000–1200 BCE)." Pages 129–255 in *The History of Eretz Israel: Introduction, the Early Periods*. Edited by I. Efal. Jerusalem: Yad Yitshak Ben-Tsevi.

———. 1994. "The Hurrians and the End of the Middle Bronze Age in Palestine." *Levant* 26:175–87.

———. 1997. "The Network of Canaanite Late Bronze Age Kingdoms and the City of Ashdod." *Ugarit Forschungen* 29:599–625.

———. 2012. "Hazor in the Fourteenth-Thirteenth Centuries BCE in the Light of Historical and Archaeological Research." *Eretz-Israel* 30:333–41.

Novak, M. 2004. "The Chronology of the Royal Palace of Qatna." *Agypten und Levante* 14:229–318.

———. 2013. "Upper Mesopotamia in the Mitanni Period." Pages 337–48 in *Archeologie et Histoire en Syrie*, volume 1: *La Syrie de l'Époque Néolithique à l'Âge du Fer*. Edited by W. Orthmann, M. Paolo, and M. Al-Maqdissi. Wiesbaden: Harrassowitz.

O'Connor, D. 1997. "The Hyksos Period in Egypt." Pages 45–67 in *The Hyksos: New Historical and Archaeological Perspectives*. Edited by E. D. Oren. Philadelphia: University of Pennsylvania Museum of Archaeology and Anthropology.

Oppenheim, A. L. 1956. "The Interpretation of Dreams in the Ancient Near East: With a Translation of an Assyrian Dream-Book." *Transactions of the American Philosophical Society* 46.3:179–373.

Panitz-Cohen, N. 2009. "The Organization of Ceramic Production During the Transition from the Late Bronze Age to Iron Age I: Tel Batash as a Test Case." Pages 186–92 in *Forces of Transformation: The End of the Bronze Age in the Mediterranean*. Edited by C. Bachhuber and R. G. Roberts. Oxford: Oxbow.

———. 2014. "The Southern Levant (Cisjordan) During the Late Bronze Age." Pages 541–60 in *The Oxford Handbook of the Archaeology of the Levant, c. 8000–332 BCE*. Edited by M. L. Steiner and A. E. Killbrew. Oxford: Oxford University Press.

Panitz-Cohen, N., and A. Mazar, eds. 2009. *Excavations at Tel Beth-Shean, 1989–1996*, volume 2: *The 13th–11th Century BCE Strata in Areas N and S*. Jerusalem: Israel Exploration Society.

Pantou, P. A. 2014. "An Architectural Perspective on Social Change and Ideology in Early Mycenaean Greece." *American Journal of Archaeology* 118.3:369–400.

Parr, P. J. 1997. "Tell Nebi Mend." Pages 114–15 in *The Oxford Encyclopedia of Archaeology in the Near East*. Edited by E. Meyers. New York: Oxford University Press.

Pfälzner, P. 2007. "Archaeological Investigations in the Royal Palace of Qatna." Pages 29–64 in *Urban and Natural Landscapes of an Ancient Syrian Capital: Settlement and Environment at Tell Mishrifeh/Qatna and in Central-Western Syria*. Edited by D. Morandi Bonacossi. Udine: Forum.

Pinnock, F. 2014. "The Ceramic Horizon of Middle Bronze I–II in North Inner Syria: The Case of Ebla." Pages 227–46 in *Tell Tuqan Excavations and Regional Perspectives: Cultural Developments in Inner Syria from the Early Bronze Age to the Persian/Hellenistic Period*. Edited by F. Baffi, R. Foorentino, and L. Peyronel. Leece: Left Coast.

Quirke, S. J. 2001. "Second Intermediate Period." Pages 260–65 in *The Oxford Encyclopedia of Ancient Egypt*. Edited by D. B. Redford. Oxford: Oxford University Press.

Rapoport, A. 1990. *The Meaning of the Built Environment: A Nonverbal Communication Approach*. Tuscon: Sage.

Rathje, W. L. 1975. "The Last Tango in Mayapan: A Tentative Trajectory of Production-Distribution Systems." Pages 409–48 in *Ancient Civilization and Trade*. Edited by J. A. Sabloff and C. C. Lamberg-Karlovsky. Albuquerque: University of New Mexico Press.

Redford, D. B. 1979. "A Gate Inscription from Karnak and Egyptian Involvement in Western Asia During the Early 18th Dynasty." *Journal of the American Oriental Society* 99.2:270–87.

———. 1992. *Egypt, Canaan, and Israel in Ancient Times*. Princeton: Princeton University Press.

———. 1997. "Textual Sources for the Hyksos Period." Pages 1–44 in *The Hyksos: New Historical and Archaeological Perspectives*. Edited by E. D. Oren. Philadelphia: University of Pennsylvania Museum of Archaeology and Anthropology.

———. 2003. *The Wars in Syria and Palestine of Thutmose III*. Leiden: Brill.

Rice, P. M. 1984. "The Archaeological Study of Specialized Pottery Production: Some Aspects of Method and Theory." Pages 45–54 in *Pots and Potters: Current Approaches in Ceramic Archaeology*. Edited by P. M. Rice. Los Angeles: Institute of Archaeology–University of California.

———. 1987. *Pottery Analysis: A Sourcebook*. Chicago: University of Chicago Press.

Roaf, M. 1990. *Cultural Atlas of Mesopotamia and the Ancient Near East*. New York: Facts on Files.

Rowan, Y. M., and J. Golden. 2009. "The Chalcolithic Period of the Southern Levant: A Synthetic Review." *Journal of World Prehistory* 22:1–92.

Savage, S. H, and S. E. Falconer. 2003. "Spatial and Statistical Inference of Late Bronze Age Polities in the Southern Levant." *Bulletin of the American Schools of Oriental Research* 330:31–45.

Schloen, D. J. 2001. *The House of the Father as Fact and Symbol: Patrimonialism in Ugarit and the Ancient Near East*. Winona Lake, IN: Eisenbrauns.

Schwartz, G. M. 2008. "Problems of Chronology: Mesopotamia, Anatolia and the Syro-Levantine Region." Pages 450–52 in *Beyond Babylon: Art, Trade and Diplomacy in the Second Millennium B.C*. Edited by J. Aruz, K. Benzel, and J. M. Evans. New York: Metropolitan Museum of Art.

Shabo, S. 2015. "Le Quartier d'Habitation dans le Chantier de la Coupole de Loth à Qatna." Pages 407–13 in *Qatna and the Networks of Bronze Age Globalism (Proceedings of an International Conference in Stuttgart and Tubingen in October 2009)*. Edited by P. Pfälzner and M. Al-Maqdissi. Weisbaden: Harrassowitz.

Sharon, I. 2014. "Levantine Chronology." Pages 38–60 in *The Oxford Handbook of the Archaeology of the Levant, c. 8000–332 BCE*. Edited by M. L. Steiner and A. E. Kilbrew. Oxford: Oxford University Press.

Shaw, I., ed. 2000. *The Oxford History of Ancient Egypt*. Oxford: Oxford University Press.

Sherratt, A., and S. Sherratt. 1991. "From Luxuries to Commodities: The Nature of Mediterranean Bronze Age Trading Systems." Pages 351–86 in *Bronze Age Trade in the Mediterranean*. Edited by N. Gale. Jonsered: Astroms.

Smith, A. 2007. *An Inquiry into the Nature and Causes of the Wealth of Nations*. Edited by J. B. Wight. Hampshire: Electric Books.

Smith, S. T. 1995. *Askut in Nubia: The Economics and Ideology of Egyptian Imperialism in the Second Millennium BC*. London.

Steel, L. 2002. "Consuming Passions: A Contextual Study of the Local Consumption of Mycenaean Pottery at Tell el-'Ajjul." *Journal of Mediterranean Archaeology* 15.1:25–51.

Stein, G. J. 1998. "World System Theory and Alternative Modes of Interaction in the Archaeology of Culture Contact." Pages 220–55 in *Studies in Culture Contact: Interaction, Culture Change, and Archaeology*. Edited by J. G. Cusick. Carbondale: Southern Illinois University Press.

Steinmetz, G. 2014. "The Sociology of Empires, Colonies, and Postcolonialism." *Annual Review of Sociology* 40:77–103.

Stepansky, Y. 1999. "The Periphery of Hazor During the Bronze Age, the Iron Age and the Persian Period: A Regional—Archaeological Study." MA thesis, Tel Aviv University.

Stockhammer, P. W. 2012. "Entangled Pottery: Phenomena of Appropriation in the Late Bronze Age Eastern Mediterranean." Pages 89–103 in *Materiality and Social Practice: Transformative Capacities of Intercultural Encounters*. Edited by J. Maran and P. W. Stockhammer. Oxford: Oxbow.

Taraqji, A. F. 1999. "Nouvelles Découvertes sur le Relations avec l'Egypte à Tel Sakka et à Keswé, dans le Region de Damas." *Bulletin de La Société Française d'égyptologie* 144:27–43.

Thalmann, J. P. 2006a. *Tell Arqa I: Les Niveaux de l'Age Du Bronze*. Beirut: Institut francais du Proche-Orient.

———. 2006b. *Tell Arqa I: Les Niveaux de l'Age Du Bronze: Planches*. Beirut: Institut francais du Proche-Orient.

Van De Mieroop, M. 2007. *A History of the Ancient Near East ca. 3000–323 BC*. Chichester, UK: Wiley.

Wachtel, I. 2018. "The Upper Galilee During the Bronze and Iron Ages: Patterns of Settlement, Economy and Society." Ph.D. diss., The Hebrew University of Jerusalem.

———. Forthcoming. "Sixty Years After Aharoni: The Iron I Settlements in the Upper Galilee." In *From Nomadism to Monarchy? "The Archaeology of the Settlement Period"—30 Years Later*. Edited by O. Lipschits, O. Sergi, and I. Koch. Winona Lake, IN: Eisenbrauns.

Weinstein, J. M. 1981. "The Egyptian Empire in Palestine: A Reassessment." *Bulletin of the American Schools of Oriental Research* 241:1–28.
Wijngaarden, G. J. van. 2002. *Use and Appreciation of Mycenaean Pottery in the Levant, Cyprus and Italy (ca. 1600–1200 BC)*. Amsterdam: Amsterdam University Press.
Wilhelm, G. 2013. "Washukanni." Page 7062 in *The Encylopedia of Ancient History*. Edited by R. G. Bagnall, K. Broderson, C. B. Champion, A. Erskine, and S. R. Huebner. Oxford: Wiley Blackwell.
Wood, B. G. 1990. *The Sociology of Pottery in Ancient Palestine: The Ceramic Industry and the Diffusion of Ceramic Style in the Bronze and Iron Ages*. Sheffield: JSOT.
Woolley, L. 1955. *Alalakh: An Account of the Excavations at Tell Atchana*. Oxford: Society of Antiquaries of London.
Wright, J. E. 1961. "The Archaeology of Palestine." Pages 73–112 in *The Bible and the Ancient Near East: Essays in Honor of William Foxwell Albright*. Edited by J. E. Wright. Garden City, NY: Doubleday.
Yadin, Y. 1972. *Hazor: The Head of All Those Kingdoms Joshua 11:10 with a Chapter on Israelite Megiddo; The Schweich Lectures of the British Academy, 1970*. London: British Academy.
———. 1975. *Hazor: The Rediscovery of a Great Citadel of the Bible*. London: Weidenfeld & Nicolson.
Yadin, Y., Y. Aharoni, R. Amiran, T. Dothan, M. Dothan, I. Dunayevsky, and J. Perrot. 1961. *Hazor III–IV: An Account of the Third and Fourth Seasons of Excavations, 1957–1958: Plates*. Jerusalem: Israel Exploration Society.
Yadin, Y., Y. Aharoni, I. Dunayevsky, T. Dothan, R. Amiran, and J. Perrot. 1958. *Hazor I: An Account of the First Season of Excavations, 1955*. Jerusalem: Israel Exploration Society.
———. 1960. *Hazor II: An Account of the Second Season of Excavations, 1956*. Jerusalem: Israel Exploration Society.
Yasur-Landau, A., E. C. Cline, A. J. Koh, D. Ben-Shlomo, N. Marom, A. Ratzlaff, and I. Samet. 2015. "Rethinking Canaanite Palaces? The Palatial Economy of Tel Kabri During the Middle Bronze Age." *Journal of Field Archaeology* 40.6:607–25.
Zeeb, F. 2004. "The History of Alalah as a Testcase for an Ultrashort Chronology of the Mid-2nd Millennium BCE." Pages 81–95 in *Mesopotamian Dark Age Revisited*. Edited by H. Hunger and R. Pruzsinszky. Vienna: Oesterreichischen Akademie der Wissenschaften.
Zuckerman, S. 2003. "The Kingdom of Hazor in the Late Bronze Age: Chronological and Regional Aspects of the Material Culture of Hazor and Its Settlements." PhD diss., The Hebrew University of Jerusalem.
———. 2007. "Anatomy of a Destruction: Crisis Architecture, Termination Rituals and the Fall of Canaanite Hazor." *Journal of Mediterranean Archaeology* 20.1:3–32.
———. 2010. "'The City, Its Gods Will Return There . . .': Toward an Alternative Interpretation of Hazor's Acropolis in the Late Bronze Age." *Journal of Near Eastern Studies* 69.2:163–78.
———. 2015. "Conspicuous Consumption of Inconspicuous Pottery: The Case of the Late Bronze Age Southern Levant." Pages 135–52 in *Plain Pottery Traditions of the Eastern Mediterranean and Near East: Production, Use, and Social Significance*. Edited by C. Glatz. Walnut Creek, CA: Left Coast.

INDEX

abandonment, 33, 70–72, 85, 92, 94, 117, 120, 122, 229
Abdi Ashirta, 18, 24
Abydos, fig. 1.1, 12, 14
Aegean, 11, 24, 27, 34–35, 126, 173, 175, 195–96, 207, 213, 221, 231–32, 239
Ahmose, table 1.1, 12–15
Akhenaten, table 1.1, 18
Akkar Plain, 17, 27
Alalakh, fig. 1.1, 20–23, 25, 64
alienable, 31–32
Aleppo, fig. 1.1, 20, 22–27, 221, 230; *see also* Yamhad
altar, 43, 49, 63, 69, 237
Amarna, 11, 18, 22, 26, 229
Amenhotep II, table 1.1, 17, 19, 22
Amenhotep III, table 1.1, 17–18, 22
Amenhotep IV, *see* Akhenaten
Amenophis II, *see* Amenhotep II
Ammuru, 18
Amorites, 20
Anatolia, 11, 21, 23–24, 26, 238
Aphek, fig. 1.1, 15
Apiru, *see* Habiru
Apophis, table 1.1, 12–14
Artashumara, table 1.1, 22
Artatama, table 1.1, 17, 22–23, 227
Arzawa, 24
Ashkelon, fig. 1.1, 10
ashlars, 56, 237
Assur, fig. 1.1, 17, 24–25, 40
Assyria, 21–23, 26

attached specialist, 29–32, 35, 219–21, 232–34, 236

Babylon, fig. 1.1, 4, 17, 20, 23–26, 230
Battle of Megiddo, 3, 5, 16, 19, 227
Battle of Kadesh, 24, 27
Beth Shean, fig. 1.1, 3–4, 10, 15, 27, 33, 74, 83–89, 121–23, 125–26, 128, 131–34, 136–37, 139, 141, 143, 145–46, 149–51, 156, 159–60, 162–63, 165, 179, 196–209, 221, 223–25, 227
Black Sea, 23
bowls, 59, 64, 90, 130, 132–39, 142, 145, 159–60, 162–63, 166–68, 176–79, 186–88, 195–99, 205, 208–9, 214, 216, 220, 236
  closed carinated bowls with short neck (CB1), 133, 135, graph 4.5, 136–37, 139, 167–68, 176, 178, 185–86, 195, 197, 207–8, 214, 216
  closed carinated bowls with high neck (CB2), 133, 135, graph 4.6, 137, 139, 167–68, 176, 178, 185–86, 197, 207–8, 216
  deep bowls (DB), 132–34, graph 4.2, 162, 166, 178, 186, 197, 208, 214, 176
  hemispheric bowls (HB), 133–34, graph 4.3, 197, 208, 185
  open bowls (OB) 132–34, graph 4.4, 159, 176, 216
  open shallow carinated bowls (CB3), 133, graph 4.7, 138, 168, 176, 178, 186, 198, 208

Index

open deep carinated bowls (CB4), 133, graph 4.8, 138–39, 168, 176, 178, 186, 199, 208–9, 215–16, 222
shallow bowls (SB), 90, 130–33, graph 4.1, 134, 162, 166, 176, 185–86, 197, 208
Byblos, fig. 1.1, 25

C14, *see* radiocarbon
Canaan, 1–3, 8–11, 14–19, 28–29, 33, 74, 220–21, 224–27, 230–31, 233–39
Carchemish, fig. 1.1, 16, 27n12
Central Hill, 10–11, 16n8, 18, 227
chalice, 159
Charom Ware, 127, 162, graph 4.38, 175, 184, 194
Chocolate on White, 127, 160, graph 4.35, 173, 175, 184, 194, 204, 207
Cisjordan, 3, 74, 216
cistern, 37n3, 39, 46
citadel, 51
conflagration, 45, 79, 81, 92, 94, 97, 99, 103, 108, 110, 105
cooking pots, 90, 125, 127, 145–49, 166, 170–71, 176, 180–81, 184, 189–91, 195, 201–2, 207, 211–12, 214, 217, 219, 232
holemouth cooking pots (HCP), graph 4.22, 144, 149, 181, 185, 195, 202, 207, 212
miniature cooking pots (MCP), graph 4.23, 144, 149, 176, 181, 189, 202, 212
rounded cooking pots (CP1), graph 4.18, 144, 146–47, 149, 171, 176, 180, 189, 191, 202
rounded cooking pots with gutter rim (CP4), graph 4.21, 144, 147–49, 181, 191, 202
rounded cooking pots with thickened rim (CP2), graph 4.19, 144, 146–47, 171, 176, 180, 185, 189, 191, 195, 202
rounded cooking pots with triangular rim (CP3), 125, 144, graph 4.20, 147, 171, 176, 180–81, 184–85, 189–91, 195, 202, 207, 212, 214, 217, 222
upright cooking pots (UCP), 144–45, graph 4.17, 170, 176, 180, 189, 201, 207, 212
Crete, 10, 14, 231

crisis architecture, 37, 70–71, 73, 228–30
cup and saucer, 159
Cusae, fig. 1.1, 14
Cypriot Bichrome Ware, graph 4.39, 163, 184, 194, 207
Cypriot imports, graph 4.41, 14, 165, 174, 184, 195, 213, 231–32, 239
Cyprus, 10, 14, 24, 231–32

Damascus, fig. 1.1, 18, 24
Deir el Balah, 221
dendrochronology, 21
destruction, 2, 5, 10, 22, 24–25, 28, 33, 46, 49–51, 53–54, 70, 81, 85, 92, 94, 97, 103, 108, 110–11, 122–23, 229–30, 236–37
deterioration, 29, 56, 72
distribution, 30, 32, 228, 234, 236
pottery distribution, 31, 134, 151, 159, 166, 168, 171, 179, 184, 188–89, 196–99, 202, 218, 220, 224, 230, 232, 236, 239
redistribution, 31

Ebla, fig. 1.1, 5, 25, 111n10, 230
economic decline, 3, 35, 72–73, 225, 228–30, 234, 238–39
economy of scale, 220
Edfu, fig. 1.1, 12
efficiency, 29–30, 35, 232
Eggshell Ware, graph 4.37, 56, 160, 173, 184, 194, 207
Egyptian Empire, 3, 8, 11, 19, 27, 35, 124, 224, 227, 234–35, 238–39
Ekallatum, 24–25, 27
el Amarna archive, *see* Amarna
Elam, 20, 25
Emar, fig. 1.1, 22, 27
Euphrates, 16, 21, 23, 27

fire, *see* conflagration
flask (FL), graph 4.34, 154, 159, 184, 192, 204

Galilee, 19, 225, 228, 230, 235
gate, 32, 37, 51, 53–54, 60, 64, 66, 69, 117
Gaza, 18
Gezer, fig. 1.1, 17, 220
Giloh, 221

Gina, 18
glacis, *see* rampart
goblet, 160

Habiru, 11, 22
Habur, 27
Habur River, 21n10
Habur Valley, 24
Hammurabi, 20, 25, 230
Hatshepsut, table 1.1, 15–16, 19
Hatti, table 1.1, 8, 17, 22–24, 26–27
Hattusa, fig. 1.1, 17, 23–24
Hattusili, table 1.1, 18, 23
Hazor, fig. 1.1, 3–4, 8–10, 18, 25–28, 32–35, 36–73, 74, 89n2, 121–23, 126–28, 130–34, 136–37, 139–52, 156, 159–60, 162–63, 165, 166–76, 179, 186, 188, 199, 202, 209, 212, 215, 220, 222–24, 227–30, 234–37, 239
Hinterland, 19, 228–29, 235
Hittite, 5, 10n6, 18, 20–25, 27, 221, 226
Horemheb, 18
household (production), 103, 219–21
Hurrians, 9–11, 20, 22, 26, 29
Hyksos, 1–3, 5, 7–8, 10–12, 14–15, 18, 25, 35, 72–73, 224–27, 229–30, 236, 238

Idrimi, table 1.1, 21–22
imitations, 10, 30
inalienable, 31
independent specialist, 29, 31–32, 35, 219, 232–34, 236–37, 239
infant burial, 45, 131n2
Intermediate Bronze Age, 1, 4, 9, 225
Ishme Dagan, table 1.1, 24–25
Israelite, 7–8

Jaffa, fig. 1.1, 15
Jezreel Valley, 19
Jordan River, 4
Jordan Valley, 4, 10–11, 19
Josephus, 8, 14
juglets, 153, 156–58, 163, 173, 184, 186, 192, 204, 212, 214
   dipper juglets (JT2), 156, graph 4.32
   with simple rim (JT1), 156, graph 4.31
   with worked rim (JT3), 156, graph 4.33, 176

jugs, 145, 153–56, 159, 163, 173, 183–84, 186, 192, 204, 212
   biconical jugs (J4), graph 4.30, 153, fig. 4.4, 156, 183, 192
   dipper jugs (JT3), graph 4.29, 153, fig. 4.4, 183–85, 204
   with simple rim (J1), graph 4.27, 153, fig. 4.4, 183, 192, 217
   with worked rim (J2), graph 4.28, 153, fig. 4.4, 173, 183, 192, 204, 212, 217

Kabri, 10n5, 26n11, 230
Kadesh (Tell Nebi Mend), fig. 1.1, 17, 22, 24, 27
Kamares Ware, 231
Kamid el-Loz, fig. 1.1, 18, 74, 91–103, 121–23, 127
Kamose, table 1.1, 12, 14–15
Kerma, 12, 15
Khamudi, table 1.1, 12
Kili-Teshub, table 1.1, 23
kiln, 39, 49, 113
Kizzuwatna, 22
kraters, 67, 114, 126–27, 131, 139–45, 149, 163, 166, 168–71, 176, 179, 188–89, 195, 199–201, 207, 210–11, 214–15, 216–17, 222, 232
   bowl-like kraters (K1), graph 4.15, 142, fig. 4.2, 189, 199, 207, 210, 217
   closed kraters (CK), fig. 4.1, 139, graph 4.10, 169, 176, 179, 185, 189, 195, 199, 207, 216
   closed kraters with ridged rim (CKR), graph 4.11, fig. 4.1, 139, 168–69, 176, 179, 189
   necked kraters (NK), graph 4.12, fig. 4.1, 141, 145, 168–69, 176, 179, 185, 189, 195, 199, 207, 210–11, 214, 217, 222
   necked kraters with gutter rim (NKY), graph 4.14, fig. 4.1, 141, 149, 179, 189, 199, 210
   necked kraters with ridged rim (NKR), graph 4.13, fig. 4.1, 141, 168–69, 176, 179, 189, 199, 210, 215, 217
   pithos-like kraters (K2), graph 4.16, fig. 4.2, 145, 169, 176, 189, 199, 210, 217
Kush, 12, 14–15, 226

260 *Index*

Laba'yu, 18
Lachish, 27, 220
Larsa, 20, 25
Lebanese Biqa, 4
Lebanon, 16, 74, 90–109, 125
Libya, 16
low chronology, 11, 20, 25
Lower Egypt, 1, 12, 14, 225, 227, 238
luxury goods, 30–31, 232, 234–35

macrotypology, 33, 35, 225
Mari, fig. 1.1, 3, 24–26, 36, 119, 221, 229–30
market economy, 31, 219
market exchange system, *see* market economy
material culture, 1–3, 7, 10, 14, 27–29, 32–33, 35, 72, 126, 129, 219, 221–26, 233–34, 236, 239
Mediterranean Sea, 4, 231
Megiddo, fig. 1.1, 3, 10, 16, 27–28, 77, 89–90, 129, 237
Mesopotamia, table 1.1, 3, 12, 20–21, 24–26, 120, 221, 227
middle chronology, table 1.1, 20–21, 25
Middle Kingdom, 12, 14–15, 23, 73
miniature vessels, graph 4.9, 139, 168, fig. 4.1
Minoans, *see* Crete
Mitanni, table 1.1, 16–24, 26–27, 221, 226–27, 234
monoliths, *see* ashlars
Mursili I, table 1.1, 20, 23, 25
Mursili II, table 1.1, 24
Muwatalli, 24, 27
Mycenaean imports, graph 4.40, 163, 174–75, 184, 195, 207, 214, 231–32
Mycenaean ware, *see* Mycenaean imports

Naram Sin, table 1.1, 24
Negev, 10–11, 15
new chronology, 21, 25
New Kingdom, 1, 5–6, 11, 14–16
northern Levant, 5, 8, 14, 20–27, 74, 90–121, 216, 222, 234, 238
Nubia, 12, 15, 18, 33–34, 226–27, 233
Nuzi, fig. 1.1, 20, 22

offering table, 46, 62
orthostats, 50–51, 54, 59, 65, 237

palace, 1, 8, 14, 25, 37, 39, 56, 59–65, 71, 91–95, 110–11, 113–14, 116–22, 216, 219
Parrattarna, table 1.1, 22
Phoenicia, 18
pithoi (P), graph 4.24, 59, 108, 131, 149–52, 171–73, 176, 181–82, 184, 191–92, 195, 202–3, 207, 212, 215, 217, 222
plague, 24
Punt, 16

Qatna, fig. 1.1, 4, 16, 18, 20, 22, 24–26, 74–76, 111–21, 122–23, 127, 216–18, 221–23, 225, 232, 234–35

radiocarbon, 5–7, 21, 26, 91, 226, 230
rampart, 46–47, 51, 54, 105, 111, 76, 79, 81
Ramses II, table 1.1, 18, 24, 27
rebellion, 22, 25
Red, White, and Blue, 160, graph 4.36, 173, 175, 184, 194, 207

Sarepta, 74
Sasuiluna, table 1.1, 25
scarabs, 1–2, 14, 28, 91
Second Intermediate Period, 12–15, 226
Seti I, table 1.1, 27
Shamshi Adad, table 1.1, 21, 24–26
Sharuhen, 15
Shasu, 11, 16
Shechem, fig. 1.1, 18
Shephelah, 10–11, 227, 235
Shuttarna III, 23
Sidon, fig. 1.1, 74, 90–91, 121, 127
silo, 39, 45–46, 107–8, 117
Sinai, 16
slabs, 46–47, 51, 90–91
southern Levant, 1–4, 9–11, 14–15, 17–22, 25, 27–29, 31, 33, 35, 68, 72–74, 76–90, 111n10, 124, 126, 129, 151, 156, 163, 165, 171, 208, 212, 215–17, 219, 224–27, 230–31, 234, 237–38
specialization, 29–31, 232–33
standardization, 29–30, 35, 220–21, 232–33

standing stone, 37, 61–62, 64–65, 69, 71, 85, 171
storage jars, 45, 105, 108, 152–53, 173, 181, 192, 203, 207, 212, 215, 219, 221–22, 236
　with simple rim (SJ1), graph 4.25, fig. 4.3, 152, 171, 181, 192, 203, 217
　with worked rim (SJ2), graph 4.26, fig. 4.3, 152, 172–73, 181–82, 185, 192, 203–4, 217
Sumur, 18
Suppiluliuma I, table 1.1, 5, 21, 23–24
Syria, 3, 4n2, 8, 10n6, 11, 16–19, 21, 23–27, 35, 59, 74, 110–21, 125, 216, 221, 226–27, 230–31, 234–35

tabun, 81, 90, 103, 105
tax, taxes, *see* taxation
taxation, 14, 18, 229, 232–33, 235–36
Tel Batash, 219–20
Tel Dan, 27, 151, 162
Tel Miqne/Ekron, 221
Tel Qashish, fig. 1.1, 10, 27–28, 33, 76–78, 121–23, 125–26, 128, 131, 134, 136–37, 139–41, 143, 145, 148, 151, 156, 162–63, 165, 176–85, 186, 188, 196–97, 224, 237
Tell Arqa, fig. 1.1, 17, 33, 74, 105–9, 122–23, 126, 129, 131, 134, 137, 139–41, 143, 145, 148, 151–52, 156, 159, 162–63, 165, 179, 186, 199, 204, 208–15, 217, 222–24, 234, 237
Tell ed-Dabʻa, fig. 1.1, 2, 6, 12, 14
Tell el-Ghassil, fig. 1.1, 74, 103–5, 122–23, 127
Tell Hadidi, 22
Tell Sakka, fig. 1.1, 4n2, 74, 110, 122–23, 127
temple, 1, 14, 17, 37–40, 42–43, 46–47, 49–51, 59–61, 63–66, 68–71, 85, 87–88, 90–91, 94–99, 102–3, 111, 114, 121, 168, 219–20, 237
Thebes, fig. 1.1, 12, 17–18
Thutmose I, table 1.1, 16, 19

Thutmose II, table 1.1, 16
Thutmose III, table 1.1, 2–3, 11, 14–19, 22, 28–29, 35, 87, 122, 124, 224–28, 234–36, 238
Thutmose IV, table 1.1, 5, 17, 19, 23, 227, 235
Tigris, 21
Timnah, 10
tomb, 12, 39, 42–43, 45, 94–95, 105, 111, 126, 128
tower, 10, 40, 51, 54, 76–77, 79, 108
Tunip, 17
Turin King List, 12
Tushratta, table 1.1, 22–23
Tuttul, fig. 1.1, 24

Ugarit, fig. 1.1, 24–25, 27, 235
ultra-high chronology, 20
ultra-low chronology, 5, 21
Upe, 18, 26
Upper Egypt, 12
Upper Mesopotamia, 24–25

vassal, 16, 19, 22–24, 26–27, 226, 228, 234, 239
via maris, 17

Washukanni, 21
watchtower, *see* tower
workshop, 38, 46, 59, 65–66, 68, 71, 94, 111, 113–14, 117, 121–22, 219–22, 236–37

Yahdum Lim, 24
Yamhad, 20, 23, 230; *see also* Aleppo
Yasmah Addu, table 1.1, 24
Yoqneʻam, fig. 1.1, 27–28, 33, 74, 76, 79–82, 121–23, 125–26, 128, 131, 134, 137, 139, 141, 145, 148, 151–52, 156, 159–60, 162–63, 165, 185–96, 197, 204, 222–24, 237

Zimri Lim, table 1.1, 25–26

www.ingramcontent.com/pod-product-compliance
Lightning Source LLC
Chambersburg PA
CBHW030546080526
44585CB00012B/276